Labour Law in Namibia

Collins Parker

UNAM PRESS
UNIVERSITY OF NAMIBIA

University of Namibia Press

Private Bag 13301

Windhoek

Namibia

© Collins Parker, 2012

All rights reserved. No part of this publication may be reproduced, stored in any retrieval system or transmitted in any form, or by any means, e.g. electronic, mechanical, photocopying, recording or otherwise without prior permission of the author.

First Published: 2012

Design & Layout: John Meinert Printers, Windhoek

Printed by: John Meinert Printers, Windhoek

ISBN: 978-99916-870-1-8

Distributed internationally by the African Books Collective:
www.africanbookscollective.com

CONTENTS

Preface and Acknowledgements ix

1 Introduction 1
    1.1   What is Labour Law? .1
    1.2   Who is an Employee? 2
          1.2.1   At Common Law 2
          1.2.2   Tests Applied in Identifying Employees 5
          1.2.3   Statutory Provisions 15
    1.3   Who is an Employer? 22
          1.3.1   At Common Law 22
          1.3.2   Statutory Definition 22
    1.4   Interpretation of the Labour Act 2007 23
    1.5   Application of the Labour Act 2007 23

2 The Employment Relationship **25**
    2.1   Contract of Employment 25
    2.2   Essential Elements of Contract of Employment 25
          2.2.1   Agreement 26
          2.2.2   The Parties 35
          2.2.3   Duties of an Employee 36
          2.2.4   Duration 37
          2.2.5   Remuneration 38
          2.2.6   The Employer's General Right of Control and Supervision . . . 39

3 Duties of Employees **41**
    3.1   Introduction 41
    3.2   Personal Service 41
    3.3   Not to be Absent from Work 42
    3.4   Punctuality 45
    3.5   Obedience to Reasonable and Lawful Instructions 45
    3.6   Furthering the Interests of the Employer 47
          3.6.1   Devotion of the Employee's Energy and Skill 48
          3.6.2   Using Information Gained in the Course of Employment 48
          3.6.3   Employees' Inventions 48
          3.6.4   Fiduciary Duties 49
    3.7   Competence and Efficiency 50
    3.8   Adaptability 52
    3.9   Not to be Guilty of Misconduct or Improper Behaviour 52
          3.9.1   Introduction 52
          3.9.2   Dishonest Act 53
          3.9.3   Negligence 56
          3.9.4   Drunkenness and Use of Unprescribed Drugs and Substances . . 56
          3.9.5   Indolence 57
          3.9.6   Insolence 57

	3.9.7	Fighting and Similar Forms of Misconduct		58
	3.9.8	Fraud		60
	3.9.9	Damage to Property		61
	3.9.10	Unauthorized Use of Employer's Motor Vehicle		61
	3.9.11	The Rule in Hollington's Case		62
3.10		Duties of Employee after Separation		63
	3.10.1	Restraint of Trade		63
	3.10.2	Using Trade Information after Separation		67

4 Duties of Employers **69**

4.1	Introduction.	69
4.2	Provision of Work	69
4.3	Payment of Remuneration	71
	4.3.1 Payment of Remuneration during Illness	72
	4.3.2 Form and Method of Payment	72
	4.3.3 Prohibited Deductions	73
	4.3.4 Permitted Deductions	75
4.4	Provision of Medical Services	76
4.5	Provision of Certificate of Service	76
4.6	Keeping of Prescribed Records	78
4.7	Observation of Prescribed Hours of Work	79
	4.7.1 Ordinary Hours of Work	79
	4.7.2 Overtime	80
	4.7.3 Meal Intervals	81
	4.7.4 Daily Spread-Over and Weekly Rest Period	81
	4.7.5 Night Work	81
	4.7.6 Work on Sundays	82
	4.7.7 Work on Public Holidays	83
4.8	Granting of Paid Leave of Absence	84
	4.8.1 Annual Leave	84
	4.8.2 Sick Leave and Compassionate Leave	86
	4.8.3 Maternity Leave	88
4.9	Provision of Accommodation	90

5 Duties Common to Employees and Employers **91**

5.1	Discrimination.	91
5.2	Duty to Bargain in Good Faith	95
5.3	Health and Safety at the Workplace	96
5.4	Indemnity	97
5.5	Sexual Harassment	103

6 Remedies of Employees and Employers. **107**

6.1	Introduction.	107
6.2	Remedies of Employees	107
	6.2.1 Termination of Contract by or without Notice	107
	6.2.2 Claim for Wages	110
	6.2.3 Damages	111
	6.2.4 Application for Reinstatement	111
	6.2.5 Interdict	112

Contents v

		6.2.6	Strike	113
	6.3	Remedies of the Employer		113
		6.3.1	Dismissal	113
		6.3.2	Non-Payment of Wages	114
		6.3.3	Damages	115
		6.3.4	Specific Performance	116
		6.3.5	Interdict	116
		6.3.6	Lockout	116
		6.3.7	Secret Profits and Commissions	117

7 Termination of the Employment Relationship **119**

	7.1	Introduction		119
	7.2	Termination not based on Notice		120
		7.2.1	Expiration of Contract	120
		7.2.2	Performance of Contract	126
		7.2.3	As a Result of Supervening Impossibility	126
		7.2.4	As a Result of Employee's Sickness or Incapacity	126
		7.2.5	By Death and Other Causes	127
		7.2.6	By Sequestration	127
		7.2.7	By Repudiation	128
	7.3	Termination by Notice or Without Notice		128
		7.3.1	Termination by Notice	128
		7.3.2	Termination without Notice	135
	7.4	Severance Pay		135

8 Unfair Dismissal and Disciplinary Actions. **139**

	8.1	Unfair Dismissal		139
		8.1.1	What is Unfair Dismissal?	140
		8.1.2	Substantive Fairness	143
		8.1.3	Procedural Fairness	147
		8.1.4	Substantive and Procedural Requirements Peremptory	156
	8.2	Inevitably Unfair Dismissal: Certain Grounds		157
	8.3	Redundancy or Collective Termination		158
	8.4	Unfair Disciplinary Actions other than Dismissal		165
		8.4.1	Introduction	165
		8.4.2	Warning	166
		8.4.3	Suspension	168
		8.4.4	Demotion	168

9 Industrial Disputes **169**

| | 9.1 | What is an Industrial Dispute? | 169 |
| | 9.2 | The Two Types of Industrial Dispute | 171 |

10 Conciliation, Mediation and Arbitration **175**

	10.1	Conciliation and Mediation		175
		10.1.1	Introduction	175
		10.1.2	Statutory Provisions	176
	10.2	Arbitration		180
		10.2.1	Introduction	180

| | | 10.2.2 | Statutory Provisions | 182 |

11 Industrial Disputes and the Labour Court **205**

11.1	Introduction	205
11.2	Establishment and Composition of the Labour Court	205
11.3	Exclusive Jurisdiction of the Labour Court	206
	11.3.1 Appeal and Review Powers of the Labour Court	206
	11.3.2 Setting Aside of Arbitral Awards	210
	11.3.3 Declaratory Orders	215
	11.3.4 Urgent Relief	215
	11.3.5 Exclusive Jurisdiction in Respect of Other Matters	216
11.4	The Labour Court's Power to Order Costs	216
11.5	The Labour Court's Power of Referral	217
11.6	Rules Board	217
11.7	General Powers of the Labour Court	218

12 Agreement to Settle Industrial Disputes **219**

13 Disputes of Interest and Industrial Action **223**

13.1	Introduction	223
13.2	Strike	223
	13.2.1 What is a Strike?	223
	13.2.2 The Right to Strike	226
	13.2.3 Protection of Strikers	230
	13.2.4 Circumstances under which Strikes are Prohibited	234
	13.2.5 Designation of Essential Services	234
13.3	Picket	237
13.4	Lockout	239

14 Trade Unions and Employers' Organizations **241**

14.1	Introduction	241
14.2	What is a Trade Union?	242
14.3	The Right to Form or Join a Trade Union	243
14.4	Unionizable Employees	244
14.5	Registration	246
14.6	Elements of the Constitution of a Trade Union	248
	14.6.1 Name of the Trade Union	248
	14.6.2 Objects of the Trade Union	248
	14.6.3 Industry or Industries in its Scope	248
	14.6.4 Qualification for Admission to Membership	249
	14.6.5 Membership Fees	249
	14.6.6 Termination of Membership	250
	14.6.7 Office-Bearers and Officials	251
	14.6.8 Workplace Representatives	251
	14.6.9 Meetings	252
	14.6.10 Financial Provisions and Acquisition and Control of Property	252
	14.6.11 Affiliation and Amalgamation	253
	14.6.12 Amendment of Constitution	253
	14.6.13 Winding up of a Trade Union	254

14.7	Consequences of Registration and Rights of Registered Trade Unions	. . 254
14.8	Consequences of Registration and Individual Membership Rights	 256
14.9	Cancellation of Registration of Trade Union	. 257
14.9.1	Cancellation in Terms of Section 61 of the Labour Act	 257
14.9.2	Cancellation in Terms of Section 62 of the Labour Act	 257

15   Collective Bargaining and Agreements **259**

15.1	Introduction.	. 259
15.2	Exclusive Bargaining Agents	. 260
15.3	Disclosure of Information	. 264
15.4	Duty to Bargain in Good Faith	. 268
15.5	Collective Agreement	. 269
15.6	Disputes Regarding Collective Agreement	. 273

16   Transitional Provisions of the Labour Act 2007 . . . . **275**

Appendix I Table of Statutes. **277**

Appendix II Table of Cases **281**

Bibliography. **301**

Index **305**

PREFACE AND ACKNOWLEDGEMENTS

This book is a comprehensive work on labour (or employment) law in Namibia, where the common law of master and servant forms its fundamentality, as it does in other common law jurisdictions. However, today, labour law in Namibia (and in other common law countries) is dominated by statute. Thus, the Labour Act 2007 (Act No. 11 of 2007) represents the sum and substance of much of Namibia's labour law, which governs employment contracts.

The book deals with the common law principles of employment relations applicable to Namibia and statutory modifications and amplifications of those principles by the Labour Act. It also treats other employment issues that are not even contemplated in the common law. Thus, the book examines, for instance, certain elements of labour law in Namibia that epitomize the political, social and economic realities of present-day employment relations that are found in most modern democratic and free societies like Namibia. Examples of those elements are the right of employees to form or join trade unions as employees' interests-promotion organizations, the right of employees to strike, the concept of unfair dismissal, collective bargaining, collective agreements, paid maternity leave, alternative dispute resolution mechanisms (i.e. conciliation, mediation and arbitration) and the Labour Court. In this connection, comparative references are made to the labour laws of some other Commonwealth countries, notably, South Africa, Swaziland, Zambia and the United Kingdom. Like Namibia's legal system, the legal system of the first two of these countries is based on the Roman–Dutch common law. Moreover, the first three countries and Namibia are all members of the Southern African Development Community (SADC).

In a period of barely eighteen years, Namibia has endeavoured, and to a large part succeeded, to move away from the apartheid-infested system of employment relations to a system that is in tune with its democratic milieu and which conduces to the fulfilment of its international obligations under the relevant International Labour Organization (ILO) Conventions and Recommendations. The repealed Labour Act 1992 (Act No. 6 of 1992) did well to bring Namibia's labour law and practices to the level of international standards, particularly standards under ILO Conventions, to which Namibia is a State Party, and some ILO Recommendations.

On the whole, the Labour Act 2007 has maintained the standards attained by the repealed Labour Act 1992. In that sense, the Labour Act 2007 does not depart markedly from the general policies and principles that shaped the repealed Labour Act 1992. There are, however, some remarkable features of the Labour Act 2007. It provides for comprehensive alternative dispute resolution mechanisms, namely conciliation, mediation and arbitration, and procedures for their implementation. It has done away with the power of magistrates' courts to sit as a labour court of first instance: the new Act has instead created a new Labour Court as a court of first instance in labour matters that fall under the Act. Another key feature of the Act is that it introduces fully paid maternity leave for employees who are subject to the Act. Lastly, for the first time in Namibia, the concept of unfair labour practice has found expression in Namibia's labour law.

My profound gratitude goes to my wife, who typed the entire manuscript of this book with exemplary diligence and a superb sense of forbearance, albeit the task is outside the bounds of her conjugal duty.

I am grateful to the publishers of *Labour Court Reports (Republic of Namibia)*, NLLP, Human Capital Consulting Ernst & Young (Namibia), and the publishers of *Namibia Law Reports*, Legal Assistance Centre. I have referred to some cases reported in those publications. I wish to register my profound gratitude to Ms Helen Vale of the University Central Consultancy Bureau, UNAM, for her impeccable editing of the manuscript. I am also grateful to Ms Jane Katjavivi, the consultant appointed by UNAM Press to do the final editing of the manuscript to get it print-ready. Above all, my esteemed gratitude goes to UNAM Press as the publishers of the book.

Collins Parker
Windhoek, Namibia

1 INTRODUCTION

1.1 What is Labour Law?

Labour law or employment law – the two terms can be used interchangeably – may be described as that branch of law that is concerned with persons in the employment relationship. Tebutt, JA put it succinctly in this way: 'Briefly speaking Labour Law is to be understood as the common law of master and servant as expanded and otherwise modified by Industrial Legislation.'[1] Put simply, labour law governs the contractual relationship between an employer and an employee.[2] Flowing from that relationship, employers and employees have certain rights, obligations and liabilities under the law.

Principles of other branches of law are deeply embedded in labour law. Chief among these are principles of the law of contract, law of delict, criminal law, statute law, administrative law, constitutional law and human rights law.

Central to labour law, as already mentioned, is the contractual relationship between an employer and an employee. Therefore, principles of the law of contract are applied to explain the nature and consequences of the employment relationship. The law of delict is also employed to determine the civil liability of employees, employers and third parties in employment situations. Many countries have eschewed penal sanctions in labour relations, although criminal law still plays an important role in labour relations, especially with regard to unlawful strike, lockout, or picket, and the employment of minors. For example, it is an offence under s. 3(6) of the Labour Act 2007[3] for a person to employ, or require or permit, a child who is under the age of fourteen years to work in any circumstances prohibited by the Act. An employer found guilty of this offence is liable to a fine not exceeding N$20,000.00, or to imprisonment for a period not exceeding four years, or to both.

Labour law also cuts into the domain of administrative law since administrative law deals with the question of the exercise of governmental power by public authorities, and control of such power by the courts. Nowadays, the exercise of governmental power by

---

1   *Sibongile Nxumalo and others v Attorney-General and others* Swaziland CA 25/96, 28/96, 29/96, 30/96 (consolidated) at p.15 (unreported).

2   'Labour law' has been chosen as the title of this book because Namibia's employment statute is called the Labour Act.

3   Act No. 11 of 2007. This is how the new Labour Act will be referred to throughout the book without any footnoting.

public officials, e.g. labour commissioners, employees' compensation commissioners and registrars of trade unions in labour relations, is well known. The principles of administrative law are, therefore, called to assist in judicial review proceedings to determine the limits of the powers of such public bodies or public officials and the lawfulness and fairness of their actions under the Labour Act.

The right to join or form trade unions within the wider right to freedom of association is protected by constitutional bills of rights in many countries. For instance, Art. 21(1)(e) of the Namibian Constitution provides, 'All persons shall have the right to freedom of association, which shall include freedom to form and join…unions, including trade unions.'[4]

The intrinsic element of labour law is the employer-and-employee relationship and the various rights, duties and liabilities that arise from the relationship. For this reason, the meaning of 'employee' and of 'employer' is fundamental to the whole gamut of labour law.[5] Consequently, our discussion will continue with determining who an employee is, and who an employer is, both at common law and in statute law.

1.2　Who is an Employee?

1.2.1　At Common Law

The provenance of Namibia's common law contract of employment or contract of service is traceable to a genre of *locatio conductio* of Roman law.[6] Roman law recognized three species of *locatio conductio*, i.e. letting and hiring. The first was *locatio conductio rei*, i.e. the letting and hiring of a specified thing for a monetary reward. Thus, since Roman legal and political thought recognized the institution of slavery,[7] a slave could form the 'thing' in a *locatio conductio rei*. The master of a slave could, therefore, lend him to another person. The reason was that a slave was a thing (*res*), and so 'he himself was incapable of letting his labour or services but if his owner did so then such a contract was construed as a letting of the slave as a thing (*res*), i.e. *locatio conductio*.'[8] In this arrangement, the slave was neither a *locator operarum* (an employee) nor a *conductor operis* (an independent contractor).

4　1990. This is how the Namibian Constitution will be referred to throughout the book without any footnoting. See also, e.g., s. 88 of Swaziland's Industrial Relations Act 2000 (Act No. 1 of 2000).

5　See E. Mureinik, 'The Contract of Service: An Easy Test for Hard Cases', *SALJ* 97, 246.

6　The two terms bear the same meaning but it appears that the former is 'a better-sounding term to democratic ears': *De Beer v Thomson & Son* 1918 TDP 70 at 76.

7　Collins Parker, 'Executive Discretion and Personal Freedom', LLM Thesis, Dalhousie University, 1979, 2.

8　*Smit v Workmen's Compensation Commissioner* 1979 (1) SA 51 (A), at 56D.

The second species of letting and hiring was *locatio conductio operas (faciendi)*, i.e. the present-day independent contractor. This was the letting and hiring of a particular piece of work or job to be done as a whole (*opus faciendum*). Joubert, JA explained it graphically in *Smit v Workmen's Compensation Commissioner* supra thus:

> This was a consensual contract whereby the workman as employee or hirer (conductor or redemptor operas) undertook to perform or execute a particular piece of work or job as a whole (opus faciendum) for the employer as letter or lessor (locator operis) in consideration of a fixed money payment (merces). Here there was a switch of terminology. The workman who undertook to perform or execute the work was deemed to be the hirer of the work (conductor or redemptor operis) whereas the employer who undertook to pay the merces for the execution of the work was considered to be the letter or lessor of the work (locator operas). What the parties to the contract contemplated was not the supply of services or a certain amount of labour but the execution or performance of a certain specified work as a whole. [9]

The third species was *locatio conductio operarum*, i.e. the letting and hiring of personal service in return for a monetary return. As Joubert, JA explained:

> This was consensual contract whereby a labourer, workman or servant as employee (locatio operarum) undertook to place his personal services (operae suae) for a certain period of time at the disposal of an employer (conductor operarum) who in turn undertook to pay him the wages or salary (merces) agreed upon in consideration of his services. [10]

The central difference between the second and third types of letting and hiring is this: the subject matter of the contract under the second type was not the supply of services or labour but the product or result of labour. Where a contract obliges one party to build for the other, providing at his own expense the necessary plant and materials, this is not a contract of service, although the builder may be obliged to use his own labour only and to accept a high degree of control. Such a contract is a building contract. MacKenna, J explained: 'It is not a contract to serve another for a wage, but a contract to produce a thing (a result) for a price.'[11]

---

9   Ibid. at 57C-E.

10   Ibid. at 56E.

11   *Ready Mixed Concrete (South East) v Minister of Pensions* [1968] 2 QB 433 at 440.

This distinction is, therefore, fundamental: 'The contract between master and servant is one of letting and hiring of service (*locatio conductio operarum*) whereas the contract between the principal and a contractor is the letting and hiring of some definite piece of work (*locatio conductio operis*).'[12] The latter is a contract for work or *locatio conductio operis*, which is in English law equivalent to a contract for services.

Seminal to this distinction is the point that if X is not bound to render his personal service to Y, then X cannot be said to be 'working for' Y, i.e. X is not Y's employee.[13] This proposition can be couched in a positive statement in this way: 'An employee agrees...he will provide his own work and skill in the performance of some service for his master.'[14] Consequently, at common law, the hallmark of the contract of service is the rendering of personal service by the *locator operarum* (servant) to the *conductor operarum* (master). In this way the service so rendered is the object of the contract.

The servant in a contract of service is under the orders of the master to render his personal service upon the master's personal command. The service that is to be rendered is, therefore, subject to the orders and decisions of the master, and the servant is subordinate to the disposition of the master. He is, therefore, obliged to obey the lawful commands or instructions of the master who has the right of supervising and controlling him by prescribing to him what work he has to do, as well as the manner in which it has to be done.[15] There is also an important feature of a contract of service or contract of employment with regard to termination: a contract of employment is terminated by the death of the servant or upon expiration of the period of service.

In summary, at common law, the law governing the master-and-servant relationship is based on the Roman law contract of letting and hiring of service (*locatio conductio operarum*). It has been said of the South African law of employment that its basis lies in the harmonization of Roman–Dutch common law and the English common law.[16] Doubtless, it is submitted, the same is true of Namibian labour law.

---

12 *Colonial Mutual Life Assurance Society Ltd v Workmen's Compensation Commissioner* 1931 AD 412, *per* De Villiers, CJ at 433.

13 See *The State v A.M.C.A. Services (Pty) Ltd* 1962 (4) SA 537 (A); *Stellenbosch Farmers Winery Ltd v Stellenvale Winery (Pty) Ltd* 1957 (4) SA 234 (C); *Ongwevallekommissaris v Onderlinge Versekeringsgenootskap AVBOB* 1996 (4) SA 446 (A); *Smit v Workmen's Compensation Commissioner* supra.

14 *Ready Mixed Concrete v Minister of Pensions* supra at 440.

15 *Smit v Workmen's Compensation Commissioner* supra.

16 J. Grogan, *Riekert's Employment Law*, 2nd edn, Cape Town, Juta, 1993, p. 2.

1.2.2 Tests Applied in Identifying Employees

It need hardly be said that while the definition of the employee in labour law has been enigmatic at times, in most cases, it is not difficult to identify the employee. However, because employment practices have changed considerably over the years and because government, commerce and industry have become highly complex and technical, requiring specialist expertise, problems do at times arise in identifying the modern-day employee. Consequently, over the years the courts have developed and applied various tests or approaches in their effort to determine who is an employee. Those tests or approaches will now be examined.

1.2.2.1 The Supervision and Control Test

In simple terms, this approach states that the higher the degree of supervision and control that the alleged employer (or master) exercises or is allowed to exercise over the work of the alleged employee (or servant) and over the manner in which the latter performs his work, the stronger is the indication that such a person is an employee (or a servant).[17] Curlewis, J observed in *De Beer v Thomson & Son,*[18] that certain elements in the employer-and-employee relationship might raise the probability that a person is an employee, but certain circumstances may not raise such probability: today the most important element seems to be the question of control.

The provenance of the supervision and control test lies in English law. The much-cited test was formulated by Bramwell, LJ in *Yewens v Noakes* as far back as 1880, thus: 'A servant is a person subject to the command of his master as to the manner in which he shall do his work.'[19] The Appellate Division of the Supreme Court (now the Supreme Court of Appeal) of South Africa adopted the supervision and control test under English law in *Colonial Mutual Life Assurance Ltd v MacDonald* supra, in deciding whether an insurance agent was an employee. De Villiers, CJ formulated the test as follows:

> The tests to be applied in deciding whether a person is a servant or an independent contractor have been dealt with recently in an instructive manner by McCardic, J. in Performing Right Society Ltd v Mitchell and Booker (Palais de Danse) Ltd (1924, 1 K.B. at p. 766), where he shows the difficulty of putting one's hand upon any one test which is conclusive. But while it may sometimes be a matter of extreme delicacy to decide whether the control

---

17   *Smit v Workmen's Compensation Commissioner* supra.

18   *De Beer v Thomson* supra.

19   *Yewen v Noakes* [1880] 6 QBD 530 at 532-533, *per* Bramwell, LJ.

reserved to the employer under the contract is of such a kind as to constitute the employer the master of the workman, one thing appears to me to be beyond dispute and that is that the relation of master and servant cannot exist where there is a total absence of the right of supervising and controlling the workman under the contract; in other words, unless the master not only has the right to prescribe to the workman what work has to be done, but also the manner in which that work has to be done. In The Queen v Walker (27 L.J.M.C. 207) Bramwell, B. (as he then was), put it in this way: 'A principal has the right to direct what the agent has to do; but a master has not only that right, but also the right to say how it is to be done.' In Yewens v Noakes (1880, 6 Q.B.D. 530) the same learned judge applied the same test. Pollock on Torts (12th ed., pp. 79, 80) draws the same distinction: 'A servant is a person subject to the command of his master as to the manner in which he shall do his work.' So also does Salmond, Law of Torts (6th ed., p. 96), in the following passage: 'A servant is an agent who works under the supervision and direction of his employer… A servant is a person engaged to obey his employer's orders from time to time.'[20]

The essence of the supervision and control test is the right of the employer to lay down rules regarding:

1   the object to be attained (the 'what');
2   the means of attaining the object (the 'how');
3   the time within which the object should be attained (the 'when'); and
4   the place where the object should be attained (the 'where').

Thus, in *Ready Mixed Concrete v Minister of Pensions* supra McKenna, J put it succinctly in the following passage:

Control includes the power of deciding the thing to be done, the way in which it shall be done, the means to be employed in doing it, the time when, and the place where it shall be done. All these aspects of control must be considered in

---

20   *Colonial Mutual Life Assurance v MacDonald* supra at 434-5.

deciding whether the right exists in a sufficient degree to make one party the master and the other the servant.[21]

In *Smit v Workmen's Compensation Commissioner* supra, Joubert, JA reminds us, '[I]t is indisputably clear…that the so-called test of supervision is firmly rooted in Roman–Dutch soil.'[22]

The supervision and control test ruled the legal waves in an age during which the owners of two of the three means of production, i.e. land and capital (the third is labour), usually had the expertise required to supervise and control the labour that they hired. In that age, the brewery manager or the coal mine manager, for instance, usually possessed managerial and technical skills, which his employees did not possess. Such a manager could, therefore, actually supervise and control his employees. But, today, many employees are not practically subject to the kind of supervision and control to which their counterparts in the period before or immediately after the Industrial Revolution were subjected. As a result, to insist today on the supervision and control test as the determining factor in the identification of the employee, will be artificial. To sum up, the control test may be difficult to apply where the so-called servant exercises professional skills or performs work of a highly technical nature.[23]

Indeed, the courts have recognized the danger of making the control and supervision test decisive. It has, therefore, been stated, 'Notwithstanding its importance the fact remains that the presence of such a right of supervision and control is not the sole *indicium* but merely one of the *indicia*, albeit an important one, and there may also be other important *indicia* to be considered depending upon the provisions of the contract in question as a whole.'[24] Thus, Lord Wright made the following terse observation in *Montreal Locomotive Works Ltd v Montreal and Attorney-General for Canada*: 'Control in itself is not always conclusive.'[25] MacKenna, J also noted in a similar vein that an 'obligation to do work subject to the other party's control is a necessary, though not always a sufficient, condition of a contract of service.'[26] Consequently, the courts have recognized that the requirements of supervision and control as an indication of the existence of the employer-and-employee relationship

---

21   *Ready Mixed Concrete v Minister of Pensions* supra at 440.

22   *Smit v Workmen's Compensation Commissioner* supra at 62C.

23   T.E. Lewis, *Winfield on Tort*, 6th edn, London, Sweet & Maxwell, 1954, p. 139.

24   *Smit v Workmen's Compensation Commissioner* supra at 62F.

25   *Montreal Locomotive Works Ltd v Montreal and Attorney-General for Canada* [1947] 1 DLR 161 at 169.

26   *Ready Mixed Concrete v Minister of Pensions* supra at 440.

need to be qualified.[27] The following observation of Roper, J in *R v Feun* is apposite in this regard: [28]

> the question (often extremely difficult) whether the relationship of master and servant exists depends mainly if not entirely upon the degree of control exercised by the employer over the manner in which the work is to be performed. Complete control in every respect is in my view not essential to the master-and-servant relationship, and some degree of freedom from control is not incompatible with the relationship.[29]

The learned judge goes on to illustrate his point with great clarity, thus:

> For example, a chef may be engaged on the understanding that his mistress is to have no say in the manner in which he prepares his dishes, but he may nevertheless be a servant. As it was put by Curlewis (Hon) J., in De Beer v Thomson 1918 T.P.D. 70 at p.76, a large amount of direct control exercised over the person engaged would tend to raise a presumption that he was a workman, whereas if he was entirely independent and free of the control of the person engaging him that would tend to show that he was not a workman. Whether the control exercised is such as to lead to the inference that the engaged person is a servant is therefore a question of degree.[30]

It may be distilled from the authorities that while supervision and control may no longer be decisive factors in determining who an employee is, the presence of 'a right of supervision and control is indeed one of the most important *indicia* that a particular contract is in all probability a contract of service'.[31] Frank, AJ put it concisely thus in *Engelbrecht and others v Hennes* : 'Whereas the question of the exercise of control is no longer the determining factor but one of the factors to be considered the total absence of control would in my view be fatal to any claim to being an employee.'[32] In *Hannah v Government of the Republic of Namibia*, Ngoepe, AJ observed, 'Although not in itself conclusive, the presence

---

[27] *Smit v Workmen's Compensation Commissioner* supra.

[28] *R v Feun* 1954 (1) SA 486 (T).

[29] At 60H-61A.

[30] Ibid.

[31] *Smit v Workmen's Compensation Commissioner* supra at 62D.

[32] *Engelbrecht and others v Hennes* 2007 (1) NR 236 at 239B.

or absence of supervision and control will be a relevant factor: a considerable measure of supervision and control will tend to indicate a master-and-servant relationship... There are several authorities on this point'.[33]

In *Hannah v Government of Namibia* supra, the respondent raised a point *in limine* as follows: the applicant, being a Judge of the High Court, was not an employee of the State in terms of the repealed Labour Act 1992[34] because the definition of 'employee' in the Act did not include a Judge. That being the case, it was argued, the Labour Court had no jurisdiction. The Court observed that when deciding whether the applicant came within the definition of 'employee' under the repealed Labour Act 1992, one had to consider not only the question of the absence of supervision and control, but also the prohibition of any interference by the State and its agents with a Judge in the execution of his or her judicial functions in terms of the Namibian Constitution.

Upon the authority of the Indian case of *Union of India v Pratibha Bonnerjea*,[35] the Court found that it was difficult to reconcile an employer-and-employee relationship with judicial independence as guaranteed in the Namibian Constitution. The Court observed further that matters such as the control that the State had concerning times when Judges worked, the place where they worked, their vacations, their pension, medical contributions, deductions for the purpose of income tax on a pay-as-you-earn (PAYE) basis, etc. were peripheral to a Judge's judicial function. In the result, the Court held that the applicant had not proved on a balance of probabilities that he was an 'employee' as defined in the repealed Labour Act 1992.

1.2.2.2 *The Organization or Integration Test*

Denning, LJ (as he then was) enunciated the organization or integration test in *Cassidy v Ministry of Health*,[36] and applied it in *Stevenson, Jordan and Harrison Ltd v MacDonald and Evans*,[37] as a criterion for distinguishing a contract of employment from a 'contract for services' (i.e. independent contractor). He stated, 'One feature which seems to run through instances is that, under a contract of service, a man is employed as part of the business, and his work is done as an integral part of the business, whereas, under a contract for services, his work, although done for the business, is not integrated into it but is only accessory to it.'[38] He also referred to the organization test in *Bank voor Handel en Scheepvaart NV v*

---

33 *Hannah v Government of the Republic of Namibia* 2000 NR 46 (LC) at 50C. See also *Engelbrecht v Hennes* supra.

34 Act No. 6 of 1992. This is how Namibia's repealed Labour Act will be cited without footnoting.

35 *Union of India v Pratibha Bonnerjea* (1976) AIR SC 690 at 695.

36 *Cassidy v Ministry of Health* [1951] 2 KB 353.

37 *Stevenson, Jordan and Harrison Ltd v MacDonald and Evans* [1952] 1 TLR 100.

38 Ibid. at 111.

Slatford and another, where he observed that: 'the test of being a servant does not rest nowadays on submission to orders. It depends on whether the person is part and parcel of the organization.'[39]

The approach underlying the organization or integration test is that a person is an employee if he is integrated into the enterprise or business. Those who are sufficiently integrated into the enterprise or business are employees; those who are not so integrated are not. While in some simple cases it may not be difficult to apply the organization or integration test, it may not be so easy to apply it to borderline cases. It is in respect of such cases that criticisms have been levelled against the organization test. In *Ready Mixed Concrete v Minister of Pensions*, MacKenna, J opined in this way about the organization test: 'This [the organization test] raises more questions than I know how to answer. What is the meaning of being "part and parcel of an organization"? Is every person who answers this description a servant? If only some are servants, what distinguishes them from the others if it is not their submission to orders?'[40] Joubert, JA expressed his view tersely about the apparent vagueness of the organization test in *Smit v Workmen's Compensation Commissioner* thus: 'In my view the organization test is juristically speaking of such a vague and nebulous nature that more often than not no useful assistance can be derived from it in distinguishing between an employee (*locator operarum*) and an independent contractor (*conductor operis*) in our common law.'[41]

1.2.2.3 The Proprietary Test

It seems that the organization test offers useful assistance in deciding whether a person is an employee if it is applied in conjunction with the proprietary test to which it appears to be akin. The Court in *Ready Mixed Concrete v Minister of Pensions* supra approached the issue of whether a master-and-servant relationship existed by invoking what has been referred to as the 'proprietary' test, together with other tests.[42] In that case, MacKenna, J referred to the following opinion of Lord Wright in *Montreal Locomotive Works Ltd v Montreal and Attorney-General for Canada*:

> In many cases the question can only be settled by examining the whole of the various elements which constitute the relationship between the parties. In this way it is in some cases possible to decide the issue by raising as the crucial

---

39 *Bank voor Handel en Scheepvaart NV v Slatford and another* [1953] 1 QB 248 at 295.

40 *Ready Mixed Concrete v Minister of Pensions* supra at 445.

41 *Smit v Workmen's Compensation Commissioner* supra at 63F-G.

42 *Ready Mixed Concrete v Minister of Pensions* supra at 443.

question whose business is it, or in other words by asking whether the party is carrying on the business in the sense of carrying it on for himself or on his own behalf and not merely for a supervisor.[43]

MacKenna, J went on to observe:

> If a man's activities have the character of a business, and if the question is whether he is carrying on the business for himself or for another, it must be relevant to consider which of the two owns the assets ('the ownership of the tools') and which bears the financial risk ('the chance of profit', the 'risk of loss'). He who owns the assets and bears the risk is unlikely to be acting as an agent or servant. If the man performing the service must provide the means of performance at his own expense and accept payment by results he will own the assets, bear the risk and be to that extent unlike a servant.[44]

Thus, relying on *Queensland Stations Pty Ltd v Federal Commissioner of Taxation*,[45] and *Montreal Locomotive Works Ltd v Montreal and Attorney-General for Canada* supra, MacKenna, J held that the common law test should not be limited to the power of control over the manner of performing service, but the test is wide enough to take account of investment and risk.[46] The proprietary test was applied in the South African case of *Tshabalala v Moroka Swallows Football Club Ltd.*[47]

According to the proprietary test, it is more likely than not that the person who has ownership of the assets of the business and bears the financial risk of the business is not an employee of the enterprise: such a person is carrying on the business as his own account. It has, therefore, been held that a director of a company, who held all the shares in a company, except one, was not an employee unless he had a service contract with the company.[48] Accordingly, in *Boulting v Association of Cinematograph, Television and Allied Technicians*,[49] Lord Denning, MR refused to accept the claim that the joint managing directors of a company were employees.

---

[43] *Montreal Locomotives v Montreal and Attorney-General* supra at 169.

[44] *Ready Mixed Concrete v Minister of Pensions* supra at 443.

[45] *Queensland Stations (Pty) Ltd. v Federal Commissioner of Taxation* (1945) 70 CLR 539.

[46] *Ready Mixed Concrete v Minister of Pensions* supra at 444.

[47] *Tshabalala v Moroka Swallows Football Club Ltd* (1991) 12 *ILJ* 389.

[48] *Lee v Lee's Air Farming Ltd* [1961] AC 12; *Robinson v George Sorby Ltd* (1960) 2 ITR 148.

[49] *Boulting v Association of Cinematograph, Television and Allied Technicians* [1963] 2 QB 606 (CA).

1.2.2.4 The Dominant Impression Test

In some cases, the question whether a person is an employee is a difficult one, because the applicable contract may have some of the features of an agency agreement and yet be a service contract or vice versa. It is to deal with such borderline cases that the courts have resorted to the dominant impression approach as a guide in determining whether a person is an employee. 'It is in the marginal cases where the so-called dominant impression test merits consideration,' Joubert, JA stated in *Smit v Workmen's Compensation Commissioner* supra.[50] Consequently, in that case, the Court did not apply either the supervision and control test or the organization test. It rather followed the judicial path it had trodden in *Ongwevallekommissaris v AVBOB* supra. The essence of the dominant impression test is this: Where the relationship has indications tending to show the existence of employer-and-employee relationship and some other relationship, one must, considering all the facts, endeavour to determine which sort of relationship comes off best, or what 'dominant impression' such a contract leaves on one's mind.

Although it has been argued that the formulations by the Court in *Smit* supra and *AVBOB* supra contain inadequacies so much so that they cannot be of assistance in determining the question whether a person is an employee at common law,[51] in *Stein v Rising Tide Productions CC*,[52] the court paid particular attention to the dominant impression test in determining whether the contract in question was one of employment. The case concerned an action instituted by the plaintiff, a photographic sports model stuntwoman and sports-therapy masseuse, against the defendant, a close corporation carrying on business as a film production service corporation. In the action, the plaintiff claimed damages for loss allegedly suffered by her as a result of injuries that she had sustained while engaged in a modelling photographic shoot in Cape Town in April 1999. While performing a kickboxing routine in the course of the photographic shoot, she had fallen and allegedly twisted her leg, resulting in a rupture of the anterior cruciate ligament in her knee. The plaintiff alleged that she fell and injured herself during the photographic shoot as a consequence of the negligence of the servants of the defendant, who, acting within the course and scope of their employment, were negligent when operating the camera for the photographic shoot. Applying the dominant impression test formulated by Joubert, JA in *Smit v Workmen's Compensation Commissioner* supra, as developed in South African case law, to the evidence before it, the Court found that the technicians hired by the defendant and to whom the plaintiff sought to attribute negligence were not the employees of the defendant. Thus, the South African Labour Appeal Court observed in *Dempsey v Home & Property*:

---

50   *Smit v Workmen's Compensation Commissioner* at 62G.

51   See Mureinik, 'The Contract of Service: An Easy Test for Hard Cases', pp. 258-60.

52   *Stein v Rising Tide Productions cc* 2002 (5) SA 199 (C).

no single factor is considered determinative and the Court has to examine the relationship in its totality to identify those aspects of their relationship which tend to indicate the existence of an employment relationship, and those which indicate a relationship other than that of master and servant. The factors are then weighed against each other and where the dominant impression indicates the existence of a contract of service, the court has to rule accordingly.[53]

1.2.2.5 *The Multiple Test*

Faced with the difficulty of putting their fingers on any one assured and decisive test, the courts have also at times fallen on the multiple test in order to determine who is an employee.[54] Indeed, the multiple test is not so different from the dominant impression test. Under the multiple test, too, what are seen to be relevant *indicia* are considered in relation to the particular situation, and the court embarks upon the exercise of balancing the various *indicia* against one another to determine what weight ought to be attached to each one of them. For instance, in *Colonial Mutual Life Assurance Society Ltd v MacDonald* supra, the court referred to some criteria of the multiple test outlined in *Performing Rights Society v. Mitchell and Booker:*[55] the nature of the job or task at hand; the freedom of action of the alleged employee; the magnitude of the contract amount; the manner of payment of remuneration; the locus of the power of dismissal; the circumstances under which payment of remuneration may be withheld; and the exercise of control and supervision.

The Court in *Ready Mixed Concrete v Minister of Pensions* supra set out three conditions necessary for the existence of a contract of employment:

1 agreement by a person X in consideration of a wage or other remuneration to provide his own work and skill in the performance of some service for another Y;

2 express or implied agreement by X that in the performance of that service he will be subject to Y's control in a sufficient degree so as to make Y the master; and

3 the other provisions of the contract are such that they are not inconsistent with it being a contract of employment.

---

[53] *Dempsey v Home and Property* (1995) 16 *ILJ* 378 (LAC) at 381B-C.

[54] The court in *Morren v Swinton & Pendlebury Borough Council* [1965] 1 WLR 576 applied the multiple test in order to reach the conclusion that a resident engineer appointed by a local authority and who worked under the instructions of a firm of consulting engineers, was an employee of the local authority.

[55] *Performing Rights Society Ltd v Mitchell and Booker (Palais de Dance) Ltd* [1924] 1 KB 762 at 767.

In English law, there must be a wage or other remuneration, otherwise, there is no consideration, and without consideration there is no contract of any kind. *Conradie v Rossouw*[56] settled the law in South Africa that the English doctrine of consideration forms no part of the South African law of contract, which is based on Roman–Dutch common law. There is no reason why the principle in *Conradie v Rossouw* should not apply to Namibian law of contract, which is also based on the Roman–Dutch common law. Nevertheless, what Christie states with regard to South African law of contract must be borne in mind, namely that the English doctrine of consideration has not been forgotten entirely in South African law of contract.[57] Thus, while payment of wages or other remuneration (*merces*) formed an element of the Roman law of *locatio conductio operarum*, it is not an essential element of the contract of employment at common law.[58] However, as we shall see in chapter 2 (para. 2.2.5 below), this aspect of the common law has been changed by statute law as far as employment contracts are concerned, for in terms of s. 1 of the Labour Act 2007, the payment of remuneration is an essential element of a contract of employment.

However, the nature of the remuneration payable is not in itself an indication that an employer-and-employee relationship exists. For instance, the payment of a commission is not necessarily incompatible with the existence of the employer-and-employee relationship; nor does it necessarily follow that because a person is paid a share of the profits of an undertaking that he is not an employee.[59]

1.2.2.6 The Pragmatic Approach

Finally, in recent times the courts have found it fit to adopt a more pragmatic approach when determining who an employee is, instead of applying mechanically the tests and approaches discussed above. Indeed, in *Hall (HM Inspector of Taxes) v Lorimer*,[60] having warned against applying any of the above tests and approaches impulsively, the Court of Appeal held that each case should be determined on the particular facts available to the court. In *Lane v Shire Roofing Co (Oxford) Ltd*,[61] too, the Court of Appeal referred with approval to a number of authorities in which the various tests have been applied, and held that the facts of the particular case must be considered and the tests that are applied must have relevance to modern employment practices.

---

56 *Conradie v Rossouw* 1919 AD 279.

57 R.H. Christie, *The Law of Contract in South Africa,* 5th edn, Durban, Butterworths, 2006, p. 10 (fn53).

58 Mureinik, 'The Contract of Service: An Easy Test for Hard Cases', p. 262.

59 *De Beer v Thomson* supra. See also *Dempsey v Home & Property* supra.

60 *Hall (HM Inspector of Taxes) v Lorimer* [1994] IRLR 171.

61 *Lane v Shire Roofing Co (Oxford) Ltd* [1995] IRLR 493.

Introduction **15**

In closing, an important question that arises is this: is the issue whether a person is an employee a question of law or fact? In *O'Kelly v. Trusthouse Forte Plc*,[62] the Court of Appeal stated that for over seventy years in England the issue of whether a person is an employee is a question of fact. The Privy Council expressed a similar view in *Lee v. Chung and Shun Shing Construction & Engineering Co Ltd.*[63] It is therefore submitted that whether a person is an employee is a question to be resolved by the determiner of fact.[64] However, where the question whether a person is an employee turns solely on the interpretation and application of a written contract of employment, then the question is a question of law.[65]

1.2.3 Statutory Provisions

Many statutory definitions of 'employee' are not definitions in sensu stricto; they merely provide statutory descriptions, which are invariably synonyms and not definitions, or are in the form of circular reasoning.[66] For instance, s. 230(1) of the Employment Rights Act (United Kingdom) states: 'In this Act "employee" means an individual who has entered into or works under (or, where the employment has ceased, worked under) a contract of employment.'[67] The Act goes on to provide in s. 230(2) that: 'In this Act "contract of employment" means a contract of service or apprenticeship, whether express or implied, and (if it is express) whether oral or in writing.' In terms of s. 1 of Swaziland's Employment Act,[68] a 'contract of employment means a contract of service, apprenticeship or traineeship.' Furthermore, s. 1 of Zambia's Employment Act[69] defines 'employee' as 'any person who has entered into or works under a contract of service, whether the contract is express or implied, is oral or in writing'. Those Acts do not define precisely 'contract of service' or 'contract of employment'.

Unlike the formulations in the Swaziland, English and Zambian definitions, the South African formulation appears to be in the form of a definition. Section 213 of South Africa's Labour Relations Act 1995[70] defines 'employee' as '(a) any person, excluding an independent contractor, who works for another person or for the State and who receives, or is entitled to

---

62 *O'Kelly v Trusthouse Forte plc* [1983] 2 All ER 456.

63 *Lee v Chung and Shun Shing Construction & Engineering Co Ltd*
    [1990] IRLR 236.

64 See *Edwards v Bairstow* [1956] AC 14; *Rumingo and others v Van Wyk* 1997 NR 102 (HC).

65 *The President of the Methodist Conference v Parfitt* [1984] IRLR 141.

66 C.D. Drake, *Labour Law,* 2nd edn, London, Sweet & Maxwell, 1973, para. 35.

67 Employment Rights Act (UK) 1996 (c. 18).

68 Act No. 5 of 1980.

69 Cap. 512 of the Laws of Zambia.

70 Act No. 66 of 1995.

receive, any remuneration; and (b) any other person who in any manner assists in carrying on or conducting the business of the employer.'

The South African formulation is substantially the same as the formulation in the Labour Act 2007, s.1 of which provides:

'employee' means an individual, other than an independent contractor, who –

(a)   works for another person and who receives, or is entitled to receive, remuneration for that work; or

(b)   in any manner assists in carrying on or conducting the business of an employer.

The words in the first part of the definition, paragraph (a), are primarily based on the common law contract of employment (*locatio conductio operarum*).[71] Consequently, one has to look to the common law for guidance in construing the provision by resorting to the tests and approaches explained and developed by the courts, and discussed previously (see para 1.2.2 above).

The second part of the definition, in paragraph (b), extends the common law definition of 'employee'. In *Borcherds v C W Pearce & F. Sheward t/a Lubrite Distributors* (IC) supra, the applicant contended that the ordinary grammatical meaning of the words 'assists in the carrying on or conducting the business of an employer' in the repealed South Africa's Labour Relations Act 1956[72] was so wide that they were capable of including independent agents who did assist in the carrying on or conducting the business of the respondent. In that case the respondent conducted business exclusively through independent agents, and would not conduct any business, if those agents did not assist in it. Thus, if the words were given their ordinary grammatical meaning, then the applicant would be an employee within the meaning of the statutory provision. This, the Industrial Court conceded. The Court, nonetheless, refused to construe these words in their ordinary grammatical sense. De Kock, SM argued: 'Giving the words used their ordinary grammatical meaning would give the word "employee" a meaning which was so wide that it would lead to anomalous and absurd situations.'[73]

The Industrial Court then proceeded to give two incisive examples to illustrate the absurdity of accepting the ordinary grammatical meaning of the statutory definition of 'employee' in

---

71   *Borcherds v. C W Pearce & F. Sheward t/a Lubrite Distributors* (1991) 12 *ILJ* 383 (IC). See also para. 1.2.1 above.

72   Act No. 28 of 1956.

73   *Borcherds v Pearce* 1991 (IC) supra at 387F.

that provision: the wife and children who assist the husband and father to run the local corner café would be 'employees', as they assist him in conducting his business, and the attorney who advises his client on how to structure his business or minimise tax obligations would be an employee, as he assists him in conducting his business. The Industrial Court then concluded that the Legislature could not have intended such anomalous and absurd consequences. For that reason, the Industrial Court was prepared to place some limitation on the very wide import of the words of the statute. In this connection, the Industrial Court stated that the definition of 'employee' ought to be limited by the following considerations:

(a) There is a distinction between assisting an employer in carrying on his business and performing work which is of assistance to the employer in the carrying on or conducting of his business. Work of the later category is not assistance within the meaning of that word as used in the (1956) Act.

(b) The assistance must be intended to be repeated with some form of regularity. Assistance on an ad hoc basis or on a single isolated occasion such as a friend helping out in the case of need, will not make the one who assists an employee.

(c) Assistance rendered at the will of and in sole discretion of the one assisting will not make him an employee. Such a relationship creates only social and not legal obligations. Those who voluntarily and without any obligation, except perhaps social, assist at the school tuck-shop are not employees despite the fact that they may have to follow the instructions of the one in charge. Chaos would reign if no one had the authority to instruct and direct.

(d) The obligation to assist must not arise from some other legal obligation to render that assistance. The obligation may arise ex contractu or ex lege. The agent assists qua agent and not qua employee. The wife assists in the café not as an employee but as part of her duty of mutual support.[74]

The Industrial Court, therefore, found that the applicant did assist in the carrying on of the respondent's business but that assistance arose out of his obligation as agent in terms of an agency agreement. The Court applied the control test, and dismissed it as being inapplicable. It then applied the dominant test and held that '[t]he applicant was in my opinion not an employee in terms of a common-law contract of employment. The applicant

---

[74] Ibid. 388D-H.

was an independent agent who was his own master. He was bound by his own contract but not by his employer's orders.'[75]

The Labour Appeal Court – albeit by a different route – also came to the conclusion that the appellant was an independent contractor and was not an employee, either at common law or for the purposes of the Labour Relations Act and, accordingly, there was no employer-and-employee relationship between the appellant and the respondent.[76]

From *Borcherds v Pearce* (IC) supra, the following useful principles emerge in respect of the interpretation and application of the second part of the definition of 'employee' in South Africa's repealed Labour Relations Act 1956, where the words used, as has been shown above, are substantially the same as those used in the second part of the definition of 'employee' in the Labour Act 2007. First, the nature of the legal agreement would determine whether a person assists in the carrying on or conducting the business of an employer and the nature of the assistance would determine the nature of the legal agreement between the parties. Second, the general words cast in very wide terms do not have the effect of extending the meaning of 'employee' to independent contractors because independent contractors are not bound to render personal service to the hirer of their service but are bound merely to produce a certain result by their own labour or the labour of others under their control and supervision. Third, some limitation must be read into the wide terms defining 'employee' because there is a distinction between assisting in the carrying on or conducting business and performing work or service, which is of assistance to another person. Work of the latter is not assistance within the meaning of 'assistance' as used in the definition of 'employee' in the Act. Fourth, the words in the second part of the definition of 'employee' do not have the effect of changing the common law: it is obvious that to alter any well-established principle of the common law, clear and positive legislation is necessary;[77] nor may legislation be presumed to make any alteration in the common law further otherwise than the Act does expressly declare.[78] Lastly, the question is always this: has the individual X who is assisting another person Y surrendered his or her productive capacity to Y. If X has not and X works for himself, he is outside the protective net of the Labour Act.

The interpretation and application of 'employee' in terms of s. 1 of the repealed Labour Act 1992 came up for determination in *Paxton v Namib Rand Desert Trails (Pty) Ltd.*[79] In that case, the applicant applied to the Labour Court for an order declaring that she was an

---

[75] *Borcherds v Pearce* 1991 (IC) supra at 387A. The control test is discussed in para. 1.2.2.1 and the dominant test in para. 1.2.2.4 above.

[76] *Borcherds v C W Pearce & F Sheward t/a Lubrite Distributors* (1993) 14 *ILJ* 1162 (LAC).

[77] See S.G.G. Edgar, *Craies on Statute Law,* 7th edn, London, Sweet & Maxwell, 1971, p. 121.

[78] *Du Toit v Office of the Prime Minister* 1996 NR 52; *Secretary of State for India v Bank of India* (1938) 159 LT 101 (Privy C.) at 104 *per* Lord Wright.

[79] *Paxton v Namib Rand Desert Trails (Pty) Ltd* 1996 NR 109 (LC).

employee of the respondent during the periods 1 June 1989 to 31 May 1992 and 1 June 1992 to 31 May 1993 in terms of the repealed Act. The facts of the case were briefly these: The applicant was the wife of *P* who was employed from June 1989 to 31 May 1993 by the respondent as game ranch manager of a farm which belonged to the respondent's company. The applicant did assist her husband and rendered certain services on an ad hoc basis and intermittently at Namib Rand Desert Trails from 1 June 1989 to 31 May 1993. The services included keeping the guestroom at Wolwedaans clean and habitable and stocked for use by tourists, assisting in game-culling in 1991 and 1992, and rendering support and assistance to her husband, *P*, in connection with his duties, particularly when he was absent from work. In a letter dated 17 August 1992, the applicant declined to negotiate any arrangement with the respondent. She confirmed that she wished to adhere to the arrangements then existing and that she was unsure at that stage whether she wanted to be employed.

Having reviewed South African authorities (textual and case-law), O'Linn, J enunciated the following principle:

> Although the exercise of control has been watered down to 'being an important yardstick or testing' but not 'decisive', it seems to me that it remains a very important yardstick and perhaps even an indispensable one when deciding the issue of who is an 'employee' in the context of the provisions of the Namibian Labour Act. I say this inter alia because of Part V of the Labour Act which provides for basic conditions of employment, which must be complied with and where failure to comply even carries a criminal sanction. Compliance with these conditions or at least several of them necessitates a substantial degree of control by the employer over the employee. If the relationship between the parties does not have such control or provide for such control as an element, whether express or implied, then the fact must be a very important, if not decisive, pointer that the relationship is not that of employer-and-employee.[80]

After applying the law to the facts of the case, O'Linn, J held that in the period subsequent to the applicant's letter of 17 August 1992, it could not be controverted that the applicant was not an employee, 'notwithstanding the widest possible interpretation of the statutory definition of "employee", "employer", and "employment"' in the repealed Labour Act 1992. The court further held that the applicant was at best an independent contractor.

---

[80] *Paxton v Namib Rand* supra at 114E.

It is submitted that the conclusions and decisions in *Borcherds* (IC) supra and *Paxton* supra should apply with equal force to the application and interpretation of the second part, i.e. paragraph (b), of the definition of employee under the Labour Act 2007. The reason is that the words in the Labour Act 2007 are, as has been said above, substantially similar to the words used in both the repealed South African statute[81] and the repealed Labour Act 1992. The principles proposed in those two cases clearly show that if the words 'assists in carrying on or conducting the business of an employer' were interpreted literally, they would be too wide and also carry a restrictive interpretation.[82]

It deserves to be mentioned that there must be a contract of employment for the employer-and-employee relationship to exist. How else can the existence of an employment relationship and the terms governing such a relationship be established, if not by reference to a contract of employment? In this regard, O'Linn, J's views in the following passage from *Paxton v Namib Rand* supra are instructive:

> It seems to me that in order to establish there is in fact an employment relationship, an agreement of some sort, indicative of the alleged relationship, would be an almost indispensable feature of the relationship. Such agreement of course need not be a formal agreement, reduced to writing. The agreement can be in whole or in part in express terms or implied or tacit. Such implied or tacit terms can be inferred from conduct of the parties.[83]

At times a contract of employment may be subject to a suspensive condition; in that case, such a contract would only inure when the condition is fulfilled. Therefore, the party, who pleads that there is no enforceable contract because the other party has failed to fulfil any suspensive condition, bears the onus of proving the suspensive condition and its non-fulfilment.[84]

This brings us to a related, practical issue: suppose, for example, an employer X enters into a contract of employment with an individual Y. Before Y starts to work for X, X changes his mind and informs Y that he is no longer required to work for X. The question that arises is: did Y become an employee of X the moment he accepted an offer of employment under the Labour Act 2007? If according to the letter, or the oral intimation, of appointment of Y, Y was to assume duty at a later date, and before he assumed duty on that appointed date X

---

81   Labour Relations Act No. 28 of 1956, s. 1.

82   See *Ellis Park Stadium Ltd v Minister of Justice and another* 1989 (3) SA 898 (T).

83   *Paxton v Namib Rand* supra at 115B.

84   *Bucher v Kalahari Express Airlines* NLLP (2002) (2) 104 NLC.

set aside the appointment, then *Y* never became an employee of *X*. In that case *Y* cannot look to the Labour Act 2007 for assistance: *Y* was not an employee of *X* within the meaning of 'employee' in s. 1 of the Labour Act. The remedy of *Y* lies in contract – at common law.[85] The reason is that it cannot be said that *Y* is a person '*who works for*' *X*, 'and who receives, or is entitled to receive, remuneration *for that work*, or *in any manner assists*' *X* 'in carrying on or conducting the business of' *X*, within the meaning of s. 1 of the Labour Act 2007.[86]

In order to ascertain the relationship between the parties it is always necessary to look at the terms of the contract. It is equally important to note that the name the parties may give to their agreement is not determinative either way. Thus, the title or designation by which a person is described or called is not conclusive that he is an employee: it is the duty of the court or arbitrator to determine the relationship between the parties. Thus, when required, the court or arbitrator is duty-bound to determine the true and real nature of the parties' relationship; the court or arbitrator must not make a determination solely on the basis of how the parties have chosen to describe their relationship in their contract.[87] In *Dempsey v Home and Property* supra, the Labour Appeal Court accepted submission of the respondent's counsel that little emphasis must be placed on the fact that the appellant was designated a sales manager and that the Court must make an attempt to determine the true relationship between the parties. In the words of Fannin, J in *Goldberg v Durban City Council*, 'It is not enough for the parties to describe their contract as one whereby Dipppenaar is appointed an independent contractor, for it is the duty of the court to have regard to the realities of their relationship, and not regard itself as bound by what they have chosen to call it.'[88]

---

[85] *Whitehead v Woolworths (Pty) Ltd* (1999) 20 *ILJ* 2133 (LC).

[86] However, see the South African case of *Wyeth SA (Pty) v Manqele and others* [2005] 6 BLLR 523 (LAC), where the South African Labour Appeal Court held that in terms of the South African Labour Relations Act 1995 (Act No. 66 of 1995) an 'employee' includes a person who has concluded an employment contract which will commence at a future date. It is submitted that the decision cannot apply in the Court in Namibia in the light of the correct interpretation of 'employee' under Namibia's Labour Act 2007. Therefore, the principle laid down in *Whitehead v Woolworths (Pty) Ltd* supra is preferred because it is in line with the correct interpretation of 'employee' under the Labour Act 2007. But see s. 5(7)(a) of the Labour Act 2007, which provides that for the purposes of s. 5(8), (9) and (10) of the Act, 'employee includes a prospective employee'. It is submitted that the special definition of 'employee' under s. 5(7)(a) is only applicable when dealing with sexual harassment under the Labour Act 2007. Sexual harassment is discussed in chapter 5, para. 5.5 below.

[87] *Denel (Pty) Ltd v Gerber* [2005] 9 BLLR 849 (LAC).

[88] *Goldberg v Durban City Council* 1970 (3) SA 325 (N) at 331B-C.

1.3 WHO IS AN EMPLOYER?

1.3.1 At Common Law

Who an employee (*locator operarum*) is at common law has been discussed above (see para. 1.2). By deduction, an employer (*conductor operarum*) at common law is any person – natural or legal – who has entered into a contract of employment with a natural person who has contracted to render his personal service to this other person.[89]

1.3.2 Statutory Definition

Here, too, it must be said that the two points made in respect of the statutory definition of employee (see para. 1.2 above) apply with necessary modifications to the statutory definition of 'employer'. Section 1 of the Labour Act 2007 provides:

'employer' means any person, including the State who –

(a)   employs, or provides work for, an individual and who remunerates or expressly or tacitly undertakes to remunerate that individual;

(b)   permits an individual to assist that person in any manner in the carrying on or conducting that person's business;

In terms of s. 1 of the Labour Act 2007, 'employer' includes a natural person, a legal person or the State. 'State' should be understood to mean any organ of State and agents of those organs, including parastatal organizations, regional councils,[90] and local authority councils and their representatives.[91]

The definition of 'employer' under English law is succinct. Section 230(4) of the Employment Rights Act, (United Kingdom) states: 'In this Act "employer", in relation to an employee or a worker, means the person by whom the employee or worker is (or where the employment has ceased, was) employed.'[92]

---

89   See *Smit v Workmen's Compensation Commissioner* supra.

90   Councils established under the Regional Councils Act 1992 (Act No. 22 of 1992).

91   Councils established under the Local Authorities Act 1992 (Act No. 23 of 1992).

92   Employment Rights Act (UK) 1996 (c.18).

1.4 Interpretation of the Labour Act 2007

It is worth making the point that in interpreting and applying the statutory definitions under the Labour Act 2007, one must take into account the well-known canons of construction of statute, e.g. that one must have regard to the Act in question as a whole and not just to a particular section of it, and that it is also permissible to look at the object and purpose of the legislature in passing the Act. In *Nkumbula v Attorney-General of Zambia*, Baron, DCJ had this to say: 'No provision can be read in isolation and construed in isolation: any word or phrase or provision in an enactment must be construed in its context.'[93] In the celebrated House of Lords case of *Attorney-General v HRH Prince Augustus of Hannover*, Viscount Simonds stated, 'words, and particularly general words, cannot be read in isolation; their colour and content are derived from their context.'[94] In *Paxton v Namib Rand* supra,[95] O'Linn, J referred with approval to the judgement of Joubert, JA in *Adampol Pty Ltd v Administrator, Transvaal*, where it was said that:

> The plain meaning of the language in a statute is the safest guide to follow in construing the statute. According to the golden or general rules of construction the words of a statute must be given their ordinary, literal and grammatical meaning and if by so doing it is ascertained that the words are clear and unambiguous, then effect should be given to their ordinary meaning unless it is apparent that such a literal construction falls within one of those exceptional cases in which it would be permissible for a court of law to depart from such a literal construction, e.g. where it leads to a manifest absurdity, inconsistency, hardship or a result contrary to the legislative intent.[96]

1.5 Application of the Labour Act 2007

The application section, i.e. s. 2 of the Labour Act 2007, prescribes the scope of application of the Act. The section is meant to remove uncertainties as to the scope of application of the Act, including subject matter, connected statutes, persons and bodies that are subject to the Act or any part of it.

---

93   *Nkumbula v Attorney-General* (1972) ZR 202 (SC) at 211.

94   *Attorney-General v HRH Prince Augustus of Hannover* [1957] 2All ER 45 at 53.

95   *Paxton v Namib Rand* supra at 111A-D.

96   *Adampol Pty Ltd v Administrator, Transvaal* (1989)(3) SA 733 (A) at 804A-G.

According to s. (2)(1) of the Act, s. 5 of the Act, which deals with prohibition of discrimination and sexual harassment in employment, applies to all employees and employers. Furthermore, according to s. 2(2) and subject to subsections (3), (4), and (5) of the Act, all other sections of the Act apply to all employers and employees, except members of the Namibian Defence Force, unless the Defence Act 2002 provides otherwise;[97] the Namibian Police Force and a municipal police service referred to in the Police Act 1990, unless the Police Act 1990 provides otherwise;[98] members of the Namibian Central Intelligence Service, unless the Namibia Central Intelligence Service Act 1997 provides otherwise;[99] and members of the Prison Service, unless the Prisons Service Act 1998, provides otherwise.[100]

In terms of s. 2(3) of the Labour Act 2007, the Minister responsible for Labour may, by notice in the *Gazette*, declare that (1) any of the laws listed in s. 2(5), namely, the Apprenticeship Ordinance 1938,[101] the Merchant Shipping Act 1951,[102] or any law on the employment of persons in the service of the State does not apply to an employee, in so far as any such statute relates to the employee's remuneration or other conditions of service and such statute is in conflict with any provision of the Labour Act 2007, or (2) that a provision of the Labour Act applies, with such modifications as the Minister may specify in the notice, to employees referred to in (1).

Lastly, according to s. 2(4) of the Labour Act 2007, where there is a conflict between a provision of the Labour Act and a provision of a law mentioned in s. 2(5) in respect of which the Minister has not made the declaration referred to in s. 2(3), the conflict must be resolved in favour of the latter provision, so long as that provision is more favourable to the employee; otherwise the conflict should be resolved in favour of the former provision in any other case.

---

[97] Act No. 1 of 2002.

[98] Act No. 19 of 1990.

[99] Act No. 10 of 1997.

[100] Act No. 17 of 1998.

[101] Ordinance No. 12 of 1938.

[102] Act No. 57 of 1951.

2 THE EMPLOYMENT RELATIONSHIP

2.1 CONTRACT OF EMPLOYMENT

At the outset, we must make the fundamental point that the general principles of law of contract apply equally to a contract of employment. Thus, in *Paxton v Namib Rand Desert Trails (Pty) Ltd*,[1] O'Linn, J stated that a contract of employment need not be reduced to writing: the terms of the contract may be wholly or partly express, implied or tacit. Unlike in Namibia, in the United Kingdom, there is a statutory definition of 'contract of employment'. According to s. 230(2) of the Employment Rights Act, '"contract of employment" means a contract of service or apprenticeship, whether express or implied, and (if it is express) whether oral or in writing'.[2]

2.2 ESSENTIAL ELEMENTS OF CONTRACT OF EMPLOYMENT

Any attempt at defining 'contract of employment' is not free from difficulty, and we are reminded of the solemn warning of Thesiger, LJ that definitions are proverbially dangerous.[3] With this judicial caution in mind, we will proffer a definition distilled from the principles developed by the courts and the writers, and thereafter the essential element of contracts of employment will be examined.

In simple terms, a contract of employment is an agreement between two parties who have the legal capacity to enter into such agreement whereby one of the parties (the employee) agrees to render personal service to the other party (the employer) for an indefinite or definite period in return for an ascertainable wage or other remuneration. The agreement also entitles the employer, among other things, to determine what the employee's personal service will be, to generally supervise the employee when performing his personal service, and to generally control the manner in which the employee discharges such personal service. Van den Heever, AJ put it thus in *National Automobile & Allied Workers Union (now known*

---

1   *Paxton v Namib Rand Desert Trails (Pty) Ltd* 1996 NR 109.

2   Employment Rights Act (UK) 1996 (c.26).

3   *Yewens v Noakes* (1880) 6 QBD 530 at 538.

as *National Union of Metalworkers of SA) v Borg-Warner SA (Pty) Ltd*: 'Under the common law, parties conclude a contract under which one of them is to provide services in return for payment. Their agreement determines when the relationship so constituted starts; what reciprocal rights and duties are acquired and incurred by each; and, if it is to be of indefinite duration, how it may be terminated.'[4]

The definition of 'contract of employment' given above may be broken down into the following main components, which also constitute its essential elements:

1   an agreement;

2   the parties;

3   an undertaking of the employee to perform personally specified or implied service for the employer;

4   the carrying out of such service for an indefinite or definite period;

5   the employer's agreement to pay to the employee an ascertainable wage or other remuneration; and

6   the employer's general right to assign work to the employee and to exercise – directly or indirectly – control over the employee, and to supervise generally the manner in which the employee performs his service.

It is now proposed to examine in detail these essential and discernible elements of contract of employment.

2.2.1   Agreement

2.2.1.1   *Freedom of Contract*

When parties freely enter into an agreement, they are taken to be aware of the duties, obligations, and rights that form the terms of the agreement. The fact that a contract of employment must be entered into voluntarily brings about certain considerations. First, freedom of contract of employment means no one can lawfully be forced to render his personal service; neither can an employer be forced to employ any person. The Namibian Constitution and the Labour Act 2007 provide for the outlawry of forced labour. Article 9(2) of the Constitution provides: 'No persons shall be required to perform forced labour.' According to s. (4)(1) of the Labour Act 2007, 'A person must not directly or indirectly

---

4   *National Automobile & Allied Workers Union (now known as National Union of Metalworkers of SA) v Borg-Warner SA (Pty) Ltd* (1994) 15 *ILJ* 509 (A) at 515G.

The Employment Relationship **27**

cause, permit or require any individual to perform forced labour.' A person breaches this prohibition on the pain of severe punitive measures under s. 4(3) of the Act. The International Labour Organization (ILO) defines 'forced labour' in Convention No. 29 as 'all work or service, which is exacted from any person under the menace of any penalty and for which the said person has not offered himself voluntarily'.[5] Second, freedom of contract means that the parties are free to settle terms that are mutually acceptable. For instance, they are free to agree the nature of work to be performed, so long as the work is not illegal or is not for an unlawful purpose.

2.2.1.2 *Illegal and Unenforceable Agreements*

The parties' freedom of contract is subject to the limitation that the nature of work involved should be such that it is neither against public morals nor illegal. Thus a contract of employment like any other contract must not be for an illegal or immoral purpose. The illegality may arise from the nature of the personal service to be performed, e.g. where X employs Y to carry to X's warehouse stolen goods from the store where the goods were stolen. The illegality may also arise from the breach of a statutory provision, e.g. where an employer employs a child under the age of fourteen years. Yet again, the illegality may result from the object or purpose of the contract.

In *Napier v National Business Agency*,[6] the applicant was employed at a fixed weekly salary. In addition, he was paid a fixed sum per week for expenses, which both the applicant and respondent knew was substantially in excess of the applicant's actual expenses. The applicant was summarily dismissed. He claimed, in default of notice, his salary, to which, according to him, he was entitled but he claimed no amount in lieu of expenses. The court held that the inclusion of an amount for fictitious expenses made the contract illegal because the purpose of the fictitious expenses was to defraud the revenue office. Then in *Pearce v Brooks,*[7] a jobmaster could not recover from a sex worker his charges for the hire of his cab, because he knew the nature of the hirer's profession, and that she was using the cab to carry out her illegal business.

The result is that the whole contract may be declared invalid; but it may happen that only a part of the contract is declared invalid. The question then arises whether there can be a severance of the illegal part of the contract so as to leave the remainder of the contract enforceable. If the contract is an indivisible arrangement, then there can no room for severing the illegal part and leaving the other part to be enforced without truncating the agreement.

---

5   ILO. C29 Forced Labour Convention, 1930, Art. 2(1).

6   *Napier v National Business Agency* [1951] 2 All ER 204.

7   *Pearce v Brooks* (1866) 1 Ex 213.

28   Labour Law in Namibia

But, if the contract is divisible, then the illegal part of the contract is severable; provided that what remains reflects substantially the parties' original intention.[8] The principle regarding severability of terms of a contract applies to contracts created by statute or the common law.

2.2.1.3   *Formalities*

As was mentioned previously (para. 2.1 above) at common law, the agreement may be a formal agreement, in the sense that the agreement is reduced to writing, or it may be an oral agreement. The terms of the agreement may also be wholly or partly express or implied. The common law does not require the parties to observe any formalities when concluding a contract of employment: so long as there is agreement on the nature of the rights and duties of the employer and the employee, including the employee's right to a wage or other remuneration, the agreement becomes operative and enforceable. Nevertheless, it is always advisable to reduce an oral contract of employment to writing; for the agreement may be settled in simple terms and may contain just the minimum requirements, especially in respect of jobs that do not require high qualifications and expert skills.

In some Commonwealth countries, legislation has modified the common law rule that a contract of employment need not be in writing. The object of such legislation is to remedy situations like those where some employees, because of their little, or lack of, education are ignorant of even the most basic terms of their contract such as the amount of wage they must get and at what intervals they must receive those wages. For instance, in Zambia, in terms of s. 24 of the Employment Act,[9] every employer is obliged to prepare and maintain a record of contract for every employee he has employed under an oral contract. The record, which must be prepared on a prescribed form, must contain the following vital information:

1   the name and sex of the employee and his nationality;

2   the name, address and occupation of the employer;

3   the date of the employee's engagement and the capacity in which he is to be employed;

4   the type and duration of contract;

5   the place of engagement;

6   the rate of wages and any additional payment in kind; and

7   the intervals of payment.

---

8   *Sasfin (Pty) Ltd v Beukes* 1987 (1) SA 1 (A). See also R.H. Christie, *The Law of Contract in South Africa*, 5th edn, Durban, Butterworths, 2006, pp. 366-8.

9   Cap 512 of the Laws of Zambia.

In the United Kingdom, in terms of s. 1 of the Employment Rights Act,[10] every employer must give to each of his employees, within two months of commencement of employment, a written statement of certain particulars of the employment. A section 1 statement must include:

1   the names of the employer and employee;

2   the date when the employment began;

3   the date on which the employee's period of continuous employment began, which would take into account any employment with a previous employer which counts as continuous;

4   the scale or rate of remuneration or the method for calculating remuneration;

5   the intervals at which remuneration is paid;

6   any terms and conditions relating to hours of work;

7   details regarding holidays and holiday pay;

8   details regarding sickness or injury, including any provision for sick pay;

9   pensions and pension schemes;

10   notice periods;

11   the title of the job which the employee is employed to do or a brief description of the work for which he is employed;

12   duration of the contract; and

13   any collective agreement, which directly affects terms and conditions of the employment.

Under Zambian labour law, a section 24 record is so crucial that if a dispute arises as to the terms of an oral contract of an employee (other than a casual employee) and the employer fails to produce a record of such contract, the statement of the employee regarding the terms of the contract will be receivable as evidence of such terms unless the employer satisfies the court to the contrary. In the United Kingdom, on the other hand, a section 1 statement is not in itself a contract unless signed by the employer and the employee,[11] but the statement constitutes prima facie evidence of the contents of the contract of employment.[12] There is no comparable record having a similar effect under the Labour Act 2007: the United Kingdom

---

10   Employment Rights Act 1996 (c.18) (UK).

11   *Gascol Conversions Ltd v Mercer* [1974] ICR 420.

12   *System Floors (UK) Ltd v Daniel* [1982] ICR 54.

30   Labour Law in Namibia

and Zambian records stand in contradistinction to the Namibian 'records and returns' that employers are obliged to keep in terms of s. 130 of the Labour Act 2007. The Namibian records and returns are primarily for statistical purposes. The contents of the Namibian record are discussed in chapter 4, para. 4.6 below.

2.2.1.4 Implied Terms

It will be remembered that the bare bones of a contract of employment are the nature of the employee's duties and entitlement to a wage or other remuneration and the employer's obligations and rights (see chapters 3 and 4 below). However, there are terms that are usually implied in a contract of employment, as is the case with other contracts. There are terms implied either by law or fact. Those implied by fact are also known as tacit terms. Terms implied by law may be so implied at common law or in terms of a statute. Terms implied by law are legal duties, which in labour law a contract of employment must be thought to contain even if the parties did not express them in their contract or did not even know they existed.

Many of the implied duties of employees and employers under contracts of employment that are subject to the Labour Act are set out in Chapter 3 of the Act, entitled 'Basic Conditions of Employment', and are discussed in chapters 3, 4 and 5 below. As its title declares, Chapter 3 contains minimum conditions that are implied in any contract of employment that is subject to the Act, even if they are not expressly provided for in the contract or the parties did not know they existed. Some of them are: maximum weekly ordinary working hours, overtime, enjoyment of public holidays, calculation and payment of remuneration, and prohibition of certain acts relating to payment of remuneration, paid annual leave, sick leave, and maternity leave, and prohibition of child labour. Another important statutorily implied term is the employee's constitutional right to form and join trade unions, a topic which is treated in chapter 14, para. 14.3 below.

The following are good examples of common law implied terms: that the employee will carry out the lawful instructions of his employer; that the employee will submit to the control and supervision of his employer; and that an employee will not render personal service to another person during official working hours without the express consent of his employer.

Terms implied in fact in an agreement, i.e. tacit terms, are those terms which derive from the presumed intention of the parties and which are implied in order to give the agreement business efficacy.[13] Corbett, AJA described such terms as 'an unexpressed provision of the contract which derives from the common intention of the parties, as inferred by the Court

---

13   C. Drake, *Labour Law,* 2nd edn, London, Sweet & Maxwell, 1973, para. 46.

from the express terms of the contract and the surrounding circumstances. In supplying such an implied term the Court, in truth, declares the whole contract entered into by the parties.'[14] In *Joel Melamed and Hurwitz v Cleveland Estates Ltd; Joel Melamed and Hurwitz v Vorner Investments (Pty) Ltd*, the same learned Judge observed, 'it is stated that a court may hold a tacit contract has been established where, by a process of inference, it concludes that the most plausible probable conclusion from all the relevant proved facts and circumstances is that a contract came into existence.'[15]

For instance, the courts will read into a contract of employment an implied duty on the part of an employee not to steal from his employer or set up a business in direct competition to that of his employer. In *Reigate v Union Manufacturing Co (Ramsbottom)*, Scrutton, LJ explained the application of a tacit term in the following passage:

> A term can only be implied if it is necessary in the business sense to give efficacy to the contract, i.e. if it is such a term that it can confidently be said that if at the time the contract was being negotiated someone ('the officious bystander') had said to the parties: 'What will happen in such a case?' they would both have replied: 'Of course so and so will happen; we did not trouble to say that; it is too clear'.[16]

2.2.1.5 Variation

As stated above, a contract of employment, like any other contract, is an agreement by consent of two or more parties and, therefore, the parties to a contract of employment are free to settle any terms they wish, so long as the terms are neither illegal nor against public policy or good morals. Thus, once a contract has been concluded, the terms it contains are fixed and it is not up to a party to vary them unilaterally: a party may only do so if the contract provides for a variation.[17] But even then, a party may not vary the terms unilaterally unless such was the understanding and in respect of specific matters. For instance, in a contract of employment, it is not uncommon for the contract to provide for agreed annual increments in wages which can be effected without the employer getting the consent of the employee before such term is implemented.

---

14 *Alfred MacAlpine & Sons (Pty) Ltd v Transvaal Provincial Administration* 1974 (3) SA 506 (A) at 531H-532A.

15 *Joel Melamed and Hurwitz v Cleveland Estates Ltd; Joel Melamed and Hurwitz v Vorner Investments (Pty) Ltd* 1984 (3) SA 155 (A) at 165B, *per* Corbett, JA.

16 *Reigate v Union Manufacturing Co. (Ramsbottom)* [1918] 1 KB 592 at 605.

17 *Smit v Standard Bank Namibia* 1994 NR 366 (LC).

There is generally only one lawful way in which terms of a contract of employment may be varied, and that is through agreement between the employer and the employee. In *Smit v Standard Bank Namibia* supra, the Labour Court held that the only way in which a change in the contract of employment between the applicant and the respondent could be effected lawfully was by way of negotiation and mutual agreement in the way provided by the repealed Labour Act 1992. There is no good reason why the principle in *Smit v Standard Bank Namibia* supra should not apply to the Labour Act 2007. Indeed, in terms of s. 50(1)(e) of the Labour Act, it is an unfair labour practice for an employer or an employers' organization to unilaterally alter a term or condition of employment.

In *Cowey v Liberian Operations Ltd*,[18] the employer circulated a notice purporting to vary the contract of employment by making the period of notice to be given in respect of termination one month. It was held that the employer could not vary the terms of employment without the consent of the affected employees. The courts have held that unilateral variation is invalid and that, subject to the extent and nature of the variation, it amounts to a repudiation of the contract that may result in constructive dismissal (also treated in chapter 6, para. 6.2.1.1 below). Thus, where an employer unilaterally changes terms of the employment contract, the employee may terminate the contract and claim constructive dismissal. In *Halgreen v Natal Building Society*,[19] Rees, SC expressed himself on the law in this way:

> It now becomes necessary to ascertain what the law on the subject is. Although the phrase 'constructive dismissal' appears in a number of English decisions to which Mr McCall has referred the court I do not consider it necessary to deal with the effect of those decisions since it is recognized in the South African law that where the conduct of an employer amounts to a fundamental breach of the contract of employment, then although the employer does not actually dismiss the employee the employee may accept the conduct as a breach of the contract of employment and the effect will be the same as if he had been summarily dismissed.

> In Smith v Clyde & Motor Trade Supply Co 1922 TPD 324 it was held at 325-6:

> 'An employer who employs a servant for a particular work, and gives him a particular status is not entitled to alter the character of that contract. The contract remains intact until both parties agree to alter it; it cannot be altered at

---

18   *Cowey v Liberian Operations Ltd* [1966] 2 Lloyd Reports 45.

19   *Halgreen v Natal Building Society* (1986) 7 *ILJ* 769 (IC).

the instance of one of the parties. The employer cannot say to his employee 'I am now going to alter the contract between us – which is that you shall act as manager of the local branch at Johannesburg – into another contract that you shall act as bookkeeper at the Johannesburg Branch.'

In Stewart Wrightson (Pty) Ltd v Thorpe 1974 (4) SA 67 (D) Miller J held:

'The Plaintiff not only denied the Defendant the opportunity of performing the specific work for which he had been engaged but, in effect, ordered him off the premises and forbade him to return. It denuded him of the authority, power and status, which the office to which he had been appointed conferred upon him. By compelling the Defendant to sever all connections with the office to which he had been appointed and with the business, which the Defendant was appointed to manage, it destroyed the very being of the contract.'[20]

In *Nhlanhla M.K. Vilakati v Attorney-General*,[21] the applicant who was a senior magistrate had been charged with theft of a motor vehicle but was acquitted. Thereafter, the Swaziland Judicial Service Commission brought him before a disciplinary enquiry and charged him with misconduct. The enquiry found that the applicant was innocent of any misconduct; consequently, it dismissed the charge of misconduct. In a period of sixteen months, the applicant, who had been allowed to go back to his job as senior magistrate, was transferred to three different duty stations in that short space of time. The applicant protested to the Judicial Service Commission against the incessant transfers, which, according to him, had a detrimental effect on him and his family life. The Judicial Service Commission rejected his protestations out of hand.

A few days later, the Judicial Service Commission varied the applicant's appointment from senior magistrate (which is a judicial office) to assistant judicial commissioner (a non-judicial post). The applicant contended that the variation of his appointment was unlawful and that the conduct of the respondent and its organs towards him amounted to victimization. He averred that the variation and victimization had been such that he could no longer reasonably be expected to continue in his employment, and for that reason he accordingly resigned his employment without notice. He considered the respondent's action and conduct as constructive dismissal. The respondent denied that. The Industrial Court found that the unlawful variation of the applicant's post from that of senior magistrate to that

---

20   *Halgreen v Natal Building Society* At 775G-776C.

21   *Nhlanhla M. K. Vilakati v Attorney-General* Swaziland IC 88/96 (unreported)

of assistant judicial commissioner was a demotion, and it amounted to a loss of status and job satisfaction because the applicant was asked to perform an entirely different job.

Relying on the authorities, the Industrial Court in *Vilakati* found that by unlawfully varying the appointment of the applicant, the Judicial Service Commission had committed a fundamental breach of the contract of employment. However, as in other contracts, this did not in itself end the contract, but served only to vest the respondent with election either to stand by the contract or terminate it.[22] In the result, the Industrial Court held that by varying the applicant's appointment, the Judicial Service Commission had repudiated the contract between itself and the applicant, entitling the applicant to cancel the contract, which he did, and to treat the action of the Judicial Service Commission as constructive dismissal.

In *Stewart Wrightson (Pty) Ltd v Thorpe*,[23] the Court cited with approval the proposition in *Denny v S.A. Loan, Mortgage and Mercantile Agency Co Ltd*[24] that 'a defendant who had deprived the plaintiff of his position of manager and "degraded him to position of clerk" had in effect summarily dismissed him.' 'The test as to whether conduct amounts to such repudiation is whether fairly interpreted it exhibits a deliberate and unequivocal intention no longer to be bound.'[25]

A variation of a term of a contract of employment that results in a demotion, but the employee continues to remain in his employment as varied under protest, does not amount to a waiver of the employee's right to claim constructive dismissal. In *Marriot v Oxford & District Cooperation Society (No. 2)*,[26] the Court of Appeal held that the demotion of a foreman and the resultant reduction in his wages amounted to a constructive dismissal which had not been waived by his continuance under protest for a time in his employment as varied.

Variation of the terms of a contract should be distinguished from what is termed 'managerial prerogative'. The latter concerns matters relating to new and different methods by which jobs are to be performed. In *CDM (Pty) Ltd v Mineworkers Union of Namibia and others*, Frank, J relied on Wallis: *Labour and Employment Law* to explain the difference between variation of contractual rights and changes falling under the scope of managerial prerogative:

---

[22] See *Stewart Wrightson (Pty) Ltd v Thorpe* 1977 (2) SA 943 (A); and Christie, *The Law of Contract in South Africa,* pp.539-40 and the cases there cited.

[23] *Stewart Wrightson (Pty) Ltd v Thorpe* 1974 (4) SA 67.

[24] *Denny v SA Loan, Mortgage and Mercantile Agency Co. Ltd* 3 EDC 47. See also *Donaldson v Webber* 4 HCG 403.

[25] *Street v Dublin* 1961 (2) SA 4 (W) at 10B and the texts referred to *per* Williamson, J fn 25.

[26] *Marriott v Oxford & District Cooperation Society (No.2)* [1970] 1 QB 187.

The terms (of a contract of employment) will inevitably include the remuneration payable to the employee, the period of the contract if it is for a fixed term and some description of the job to be performed. In regard to the latter it is unlikely to be construed inflexibly provided that the fundamental nature of the work to be performed is not altered. The fact that some tasks are added and others removed or different methods to those initially used are to be adopted will not constitute a breach of contract.

Once the terms of a particular contract of employment have been ascertained it will be possible to identify those situations which involve a variation of contractual rights and distinguish them from situations falling within the scope of managerial prerogative. The former will require all the elements of a contract while the latter are exercises of discretion supported and sustained by the employee's 'duty of obedience to lawful orders'.[27]

Thus, while variation of contractual rights like those relating to remuneration and duration of the contract require the consent of the employee before they can be effected, the variation of matters under managerial prerogative do not necessarily require the employee's consent.

2.2.2 The Parties

Like any other kind of contract, a contract of employment requires two parties to effect it; it envisages two mutually exclusive entities as parties to the contract, i.e. an employer and an employee.[28] What this means is that in law an employer cannot be both the employer and employee at the same time, and vice versa. One's capacity to enter into a contract of employment is governed by the general principles of contract as modified by statute. Although the age of majority in Namibia according to the Age of Majority Act is 21 years,[29] as far as the Labour Act 2007 is concerned, a person who has attained the age of 18 years has the legal capacity to enter into a contract of employment.

Nokes v Doncaster Amalgamated Collieries Ltd[30] is authority for the proposition that an employee cannot be assigned to another employer like a chattel. The principle is predicated

---

27 *CDM (Pty) Ltd v Mineworkers Union of Namibia and others* 1994 NR 180 (LC) at 183F-G. See M.J.D. Wallis, *Labour and Employment Law*, Durban, Butterworth, 1992. The Court also relied on the Court of Appeal's decision in *Creswell and others v Board of Inland Revenue* [1984] 2 All ER 713.

28 *Boulting v Association of Cinematograph, Television and Allied Technicians* [1963] 2 QB 606 (CA).

29 Act No. 57 of 1972.

30 *Nokes v Doncaster Amalgamated Collieries Ltd* [1940] AC 1014.

upon the common law rule that an employee 'agrees that in consideration of a wage or other remuneration he will provide his own work and skill in the performance of some service to his master.'[31] We saw in chapter 1, para. 1.2.1 above that *locatio conductio rei* (the letting and hiring of a specified thing) in return for a monetary reward stands in contradiction to *locatio conductio operarum* (the letting and hiring of personal service) for monetary reward. Seminal to the principle of the unassignability of an employee to another employer is the principle of the unassignability of the rights of an employer or employee under a contract of employment to a third party without the consent of the other.[32] It is also based on the fundamental notion of the parties' freedom of contract.

To sum up, one employer cannot let the service of his employee to another without the employee's consent. Denning, LJ (as he then was) put it succinctly thus: 'No contract of service can be transferred from one employer to another without the servant's consent and the consent is not to be raised by operation of law.'[33] The converse is also true: an employee cannot compel his employer to take on another person in his place.

So firmly embedded in the law is the principle of unassignability of a right under a contract of employment, that even where one employer transfers his ownership of a business to another, the principle still applies.[34] Lord Atkin declared in *Nokes v Doncaster Amalgamated Collieries Ltd* supra, 'I had fancied that ingrained in the personal status of a citizen under our laws was the right to choose for himself whom he would serve, and that this right of choice constituted the main difference between a servant and a serf.'[35] Further on he said: 'The principle that a man is not to be compelled to serve a master against his will is...deep-seated in the common law of this country.'[36] It is submitted that the principle is also deeply rooted in Namibian labour law, given the many human rights guaranteed to individuals by the Namibian Constitution and the protection of the legal rights of employees and employers under the Labour Act 2007.

2.2.3 Duties of an Employee

The duties of an employee are left to be settled by the parties to the contract of employment establishing the employer-and-employee relationship, so long as what the parties agree to be bound by are within the four corners of the law. One primary duty of an employee is that he undertakes to provide his own skill in the performance of some agreed service for

---

31   *Ready Mixed Concrete (South East) v Minister of Pensions* [1968] 2 QB 433 at 440.

32   *Isaacson v Walsh & Walsh* (1903) 20 SC 56.

33   *Denham v Midland Employers Mutual Assurance Ltd* [1955] 2 QB 437 at 443; [1955] 2 All ER 561 at 564.

34   *MacLoughlan v Alexander Paterson Ltd* [1968] 1 TR 251.

35   *Nokes v Doncaster Amalgamated Collieries* supra at 1030.

36   Ibid. at 1033.

his employer. It is worth pointing out that apart from the express terms of a contract of employment outlining the duties of the employee, the law, as we saw previously (para. 2.2.1.4 above) reads certain terms into such contracts. Such terms may be put into two classifications.[37] The first are those terms that are imposed by law and, therefore, the parties are not free to agree that such terms should not form a part of their contract. For instance, under s. 17(1) of the Labour Act 2007, an employer must not require or permit an employee to work more than ten hours of overtime a week, and in any case, not more than three hours of overtime a day. The second are those terms that the courts will hold they apply, even if they have expressly been excluded from the contract. An example, which readily comes to mind, is the employee's duty to render his personal service exclusively to his employer during official working hours (see para. 2.2.1.4 above).

Apart from terms that the law imports into contracts of employment, there are terms that the courts may apply to a particular contract of employment because of the existence of some trade usage in relation to the particular job to be performed. Thus, an employee may be presumed to have entered into a contract of employment with his employer against the backdrop of some trade usage. From the authorities,[38] it is clear that a court will import a trade usage into a contract of employment only if it is satisfied that the usage is universally and uniformly observed within the relevant trade and is long established, reasonable, well-known and certain, and does not conflict with any law. It needs hardly saying that even where all the six conditions are fulfilled, a court will not apply the usage if its invocation will invalidate or vary an express term of the contract of employment.[39]

The duties of employees are examined in chapter 3, those of employers in chapter 4 and those common to employees and employers in chapter 5. The remedies that employers and employees have in the event of breaches are treated in chapter 6.

2.2.4 Duration

2.2.4.1 Contracts for Fixed Terms

An employment contract may be for a fixed term or for an indefinite duration. The parties may either agree that the contract should run for a fixed term or they may leave its duration undefined.[40] A contract for a fixed term is one whose duration is certain, e.g. a contract

---

37 Drake, *Labour Law,* paras 129-30.

38 *Crook v Pedersen Ltd* 1927 WLD 62; *Estate Duminy v Hofmeyr & Sons Ltd* 1925 CPD 115; *Freeman v Standard Bank of South Africa Ltd* 1905 TH 26; *Golden Grapefruits (Pty) Ltd v Fotoplate (Pty) Ltd* 1973 (2) SA 642 (C); *McLeod & Co v Dunnell, Ebden & Co* (1868) 1 Buch 182; *Meythal v Baxter* 1916 OPD 122; *Sagar v Ridehalgh* [1931] 1 Ch 310.

39 *Orman v Saville Sportswear Ltd* [1960] 1 WLR 1055.

40 *Tiopaizi v Bulawayo Municipality* 1923 AD 317.

for a specified number of days, months or years, e.g. thirty days, six months or two years. Where the fixed term is expressly provided in a contract of employment, it is not open to a court to import any implied term relating to duration. There is authority for the view that if upon the expiration of the fixed term, the employee continues to render his service to the employer in return for an agreed wage or other remuneration, the contract may be taken to have been tacitly renewed for a further term. However, for this imputation to be made, the court or tribunal will take into account the circumstances of the particular case, especially the conduct of the employer and the employee.[41] Where a new contract is deemed to have come into existence in this way, the terms and conditions will generally be taken to be the same as those in the original contract. However, with regard to duration, the new contract will be found to be either for the same period as the old contract or to continue indefinitely subject to satisfactory performance of duties, and terminable upon reasonable and fair notice being given by either party.[42] Whether the new contract will assume the character of a fixed-term contract or an indefinite-term contract will depend largely upon the circumstances of each case.

2.2.4.2 *Indefinite-Term Contracts*

Where parties to a contract of employment do not specify the duration of the contract, the contract is for an indefinite period. Of course, the parties themselves may specify that the contract be for an indefinite term. A contract for an indefinite term continues subject to termination upon the employee reaching retirement age or upon giving reasonable and fair notice in accordance with the terms of the contract or the Labour Act 2007, if the contract is subject to that Act. It may also be terminated by agreement or by fundamental breach committed by one party as was discussed earlier (para. 2.2.1.5 above) Termination of contracts of employment is treated more fully in chapter 7.

2.2.5 Remuneration

It will be remembered (from chapter 1, paras 1.2.3 and 1.2.2.5 above) that payment of remuneration is not an essential element of a contract of employment at common law; however, as stated previously, in terms of the Labour Act 2007, payment of remuneration is a statutory requirement, and therefore an essential element of a contract of employment subject to the Act.

---

41 *Redman v Colbeck* 1917 EDL 35.

42 The question of fairness or unfairness of failure to renew fixed term contracts is examined in some detail in chapter 7, para. 7.2.1 below.

The employee's remuneration must be fixed, and must be paid in cash. At common law an employee may be paid in money or anything sounding, or capable of sounding, in money. Thus, an employee may be paid wholly in money, wholly in kind or partly in money and partly in kind.[43] As we shall see later (in chapter 4, para. 4.3) at common law the specific amount payable may be expressed by the parties or implied.

2.2.6 The Employer's General Right of Control and Supervision

We saw in chapter 1(para. 1.2.2 above) that one of the most essential requirements of a contract of employment is the employer's general right of supervision and control over the manner in which the employee renders his personal service. It was also mentioned in that chapter that the degree of control depends largely upon the nature and complexity of the work assigned to the employee, the skills required to do the work and the location of the employee's duty station. If operations of an employer's business are located in one small area, the closer would be the employer's supervision of the operations. However, if the business operations are scattered over different countries on different continents, the more tenuous would be his supervision. Similarly, if an employee possesses skills that the employer does not have, then the degree of control exercised by the employer in respect of the manner in which the employee performs his duties will be a mere supposition.

Nevertheless, no matter how weak the employer's power of supervision and control might be, the reality of the employment relationship remains that an employee stands in a position of submission and subordination, allowing the employer to regulate to some degree the employer-and-employee relationship. Of course, with the intervention of statutes governing employment relations, the degree of submission and subordination has attenuated to a marked degree compared with the position of an employee at common law. In most cases, employees have the statutory right to form and join trade unions so as to protect their rights and interests as employees, and to challenge unreasonable and unfair conduct of their employers. We shall see in chapter 8 that the Labour Act 2007, for instance, protects employees from dismissal based on invalid and unfair reasons and unfair procedure. Consequently, the seemingly unfettered common law power of the employer to terminate the services of his employee at will has diminished in the face of present-day labour legislation like the Labour Act 2007.

---

43   J. Grogan, *Riekert's Employment Law,* 2nd edn, Cape Town, Juta, 1993, p. 22 and the cases cited.

3 DUTIES OF EMPLOYEES

3.1 INTRODUCTION

We saw in chapter 2 (para. 2.2 above) that the employer-and-employee relationship is fixed by the express and implied terms of their contract, and these terms govern the duties of employees (as well as their rights). In the labour law of common law countries, the implied terms, as we saw in chapter 2, may be based either on the common law or legislation. But, of course, national differences exist with regard to the duties that are subject to the common law and those that are governed by statute law. For instance, while under Swaziland's Employment Act[1] the general duties of an employee are specifically listed in s. 36 of that Act, there is no such express enumeration of the general duties of an employee in any one particular section of the Labour Act 2007. Consequently, it is to the common law and the various sections of the Labour Act and provisions of other applicable statutes,[2] that one must direct one's attention in this regard. The basic duties that the employee owes to his employer will now be discussed.

3.2 PERSONAL SERVICE

We saw in chapter 1 (para. 1.2.1) that the primary and central duty of an employee is to make over his or her capacity to produce to his employer.[3] As Joubert, JA put it in *Smit v Workmen's Compensation Commissioner*, the primary duty of an employee (*locator operarum*) is the rendering of personal service to his employer (*conductor operarum*).[4] Flowing from this principle is that the primary duty of an employee to his employer is to perform personal service in return for a wage or other remuneration. Thus, at common law, the failure of an employee to carry out this basic obligation will disentitle him to any wage. It has been held that it matters little if the employee has a reason for his failure to render such service.[5]

---

1   Act No.5 of 1980.

2   For instance the Public Service Act 1995 of Namibia (Act No. 13 of 1995).

3   M.S.M. Brassey et al., *The New Labour Law*, Cape Town, Juta, 1987, p. 899.

4   *Smit v Workmen's Compensation Commissioner* 1979 (1) SA 51 (A).

5   *Potchefstroom Municipal Council v Bouwer NO* 1958 (4) SA 382 (T).

The converse is also true, i.e. an employee who tenders his service but is prevented from working is entitled to his wages. Therefore, so long as the contract of employment subsists, the employee is under an obligation to perform personal service to his employer. All these are subject to legal strike and lockout, which are discussed in chapter 13 below.

3.3 Not to be Absent from Work

Related to an employee's duty to render personal service to his employer while the contract of employment is in force is the matter of absence from work. An employee is obliged by the contract of employment not to be absent from work. At common law, a contract of employment requires an employee to report for work and to remain at work in order to furnish his personal service for the duration of the agreed daily hours of work. Therefore, an employee has a duty not to absent himself from work without lawful excuse. The common law duty has been buttressed by legislation. For instance, in terms of s. 25(1) of the Public Service Act 1995,[6] a staff member is guilty of misconduct if he absents himself from work without leave or valid reason.

The question is: what is the effect of absence from work? In considering the question, it is necessary to distinguish between intentional (i.e. wilful) absence from work without lawful or reasonable excuse, and absence from work due to some provable or proven illness or injury. In this connection, the words 'without leave or valid reason' in the Public Service Act 1995, for example, refer to wilful and blameable absence. Wilful and blameable absence from work is, as a general rule, prima facie breach of duty to render personal service, which may result in dismissal. It should be noted that wages cannot be claimed as of right during the period of wilful and blameable absence from work. A key factor an employer faced with this problem ought to take into account is whether there have been only occasional and isolated incidences of absence from work, or the employee's behaviour has become a pattern or a persistent practice. Absence from work, which has become a pattern or a persistent behaviour, is referred to as absenteeism. While absenteeism may attract the serious sanction of dismissal, absences from work, which are few and far between, may not, especially if such absences have had minimal or no detrimental effect on the business operations of the employer.[7]

---

6   Act No. 13 of 1995. This is how the Public Service Act 1995 will be referred to in the rest of the book without footnoting.

7   *Schneir & London Ltd v Bennet* 1927 TPD 346; *Negro v Continental Spinning & Knitting Mills* 1954 SA (2) 203 (W).

In short, the question to be determined is whether an employee's absenteeism amounts to a breach of a fundamental term, i.e. a breach that goes to the root of the contract of employment?[8] In deciding whether the employee's absence amounts to a fundamental breach, the employer may take into account factors such as the following.

1 How critical to the smooth operation of the organization is the employee's individual personal service? On this score, the decision in *Kaplin v Penkin*[9] cannot be supported. In that case it was held that the employer was not entitled to dismiss his employee, a cinema projectionist. The employee arrived at the cinema ten minutes late and found a fault in the projector. He could not repair the fault on time, and this led to a scheduled performance being cancelled. The employee's personal service to the cinema business was crucial; any show depended upon his punctual arrival at his place of work. The view of the court in *Brown v Sessel*[10] appears to be the correct view. There, Wessels, J. stated:

> It is perfectly clear that absence from duty is under certain circumstances, a good ground for dismissal. But from the authorities it appears to me very difficult to lay down any general rule. Each case depends upon the nature of the contract between the employer and the employee, and what the result of the employee's absence was to the employer. And it appears to me prejudice to the employer is a very important element in determining whether or not he has a right to dismiss the servant.[11]

2 For how long has the employee been in the employment of the employer and on how many occasions has he been absent from work?

3 At what times of the month is he absent from work? For instance, does he absent himself immediately after receiving his wage, which may indicate that he is only interested in the wage, not in rendering his personal service?

4 Does the employee furnish a lawful excuse for his absence immediately he reports back for work or before he reports back for work?

---

8   *Strachan v Prinsloo* 1925 TDP 709.

9   *Kaplin v Penkin* 1933 CPD 233.

10   *Brown v Sessel* 1908 TS 1137.

11   Ibid. at 1139-40.

5 Has the employee ignored warnings in the past to refrain from absenting himself from work?

6 Are there any regulations in the employer's enterprise against absenteeism, and are employees made sufficiently aware of such regulations?

In terms of s. 24(5) of the Public Service Act 1995, for instance, a staff member who absents himself from work for more than thirty days without leave or valid reason is considered as having absconded from the public service and, therefore, is summarily dismissible. The basis of this rule is that by so absenting himself for such a long time without valid reason or leave, the civil servant has breached the duty to render personal service to the public service, which is a term that goes to the root of the contract of employment, entitling the Government, as his employer, to terminate the contract of employment summarily.

There are occasions when absence is due to an illness or injury or some event beyond the employee's control, such as where because of some serious civil commotion, the police order certain sections of the population of a town to remain indoors so as to enable the security forces to contain the situation, and the employee is affected by the police order. In the case of sickness or injury, it is necessary to draw a line between sickness or injury that makes the continued rendering of personal service impossible and sickness or injury that does not have such consequence. In the later situation, it is a common practice that the employee should apply for and be given sick leave. If an application cannot be made in advance, the employee should deliver or cause to be delivered to the employer within a reasonable time a recommendation by an authorized medical practitioner that he be granted leave of absence from work due to illness or injury.

One important point deserves to be made. As was rightly noted in *Ellerines Furniture Namibia (Pty) Ltd t/a Furncity Furniture v De Vos*, 'Going to hospital or honouring a doctor's appointment is not a ground for abandoning one's workstation without permission unless the circumstances are such that it was not necessary to seek permission before leaving.'[12] Where the employee's illness or injury is such that it is impossible for him to continue to work, the employer may take the necessary steps according to laid down procedures to have a medical practitioner examine the employee to determine whether it is not in the interest of both the employee and the employer or either of them to terminate the contract of employment.[13]

On the question of whether wages are due and payable to an employee who has been absent due to illness or injury, Pilcher, J pronounced himself on the law in the following passage in *Orman v Saville Sportwear Ltd*:

---

12   *Ellerines Furniture Namibia (Pty) Ltd t/a Furncity Furniture v De Vos* NLLP 2004 (4) 35 NLC at 41.

13   See e.g. s. 24 of the Public Service Act 1995.

Where the written terms of contract of service are silent as to what is to happen in regard to the employee's rights to be paid whilst he is absent from work due to sickness, the employer remains liable to continue paying so long as the contract is not determined by prior notice, except where a condition to the contrary can properly be inferred from all the facts and evidence in the case.[14]

Thus, as a general rule, the employer is not obliged to remunerate an employee during his absence from work due to illness or injury.[15] However, he is not entitled to dismiss him just because he is not able to render his personal service for a short period due to illness or injury, and what constitutes a short period will depend upon the circumstances of each case. The reason is that the contract of employment is still in force.[16] It must be borne in mind that the Labour Act 2007 has changed the general rule with regard to employment contracts subject to the Act.

It is worth pointing out that where an employee absents himself from work for a considerable length of time without leave or lawful excuse, and the contract of employment is terminated, it is the employee who repudiated the contract in the first place: in law, he was not dismissed.[17]

3.4 PUNCTUALITY

As a general rule, persistent unpunctuality of an employee may result in his dismissal. However, the considerations discussed above (in para. 3.3) with regard to absence from work, should apply with necessary changes when the employer is considering dismissal on the ground of unpunctuality.

3.5 OBEDIENCE TO REASONABLE AND LAWFUL INSTRUCTIONS

An employee's obedience to the lawful and reasonable instructions of his employer is the touchstone of the employer-and-employee relationship. The employee must carry out a

---

14 *Orman v Saville Sportwear Ltd* [1960] 1 WLR 1055 at 1064.

15 *Boyd v. Stuttaford & Co* 1910 AD 101. See also chapter 4, para. 4.8.2 below, where statutory paid sick leave is discussed.

16 *Magawo v Caledon Divisional Council* 1972 (3) SA 365 (C).

17 *Cross Country Carriers v Farmer* NLLP 1998 (I) 226 NLC; *Johannes Swartbooi v Deon Heunis* Case No.: LCA 6/2001 (unreported).

lawful order that is within the scope of the express or implied terms of his contract of employment.[18] Failure to do so is insubordination, i.e. the wilful disobedience of the lawful and reasonable commands of the employer. Insubordination may take the form of sheer insolence, benign refusal to carry out the lawful orders of the employer, or verbal defiance accompanied by vitriolic vituperations.

It is worth noting that an employee cannot be required to carry out an unlawful order or to perform a service outside the scope of his employment,[19] for as we saw in chapter 2 (para. 2.2.1.5 above), an employee is entitled to hold the office or job to which he was employed: any changes must be negotiated and accepted by both parties.

It has been explained that disobedience is when the employee refuses to obey a lawful and reasonable command or request and the refusal is wilful and serious (wilful disobedience), or when the employee's conduct poses a deliberate (wilful) and serious challenge to the employer's authority.[20] An incidence of disobedience of a lawful order cannot simply, without more, amount to a repudiation of the contract of employment: the courts ought to take into account all the circumstances of the particular case. In *Monareng v Midrand Motolek cc*[21] the court referred with approval to a proposition by Brassey et al.[22] and found that irrespective of the lawfulness and reasonableness of the employer's orders or instructions, the courts will not hold that the employee has repudiated the contract of employment where there is evidence tending to show that the failure to obey was justified or reasonable, such as where employees feared for their safety if the order or instruction was carried out. Such a factor was taken into account by the Industrial Court in *SALDCDAWU v Advance Laundries t/a Stork Napkins*[23] where employees failed to obey their employer's instructions not to leave their workplace before a certain appointed time under circumstances where they feared for their lives. Similarly, it is not a reasonable or lawful order where the carrying out of the order exposes the employee to immediate and real danger.[24]

Insubordination will justify dismissal, especially if it is wilful or repeated because a wilful and repeated disobedience shows a complete disregard for a term essential to the contract of service, namely, that an employee must obey the lawful and reasonable orders of his employer. Unless he does so, the employment relationship is destroyed.[25] In *Kausiona*

---

18   *Khan v Rainbow Chicken Farms* (1985) 6 *ILJ* 60 (IC).

19   *Morrish v Henlys (Folkestone) Ltd* [1973] ICR 482.

20   *CCAWUSA v Wooltrul Ltd. t/a Woolworths (Randburg)* (1989) 19 *ILJ* 331 (IC).

21   *Monareng v Midrand Motelek cc* (1991) 12 *ILJ* 1348 (IC)

22   Brassey et al., *The New Labour Law*, p. 431.

23   *SALDCDAWU v Advance Laundries t/a Stork Napkins* (1985) 6 *ILJ* 544 (IC).

24   *Ottoman Bank v Chakarian* [1930] AC 277.

25   *Madlala v Vynne & Tedder t/a Thorville Engineering* (1990) 11 *ILJ* 394 (IC); *Mqhayi v. Van Leer SA (Pty) Ltd* (1984) 5 *ILJ* 179 (IC).

v Namibia Institute of Mining and Technology,[26] the Labour Court accepted the contention of the respondent's counsel that insubordination strikes at the heart of the employment relationship between the parties and held that the district labour court was, therefore, correct in finding that the respondent had a valid and fair reason when he dismissed the appellant for insubordination (see chapter 8 para. 8.1 where unfair dismissal is discussed). In terms of s. 25(1)(c) of the Public Service Act 1995, for instance, a public servant who disobeys a lawful order or is insubordinate is guilty of misconduct and may be dismissed.

It has been said that a single and isolated act of insubordination may not amount to a repudiation of the contract of employment.[27] What ought to be taken into account in determining whether the disobedience amounts to repudiation of the contract does not hinge only on how many times disobedience takes place, but also on whether the nature of the disobedience and the form that it takes are so serious and malicious that only one logical and reasonable conclusion can be drawn, namely, the intention of the employee to refuse to be bound by the contract of employment. In *Pepper v Webb*,[28] the employee's refusal to obey a reasonable and lawful order of his employer was accompanied by insulting words and insolent behaviour. The House of Lords held that the employee had repudiated his contract. In so holding, the House of Lords took into account the employee's past incidences of insolence and insubordination. Thus, only serious, persistent, depraved, and intentional disobedience, such as where the refusal is accompanied by vituperations and insolent conduct, would amount to a repudiation of the contract of employment.[29] When an employee is disobedient he repudiates his contract of employment,[30] and in determining whether there has been repudiation all the surrounding circumstances and the nature of the contract ought to be taken into account.

3.6 Furthering the Interests of the Employer

Connected to his duty to obey the reasonable and lawful orders of his employer, is an employee's duty to further the interests of the employer. Of course, it is not easy to determine in a vacuum the parameters of an employee's duty to serve faithfully the interests of his employer. However, in practice, it may not be so difficult to determine those acts and

---

26   *Kausiona v Namibia Institute of Mining and Technology* NLLP 2004 (4) 43 NLC.

27   *Laws v London Chronicle* (1959) 1 WLR 698.

28   *Pepper v Webb* [1969] 1 WLR 514.

29   *Chemical Workers Industrial Union & another v AECI Paints (Pty) Ltd* (1988) 9 *ILJ* 1046 (IC).

30   *Monareng v Midrand Motolek* supra.

3.6.1 Devotion of the Employee's Energy and Skill

An employee is obliged by the contract of employment to devote all his energy and skill to the attainment of the objects of his employer's business during official working hours. He cannot enter into a contract of employment with another person whereby he has to furnish his personal service to that other person during the official working hours of his employer's business without his employer's consent.[31] However, the courts are wary or unwilling to place undue restrictions on an employee's spare time.[32] The justification for restraining an employee from performing personal service for someone other than his employer is the need to ensure the employee's absorption in the service he is performing for his employer.[33]

3.6.2 Using Information Gained in the Course of Employment

During employment, it is not furthering the business interests of his employer if an employee uses specific information gained in the cause of employment in a way that endangers the business interests of his employer.[34] Therefore, divulging confidential information gained in the course of employment to an unauthorized person constitutes a breach of the employee's duty to faithfully serve the employer and further his business interests. As was held in *Prism Holdings Ltd and another v Liversage and others*,[35] the respondents were not entitled to use confidential information gained during the period of their employment with the applicants to compete with the applicants.

3.6.3 Employees' Inventions

A contract of employment may regulate the right of an employee to exploit his own invention. If there is no such express provision in the contract, an employer may, taking into account the circumstances of the case, have the right to his employee's invention which arose out of the employee's performance of his service to the employer.[36]

---

31   *Harrismith Building Society v Taylor* 1938 OPD 36.

32   A.C. Bell, *Employment Law in a Nutshell*, London, Sweet & Maxwell, 2000, p. 18.

33   *Esso Petroleum Co v Harper's Garage (Sturport) Ltd* [1968] AC 269.

34   *Pelunsky v Teron* 1913 WLD 34.

35   *Prism Holdings Ltd and another v Liversage and others* 2004 (2) SA 478 (W).

36   *Sterling Engineering Co v Patchett* [1955] AC 534.

3.6.4 Fiduciary Duties

It has been said that the employee's duty to act in good faith in the furtherance of the business interests of the employer is a fiduciary one. In *Ganes and another v Telecom Namibia Ltd*,[37] the Supreme Court of Appeal stated that in the absence of an agreement to the contrary, an employee owes the employer a duty of good faith, which means that, in the course of his employment or by means of his position as an employee of the employer, the employee is obliged not to act against the employer's interests; not to place himself in a position where his interests conflict with those of the employer; not to make a secret profit or commission at the expense of the employer; and not to receive a bribe from a third party. According to the Court, if these duties are breached, the employer may claim from the employee any secret profit or commission or a bribe received by the employee without the consent of the employer: the employer's remedy in this regard is based on the fiduciary duty the employee owes to him.

In *Boston Deep Sea Fishing & Ice Co. v. Ansell*,[38] a managing director of a fishing company took a secret commission from a supplier. He was dismissed, and he brought a suit to the Court for wrongful dismissal. The Court held that he had broken his duty of good faith and therefore the dismissal was valid. And in *Phillips v Fieldstone Africa (Pty) Ltd and another*,[39] the appellant, an employee of the respondent, acquired shares in a company with which he was dealing for his own interest and not in the furtherance of the interests of his employer. The South African Supreme Court of Appeal held that the appellant was in a position of trust in relation to the business of his employer, and that required him to place his employer's business interests above his own interests whenever there was a real likelihood of conflict of interests. According to the Court, the duties of the appellant as an employee included the furtherance of his employer's business interests, which included the duty to disclose to his employer such information that came to his knowledge, which might reasonably be thought to have a bearing on the employer's business. Having failed to inform his employer about the offer made to him to buy the shares, he had breached his duty to his employer, and in that regard, in the face of a potential conflict of interest between his duty to his employer and his own self-interest, the employee had placed his self-interest above the business interests of his employer. Therefore, the employee had to account for the profit

---

37 *Ganes and another v Telecom Namibia Ltd* 2004 (3) SA 615 (SCA); See also *Daewoo Heavy Industries (SA) (Pty) Ltd v Banks and others* 2004 (4) SA 458 (C); *Gerry Bouwer Motors (Pty) v Preller* 1940 TPD 130 and the English cases of *Sanders v Parry* [1967] 2 All ER 145; *Hivac Ltd v Park Scientific Instruments Ltd* [1946] Ch 169. Cf. J. Grogan, *Riekert's Employment Law,* 2nd edn, Cape Town, Juta, 1993, p. 41, where it is said that the duty to act in good faith in the furtherance of the business interests of the employer comes close to being a fiduciary one.

38 *Boston Deep Sea Fishing & Ice Co. V Ansell* (1889) 39 Ch D 339.

39 *Phillips v Fieldstone Africa (Pty) Ltd and another* [2004] 1 All SA 150 (SCA).

made. In *Gerry Bouwers Motors (Pty) Ltd v Preller*,[40] the Court dismissed an appeal by a car salesman against dismissal for receiving a secret commission. The decisions in the above cases are, therefore, authority for the proposition that an employee has a duty to account for secret commission and profits made, and bribes received, by him in the course of his employment and through his position as an employee without the consent of the employer.

3.7 COMPETENCE AND EFFICIENCY

It is an implied term of a contract of employment, even if there is no express term, that the employee will furnish his service in a competent and efficient manner.[41] Any representation made by an employee in his application or at an oral interview during the recruitment process binds the employee. If he does not live up to the level of skill and competence he held out to the employer that he possessed, that would amount to a breach of the employment contract. The level of competence and efficiency expected of an employee is that displayed by others who have comparable academic qualification, skill and experience. The competence and efficiency of an employee can also be measured in terms of the reasonably expected output of the employee's performance, particularly in the manufacturing and retail industries.

In *O'Reilly v Graaff-Reinetse Kooperatiewe Winkels Bpk*,[42] the respondent's (employer's) business consisted of seven departments. Each department had its own manager. Since 1989, the applicant (employee) had been the manager of the grocery department – by far the largest department in the respondent's business. Initially, the applicant performed his duties satisfactorily. However, in the 1990-91 financial year, the gross profit of the grocery department fell from 12.76 per cent of the previous year to 7.6 per cent. In comparison, the other departments were doing very well as far as gross profit was concerned. The poor performance of the applicant caused the employer severe losses. The general manager discussed the employee's poor performance with him. The employee also received counselling. As the Industrial Court found, the employee had ample opportunities to improve his performance but failed to do so. The Court, therefore, accepted the employer's contention that the employee was incompetent.

---

[40] *Gerry Bouwers Motors (Pty) Ltd v Preller* 1940 TPD 130. See *Commercial Bank of Namibia Ltd v Van Wyk.* NLLP 2004 (4) 250 NLC at 253, where the Labour Court referred with approval to *Preller.*

[41] *Friedlander v Hodes* 1944 CPD 169.

[42] *O'Reilly v Graaf-Reinetse Kooperatiewe Winkels Bpk* (1991) 12 *ILJ* 1360 (IC).

The courts have accepted that an employer has a right in principle to dismiss his employee for incompetence.[43] If an employee is found to display incompetence in the performance of his service and yet refuses to be trained, the employer is entitled to dismiss him.[44] In *Rossam v Kraatz Welding Engineering (Pty) Ltd,*[45] the employee as head of the steel sales department failed to act and rectify shortcomings in his department, although the shortcomings had been pointed out to him by management. The court held that indeed a case of poor work performance had been made out against him.

An employer has the right to dismiss his employee where the employee's performance has been so poor or unsatisfactory that the employer cannot reasonably be expected to continue employing him. But in order for the dismissal for poor or unsatisfactory performance to be fair, the employer bears the onus of satisfying the court or other tribunal that he has:

1   pointed out to the employee his shortcomings and respects in which his performance is unsatisfactory;

2   given to the employee a reasonable opportunity to improve his performance; and

3   warned the employee that if he did not improve, he faced the likelihood of dismissal.[46]

In *Goagoseb v Arechenab Fishing & Development Co (Pty) Ltd,*[47] although the appellant was an administrative manager, he was really doing the work of a clerk. His poor work performance was discussed with him and appropriate remedial measures taken by the respondent. He was given a clerk to assist him, a mini training was offered to him and forms were prepared so as to simplify the work he had to do. All this notwithstanding, the appellant was not able to cope and could not meet deadlines. In the circumstances, according to the Labour Court, it would have been fair to terminate his services. Nevertheless, the respondent decided not to dismiss him but to accommodate him by offering him the opportunity to stay on at a lower salary. It was after the appellant had rejected the respondent's offer that his services were terminated. The dismissed employee approached the district labour court contending that his dismissal was unfair. The district labour court held that in the circumstances the appellant was dismissed for a fair and valid reason. The Labour Court

---

43   Grogan, *Riekert's Employment Law,* p. 38; *Madayi v Timpson Bata (Pty) Ltd* (1987) 8 *ILJ* 494 (IC). In this connection, see chapter 8, para. 8.1 below, where unfair dismissal is discussed.

44   *Building Construction and Allied Workers Union and others v Group 5/Combrink Construction* (1993) 2 LCD 117 (LAC).

45   *Rossam v Kraatz Welding Engineering (Pty) Ltd* 1998 NR 90 (LC).

46   *Johannes Swarbooi v Deon Heunis* Case No. LCA 6/2001 (unreported).s.

47   *Goagoseb v Arechenab Fishing & Development Co (Pty) Ltd* NLLP 2004 (4) 10 NLC.

found that the district labour court was correct when it held that the appellant was dismissed for a fair and valid reason. (Unfair dismissal is treated in chapter 8, para. 8.1.2 below.)

3.8 ADAPTABILITY

Related to the employee's duty to perform his service competently and efficiently, is his duty to adapt to new methods and techniques introduced in the employer's undertaking. However, the employee's duty can only arise if the employer has provided appropriate training or retraining.[48] The critical question that arises is whether the changes merely amount to an adaptation of the way in which the work is carried out or a change of the job itself. In other words, will the employee be doing a different job or he will merely be doing recognisably the same job in a different way?[49] If the changes amount to a change of work itself, which the employee cannot cope with, then the question of redundancy may arise.[50]

3.9 NOT TO BE GUILTY OF MISCONDUCT OR IMPROPER BEHAVIOUR

3.9.1 Introduction

In labour law, the term 'misconduct' covers a wide sweep of improper behaviour on the part of the employee, encompassing a range of offences in the employment relationship.[51] The following offences of an employee constitute misconduct at common law: a dishonest act, negligence, drunkenness, indolence, insolence, fighting, insulting remarks, revealing trade secrets, and absenteeism.[52] Some statutes have not only confirmed the common law instances of misconduct,[53] but they have also added to the common law list such improper behaviour as assault, fraud, damage to property, unauthorized use of motor vehicle, and sexual harassment. Absenteeism and revealing of trade secrets have already been discussed in para. 3.3 and chapter 2 para. 2.6.5 above, respectively. It now remains to discuss the other forms of misconduct, apart from sexual harassment, which falls under duties common to both employees and employers and is dealt with in chapter 5, para. 5.5.

---

48   *Creswell and others v Board of Inland Revenue* [1984] 2 All ER 713. See also *CDM (Pty) Ltd v Mineworkers Union of Namibia & others* 1994 NR 180 (LC), where *Creswell v Inland Revenue* was referred to with approval.

49   See *Creswell v Inland Revenue* supra.

50   *North Riding Garages Ltd v Butterwick* [1967] 2 QB 56. Unfair dismissal due to redundancy is treated fully in chapter 8, para. 8.3 below.

51   C.D. Drake, *Labour Law,* 2nd edn, London, Sweet & Maxwell, 1973, para. 74.

52   Grogan, *Riekert's Employment Law*, p. 47.

53   For example, the Public Service Act 1995 and the Labour Act 2007.

3.9.2 Dishonest Act

According to its ordinary meaning, a dishonest act is any act (including an omission) or conduct whose object is to cheat, steal, deceive, defraud and to tell lies.[54] From its ordinary meaning the conclusion can be drawn that a dishonest act strikes at the very core of trust, which is a *sine qua non* of the employer-and-employee relationship.

A dishonest act may manifest itself in a number of ways, e.g. the making of a false statement or representation or the withholding of information, which the employee is lawfully or reasonably required to give.[55] For instance, the employee may falsely state that he has a certain academic qualification, which results in the employer promoting him or putting him in a certain position in the organization, or the employee may fail to disclose that he has business interests in a company with which his employer has business dealings,[56] or while applying to join a benefit fund, the employee may intentionally conceal the fact that he has already received benefits from other sources. Conduct amounts to insincerity, and, therefore, a dishonest act, where the employee collects wages or other remuneration when he knows that they are not due to him.

In *Fana Ndaba v Thekwini Wholesalers*,[57] the applicant (employee) travelled from Swaziland to South Africa and borrowed R600 from the manageress of the respondent (employer) at its headquarters in South Africa. He made the manager believe that he needed the money to pay off his staff loan at the respondent's Manzini shop, but instead used it to pay off a private loan and to settle his rent arrears. In fact, the manageress had agreed to lend the applicant R600 on condition that he would use the borrowed money to pay off the Manzini store staff loan; the employee had, indeed, told her that that was the purpose of the loan. The Industrial Court found that the conduct of the employee amounted to a dishonest act because the employee was insincere and deceitful in his dealings with his employer.

In *Metropolitan Namibia Ltd v Haimbili*,[58] the respondent was found to have acted dishonestly in causing funds to be transferred from a client's account (the client was her mother) to her own account without following the laid-down procedures, and also to have abused her position by instructing her subordinate to effect the transfer on her behalf. The Labour Court, therefore, rejected the respondent's contention that there was no valid or fair reason for her dismissal by the appellant. In that case,[59] Manyarara, AJ relied on the following passage in *Standard Bank of SA Ltd v Commission for Conciliation, Mediation*

---

[54] *The Concise Oxford Dictionary*, 10th edn, Oxford, Clarendon Press, 2000.

[55] *Namibia Post Limited v Hans Eiman* Case No.: LCA 13/2005 (unreported).

[56] *Nadasen v C G Smith Sugar Ltd* (1992) 13 *ILJ* 1571 (IC).

[57] *Fana Ndaba v Thekwini Wholesalers* Swaziland IC 7/97 (unreported).

[58] *Metropolitan Namibia Ltd v Haimbili* NLLP 2004 (4) 110 NLC.

[59] Ibid. at 112.

and Arbitration and others to hold that the employer was entitled to summarily dismiss the employee (a bank employee and the respondent) for the offence of which the respondent was found guilty, viz. non-compliance with established procedures in the processing of loans by the bank:

> [I]t was one of the fundamental principles of the employment relationship that an employer should be able to place trust in the employee and that a breach of this trust or form of conduct involving dishonesty is one that goes to the heart of a relationship and is destructive of it. There can be no discounting of these principles in an environment such as the conduct of a bank. Every level and every transaction must be permeated with unqualified good faith.[60]

The Supreme Court was even more emphatic on the imperativeness of honesty on the part of bank employees in the following passage in *Hendrik Jacobus Van Wyk v Commercial Bank of Namibia Limited*: 'It is self evident that by virtue of the nature of work performed by bank employees, their employers are entitled to expect absolute integrity and absolute honesty at all times, i.e. in and out of work.'[61]

Relying on *Mahlangu v CIM Detlak, Gallant v CIM Detlak,*[62] and *Gerry Bouwers Motors (Pty) Ltd v Preller,*[63] the Labour Court found in *Commercial Bank of Namibia v Van Wyk*[64] that the dishonest conduct of the respondent rendered the continuation of the employment relationship insupportable. Consequently, the Court held that on that basis, the district labour court erred in finding that the dismissal of the applicant was unfair.[65] In that case, the Labour Court found that the respondent (employee) lied when he sought permission on the strength that he was going to visit his sister-in-law, but never visited her. He, thus, deceived his employer (appellant) and lied about his whereabouts with the knowledge that his employer would not have given him permission to go gambling during working hours. The Labour Court[66] referred with approval to the following passage in *Mahlangu v CIM Detlak, Gallant v CIM Detlak*: 'It is accepted that any act on the part of an employee in the performance of

---

60 *Standard Bank of SA Ltd v Commission for Conciliation, Mediation and Arbitration and others* 1998 19 *ILJ* 903 (LC) at 905J-906A.

61 *Hendrik Jacobus Van Wyk v Commercial Bank of Namibia Limited* Case No. SA 12/2004 (SC) at p. 4, *per* Chomba, AJA .

62 *Mahlangu v CIM Detlak, Gallant v CIM Detlak* (1986) 7 *ILJ* 346 (IC)

63 *Gerry Bouwers v Preller* supra.

64 *Commercial Bank of Namibia Ltd v Van Wyk* NLLP 2004 (4) 250 NLC.

65 The Supreme Court came to the same conclusion when the case came up on appeal in *Hendrik Jacobus Van Wyk v Commercial of Namibia* supra.

66 *Commercial Bank v Van Wyk* (Labour Court) *supra* at 253.

his employment activities, and of which dishonesty is a component, entitles the employer to dismiss the employee summarily. . . However, dishonesty must not be merely suspected, it must be proved, although this proof may be based on a balance of probabilities.[67]

Another form of dishonest act is theft, which is so serious and reprehensible that it usually attracts summary dismissal even if the employer is a first offender.[68] Theft by an employee is simply unacceptable in the employment situation. As was observed by Gibson, J in *OA-Eib v Swakopmund Hotel and Entertainment Centre*, 'Theft by an employee from an employer strikes at the trust that the employer reposes in his employee.'[69] In *Model Pick 'N Pay Family Supermarkets v Mwaala,* Damaseb, AJ (as he then was) observed: 'Theft (or dishonesty) is not to be taken lightly when it happens in the workplace, for it tends to destroy the relationship of trust between employer and employee.'[70]

As a general rule, the value of the stolen item does not matter in the least. In *Central News Agency (Pty) Ltd v Commercial Catering & Allied Workers Union and another* supra, the value of the item stolen was a paltry R50, and yet the Labour Appeal Court upheld the dismissal of the employee. In that case, De Klerk, J observed correctly as follows:

> In my view it is axiomatic to the relationship between the employer and employee that the employer should be able to rely upon the employee not to steal from the employer. This trust which the employer places in the employee is basic to and forms the substratum of the relationship between them. A breach of this duty goes to the root of the contract of employment and of the relationship between employer and employee ... [A]n employer unquestionably is entitled to expect from his employees that they would not steal from him and if an employee does steal from the employer that is such a breach of the relationship and of the contract between them and such a gross and criminal dereliction of duty that dismissal undoubtedly would be justified and fair.[71]

It is important to stress the point that in the charge of dishonest act, it is not required that the employer should necessarily have been prejudiced by the employee's dishonest act.

---

67 *Mahlangu v CIM Detlak* supra at 357F-H.

68 *Central News Agency (Pty) Ltd v Commercial Catering & Allied Workers Union & another* (1991) 12 *ILJ* 340 L (LAC).

69 *OA-Eib v Swakopmund Hotel and Entertainment Centre* 1999 NR 137 (LC) at 141A. See also *Foodcon (Pty) Ltd v Schwartz*. NLLP 2002 (2) 181 NLC.

70 *Model Pick 'N Pay Family Supermarket v Mwaala* 2003 NR 175 (LC) at 181F.

71 Ibid. at 344F-J. See also *Metcash Trading Ltd t/a Metro Cash and Carry v Fobb and another* (1998) *ILJ* 1516 (LC); *Foodcon (Pty) Ltd v Schwartz* supra.

3.9.3 Negligence

For our present purposes, negligence in the employment relationship should be understood to mean a breach of an employee's duty to exercise reasonable care in the performance of his service, i.e. the breach of standard of care that is expected of him by his employer in accordance with standards established by the employer or the vocation or profession to which the employee belongs, taking into account the nature of service that the employee performs. Thus, negligence is constituted by an act or omission or conduct that is found to be negligent.[72]

In *Empangeni Transport (Pty) Ltd v Zulu*,[73] the Industrial Court held that an employer is free to set standards, which an employee should follow in the performance of his service, and that the courts will only interfere if they find such standards to be grossly unreasonable. It is submitted that the level of 'gross unreasonableness' cannot be determined in a mechanical way. A court or tribunal must take into consideration the nature of service rendered by the employee; the standard set by the vocation or profession to which the employee belongs; the standard set by statute; and the effect of the negligent act on the operations of the employer's business and on fellow employees. For instance, a medical doctor employed by a hospital is expected to comply with the standard of care set by the hospital, as well as the standard of care set by the medical profession and supervised by the profession's controlling body, i.e. the Medical and Dental Council of Namibia.[74] Thus, a standard set by legislation ought to be taken into account. The employer bears the onus of proving that his employee has been negligent, i.e. his action or conduct has fallen short of the standard of care applicable in the particular circumstances.

3.9.4 Drunkenness and Use of Unprescribed Drugs and Substances

Drunkenness as a form of misconduct refers to the excessive consumption of alcohol or any intoxicating beverage by the employee resulting in his incapacity to perform his service to his employer. It does not matter whether the substance was consumed during or outside working hours or at his workplace or outside it: the test is whether the employee, because of drunkenness, is incapable of performing his service to his employer in terms of the contract of employment. The same considerations apply where the employee has taken unprescribed, stupefying drugs or similar substances making him incapable of performing his service to his employer.

---

72   *Anbeenco (Pty) Ltd and SACCAWU* (1991) *ARB* 8.14.10.

73   *Empangeni Transport (Pty) Ltd v Zulu* (1992) 13 *ILJ* 352 (IC).

74   The Council is established in terms of Part IV of the Medical and Dental Act 2004 (Act No. 10 of 2004).

3.9.5 Indolence

Indolence typifies a situation in which an employee does not apply his mind fully to his work because he is idle, lazy or is disinclined to perform his service. Such conduct may result in the employee not completing assignments given to him on time or not doing anything at all.[75] In order for the misconduct of indolence to be found proved against an employee, the court or tribunal will do well to take into account the performance of other employees assigned to carry out a similar task.

3.9.6 Insolence

Insolence is a form of common law misconduct, and its basis lies in the employee's obligation to show common respect and good manners toward his employer.[76] In *CCAWASU v Wooltru Ltd. T/a Woolworths (Randburg)* supra, the Industrial Court described insolence as impudence, cheekiness, disrespect and rudeness. Insolence, therefore, stands in contradistinction to insubordination, which denotes disobedience to reasonable and lawful order or instruction. Nevertheless, the line between insolence and disobedience is very fine and at times hard to draw. In *Lucas Zwane v Tip Top Holdings,*[77] the branch manager of the respondent (employer) instructed the applicant (employee) to assist three other employees to offload a filing cabinet from a truck, and carry it into the respondent's new shop. Not only did the employee refuse to carry out what seemed to be a reasonable and lawful instruction, but he also launched into a tirade of verbal abuse, calling the manager 'a stupid manager'. When the manager reminded him to whom he was talking, the employee replied, 'I don't f… care!' The Industrial Court found that the employee had not only been disrespectful, but he had also been insubordinate.

Where insolence is proved, the employee may still not suffer the ultimate sanction of dismissal unless the insolence is so gross, e.g. where the employee uses abusive and insulting language as was found in *Lucas Zwane v Tip Top Holdings* supra, or where the insolence is so recurrent as to give an indication that the employee is not prepared to abstain from such impudent or disrespectful behaviour.[78]

---

75 *Goagoseb v Arechenab Fishing* supra.

76 See P.A.K. Le Roux and A. Van Niekerk, *The South African Law of Unfair Dismissal,* Cape Town, Juta, 1994, p. 138.

77 Swaziland IC 77/95 (unreported).

78 Grogan, *Riekert's Employment Law*, p. 43.

3.9.7 Fighting and Similar Forms of Misconduct

An employee may be charged with misconduct for participating in a fight. The person against whom he fights could be a fellow employee or the employer, or a person who is neither an employee nor employer, e.g. a client or customer of the employer. It is still misconduct so long as the fighting occurs in the course or scope of the employee's employment, or if it happens on the premises or other property of the employer. Fighting is a serious form of misconduct because it brings the business of the employer into disrepute, particularly where the fight takes place in the presence of customers and other outsiders.[79] In *Mhlume Sugar Company v Jablane James Mbuli*,[80] the Court of Appeal accepted the English textual authority in the *Law of Unfair Dismissal* by S. D. Anderman (p. 146) that fighting or violence is well established as a category of misconduct for which a single offence can justify instant dismissal.

Fighting is distinguishable from assault, because, while fighting requires at least two perpetrators on opposite sides, an individual or a group of individuals is capable of perpetrating an assault against a victim or victims, i.e. another individual or a group of individuals. Therefore, with regard to fighting, the perpetrators are considered to be full and active participants. Hence, if two employees fight each other and only one is dismissed, the courts will find the dismissal unfair because of the difference in the treatment meted out.[81] But an employee who acts in self-defence may not be found guilty of misconduct so long as he is able to prove on a balance of probabilities that he was an unwilling participant or he was pushed beyond the point where he had no alternative but to defend himself against the attacker. In such a case, his response ought to be reasonably proportionate to the attack. Since, unlike fighting, an assault is perpetrated by a person against a passive victim, an assault must be viewed with even greater disapproval. The seriousness of an assault as a form of misconduct arises from the fact that it is a gross violation of the victim's personal integrity and dignity.[82] Besides, assault is not conducive to sound employment relations and interpersonal relations at the workplace.

Both fighting and assault are acts of violence, and an employee who is found guilty of such misconduct deserves little or no leniency. Therefore, the view of the Labour Appeal Court in *Scaw Metals Ltd. v Vermeulen*[83] that an employer is entitled to adopt an uncompromising approach to violence and, if it does, the Court must not interfere is very persuasive.

---

79   *CCAWUSA v Metro Cash & Carry Ltd* (1992) 1 LCD 28 (IC).

80   *Mhlume Sugar Company v Jablane James Mbuli* Swaziland CA 1/91 (unreported).

81   *ACTWUSA & others v J M Jacobsohn (Pty) Ltd.* (1970) 11 *ILJ* 107 (IC).

82   Le Roux and Van Niekerk, *South African Law of Unfair Dismissal*, p. 126.

83   *SCAW Metals Ltd v Vermuelen* (1993) 14 *ILJ* 672 (LAC).

Related to assault and fighting is intimidation, which means 'to frighten or overawe, especially to subdue or influence'[84] or 'to inspire with fear, cow, especially to influence conduct'.[85] In the employment relationship, it is misconduct for the employee to intimidate the employer so as to compel or influence the employer to carry out, or refrain from carrying out, a particular act. A good example is where the employee locks the general manager of the employer in his office and threatens to keep him there until the general manager grants him promotion or some remunerative benefit or until he removes a suspension hanging over the employee.

In *Kamanya & others v Kuiseb Fish Products Ltd.*,[86] the employee appellants were members of the crew of the *Erika*, a vessel of the respondent company, out on the open sea engaged in fishing operations. At some stage, the second mate threatened members of the crew with knives; he was subdued and disarmed by the first mate and locked in his cabin. The crew knew that the second mate was under control. Armed with spikes, spanners, knives and spades, the crew demanded to search the second mate's cabin for contraband like whisky and wine, but the skipper declined their demand. They were told to go back to their workstations and to continue with their work, but they disobeyed this lawful and reasonable order. They resorted to making noise, yelling and shouting. The situation was found to be so explosive that the first mate believed his life to be in danger. As a result of their conduct, the ship had to return to port, causing great loss to the employer respondent. Having found that their conduct was clearly threatening and intimidating, the Labour Court held that in law serious intimidation of the employer and/or co-employees was a valid reason for the summary dismissal of an employee.

Assault, fighting and intimidation ought to be distinguished from threatening violence. An example of threatening violence is what the Industrial Court found in *Lucas Zwane v Tip Top Holdings* supra. In that case, apart from his refusal to carry out a lawful and reasonable order of his branch manager and verbally abusing him, the employee walked towards the branch manager in an aggressive manner, removing his wristwatch as he walked menacingly towards him. The branch manager testified that he was afraid that the employee was going to hit him. The Industrial Court found that the applicant (employee) had threatened the branch manager with violence (see para 3.9.6 above).

To all these examples should be added the making of insulting remarks, e.g. racist remarks. In *Crown Chickens (Pty) Ltd t/a Rocklands Poultry v Kapp and others*,[87] the South African Labour Appeal Court commented on acts of racism in employment situations. The

---

84   See *The Concise Oxford Dictionary*, 10th edn.

85   *SA Allied Workers Union & others v Dorbyl Automotive Products (Pty) Ltd* (1988) 9 *ILJ* 680 (IC).

86   *Kamanya & others v Kuiseb Fish Products Ltd* 1996 NR 123 (LC).

87   *Crown Chickens (Pty) Ltd t/a Rocklands Poultry v Kapp and others* [2002] 6 BLLR 493.

Court stated that the courts should deal with matters of racism in a manner that would give expression to the legitimate feelings of outrage and revulsion that responsible members of the South African society – black and white – should have when acts of racism are perpetrated. Consequently, employees found guilty of scurrilous racist remarks and offensive utterances ought to be dismissed.[88] Given Namibia's apartheid colonial past and the signal efforts of the Government and the people to build 'One Namibia, One Nation', which eschews racism, coupled with the genuine efforts of the Government and the people to make the policy of reconciliation work, the decision in *Crown Chickens v Kapp* supra ought to be followed in Namibia.

3.9.8 Fraud

Fraud consists 'of a false representation deliberately made with the intention of being acted upon by another to his detriment'.[89] When such false representation is made with this criminal intent and with potential prejudice to the complainant the crime has been committed.' It does not matter if the unlawful, intentional and false representation causes actual prejudice or has the potential of causing prejudice to another person.[90] Fraud, like theft, is capable of undermining the very foundation of the employee-and-employer relationship, namely, trust, upon which such relationship rests. Hence, fraud is considered to be a very serious form of misconduct, which usually attracts the severest punishment, i.e. dismissal.

In order for the misconduct to attach to the employee, there must be a distortion of the truth that causes or is capable of causing prejudice or harm; in other words, the misrepresentation should have caused or has the potential of causing harm. The nature of the harm is usually financial or proprietary, but it need not always be so. Finally, it is incumbent upon the employee to prove that he did not know, or had no way of knowing, that the representation was false.

If an employee fails to disclose vital information in an application form, he can be charged with fraud, if the information was so vital in the recruitment process to such an extent that, had the full facts been disclosed, he would not have been employed or promoted. For instance, where an employee had misrepresented that he was not dismissed from his former employment, his conduct constitutes misconduct, if he would not have been employed had he disclosed this fact in his application.[91] Non-disclosure in itself will not constitute fraud unless the question of whether the employee had been dismissed from his former

---

88   See M. Oosthuizen, 'Racist language in the workplace', *De Rebus* 431 (March 2004) 46, where racist and other unacceptable remarks at the workplace are discussed with insight.

89   *Rex v Nay* 1934 TPD 52 at 54.

90   A.R. Snyman, *Criminal Law,* 3rd edn, Durban, Butterworths, 1995, p. 487.

91   *Beier Ltd v SACTWU* (1991) ARB 8.9.8.

Duties of Employees **61**

employment was asked, e.g. in an application form or during an interview, and the employee had answered in the negative, knowing that he was distorting the truth.

3.9.9 Damage to Property

It must be pointed out from the outset that it is the wilful damage to property that constitutes misconduct and not accidental or negligent damage to property. If the damage is caused by the employee's negligence, he must rather be charged with negligence. Wilful damage to property breaches the trust, which the employer-and-employee relationship places on the employee in relation to the property of the employer. Hence the employer is entitled to dismiss an employee who commits such misconduct.[92] However, whether damage to property should attract dismissal depends largely on the value of the property, how crucial the property is to the smooth operation of the business of the employer and, more importantly, the circumstances under which the property is damaged. For instance, did the employee damage the property during the commission of another form of misconduct, e.g. when the employee was drunk and incapable, or when he was engaged in a strike with a view to sabotaging the smooth running of the business of the employer?

Where damage to property is carried out with the sole purpose of sabotaging the product of the employer's business, or with the sole aim of preventing the smooth operation of the employer's business, the courts have endorsed the prompt and severe response of the employer in summarily dismissing his employee.[93] The misconduct is committed whether the property in question belongs to the employer or whether it belongs to another person but has been left in the employer's care and control.

3.9.10 Unauthorized Use of Employer's Motor Vehicle

The unauthorized use of the employer's motor vehicle is a form of misconduct that continues to gain great notoriety in many organizations. The conduct is regarded as a serious offence capable of attracting a dismissal, especially if there are clear rules prohibiting employees from using or driving the organization's motor vehicles without authorization. The unauthorized use of motor vehicles belonging to an organization carrying out the business of transport has been regarded as particularly unacceptable.[94] The offence will be viewed in a serious light if, for instance, by driving off the organization's motor vehicle without permission, the employee deprives the organization the capacity to perform an important service. This can occur where the vehicle is needed to carry some senior personnel to an important meeting,

---

92   *SA Breweries Ltd v FAWU and others* (1992) 1 *LCD* 16 (LAC).

93   *SACWU & others v Noristan Holdings Ltd and others* (1987) 8 *ILJ* 682 (IC).

94   *Machine Moving International (Pty) Ltd and TGWU* (1990) *ARB* 1.4.2.

or where because of the employee's conduct, an operation of the organization is brought to a standstill or harmed, as where a group of employees are deprived of the use of a truck that they were to use to carry goods to a customer.

An employee may also be charged with the misconduct of unauthorized use of a motor vehicle if, instead of using the vehicle for the purpose for which he was authorized, he goes on a frolic of his own with the vehicle. The arbitrator in *Interstate Matsebulas Bus Service and TGWU* [95] found the dismissal of an employee fair where the employee had not only driven the employer's vehicle without permission, but the vehicle had also been involved in an accident.

3.9.11 The Rule in Hollington's Case

In view of the rule in *Hollington v F H Hewthorn & Co Ltd*,[96] where an employee charged with misconduct had been charged with a criminal offence for that misconduct and tried in a criminal court, the evidence of the criminal conviction of the employee or employer is not admissible in civil or arbitral proceedings between different parties to prove the facts upon which such conviction was based. That the rule is alive and still applicable is borne out by a statement by Hofmann, J (as he then was) in *Land Securities plc v Westminster City Council*: 'In principle the judgment, verdict or award of another tribunal is not admissible evidence to prove a fact in issue or a fact relevant to the issue in other proceedings between different parties. The leading authority for that proposition is *Hollington v F Hewthorn & Co*.'[97]

The rule is not, however, applicable to disciplinary hearings because disciplinary hearings conducted by, for instance, an employer's disciplinary committee are not judicial or quasi-judicial 'proceedings', nor is the disciplinary committee a court or a tribunal. That being so, s. 26(10) of the Public Service Act 1995 cannot be faulted. In terms of that provision, if the misconduct with which a staff member has been charged under the Public Service Act constitutes an offence of which he has been convicted by a court, then a certified copy of the record of his trial and conviction is conclusive proof that he is guilty of the misconduct, unless the conviction has been set aside by an appeal court. In that case there is no need for a hearing to establish his guilt, for he has already had his day in court. In such a situation, all that is left for the disciplinary committee to do is to recommend an appropriate punishment.

---

[95]   *Interstate Matsebulas Bus Service and TGWU* (1991) *ARB* 10.4.6.

[96]   *Hollington v F H Hewthorn & Co Ltd* [1942] 3 All ER 35.

[97]   *Land Securities plc v Westminster City Council* [1993] 4 All ER 124 at 126 C.

3.10 Duties of Employee after Separation

Two important topics will be discussed under this heading, namely, (1) restraint of trade clauses in contracts of employment and (2) employees using information gained during employment for their own business or for the business of a new employer.

3.10.1 Restraint of Trade

The type of restraint discussed earlier (in para. 3.6) concerns the limitation imposed while the employee is still in the employment of his employer. There, 'restraint of trade' is used to refer to limitations that become operative after the employee has separated from the service of his former employer. A restraint of trade clause in a contract of employment aims to limit the freedom of the employee after he has separated from the service of his employer to set up or join a business in direct competition to his employer's business.

In *Magna Alloys and Research (SA) (Pty) Ltd v Ellis*,[98] after reviewing the authorities, the then Appellate Division of the Supreme Court stated that under South African law, unlike English law,[99] restraint of trade clauses in contracts of employment are prima facie valid and enforceable. The Court came to the conclusion that in terms of the common law, parties of equal standing are free to conclude and enforce a contract in restraint of trade unless it is proved that the contract is contrary to public policy. In *J Louw and Co (Pty) Ltd v Richter and others,* Didicott, J stated:

> Covenants in restraint of trade are valid. Like all other contractual stipulations, however, they are unenforceable when, and to the extent that, their enforcement would be contrary to public policy. It is against public policy to enforce a covenant, which is unreasonable, one which unreasonably restricts the covenantor's freedom to trade or to work. In so far as it has that effect, the covenant will not be enforced. Whether it is indeed unreasonable must be determined with reference to the circumstances of the case. Such circumstances are not limited to those that existed when the parties entered into the covenant. Account must also be taken of what has happened since then and, in particular, of the situation prevailing at the time when enforcement is sought.[100]

---

98   *Magna Alloys and Research (SA) (Pty) Ltd v Ellis* 1984 (4) SA 874 (A).

99   See e.g. *Mason v Provident Clothing & Supply Co Ltd* [1913] AC 724.

100 *J Louw and Co (Pty) Ltd v Richter and others* 1987 (2) SA 237 (N) at 243A-C.

The decision in *Magna Alloys v Ellis* was followed by the High Court in *Bauer t/a Hrabovsky Bottle Store v Piebrock t/a L' Dorado Clothing Shop.*[101]

According to the common law rule, each agreement should be examined, taking into account the circumstances of the particular case, to ascertain whether the enforcement of the agreement will be against public policy. However, it must be remembered that public policy also requires that agreements freely entered into should be respected.[102] Nevertheless, an unreasonable restriction of an individual's freedom of trade and freedom to practise his profession will be contrary to public policy. When a party avers that he is not bound by a restraint of trade clause in a contract, which he has entered into, he bears the onus of proving that the clause is not enforceable against him.[103]

It was held in *Basson v Chilwan and others*[104] that while a person should not on termination of the contract of employment be prevented from participating freely in the commercial and professional world, if the employer has a protectable proprietary interest, which requires protection, the employee can be restrained from doing anything in breach of that interest for a reasonable period of time and in a reasonably defined area. However, it must be borne in mind that in a society like Namibia, in which free economic competition is encouraged and protected, the mere desire to eliminate competition is not a protectable interest. Therefore, the courts will not uphold a restraint of trade clause that serves to do no more than eliminate and restrict competition: such a restraint is unreasonable by its very nature.[105]

In determining whether a restraint of trade clause is reasonable, the court has to weigh the freedom of the employee to work and practise his profession against the legitimate interests of the employer to protect the trade secrets of his business and the business connections he has built over the years. *Walter McNaughton (Pty) Ltd v Schwartz and others*[106] is authority for the proposition that whether information gained by an employee in the course of employment constitutes a trade secret is a factual question. For information to qualify as a trade secret, it must be useful, known to a restricted number of people, in the sense that it is not public knowledge, and be of value to the person seeking to protect it.

---

[101] *Bauer t/a Hrabovsky Bottle Store v Piebrock t/a L'Dorado Clothing Shop* 1999 NR 157 (HC).

[102] *Barkhuizen v Napier* 2007 (5) SA 323 (CC); *Wlotzkasbaken Home Owners' Association and another v The Erongo Regional Council and others* 2007 (2) NR 799; R.H. Christie, *The Law of Contract in South Africa,* 5th edn, Durban, Butterworths, 2006, p. 199.

[103] *Forwarding African Transport Services CC t/a F.A.T.S. v Manica Africa (Pty) Ltd and others* [2004] 4 All SA 527 (D).

[104] *Basson v Chilwan and others* 1993 (3) SA 742 (A).

[105] See *Ocean Diamond Mining SA v Louw and others* NLLP 2002 (2) 276 RSA HC (C).

[106] *Walter McNaughton (Pty) Ltd v Schwartz and others* [2003] 1 All SA 700 (C).

According to *Basson v Chilwan and others* supra, where the enforcement of a contract in restraint of trade is challenged, the court would do well to consider the following crucial questions in determining the issue:

1   After the termination of the contract of employment, does one of the parties to the contract have an interest worthy of protection?

2   Is the interest being harmed by the conduct or action of the other party?

3   Are there other public policy considerations that need to be enforced?

4   Does the restraint go further than is necessarily required to protect the interest of the party seeking enforcement?

In the same vein, the court will consider whether the provisions of the restraint of trade clause are too broad or oppressive. In *Commercial Plastic Ltd v Vincent*,[107] the Court struck down a restraint of trade clause because it unnecessarily set the geographical limits of the restraint globally, and it sought to limit the freedom of the employee to engage in an activity, which was different from the type of work he had done in the employer's enterprise. In *Forwarding Africa Transport Services CC t/a F. A. T. S. v Manica Africa (Pty) Ltd and others* supra, a restraint of trade clause prohibited the employee from taking up employment within one year from the date of termination of employment with the applicant (employer) with any company carrying on business, irrespective of the nature of its business, in South Africa or any other country in which the employer had in the past or during the duration of the employment contract, done business. The Court held that the restraint of trade was unreasonably wide and contrary to public policy and, therefore, unenforceable.

Thus, following the authorities, it is correct to state that at common law whether a contract in restraint of trade is enforceable must be tested against this crucial consideration, namely, the requirement that all contractual obligations must be complied with and that the courts will only interfere where an unreasonable restriction or restraint is put on a person's freedom to trade or practise his profession or vocation. The justification for this approach is predicated upon the following premise: public policy recognizes a person's right to enter into contracts and that such contracts are binding and are to be implemented in good faith (i.e. the principle of *pacta sunt servanda*), and that they must be enforced where a party is in breach of his obligations under the contracts.[108]

---

107   *Commercial Plastic Ltd v Vincent* [1965] 1 QB 623.

108   See *Woltzkasbaken Home Owners' Association and another* supra.

The question whether a particular restraint of trade clause is reasonable is a question of law not fact.[109] Consequently, evidence of persons in the trade concerning whether in their view the restraint is reasonable is not admissible to prove the unreasonableness of the restraint.[110] In the end, however, as was cautioned in *Walter McNaughton (Pty) Ltd v Schwartz and others* supra, each case must be decided on its own facts.

Article 21(1)(j) of the Namibian Constitution guarantees to the individual the right to 'practise any profession or carry on any occupation, trade or business'. It must, however, be pointed out that the human right is not absolute. A court ought to take into account relevant considerations like those discussed above in deciding whether a restraint of trade clause violates Art. 21(1)(j), on the basis, for instance, that it is unreasonable, too broad (i.e. the restraint goes further than it is necessary to protect the interest of the party seeking enforcement) or oppressive.[111]

According to *Magna Alloys v Ellis* and *Louw v Richter* supra, the party alleging that the contract in restraint of trade is unenforceable bears the onus of proving it, and *a fortiori*, according to the Namibian Constitution, it is the person alleging that his constitutional right to any of the freedoms guaranteed by Art. 21 has been infringed who bears the 'initial burden' of proving the infringement and as part thereof, satisfy the court in regard to the meaning, content and ambit of the fundamental freedom.[112]

In *Knox D'Arcy Limited and another v Shaw and another*,[113] K employed S as a management consultant. The latter agreed that he would not take up employment with K's competitors or contact K's clients for one year after termination of his employment with K. S resigned and took up employment with K's competitor, whereupon K sued to enforce the contract in restraint of trade. The Court held that the restraint was reasonable and enforceable as it sought to restrain the former employee from utilizing information received in the course of his employment for the benefit of his new employer. The legal representative of the respondents had argued that since s. 26(1) of the South African interim Constitution (now s. 22 of the 1996 Constitution) guaranteed to individuals the right to

---

[109] *Dowden and Pook Ltd v Pook* [1904] 1 KB 45.

[110] *Haynes v Doman* [1899] 2 Ch 13.

[111] See *Basson v Chilwan and others* supra.

[112] *Chairperson of the Immigration Selection Board v Frank and another* 2001 NR 107, at 132H *per* O'Linn, AJA. See also *Kauesa v Minister of Home Affairs* 1985 (2) SA 51 (NmH). The position with regard to burden of proof in cases of alleged infringement of human rights is the same in Zimbabwe: see *Zimbabwe Township Developers (Pvt) Ltd v Lou's Show (Pvt) Ltd* 1984 (2) SA 778 (ZS); *Catholic Commission for Justice and Peace v Attorney-General, Zimbabwe* 1993 (2) SACR 432 (ZS). See also Collins Parker, *Human Rights Law,* Leicestershire, Upfront Publishing, 2002, pp. 197-8, for a discussion of burden of proof of alleged human rights violations in some other jurisdictions.

[113] *Knox D'Arcy Limited and another v Shaw and another* 1996 (2) SA 651 (W).

engage freely in economic activities, the principles in *Magna Alloys v Ellis* supra should be revisited. In dismissing counsel's argument, Van Schalkwyk, J observed:

> The Constitution does not take such a meddlesome interest in the private affairs of individuals that it would seek, as a matter of policy, to protect them against their own foolhardy or rash decisions. As long as there is no overriding principle of public policy, which is violated thereby, the freedom of the individual comprehends the freedom to pursue, as he chooses, his benefit or his disadvantage.[114]

The Court held that *S* bore the onus of proving that *K* violated his constitutional right and that he had failed to discharge that onus.

Doubtless, the principle enunciated by the Court in *Knox D'Arcy v Shaw* supra is sound, and should, therefore, be followed in a case where a party challenges the enforceability of a restraint of trade clause in a contract of employment on the basis that Art. 21(j) of the Namibian Constitution guarantees to him the basic right to 'practise any profession, or carry on any occupation, trade or business'. The reason is that the content of the Namibian human right is essentially similar to that of the human right guaranteed by s. 22 of the South African Constitution.[115]

Thus, if *X* alleges that a restraint of trade clause in a contract of employment between him and *Y* (his employer) has violated his constitutional right under Art. 21(j) of the Namibian Constitution, then upon the authority of *Chairperson of the Immigration Selection Board v Frank and another* supra, *X* bears the 'initial burden' of proving such infringement. The burden of proof may shift to *Y* only after *X* has discharged his burden. In that event, *Y* must show that the restraint of trade clause falls within the reasonable derogations to the right provided by Art. 21(12) of the Constitution or that the restriction is necessary and reasonable, and not too wide, oppressive or against public policy.

3.10.2 Using Trade Information after Separation

This aspect concerns the situation where the employee applies the knowledge and skills he has gained in his previous employment in his own or another person's business once he has

---

[114] *Knox D'Arcy v Shaw* supra at 660C-D.

[115] For an insightful discussion of restraint of trade clauses in relation to public policy and the onus of proof within the context of the South African Constitution, see Q. Letsika, 'Restraint of trace clauses', *De Rebus* 425 (August 2003) 26-31.

left the service of his former employer.[116] In this computer age, where there is increased and rampant use of highly sophisticated methods of industrial espionage, the courts have shown greater sympathy towards the right of the employer to protection of his trade secrets.[117] Nevertheless, it is not any information gained by the employee in the course of employment with his erstwhile employer that would be protected by the courts: the information should be proprietary information. For that reason, the question that calls for determination is whether the information so gained is proprietary information and, therefore, protectable. In this connection, it is necessary to draw a distinction between skills or expertise developed by an employee in the course of his employment on the one hand and trade secrets and confidential information received by the employee that are proprietary to the employer and which for that reason deserve the protection of the courts. [118]

---

[116] See *Lunt v University of Cape Town and another* 1989 (2) SA 438 (C).

[117] Grogan, *Riekert's Employment Law,* p. 41, and the cases cited.

[118] See *Ocean Diamond SA v Louw* supra.

4 DUTIES OF EMPLOYERS

4.1 Introduction

From what we saw in chapters 1, 2 and 3, it would seem that both the common law and statute law place almost all the obligations arising out of the employer-and-employee relationship on the employee. Indeed, even the common-law term 'master and servant' underpins the apparently unequal positions of the parties to the employment contract; an agreement between a superior person (the master), having control, and an inferior person (the servant), who takes orders from the master and to whose *dominica potestas* he is subject.[1]

Under a common law master-and-servant contract, all that the employer needs to do is primarily to take in the employee, give him work, which he will carry out by applying his skill, and in return pay him a wage. It will be remembered that barring terms that are unlawful or against public policy, the parties are free to include any terms in their contract, and the courts may also read some implied terms into the contract (implied terms are discussed in chapter 2, para. 2.2.1.4 above). The statutory modifications of the common law are, among other things, meant to protect and promote the rights of the employee within the contextual framework of respect for human rights.

In practice, statute law takes the view that a person who furnishes his personal service to another for payment should not be treated as an inferior person who bears a great many duties and very few correlative rights. It goes without saying that it is the rights that the employee has under the law that create the correlative duties, which the employer owes to the employee. The salient duties of the employer towards his employee will now be discussed.

4.2 Provision of Work

One would have thought that the provision of work by the employer to his employee should be the *raison d'être* of the contract of employment. However, as a general rule, the employer is not obliged to provide work for his employee. In *Turner v Sawdon & Co*, Smith, MR

---

[1] C.D. Drake, *Labour Law*, 2nd edn, London, Sweet & Maxwell, 1973, para. 3.

stated: 'It is within the province of the master to say that he will go on paying the wages, but that he is under no obligation to provide work.'[2] Asquith, J put it picturesquely in *Collier v Sunday Referee Publishing Co Ltd* thus: 'It is true that contract of employment does not necessarily, or perhaps normally, oblige the master to provide the servant with work. Provided I pay my cook her wages regularly she cannot complain if I choose to take any or all my meals out.'[3] This is a correct statement of the general rule of the common law. However, as Miller, J said of the rule in *Stewart Wrightson (Pty) Ltd v Thorpe*, 'I cannot accept that it is true of all contracts of employment and all circumstances, nor has the dictum been applied in the English Courts to all cases in which the master has refused to provide work for his servant.'[4] McCardie, J agrees: 'serious results…might follow if *Turner v Sawdon & Co* supra were to apply to all types of cases'.[5]

Hence, to the general rule, the courts have applied exceptions. One such exception is where failure to provide work results in ignominy and degradation. In *In re An Arbitration between Rubel Bronze and Metal Company Ltd and Vos* supra, the plaintiff had been appointed in terms of a written contract, as general manager of the defendant's enterprise for a fixed period and at a fixed salary and commission. The defendant purportedly suspended the plaintiff from the exercise of his duties pending an investigation into his fitness, and he requested him to hand over his badge, took from him the keys of the business, and instructed him not to return to work. As if that was not enough, the defendant appointed another person to take charge of the work in the plaintiff's place. It was held that the defendant had by his conduct wrongfully repudiated the contract inasmuch as he completely forbade the plaintiff to fulfil any of his duties as a general manager.

In *Nhlanhla M K Vilakati v Attorney-General*,[6] the variation of the nature of the applicant's (employee's) duty was found to constitute repudiation by the employer of the contract of employment. In *Collier v Sunday Referee Publishing Co Ltd* supra,[7] it was held that the contract of employment under which the applicant (employee) served as a chief sub-editor of a specified paper obliged the employer to afford the employee the opportunity of performing the task for which he was employed. It has also been held that it is a breach of the employer's duty where the employer sells the business so that the specific office to which an employee was appointed for a fixed period ceases to exist.[8] For a court to come to

---

2   *Turner v Sawdon & Co* [1901] 2 KB 653 at 657.

3   *Collier v Sunday Referee Publishing Co Ltd* [1940] 4 All ER 234 at 650.

4   *Stewart Wrightson (Pty) Ltd v Thorpe* 1974 (4) SA 67 (D) at 77H.

5   *In re An Arbitration between Rubel Bronze and Metal Company Ltd and Vos* [1918] 1 KB 315 at 324.

6   Swaziland IC 88/96 (unreported). The facts of the case are outlined in chapter 2, para. 2.2.1.5 above.

7   See also *Addis v Gramophone Co Ltd* [1969] AC 488.

8   *Collier v Sunday Referee* supra.

this a conclusion, it ought to take into account the circumstances surrounding the abolition; for instance, whether it was done for ulterior motives unconnected with efforts to achieve efficiency in the business. Abolishing of posts in an organization in the course of genuine restructuring and reorganizing the business, so as to achieve efficiency, is fair and reasonable in industry and business, as well as in government administration.[9]

Another exception to the general rule in *Turner v Sawdon* is where the employee's remuneration depends largely upon the amount of personal service he performs. This usually happens where the amount of commission to which the employee is entitled is tied to the amount of work he actually performs. In that case, the employer's failure or refusal to provide work to the employee amounts to a repudiation of the contract of employment because the employee is denied remuneration, which is a fundamental term of contract of employment. Thus, in *Bauman v Hulton Press Ltd*,[10] the court held that the defendant was bound to give the plaintiff a reasonable amount of work to enable him to earn that which the parties must be taken to have contemplated. In *In re An Arbitration between Rubel Bronze and Metal Company Ltd and Vos* supra, the fact that the defendant prevented the plaintiff (employee) from exerting his opportunities as a manager to gain commission upon the net profits of the company was also considered material and decisive in deciding that there had been a repudiation of the contract by the employer (defendant).

Related to the employer's duty to provide work is his duty to admit the person with whom he has entered into a contract of employment into his service. What happens if, after the conclusion of a contract of employment, the employer decides not to admit such person into his employment? As we saw in chapter 1 (para. 1.2.3), if the employer fails or refuses to admit such person into his employment, he commits a fundamental breach of the contract of employment, and the aggrieved party's remedy lies in contract where he may sue for damages or specific performance.[11]

4.3 Payment of Remuneration

Where there has been agreement on the payment of wages but the amount has not been specified in the contract, the courts will import into the contract that the parties implied that a reasonable amount will be paid, depending upon the usage of the particular industry.

---

9   For example s. 34 of the Labour Act 2007.

10   *Bauman v Hulton Press Ltd* [1952] 2 All ER 1121.

11   *Kinemas Ltd v Berman* 1932 AD 246. We saw in chapter 1, para. 1.2.3, that such aggrieved party is not an employee in terms of the Labour Act 2007.

According to *Van der Merwe v Colonial Government*,[12] and *Johannesburg Municipality v O'Sullivan*,[13] an employer is not relieved of his duty to pay wages, if as a result of some *vis major* the employee is incapable of furnishing his service. It is important to reiterate the point that the amount of remuneration payable forms a term of the contract, and the term may be express or implied. Finally, it is also worth noting (as will be seen below in paras 4.3.2, 4.3.3 and 4.3.4) that there has been a massive statutory intervention by the Labour Act 2007 in matters concerning remuneration.

4.3.1 Payment of Remuneration during Illness

The question whether an employer is obliged to pay remuneration during the employee's absence from work due to illness or any other cause has already been discussed (chapter 3, para. 3.3 above).

4.3.2 Form and Method of Payment

At common law, the parties to a contract of employment may agree the form in which remuneration ought to be paid. The Labour Act 2007 has not taken away this aspect of freedom of contract, for s. 1 of the Labour Act defines remuneration as 'the total value of all payments in money or in kind made or owing to an employee arising from the employment of that employee'.

This formulation is fundamentally different from the formulation used in the definition of 'remuneration' under the repealed Labour Act 1992, which is rather involved and unclear. Under the repealed Act, benefits in kind, payment in compensation for travelling expenses, and daily subsistence allowance payable to an employee who is on official duty outside his duty station, were excluded from the definition.[14] Excluded from the definition under the repealed Labour Act were also retirement benefits and other separation benefits.[15] It is submitted that it is the definition of 'remuneration' under the Labour Act 2007 that does justice to the English language because it correctly defines remuneration as all payments – in cash or in kind – to an employee for his service under the contract of employment.[16] Remuneration by definition is a basic wage plus any other payments, e.g. allowances and fringe benefits, due to an employee from his employer. A basic wage is, therefore, subsumed under remuneration. In *Erongo Mining & Exploration Company Limited t/a Navachab Gold*

---

12 *Van der Merwe v Colonial Government* (1904) 21 SC 520.

13 *Johannesburg Municipality v O'Sullivan* 1923 AD 201.

14 *African Granite Company (Pty) Ltd v Mineworkers Union of Namibia & others* 1993 NR 91 (LC).

15 *Kruger v Office of the Prime Minister & another* 1996 NR 323 (LC).

16 *The Concise Oxford Dictionary,* 10th edn.

Mine v Mineworkers Union of Namibia, after reviewing the authorities and relying on the dictionary definition of remuneration, Hannah, J came to the conclusion that the ordinary meaning of remuneration was wider than wage or salary, and that it included bonuses and allowances.[17]

An employee's remuneration may be paid wholly in money or partly in money and partly in kind. If remuneration is paid in money, then it must be paid in the money having legal tender in Namibia, i.e. the Namibia Dollar. Section 10 of the Labour Act 2007 applies when, for any purpose under the Act, it is necessary to determine the applicable hourly, daily, weekly or monthly rate of pay of an employee. Section 12(2) sets out a table for the 'calculation of remuneration and basic wages' on hourly, daily, weekly and monthly rates.

In terms of s. 11 of the Labour Act 2007, a monetary remuneration payable to an employee must be paid to him on the normal or agreed pay day, which may fall due daily, weekly, fortnightly or monthly. Payment should be made not later than one hour after the employee has completed the ordinary hours of work on the agreed payday. An employer must, if the employee so desires, pay his employee's remuneration that is due in money in cash or by cheque. In that case, the employer must pay the monetary remuneration either to the employee or by a direct deposit into an account that the employee designates in writing. If an employer pays his employee in cash or by cheque, then he must put the cash or the cheque in a sealed envelope, and hand over the envelope to the employee.

A written statement of particulars in the prescribed form (usually referred to as pay-slip) must accompany every payment of monetary remuneration. The written statement must accompany the payment, if the payment is made in cash or by cheque, but if payment is made by direct deposit into an account, then the written statement must be put in an envelope and given to the employee. Lastly, an employer must not pay an employee at a shop, bottle store or a place where intoxicating liquor is sold or stored or a place of amusement in that shop, store or place, unless the employee is employed in that shop, bottle store or other place. It must be borne in mind that these provisions of the Labour Act 2007 dealing with the payment of remuneration cannot be excluded by agreement.[18]

4.3.3 Prohibited Deductions

Section 12(5) of the Labour Act 2007 forbids an employer to require his employee to:

1   buy goods from a shop either owned by the employer or run on his behalf;

---

[17] *Erongo Mining & Exploration Company Limited t/a Navachab Gold Mine v Mineworkers Union of Namibia* 2000 NR 70 at 76D.

[18] *Penman v Fife Coal Co* [1936] AC 45.

2   use the services rendered by the employer for reward; or

3   pay for any goods supplied by the employer at a price exceeding an amount equal
       to the price paid by the employer for the goods plus any reasonable costs incurred
       by the employer in obtaining the goods. [19]

It is, therefore, illegal under the Labour Act 2007 for an employer to require his employee to buy goods from a tuck shop owned by the employer or one managed for him or on his behalf by somebody else.

Additionally, in terms of s. 12(5) of the Labour Act, it is unlawful for an employer to require or permit an employee to pay back to him the remuneration that the employee has lawfully received from the employer. In *Pratt v Cook, Son & Co (St. Paul's) Ltd*,[20] the House of Lords held that a deduction of 10 Shillings dinner- and tea-money from the weekly wages of a packer in a wholesale drapery firm was illegal. It is also not permitted even if, in the opinion of the employer, the deduction is beneficial to the employee in the long run, such as deductions made by the employer and invested in stocks for the employee. In *Kenyon v Darwen, Cotton Manufacturing Co*,[21] the employer (defendant) made an agreement with its employees to raise new capital by issuing shares to them. Under the agreement the employees received the balance of wages after deducting the payment for the shares they held in the company. The Court of Appeal held that the deductions were unlawful, notwithstanding the employees' consent. The consent of the employees meant nothing because the prohibition was based on a rule of law, and, therefore, could not be waived by the parties, even by consent, for it 'is not open to the parties to agree to waive a statutory requirement'.[22]

Considering the great disparity between the powerful economic position of employers and the subordinate and inferior position of employees, an unscrupulous employer might be inclined to force his employee to acknowledge in writing that he has received the full amount of remuneration lawfully due to him, when that is not truly the case. Section 12(5)(c)(ii) of the Labour Act is, therefore, designed to protect employees from such practice. The subparagraph prohibits an employer from requiring or permitting an employee to acknowledge receipt of an amount greater than the amount of remuneration he has actually

---

[19] The prohibited practice is akin to the English 'truck' system whereby employers paid their employees in tokens exchangeable for goods: see R. Lowe, *Commercial Law,* 4th edn, London, Sweet & Maxwell, 1973, para. 194. The Truck Acts, 1831 (1& 2 Will. 4, c.37), 1887 (50 & 51 Vict. c. 46), 1896 (59 & 60 Vict. c. 48) and 1940 (3 & 4 Geo. 6, c.38) abolished the practice.

[20] *Pratt v Cook, Son & Co (St. Pauls) Ltd* [1940] AC 437.

[21] *Kenyon v Darwen, Cotton Manufacturing Co* [1936] 1 All ER 310.

[22] See *Nantex Textile Swaziland (Pty) Ltd v Swaziland Manufacturers and Allied Workers Union and others* Swaziland IC 140/97 at p. 9 (unreported). See also *Springs Town Council v MacDonald* 1967 (3) SA 229 (W); *Buthelezi & others v Labour for Africa (Pty) Ltd* 1991 12 *ILJ* 587; *Braude v Pretoria City Council* 1981 (1) SA 680 (T).

received. In addition, s. 12(5)(a) provides that an employer is prohibited from levying a fine on an employee unless it is authorized by statute or a collective agreement (which is dealt with in para 4.3.4 below). For instance, in terms of s. (26)(1)(a)(ii) of the Public Service Act 1995, a disciplinary committee may recommend that a staff member whom it has found guilty of misconduct be made to pay a fine not exceeding N$2,000.00.

4.3.4 Permitted Deductions

The Labour Act 2007 permits certain lawful deductions to be made from an employee's remuneration. This statutory permission is clearly a departure from the common law rule that prima facie all deductions from the employee's wages are unlawful. Section 12 of the Labour Act sets out deductions permitted by the Act. First, a deduction made in terms of a court order is allowable, e.g. payment in favour of a judgment creditor or payment made pursuant to a maintenance order or a garnishee order. Second, lawful deductions may be made in terms of any other statute, e.g. income tax under the Income Tax Act,[23] social security contributions under the Social Security Act,[24] and pension contributions under the National Pensions Act.[25] Third, an employer may make a deduction from his employee's remuneration if the deduction is required or permitted under a collective agreement or in terms of an arbitral award. He may also make a deduction, if the employee agrees to the deduction in writing, and the deduction is for the payment of any of the following items: (i) rent in respect of accommodation supplied by the employer; (ii) goods sold by the employer; (iii) a loan advanced by the employer; (iv) contribution to the employee's benefit fund; and (v) subscriptions or levies to a recognized trade union. The only condition is that the permitted deduction should not in the aggregate exceed one third of the employee's remuneration. For example, if the employee's monthly remuneration is N$1,500.00, the total of deductions made in a month should not exceed N$500.00.

It is worth pointing out that under Namibian labour law, an employer cannot lawfully deduct money from his employee's remuneration in favour of every third party imaginable in respect of debts the employee owes to such third party, even where the employee himself requested that the amount be deducted from his remuneration and paid over to such third party. Under the labour law, the instances under which, and the persons or institutions in whose favour, such authorization can lawfully be given by an employee are set out in s. 12 of the Labour Act, and the persons and institutions mentioned there do not cover just any third party.

---

23   Act No. 24 of 1981.

24   Act No. 34 of 1994.

25   Act No. 10 of 1992.

Finally, in terms of s. 12(4) of the Labour Act, an employer who deducts an amount of money from his employee's remuneration under the Act in favour of another person X – legal or natural - is obliged to pay the amount to X in accordance with the time limits and other requirements specified in the relevant law, court order, arbitral award or agreement.

4.4 PROVISION OF MEDICAL SERVICES

The common law does not impose a general duty on an employer to provide medical services to his employee. However, where the injury or illness is occasioned by the failure of the employer to provide a safe working environment, the employer may be held liable for expenses incurred by the employee for receiving medical attention for such injury or illness (see further chapter 5, para. 5.3 below).

4.5 PROVISION OF CERTIFICATE OF SERVICE

An employer bears no duty at common law to provide a testimonial or certificate of employment or service to an employee when the employee separates from the employer's service.[26] The common law has been modified by statute in some jurisdictions. For example, under Swaziland's Employment Act,[27] an employer has a duty to give his employee a 'certificate of employment', but the employer owes such duty only to 'employees whose services are terminated', i.e. terminated by the employer. A similar statutory duty is found in Namibian and South African labour laws but, unlike in Swaziland, in Namibia and South Africa, the employer owes the duty to all employees who separate from their employment – whether they separated voluntarily or involuntarily (for further explanation of these terms see chapter 7 below).

In terms of s. 37(5) of the Labour Act 2007, on termination of employment, an employer must give his employee a certificate of employment. The certificate must contain the following particulars:

1   the full name of the employee;
2   the employer's name and address;

---

26   J. Grogan, *Riekert's Employment Law,* 2nd edn, Cape Town, Juta, 1993, p. 74; *Carol v Bird* (1800) 3 Esp 201.

27   Act No. 5 of 1980.

3	a description of the industry in which the employer is engaged;
4	the date of commencement and date of termination of employment;
5	the employee's job description;
6	the employee's remuneration at date of termination; and
7	if the employee so requests, the reason for termination of employment, e.g. resignation, expiry of fixed-term contract or dismissal.

Apart from the certificate of employment, an employer may give the employee whose service has been terminated a testimonial or such-like certificate of good character.

A reference or testimonial, which is defamatory of the employee and which is shown to a third party, may make the employer liable to an action for defamation.[28]

A related matter needs to be discussed at this juncture. Suppose, for example, an employer gives a reference or testimonial about his employee to an inquiring prospective employer, knowing it to be false or where he ought to have known it to be false, and he knew or ought to have known that the prospective employer would place reliance on the testimonial or the reference. In English law, if the inquiring employer acts upon the reference or testimonial to his economic detriment, the employer who gave the reference or testimonial may be liable because he owes a duty of care to the inquiring employer, even though there is no contractual or fiduciary relationship between the inquiring employer and the employer who gave the testimonial or reference. In this regard, the House of Lords held in the landmark case of *Hedley Byrne & Co Ltd v Heller & Partner Ltd*[29] that liability for negligent misstatement can give rise to liability for pure economic loss without there being a contractual or fiduciary relationship between the parties. The test to apply appears to be whether, taking into account the circumstances in which the reference or testimonial was given, the employer who gave the reference or testimonial must be taken to have accepted some responsibility for his statement 'being given carefully, or to have accepted a relationship with the inquirer which requires him to exercise such care as the circumstances require'.[30] Thus, in English law, an employer who agrees to give a testimonial or reference about his employee to an inquiring prospective employer and wishes to escape liability will do well to give his answer with a clear qualification that he accepted no responsibility for it or did so without prejudice.[31]

---

28 See *Webb v East* (1880) LR 5 Ex 108. See also Grogan, *Riekert's Employment Law,* p. 74.

29 *Hedley Byrne & Co Ltd v Heller & Partner Ltd* [1963] 2 All ER 575.

30 Ibid. at 486 *per* Lord Reid. See also R.G. McKerron, *The Law of Delict,* Cape Town, Juta, 1971, p. 219.

31 *Hedley Byrne v Heller* supra.

4.6 KEEPING OF PRESCRIBED RECORDS

Section 130 of the Labour Act 2007 requires every employer to keep a proper record and returns in respect of each employee of his. The record must be current for the last five years; in the sense that the information in the record must relate to the last five years. The record and returns should contain the following particulars:

1   the name, sex, age and occupation (i.e. the specific job) of the employee;

2   the date the employee commenced employment;

3   the date on which, and the reason why, the contract of employment of the employee was terminated;

4   remuneration payable to the employee;

5   remuneration actually paid to the employee;

6   any period of absence, including annual leave, sick leave, compassionate leave, or maternity leave taken by the employee; and

7   any other information that is prescribed to be furnished or requested in writing by the Permanent Secretary responsible for Labour.

An employer must keep a record of an employee in the prescribed manner and must retain it for five years after the termination of employment of the employee concerned. An employer must submit to the Permanent Secretary responsible for Labour information contained in such record as may be prescribed. If an employer fails to comply with a provision of s. 130 or intentionally makes a false entry in a record or in the submission made in terms of s. 130, he commits an offence, and on conviction is liable to a fine not exceeding N$10,000.00 or imprisonment for a period not exceeding two years, or both.[32]

It will be remembered that the records and returns do not constitute contracts of employment, and that the legal effect of the Namibian record is different from that of the Zambian 'record of contract' because the Zambian record may be taken as a written form of an otherwise oral contract of employment (see chapter 2, para. 2.2.1.3 above).

---

[32]   Similar provisions are found in s. 22 of Swaziland's Employment Act 1980 (Act No. 5 of 1980).

4.7 Observation of Prescribed Hours of Work

4.7.1 Ordinary Hours of Work

At common law, the parties to a contract of employment are free to agree the hours of work. Where the contract does not contain a provision on hours of work, the courts have applied the hours of work known to be the custom applicable in the industry.[33] In that case, the courts may also determine whether hours of work demanded of the employee are harsh and unreasonable.

The Labour Act 2007 regulates hours of work of an employee who is subject to the Act. In terms of s. 16(1) of the Labour Act, and subject to any contrary provision in Chapter 3 of the Act, an employer is prohibited from requiring or permitting an employee to work for more than 45 hours in any week, and in any case:

1   not more than nine hours in any day, if the employee works for five days in a week or not more than eight hours in any day, if the employee works for more than five days in a week; or

2   not more than the maximum number of hours prescribed by the Minister responsible for Labour in terms of s. 15(2) of the Act for that employee's shift, if that employee works in a continuous operation.

This prohibition does not apply to an employee who is a security officer, an employee working in emergency healthcare services or an employee of a class designated by the Minister in terms of s. 16(5) of the Act.

An exception is provided by s. 16(2) to this maximum-hours-of-work rule in s. 16(1). The ordinary working hours of an employee under s. 16(1) may be extended for up to 15 minutes in a day, but not more than 60 minutes in a week, so as to enable an employee whose duties include serving members of the public, to continue performing those duties after the completion of his ordinary hours of work. Examples of such employees are hotel workers and shop assistants.

In terms of s. 16(3) of the Labour Act, and subject to Chapter 3 of the Act, an employer must not require or permit an employee who is a security officer, an employee working in emergency healthcare services or an employee of a class designated by the Minister

---

[33]   Grogan *Riekert's Employment Law*, p. 64.

responsible for Labour in terms of s. 16(15) to work for more than 60 hours in a week; and in any case, not more than:

1   12 hours in any day, if the employee works for five days or fewer days in a week; or 10 hours in any day, if the employee works for more than five days a week; or

2   not more than the maximum number of hours prescribed by the Minister in terms of s. 15(2) for that employee's continuous shift, if the employee works in a continuous operation.

In terms of s. 16(4), in determining the time worked by an employee during the week for the purposes of s. 16, any meal interval referred to in s. 18 taken by an employee mentioned in s. 16(3) must be regarded as time worked ; but a meal interval of any other employee must be disregarded. (Meal interval is discussed in para. 4.7.3 below.)

4.7.2   Overtime

The Labour Act 2007 permits only contractual voluntary overtime. What this means is that an employer should not require or permit an employee to do non-contractual overtime work.[34] In terms of s. 17(1) of the Labour Act, and subject to any contrary provision in Chapter 3 of the Act, an employer must not require or permit an employee to work overtime unless the request or permission is in accordance with an agreement made between the employer and the employee. Even where such agreement exists, overtime worked should not exceed 3 hours in a day or 10 hours in a week; and in any case, not more than three hours' overtime a day. However, in terms of s. 17(3), maximum overtime may be increased, if an employer makes application to the Permanent Secretary responsible for Labour to that effect, and an affected employee agrees. According to s. 17(4), if the Permanent Secretary grants the application, the Permanent Secretary must issue a notice, indicating the class of employees to whom the notice applies, the new limits on overtime work, any conditions concerning the working of the overtime and the duration of the application of the approved overtime. The Permanent Secretary may at any time amend or withdraw the notice. According to s. 17(5), s. 17(1), (3) and (4) do not apply to an employee who is performing urgent work.

Section 17(2) provides that where an employee works overtime, the following rate of pay will apply to him: the employer must pay to the employee for each hour of overtime worked the rate of at least one and a half times the employee's hourly basic wage. However, if an employee who ordinarily works on a Sunday or public holiday works overtime on a Sunday

---

34   *Tiger Bakeries Ltd v Food & Allied Workers Union & others* (1998) 9 *ILJ* 82 (W).

Duties of Employers **81**

or public holiday, the employer must pay him at the rate of at least double that employee's hourly basic wage. It must be borne in mind that it is only an employee who has worked overtime who is entitled to overtime payment in accordance with s. 17 of the Labour Act.[35]

4.7.3 Meal Intervals

Section 18 of the Labour Act 2007 provides for meal intervals in this way: an employer must give a meal interval to an employee who works continuously for more than five hours. The meal interval should not be less than one hour. However, the employer and the employee may agree that the latter's meal intervals be shortened to not less than 30 minutes, but such agreement is valid only if the employer has given notice of the agreement to the Permanent Secretary responsible for Labour. Section 18(3) provides that no employer should require or permit his employee to perform any work during the employee's meal interval. Where the meal interval given or taken is less than one hour or less than the agreed time, the employee concerned will be considered as having had no meal interval.

For the purposes of s. 18 of the Labour Act, work is continuous unless it is interrupted by an interval that is more than 60 minutes or the agreed shortened duration under s. 18(2). Furthermore, for the purposes of s. 18, the driver of a motor vehicle who does no work other than remaining in charge of the vehicle or its load during a meal interval, is deemed not to be working during the interval. Moreover, for the purposes of s. 18, an employee is entitled to be remunerated for any portion of a meal interval that is longer than 90 minutes. Finally, s. 18 does not apply to an employee who is engaged in urgent work, a security officer or an employee who works in a continuous shift.

4.7.4 Daily Spread-Over and Weekly Rest Period

The Labour Act 2007 limits the maximum spread-over of working hours of employees. According to s. 20, no employer may require or permit an employee, save an employee who is performing urgent work, to work a spread-over of more than 12 hours. Furthermore, an employer must not require or permit an employee, other than an employee who is performing urgent work, to work without a weekly interval of at least 36 consecutive hours of rest.

4.7.5 Night Work

Section 19(1) of the Labour Act 2007 provides that an employee is entitled to additional payment of 6 per cent of his hourly basic wage excluding overtime work, for each hour of work the employee performs between 20h00 and 07h00. However, an employer must not

---

35   See Municipality of Windhoek v Van Wyk and others 1999 NR 315 (LC).

require or permit an employee, who the employer knows or reasonably ought to know to be pregnant, to perform any work, including overtime work, between 20h00 and 07h00 at any time during eight weeks prior to her expected date of confinement or eight weeks after her confinement. The eight-week period may be extended if a medical practitioner certifies that an extension is necessary for the health of the employee or her child.

4.7.6   Work on Sundays

According to s. 21 of the Labour Act 2007, an employer must not require or permit an employee to perform work on a Sunday, unless in situations or circumstances provided under that section. The prohibition does not apply to an employer who employs an employee for the purpose of:

1   urgent work;

2   carrying on business of a shop, hotel, boarding house or hostel that is permitted by law to operate on a Sunday;

3   performing domestic service in a private household;

4   providing health and social welfare care and residential facilities, e.g. hospitals, hospices, orphanages and old age homes;

5   work on a farm that is required to be done on Sunday;

6   engaging in work in which continuous shifts are worked; and

7   any other activity approved by the Permanent Secretary responsible for Labour.

An employer may apply in writing to the Permanent Secretary to approve work on Sundays if an employee affected by the application agrees. Section 21(4) provides that if the Permanent Secretary grants the application, he must issue a notice in writing, indicating the nature of work to which the notice applies and any conditions attached to the grant.

According to s. 21(5) of the Labour Act, an employee who works on a Sunday is entitled to double his hourly basic wage for each hour worked. However, in terms of s. 21(6), an employer may pay an employee who works on a Sunday one and a half of that employee's hourly basic wage for each hour worked, so long as the employer grants that employee an equal period of time away from work during the next succeeding working week, and the employee agrees to such arrangement. In the case of an employee who ordinarily works on Sundays, an employer must pay the employee his daily remuneration plus the hourly basic wage for each hour worked.

Duties of Employers   **83**

For the purposes of s. 21, if the majority of hours worked by an employee on a shift, which extends into or begins on a Sunday, fall on a Sunday, all the hours on that shift are deemed to have been worked on Sunday, or if they fall on a Saturday or Monday, all the hours on that shift are deemed to be work on Saturday or Monday.

4.7.7   Work on Public Holidays

In terms of s. 22(1) of the Labour Act 2007, an employer must not require or permit an employee to perform any work on a public holiday, save as provided in s. 22; but certain employers are exempted from this restriction. According to s. 22(2), this prohibition does not apply to an employer who employs an employee for the purpose of:

1   urgent work;

2   carrying on business of a shop, hotel, boarding house or hostel that by law can operate on a public holiday;

3   performing domestic service in a private household;

4   health and social welfare care and residential facilities, e.g. hospitals, hospices, orphanages and old age homes;

5   work on a farm that is required to be done on a public holiday;

6   work in which continuous shifts are worked; or

7   an activity approved by the Permanent Secretary responsible for Labour.

An employer may apply in writing to the Permanent Secretary to approve work on a public holiday if an employee affected by the application agrees. Section 22(4) provides that if the Permanent Secretary grants the application, he must issue a notice in writing, indicating the nature of work to which the notice applies and any conditions attached to the grant.

In terms of the Labour Act, a public holiday is a paid holiday. Consequently, according to s. 22(5)(a), if a public holiday falls on a day on which an employee would ordinarily work, an employer must either pay the employee who does not work on the public holiday an amount that is not less than the employee's daily remuneration, subject to s. 22(6), or pay an employee who works on a public holiday an amount equal to that employee's normal daily remuneration plus his hourly basic wage for each hour worked. However, an employee who works on a public holiday may rather opt, if his employer agrees, to be paid his normal daily remuneration plus a half of that employee's hourly basic wage for each hour worked. In that

84 Labour Law in Namibia

case, in addition to the payment, an employee is also entitled to be granted an equal period of time from work during the next succeeding working week.

According to s. 22(7) of the Labour Act, if an employee works on a public holiday that falls on a day other than the employee's ordinary working day, an employer must pay double that employee's hourly basic wage for each hour worked. Section 22(6) of the Act provides that if an employee who does not work on a public holiday fails without a valid reason to work on either the day immediately before or immediately following the public holiday, then his employer is not required to pay that employee his daily remuneration in terms of s. 22(5)(a)(i).

Finally s. 22(7) of the Labour Act provides that if the majority of the hours worked on a shift, which extend into or begin on a public holiday falls on a public holiday, then all the hours on that shift are deemed to have been worked on a public holiday, but if they fall on another day, all the hours on that shift are deemed to have been worked on that day.

4.8 GRANTING OF PAID LEAVE OF ABSENCE

4.8.1 Annual Leave

The rule that vacation leave is a privilege not a right underlies the principle that an employee at common law has no right to paid leave or payment in lieu of leave: the employer's obligation to grant leave depends rather on the contract of employment.[36] In Namibia, as it is in some other countries,[37] there has been statutory intrusion into the matter of leave. Under statute law, paid annual leave is the rule rather than the exception, and is a right not a privilege.

In terms of s. 23(2) of the Labour Act 2007, every employer is obliged to grant his employee at least four consecutive weeks' annual leave with full remuneration in respect of each annual leave cycle, calculated as in the following table:

---

[36] *East London Municipal Council v Thompson* 1944 AD 61.

[37] See e.g. Chapter Three of South Africa's Basic Conditions of Employment Act 1997 (Act No. 75 of 1997); Part XII of Swaziland's Employment Act 1980 (Act No. 5 of 1980); and s. 15 of Zambia's Employment Act (Cap 512 of the Laws of Zambia).

Number of days in ordinary work week[38]	Annual leave entitlement in working days
6	24
5	20
4	16
3	12
2	8
1	4

According to s. 23(3), if an employee does not ordinarily work a fixed number of days per week, the employee is entitled to annual leave, calculated on the basis of the average number of days worked per week over the twelve months prior to the commencement of a new annual leave cycle, multiplied by four.[38]

Section 23(4) of the Labour Act provides that the number of leave days referred to in s. 23(2) may be reduced by the number of days in the annual leave cycle during which on an employee's request, an employer granted that employee as occasional leave on full remuneration. According to s. 23(5) of the Labour Act, an employer may determine when his employee may take his annual leave, so long as the leave is taken not later than four months following the end of his annual leave cycle or six months after the end of the annual leave cycle if before the end of the four-month period, the employee agreed in writing to such an extension.

Section 23(9) provides that an employer must not require or permit an employee to work for him when the employee is on annual leave. Besides, according to s. 23(7), an employer must not require or permit an employee to take annual leave when the employee is already on another leave to which he is entitled under the Labour Act. Thus when, for instance, an employee is on sick leave or maternity leave, the employer must not require or permit him to take annual leave, too.[39] An employer must grant an employee an additional day of paid leave if a public holiday falls on a day during which the employee is on annual leave and on which the employee would ordinarily have worked.

According to s. 23(6), an employer must pay the remuneration due to an employee in respect of annual leave, according to that employee's regular pay schedule, if the employee is paid by direct deposit into the employee's account in terms of s. 11(1)(b)(ii) of the Act

---

[38] According to s. 23(1) of the Labour Act 2007, for the purposes of s. 23, 'ordinary work week' means the number of days per week ordinarily worked by an employee.

[39] Sick leave is dealt with in para. 4.8.2 and maternity leave in para 4.8.3 below.

(see para 4.3.2 above). However, if any other pay schedule applies, the employer must pay the employee not later than the last working day before the commencement of his annual leave, or no later than the first pay day after the end of his leave period, if the employee requests such extension.

Finally, according to s. 23(10), except on termination of employment, an employer must not pay an employee an amount of money in lieu of annual leave to which the employee is entitled (usually referred to as 'leave pay', i.e. pay in lieu of leave), whether or not the employee requests or agrees in writing to such pay. In this connection, the question which is always raised is this: Is an employee who had declined to take leave due to him entitled to an amount of money in lieu of the leave upon his separation from his employer? In South Africa, the question was answered in the negative in *Reed v Richmond Local Board*[40] and in *Louw v University of Cape Town.*[41] The decisions in *Reed v Richmond* and *Louw v University of Cape Town* make sense. If an employee refuses to go on leave when leave to which he is entitled falls due, he should not be paid any amount in lieu of such leave. The purpose of annual leave is to enable an employee to rest so as to be able to render better service after resting. It is detrimental to productivity and efficiency in an organization if every employee refused to take any annual leave at all when such leave fell due in the hope of getting a large amount of 'leave pay' on termination of employment.

Thus, upon the authorities, it is submitted that when one is interpreting and applying s. 23 of the Labour Act, one ought to take into consideration that 'leave pay' payable on termination of contract of employment must only be in respect of annual leave that an employee could not reasonably be expected to take when it fell due, or in respect of any number of unutilized leave days, which an employee is allowed to carry forward in terms of his contract of employment or the Labour Act or any legislation.

4.8.2 Sick Leave and Compassionate Leave

4.8.2.1 *Sick Leave*

Sick leave is granted where the employee's absence from work is due to illness or injury. According to s. 24(1) of the Labour Act 2007, during any sick leave cycle, an employee is entitled to sick leave in this way: (i) not less than 30 working days, if the employee ordinarily works five days in a week, (ii) not less than 36 working days, if the employee ordinarily works six days in a week, and (iii) not less than the number of working days, calculated proportionately, *pro rata*, if the employee ordinarily works fewer than five days in a week. However, an employee is entitled to one day's sick leave for every 26 days

---

40   *Reed v Richmond Local Board* 1923 AD 50.

41   *Louw v University of Cape Town* 1945 CPD 373.

worked during the employee's first year of employment. Where the 36 working days' apply, i.e. s. 26(1)(b), the sick leave days to which an employee who does not ordinarily work a fixed number of days per week is entitled, must be calculated annually on the basis of the previous twelve months.

It is not open to an employee to take sick leave unless he is sick or injured. Therefore, for an employee to be entitled to be paid on a normal pay day an amount equal to the employee's daily remuneration for each day of absence or sick leave in terms of the Labour Act, he has to show proof of his illness or sickness. Accordingly, in terms of s. 24(4) of the Labour Act, an employer is not required to pay an employee for sick leave if the employee has been absent from work for more than two consecutive days, and has failed to produce a medical certificate by a registered medical practitioner attesting to his illness or injury or any evidence of proof of illness as may be prescribed.

Furthermore, an employer is not required to pay an employee for sick leave, if the employee is absent from work during any period of incapacity arising from an accident or a scheduled disease to the extent that the employee is entitled to payment of compensation in terms of the Workmen's Compensation Act, as amended.[42] Besides, an employer is not required to pay an employee for sick leave to the extent that the employee is entitled to payment in respect of that sick leave from a fund or organization designated by the employee, and in respect of which the employer makes contributions that are at least equal to that made by the employee and the fund or organization guarantees the payment of sick leave. Additionally, an employer is not required to pay an employee for sick leave to the extent that the employee is entitled to payment in respect of sick leave under any other legislation.

Final aspects of sick leave under the Labour Act are the following. Sick leave does not form a part of annual, compassionate or maternity leave (which is discussed in para 4.8.3 below). Additionally, sick leave does not entitle an employee to any additional remuneration on termination of employment. Furthermore, sick leave does not accumulate; if sick leave is not used during the sick leave cycle referred to in s. 24(1), it lapses at the end of that period.

4.8.2.2 Compassionate Leave

An employee is also entitled to compassionate leave under the Labour Act. Section 25(1) of the Labour Act provides that during each period of twelve months of continuous employment, an employee is entitled to five working days' compassionate leave with fully paid remuneration. An employee is so entitled to compassionate leave if there is a death or serious illness in the family.

---

42   Act No. 30 of 1941, as amended by the Employees' Compensation Act 1995 (Act No. 5 of 1995).

According to s. 25(4), for the purposes of s. 25, 'family' means a child, including a child adopted in terms of any law, custom or tradition, a spouse, parent, grandparent, brother or sister of an employee, or father-in-law or mother-in-law of an employee. It must be pointed out that if a dispute arises as to whether the family in which the death or serious illness has occurred is the family of an employee, the employee bears the onus of proving on a preponderance of probability that that family is his family. Section 25(3) of the Act provides that the Minister responsible for Labour must prescribe the form and manner in which an employee may apply for compassionate leave and any additional information that may be required to support the application. For instance, if it is a death, the Minister may prescribe that it be required that the employee attaches a certified copy of the relevant death certificate to his application.

In terms of s. 25(4) of the Labour Act, like sick leave, compassionate leave does not form a part of annual leave, sick leave or maternity leave. Yet again, like sick leave, compassionate leave, bears these two distinguishing features, namely, compassionate leave does not entitle an employee to any additional remuneration on termination of employment and compassionate leave days are not cumulative; if not used during the period of twelve months referred to in s. 25(1), they lapse at the end of that period.

4.8.3 Maternity Leave

According to s. 26(1) of the Labour Act 2007 and subject to s. 26(3), a female employee who has completed six months' continuous service in the employment of an employer is, before her confinement, entitled to not less than twelve weeks' maternity leave, calculated according to of s. 26(1)(a) and (b). Section 26(1)(a) provides that the employee is entitled to commence maternity leave four weeks before her expected date of confinement, as certified by her medical practitioner, and also to maternity leave for the entire time from the commencement of her maternity leave, i.e. four weeks before her expected date of confinement, until her actual date of confinement. In terms of s. 26(1)(b), after her date of confinement, she is entitled to eight weeks' maternity leave in every case, and in the case of an employee whose date of confinement occurred less than four weeks after the commencement of her maternity leave, the amount of additional time required to bring her total maternity leave to twelve weeks. According to s. 26(2), she must give to her employer a certificate signed by a medical practitioner, confirming the expected date of confinement before taking maternity leave and the date of confinement on her return from leave.

The Labour Act protects the employment rights of an employee who goes on maternity leave. In terms of s. 26(3) of the Act, all terms of the employee's contract of employment remain in intact and in force during any period that she is on maternity leave; and the employer must during that period pay her the remuneration payable to her, except the basic wage. In terms of s. 26(4), the Social Security Commission established under the Social Security Act 1994[43] must, during the period that an employee is on maternity leave, pay the employee part of that employee's basic wage as may be prescribed in terms of the Labour Act.

Furthermore, s. 26(5) of the Labour Act guarantees the tenure of service of an employee during, and at the expiration of, her maternity leave. Accordingly, an employer must not dismiss such employee during that period on any ground referred to in s. 34 of the Labour Act, i.e. grounds arising from collective termination or redundancy, or on any ground arising from her pregnancy, delivery, or her resultant family status or responsibility. However, the protection offered by s. 26(5) of the Act does not apply, if an employer has offered an employee comparable alternative employment and she has unreasonably refused to accept that offer. What is 'comparable alternative employment' is a question of fact to be determined after considering all the surrounding circumstances. It is submitted, 'comparable alternative employment' is employment that compares favourably in material respects to the previous one, including such terms and conditions of employment as remuneration, duty station, working environment and career development prospects. Section 27 of the Labour Act provides for an extension of maternity leave of an employee if any one or both of the following grounds exist. First, if a medical practitioner certifies that due to complications arising from pregnancy or delivery, it is necessary for the health of an employee, her employer must grant to her extended maternity leave in excess of the period mentioned in s. 26(1)(a) or (b) of the Act (and discussed above), up to a maximum period that is equal to the greater of either one month or the amount of accrued sick leave that the employee has to her credit at the time. Second, if a medical practitioner certifies that due to complications arising from birth or congenital conditions, it is necessary for the health of the employee's child, the employer must grant that employee extended maternity leave in excess of the periods mentioned in terms of s. 26(1)(b) of the Act (and discussed above) up to a maximum period that is equal to the greater of either one month or the amount of accrued sick leave that the employee has to her credit at the time.

Section 27(2) provides that if a medical practitioner issues a certificate covering both situations, then the periods of extended maternity leave must run concurrently. Furthermore, in terms of s. 27(3), a period of extended maternity leave must run immediately before or immediately after the employee's maternity leave granted in terms of s. 26. Finally, according to s. 27(4), the protection afforded by s. 26(3) to (6) to employees on maternity leave (and discussed above) apply to those on extended maternity leave under s. 27.

---

[43] Act No. 34 of 1994.

4.9 PROVISION OF ACCOMMODATION

Nowadays, in practice, except for farmers, a negligible number of employers provide their employees with board and lodging mainly because very few employees live with their employers in the same household.[44] Under the common law, the employer's obligation to provide his employee with board and lodging must be made a term of the contract of employment for it to have effect. However, in terms of s. 28(2) of the Labour Act 2007, an employer's obligation to provide lodging to his employee exists where in virtue of his job, the employee is required to live at the place of employment or reside on any premises owned or leased by the employer. If that is the case, then the employer is obliged to provide the employee with adequate housing, including sanitary and water facilities. If the employee concerned lives on agricultural land, then, in terms of s. 28(3) the accommodation and sanitary and water facilities must be adequate to meet the needs of the employee and his dependants. In addition, an employer must permit a live-in employee to keep livestock and to cultivate land in order to meet his and his dependants' reasonable needs, unless in terms of an agreement with the employee, the employer provides the employee with sufficient food to meet his and his dependants' reasonable needs, or the employer pays the employee additional amount to use for that purpose. In terms of s. 28(1), for the purposes of s. 28, 'a dependant' means the spouse and dependent children of the employee or of the spouse.[45]

One final point about accommodation that is tied to employment is that as a general rule, where the employee's employment has been lawfully terminated, his employer is entitled to evict him from accommodation that he provided.[46] Here, too, the Labour Act 2007 has stepped in to offer some protection to such employee. According to s. 28(4), an employer who terminates the employment of an employee who is required to live at the place of employment or to reside on any premises owned, leased or provided by the employer, may not require the employee to vacate the premises or place unless (i) in the case of an employee who resides on agricultural land, the employer gives to the employee three months' notice to vacate, or (ii) in the case of all other employees, the employer gives to the employee at least one months' notice to vacate. In conclusion, if the employee is unwilling to vacate the accommodation voluntarily, when the time to vacate is due, the employer needs to obtain a court order to effect an eviction.

---

44 Drake, *Labour Law,* para. 54

45 Compare with the definition of 'dependant' under the repealed Labour Act, 1992. For the purposes of s. 38 of the repealed Act, a dependant was the employee's husband or wife, as the case might be, including a common-law wife or husband, and their dependant children and the common dependant children of the wife and husband.

46 *Coin Security (Cape) v Vukani Guards & Allied Workers Union* 1989 (4) SA 234 (C).

5 DUTIES COMMON TO EMPLOYEES AND EMPLOYERS

5.1 DISCRIMINATION

At a basic level, 'discrimination' means unfavourable and prejudicial treatment based on, for example, sex, race, colour, ethnicity, political opinion or physical disability. In the employment relationship, it is unlawful to discriminate on any prohibited grounds such as the foregoing examples.

The International Labour Organization (ILO) Discrimination (Employment and Occupation) Convention 111 of 1958 defines discrimination as including 'any distinction, exclusion or preference made on the basis of race, colour, sex, religion, political opinion, national extraction or social origin, which has the effect of nullifying or impairing equality of opportunity or treatment in employment or occupation'.[1] However, the Convention recognizes that 'any distinction, exclusion, or preference in respect of a particular job based on the inherent requirements thereof shall not be deemed to be discrimination'.[2]

The definition of discrimination under the Labour Act 2007 is similar in material respects to the ILO definition. The anti-discrimination provisions of the Labour Act are in s. 5(2). According to this section, a person must not discriminate directly or indirectly in any employment decision or adopt any requirement or engage in any practice which has the effect of discriminating against an individual on any of the prohibited grounds that are set out in s. 5(2). The grounds are: race, colour, ethnic origin, sex, marital status, family responsibilities, religion, creed, political opinion, social status, economic status, degree of physical or mental disability, HIV or AIDS status and previous, existing or future pregnancy.[3] For the purposes of s. 5, s. 5(1)(b), defines 'employment decision as including':

1 access to vocational guidance, training and placement services;

---

1 ILO. Employment and Occupation Convention, 1958, Art. 1(1).

2 Ibid. Art. 2.

3 For a well-researched and comprehensive work on HIV and AIDS in Africa, see H. Jackson, *Aids in Africa: Continent in Crisis*, Harare, SAFAIDS, 2002.

2   access to employment and to a particular occupation or job, including such procedures or matters as advertising, recruitment, selection, appointment, promotion, demotion, transfer, remuneration, and other terms and conditions of employment;

3   access to, and provision, of benefits, facilities and services;

4   security of tenure;

5   discipline, suspension and termination of employment; and

6   dismissal arising from collective termination or redundancy.

Some key terms used to describe some of the prohibited grounds have been statutorily defined. For example, s. 5(1)(c) defines 'family responsibility' as the responsibility of an employee to another individual who is a parent, spouse, son, daughter or dependant of the employee and who, regardless of age, needs the care and support of that employee. 'Person with disability' is defined in s. 5(1)(e).

It is worth noting that first, the anti-discrimination provisions in s. 5(2) of the Labour Act do not cast the duty not to discriminate on employers alone but on "persons", i.e. all persons in the employment relationship or situation. Second, the provisions are meant to protect not only employees but also potential employees. Third, s. 5(2) outlaws both direct discrimination and indirect discrimination. Last, the prohibited grounds of discrimination set out in s. 5(2) are exhaustive; no other grounds can be added to the list.

Thus, according to s. 5(2) of the Labour Act, X discriminates in any employment decision against Y if on the grounds of, for example, Y's race, colour, ethnic origin, sex, marital status, family responsibilities, religion, political opinion, degree of physical or mental disability, or HIV or AIDS status, X treats Y less favourably than he treats or would treat other persons of, say, a different sex, race, ethnic origin, or having a different HIV or AIDS status. Such differential treatment constitutes direct discrimination. Another illustration can be found in s. 5(3) of the Act. According to this subsection, for the purposes of s. 5(2), it is discrimination on the grounds of sex to differentiate *without justification* in any employment decision between employees who do work of equal value, or between employees who do work of equal value, or between applicants for employment who seek work of equal value.

In England, case law has defined such situation as the 'but for' test, i.e. would the victim have been treated differently *but for* his or her race, colour, ethnic origin, sex, marital status, family responsibilities, religion, political opinion, degree of physical or mental disability or HIV or AIDS status?[4]

---

[4]   A.C. Bell, *Employment Law in a Nutshell*, London, Sweet & Maxwell, 2000, p. 33 and the case cited.

The motive for the discrimination is irrelevant: direct discrimination brought about by good intentions or even unintentionally is discrimination.[5] Thus, direct discrimination covers the more familiar instances, like those mentioned above, e.g. the withholding of some benefit or refusing to employ a person because 'he is of the "wrong" race, colour, sex or ethnic background or because he or she is HIV positive'.[6]

Indirect discrimination, on the other hand, is brought about if, for example, one class of the community (for example an ethnic minority or a racial group), because of discrimination in the past, has had less opportunity of obtaining certain educational qualifications, and that class is adversely affected if an employer makes it a requirement that his employees or potential employees must possess those educational qualifications if they are to be employed or promoted.[7] According to the European Court of Justice, proof of indirect discrimination is established by a comparison between groups, while proof of direct discrimination is established by a comparison between individuals.[8]

As we saw previously, s. 5(3) of the Labour Act provides that it is discrimination to differentiate without justification in any employment decision between employees who do work of equal value, or between applicants for employment who seek work of equal value. In *Nanditume v Minister of Defence*,[9] the applicant had applied to be enlisted in the Namibian Defence Force. A medical examination and blood test revealed that he was HIV positive. His application for enlistment was refused on this ground. From the expert evidence, the Labour Court found that people who were HIV positive would most likely only contract AIDS after eight to twelve years. Such persons would accordingly be fit for any kind of employment. In any case, there were many other members of the Defence Force who were HIV positive or who had AIDS but they had not been tested or excluded from enlistment. The Defence Force in fact practised a policy of non-discrimination. The Court also found that the applicant was in good health. In the result, the Court held that the exclusion of the applicant from the Defence Force on the ground that he had tested HIV positive constituted unfair discrimination in terms of s. 107 of the repealed Labour Act 1992.

Although the Court in *Nanditume v Minister of Defence* supra was interpreting and applying the anti-discrimination provisions under the repealed Labour Act 1992, it is submitted that the principles outlined in that case should apply equally to the interpretation and application of the anti-discrimination provisions of the Labour Act 2007. So should *SA*

---

5   Ibid.

6   Collins Parker, *Human Rights Law,* Leicestershire, Upfront Publishing, 2002, p. 141.

7   Ibid. p. 142.

8   *Enderby v Frenchay* (1994) 69 CMLR 8.

9   *Nanditume v Minister of Defence* 2000 NR 103 (LC).

Chemical Workers Union and others v Sentrachem Ltd,[10] where the Industrial Court ruled that wage differentiation based on race or any other differences between employees other than skills or experiences was unfair discrimination and therefore unlawful.

However, according to s. 5(4)(a) of the Labour Act, as is the case under Art. 2 of the ILO Convention 111 of 1958 referred to above, it is not discrimination to take an affirmative action measure aimed at ensuring that racially disadvantaged persons, women or persons with disabilities enjoy employment opportunities at all levels of employment that are at least equal to those enjoyed by other employees of the same employer, and are fairly represented in the workforce of an employer. It is also not discrimination, according to the Labour Act, where there are distinctions, exclusions or preferences on the basis of an inherent job requirement. As was mentioned previously in the present chapter, 'person with disability' is defined in s. 5(1)(3), as is 'racially disadvantaged person' defined in s. 5(1)(f).

Thus, not all forms of differentiation amount to discrimination under the Labour Act. For instance, it would not amount to discrimination if an employer rewarded employees unequally on the basis of differences in qualifications, skills and expertise required in performing different tasks.[11] Nor would an employer be guilty of discrimination if he showed preference to a particular applicant on the basis of his qualification, skills or expertise that are appropriate to an inherent job requirement. It is again not discrimination to take any measure that has been approved by the Employment Equity Commission in terms of the Affirmative Action (Employment) Act 1998.[12] Furthermore, it is not discrimination against a pregnant female employee for her employer to assign her temporarily to duties or functions, other than her normal duties or functions, which suited her condition, so long as the reassignment does not lead to a reduction in remuneration or any other benefits to which she is entitled.

To sum up, the actions or conduct of a person in any employment decision would constitute discrimination under s. 5 of the Labour Act 2007 if the facts found disclose a differential treatment and such distinction, exclusion or preference does not have any of the legitimate aims laid down in s. 5(4) of the Act. In other words, the basis of the differentiation must be rational and must have a legitimate object like any of those set out in s. 5(4) of the Act in order for such action or conduct not to attract the stigma of discrimination under the Act.[13] As Strydom, CJ stated succinctly in *Müller v President of the Republic of Namibia*

---

10 *SA Chemical Workers Union and others v Sentrachem Ltd* (1988) *ILJ* 410 (IC).

11 See *Mthembu and others v Claude Neon Lights* (1992) 13 (ILJ) 422 (IC); *SA Chemical Workers Union and others v Sentrachem* supra.

12 Act No. 29 of 1998.

13 See *Mwellie v Minister of Works, Transport and Communication and Another* 1995 (9) BCLR 1118 (NmH); *Prinsloo v Van Linde and another* 1997 (3) SA 1012 (CC); and J. Grogan, *Riekert's Employment Law,* 2nd edn, Cape Town, Juta, 1993, p. 121.

and another, 'inherent in the meaning of the word discrimination is an element of unjust or unfair treatment'.[14]

Section 5(6) of the Labour Act offers a complete defence to an employer against whom an allegation of discrimination under the Labour Act has been made. According to that provision, it is a complete defence to the allegation if the employer took the decision in compliance with both an affirmative action plan approved by the Employment Equity Commission in terms of the Affirmative Action (Employment) Act 1998 and s. 19(1) and (2) of that Act.[15] Section 19(1) provides that in filling vacancies the employer must give preferential treatment to suitably qualified persons of the designated groups, which are listed in s. 18 of the Act; and s. 19(2) provides that where two or more qualified candidates from the designated groups qualify for a position, the employer must give priority to those who are Namibian citizens, and if all of them are Namibian citizens, to the candidate who belongs to the greatest number of the designated groups. Furthermore, an employer has a complete defence if he chooses one person from a group consisting of, say, a woman, a person with a disability and a racially disadvantaged person.

5.2 Duty to Bargain in Good Faith

The duty to bargain in good faith in employment relationships rests with both employees and employers. Generally, the mere existence of an employment relationship imposes a duty on an employer to negotiate individually with any of his employees on any matter concerning their employment relationship;[16] for the right to negotiate is a personal right which attaches to the person of the individual employee. During such negotiations, both an employer and employee are obliged to negotiate in good faith. But the employee's right to bargain with his employer as an individual exists only where there is no ongoing collective bargaining between the employer and a trade union recognized by the employer as the exclusive bargaining agent on the same subject matter that the employee wishes to negotiate on. A full treatment of the obligation on both employers and trade unions recognized as exclusive bargaining agents to bargain in good faith during collective bargaining will be found in chapter 15.

---

14 *Müller v President of the Republic of Namibia and another* 1999 NR 190 (SC) at 200G.

15 Affirmative Action (Employment) Act No. 29 of 1998. See also Employment Equity Commission of Namibia, *The Employers' Guidelines to the Affirmative Action (Employment) Act 1998 (Act No. 29 of 1998)*, revised edn, Windhoek, October 2002.

16 In *Radio Television Electronic & Allied Workers Union v Tedelex (Pty) Ltd & another* (1990) 11 *ILJ* 1272 (IC).

5.3 Health and Safety at the Workplace

The aim of labour or employment law on health and safety is to prevent accidents occurring at the workplace and to promote the health of the employees at the workplace. An employer is under a common law duty to take reasonable care for the safety of his employees.[17] The common law basis of the employer's duty towards his employee's safety arises from the contract of employment. There is an implied term that an employer will take reasonable care to safeguard the safety of his employee. A breach of this duty amounts to a breach of the contract of employment. In practice, where the employer's breach has resulted in an injury to the employee, there is no point in suing in contract. The employee will do well to bring an action in delict for negligence.

In Namibia, as in some other Commonwealth countries, e.g. the United Kingdom under the Health and Safety at Work Act 1974,[18] the common law has been buttressed by legislation. Section 39(1) of the Labour Act 2007 sets out a long list of an employer's duties concerning the health and safety of his employees. Notable among the duties are the employer's duty:

1   to provide, without charge to employees, a working environment that is safe, that poses no risk to the health of employees and that has adequate facilities and arrangements for the welfare of employees;

2   to provide and maintain plant, machinery, systems of work and work processes that are safe and that poses no risk to the health of employees;

3   to provide employees with adequate personal protective clothing and equipment that are reasonably necessary;

4   to ensure that the use, handling, storage or transport of articles or substances is safe and poses no risk to the health of employees; and

5   to ensure that employees are given the necessary instructions and supervision that will enable them to work safely and without any risk to their health and safety.

In terms of s. 39(2) of the Act, an employer must report to a labour inspector in the prescribed manner whenever either there is an accident at any place where the employer's employees work, or whenever a prescribed disease is contracted at such place. In this regard,

---

[17]   *Media 24 Ltd and another v Grobler* [2005] 3 All SA 297 (SCA); *Wilson & Clyde Coal Co v English* [1938] AC 57; Grogan, *Riekert's Employment Law,* p. 63.

[18]   Health and Safety at Work etc. Act, 1974 (c. 37).

according to the Workmen's Compensation Act 1941,[19] as amended by the Employees' Compensation Act 1995,[20] an employer is liable to pay compensation to his employee for a personal injury he has sustained as a result of an accident arising from and in the course of his employment.[21]

The duty of an employee to implement his employer's regulations on health and safety also cannot be overemphasized. Section 40 of the Labour Act 2007 provides for two main duties of the employee in this regard. First, an employee has the duty to take reasonable measures to ensure his own safety and health at the workplace and the safety and health of any other person who may be affected by the employee's activities at work. An employee will, therefore, do well to get acquainted with any safety and health instructions that the employer may issue from time to time. Second, an employee has a duty to cooperate with his employer to enable the employer to perform any duty imposed by Chapter 4 of the Labour Act in respect of safety and health in the work environment.

5.4 INDEMNITY

It is an implied term of a contract of employment that the employee will exercise proper and reasonable care in the performance of his service.[22] This general principle was established in England as far back as the fifteenth century.[23] In determining what is reasonable, the courts have taken into account the circumstances of the particular case, including such factors as the role of the employee's work in the overall operation of the employer's business and the skill that the employee professes to possess.[24] Seminal to this duty is the employee's duty to indemnify his employer. The duty arises where, as a result of an employee's conduct in the course or scope of his employment, an employer is made liable to a third party in damages and costs. The indemnity arises so long as the employee's conduct purportedly giving rise to the employer's liability arose in the course or scope of employment.[25]

---

19   Act No. 30 of 1941.

20   Act No. 5 of 1995. See also Swaziland's Workmen's Compensation Act 1983 (Act No. 7 of 1983).

21   See *Khoza v Minister of Justice* 1964 SA (3) 78 (W) for a discussion on what constitutes an accident 'arising out of and in the course of employment'.

22   *Ndamase v Fyfe-King NO* 1939 EDL 259. See also chapter 3, para. 3.9.3 above, where negligence of employees is treated.

23   R. Lowe, *Commercial Law,* 4th edn, London, Sweet & Maxwell, 1973, p. 88.

24   Ibid. See also *Harmer v Cornelius* (1858) 5 CB (NS) 236.

25   The vicarious liability of an employer for his employee's delict and the meaning of 'in the course or scope of employment' are discussed later in this section.

In *Lister v Ramford Ice and Cold Storage Co. Ltd.*,[26] a lorry driver negligently injured a co-employee, who happened to be his father, while both of them were acting in the course or scope of their employment. Lister senior obtained damages and costs against the employer. The employer sought to be indemnified in respect of the damages and costs, claiming that it was an implied term of their contract of employment that Lister junior would perform his duties with proper and reasonable care. The House of Lords held that Lister junior was liable to his employer in full. Viscount Simonds stated:

> It is, in my opinion, clear that it was an implied term of the contract that the appellant would perform his duties with proper care. The proposition of law stated by Willis, J in *Hormer v Cornelius* has never been questioned: 'When a skilled labourer,' he said, 'artisan, or artist is employed, there is on his part an implied warranty that he is of skill reasonably competent to the task he undertakes – *Spondes peritam artis*... An express promise or express representation in the particular case is not necessary.' I see no ground for excluding from, and every ground for including in, this category a servant who is employed to drive a lorry which, driven without care, may become an engine of destruction and involve his master in very grave liability. Nor can I see any valid reason for saying that a distinction is to be made between possessing skill and exercising it... Of what advantage to the employer is his servant's undertaking that he possesses skill unless he undertakes also to use it?[27]

Lister junior claimed that it was an implied term of his contract of employment that the duty to indemnify did not extend to cases where the employer had insured against liability. By a majority of three to two, the House of Lords held that there was no implied duty on the master's part to insure, particularly where there is no statutory third-party insurance requirement.

The point should be reiterated that indemnity is limited to cases where the employee is performing his usual service under the contract of employment. In *Harvey v O'Dell*,[28] an employer could not claim indemnity from his employee for breach of the implied duty to take care because the employee had been employed as a storekeeper and not as a driver, and the breach occurred while acting as a driver.

---

26   *Lister v Ramford Ice and Cold Storage Ltd* [1957] AC 555.

27   Ibid. at 572-3.

28   *Harvey v O'Dell* [1958] 1 All ER 657.

The liability of an employer for the delicts of his employee is an example of vicarious liability (*respondent superior*) in delict. Under the principle of vicarious liability, X is held liable for the delict of Y committed against Z, though X is not privy to the delict. In labour law, the principle of vicarious liability states that the employer is liable for any delict that the employee commits in the course or scope of employment. In *Colonial Mutual Life Assurance Society Ltd v MacDonald* [29] Roos, JA approved the reference by the Court *a quo* to *Mkize v Maartens* [30] and *Estate van der Byl v Swanepoel* [31] from which he extracted the principle 'that a master is liable to a third party for the act of his servant, so long as the later is about the business of his master and does the act in the course of his employment'.[32] It is important to note that an employer's liability is in addition to, and not instead of, his employee's liability. Thus an employee does not cease to be liable delictually because of his employer's vicarious liability in respect of the same wrong.[33]

An employer's vicarious liability has two main elements, namely, the tortfeasor or wrongdoer must be an employee of the employer,[34] and the delict ought to have been committed in the course or scope of employment at the relevant time.[35] The first element, i.e. who an employee is, has been treated fully in chapter 1, para. 1.2, and so the subject does not require further treatment. Nevertheless, one crucial point merits re-emphasising: some employees, e.g. surgeons, jet pilots and scientists, may exercise their skills and judgment unsupervised and uncontrolled by the employer because the employer may not have the technical skill to give any orders of a technical nature. Nevertheless, such a handicap does not relieve the employer of liability.[36]

As to the second element, an employer is liable for harm caused to third parties by the negligence of his employee if such employee is acting within the 'course or scope of his employment – expressions which have been held to be synonymous'.[37] What then is meaning of the expression 'in the course or scope of employment'? The wrongful act is done in the course or scope of employment, if it is expressly or impliedly authorized by the employer or if it is an unauthorized or wrongful manner of doing an act that is authorized by the employer or the act is necessary or incidental to, or connected with, an act which the

---

29   *Colonial Mutual Life Assurance Society Ltd v MacDonald* 1931 AD 412.

30   *Mkize v Maartens* 1914 AD 382.

31   *Estate van der Byl v Swanepoel* 1927 AD 141.

32   *Colonial Mutual Life v MacDonald* supra at 423.

33   *Harnischfeger Corporation v Appleton* 1993 (4) SA 479 (W).

34   *Gibbins v Williams, Muller, Wright & Mostert Ingelyf* 1987 (2) SA 82 (T).

35   *Mkize v Maartens* supra; *Minister of Police v Mbilini* 1983 (3) SA 705 (A); *Nel v Minister of Defence* 1979 (2) SA 246 (R); *Isaacs v Centre Guards CC t/a Town Centre Security* [2004] 3 BLLR 288 (C). See also *Stein v Rising Tide Productions CC* 2002 (5) SA 199 (C): the facts of the case are sketched briefly in chapter 1, para. 1.2.2.4 above.

36   *Roe v Ministry of Health* (1954) 2 WLR 915 at 930.

37   *HK Manufacturing Co (Pty) Ltd v Sadowitz* 1965 (3) SA 328 (C) at 332C-D *per* Tebbutt, J.

100 Labour Law in Namibia

employee is authorized to do.[38] The following passage from *SAR & H v Marais* is straight to the point and instructive:

> As to the law which is applicable it is not necessary to consider the Roman-Dutch authorities as to the liability of a master for the delicts of his servant, for those authorities were considered by this Court in *Mkize v Martens* (1914 AD 382) and in *Feldman (Pty) Ltd v Mall* (1945) AD 733, 738). In *Mkize's* case Lord De Villiers, C.J., at p. 387, Innes, J.A., at pp. 389, 390 and Solomon, J.A., held that the law as laid down by Voet, 9.4.10 must be applied in South Africa, viz., that masters are liable *in solidum* for the delicts of their servants whenever they inflict injury or damage 'in the duty or service' (*in officio aut ministerio*) set them by their masters, but that the master is not liable when the delict is committed 'outside of' (*extra*) their duty or service. Potheir on *Obligations*, p. 453, who is much to the same effect as *Voet*, was quoted by Innes, J.A., at p. 390 and De Villiers, A.J.A., at p. 400. *Pothier* says (*Evans'* translation):
>
> 'Whoever appoints a person to any function is answerable for the wrongs and neglects which his agent may commit in the exercise of the functions to which he is appointed.'[39]

In practice, the requirement that an employer is only liable if the wrongful act was done in the course or scope of employment creates little difficulty in many instances of the employment relationship. It is with regard to borderline cases that the application of the rule creates considerable difficulty. Denning, LJ (as he then was) has, therefore, counselled that the expression (course or scope of employment) 'be construed liberally'.[40]

In this regard, an act is authorized if it is done so as to carry out an order of the employer, which results in the commission of a delict or so as to carry out an order, which, by necessary implication, involves the commission of a delict. But the fact that an employee acts in disobedience of orders of his employer does not necessarily absolve the employer from liability.[41] This statement needs clarification. An employee who ignores a prohibition that limits the sphere of his employment is not acting in the course or scope of his employment. Hence, an employee who is employed to drive a delivery van used solely to carry goods

---

38   T.E. Lewis, *Winfield on Tort,* 6th edn, London, Sweet & Maxwell, 1954, pp. 146-7.

39   *SAR & H v Marais* 1950 SA 610 (A) at 616E-H, *per* Watermeyer, CJ.

40   *Navarro v Moregrand Ltd* [1951] 2 TLR 674 at 681. See also *Lloyd v Grace Smith & Co* [1912] AC 716 at 736, *per* Lord Macnaghten.

41   *Fawcett Security Operations v Omar Enterprises (Pvt) Ltd* 1992 (4) SA 425 (ZSC).

Duties Common to Employees and Employers

will not be acting in the course or scope of his employment if he carries passengers in the van. However, an employee who ignores a prohibition that concerns the manner in which he caries out an act that is within the sphere of his employment is acting in the course or scope of his employment.[42]

Thus, in the above illustration, if the employee disregards his employer's injunction that he must ensure that the doors of the delivery van are always locked when it is loaded and in motion and a package falls off the van while in motion injuring a pedestrian, his employer is liable. Diplock, J stated likewise that the employer is liable if his employee carries out an authorized act in a wrongful and an unauthorized manner. He explained tersely and with insight the proposition in the following passage in *Hilton v Thomas Burton (Rhodes) Ltd*:

> I think that the true test can be expressed in these words: Was the second defendant (the employee) doing something that he was employed to do? If so, however improper the manner in which he was doing it, whether negligent as in *Century Insurance Co Ltd v Northern Island Road Transport Board* (1924) or even fraudulent as in *Lloyd v Grace, Smith & Co* (1912), or contrary to express orders as in *Canadian Pacific Railway v Lockhart* (1942), the master is liable.[43]

Therefore, in *Lister v Ramford Ice and Cold Storage Co Ltd*,[44] in carelessly backing his lorry into a slaughterhouse yard and injuring a co-employee, the driver (employee) was found to have been doing an authorized act, i.e. driving the lorry, except that he was doing so in a wrongful and an unauthorized manner. The Court in *Isaacs v Centre Guards CC t/a Town Centre Security* supra also distinguished between prohibitions that limit the sphere of employment and those that concern conduct within the sphere of employment. The Court then stated that an employee who disregards the sphere of employment is not acting within the scope of employment, but an employee who disregards a prohibition relating to a conduct within the sphere of employment is acting within the course or scope of employment.

The fact that the act giving rise to the liability is done while the employee is on duty does not *ipso facto* mean that he was acting in the scope or course of employment.[45] The converse is also true: the act or omission of the employee complained of may occur whilst the employee is engaged in the affairs of his employer and yet the employer may not be

---

42   *Moghamat v Central Guards CC* (2004) 1 All SA 221 (C).

43   *Hilton v Thomas Burton (Rhodes) Ltd* [1961] WLR 70 at 77.

44   *Lister v Ramford* supra, AC 555.

45   *Minister of Police v Mbilini* supra.

liable. Thus, in *Rossouw v Central News Agency Ltd*,[46] while driving a car on the business of his employer, an employee of the defendant (employer) gave the plaintiff a lift in the car. The car was involved in an accident caused by the negligence of the employee, which resulted in the plaintiff sustaining serious injuries. It was held that because the employee had no authority to carry passengers in the car, his act in giving a lift to the plaintiff was a personal and private act of his own and therefore outside the course or scope of his employment.

The courts have therefore held that the employer is not liable where the employee acts while he is 'on a frolic of his own'.[47] The employee is on a frolic of his own if, for instance, he deviates from his normal route so as to perform some errand for himself, a relative or a friend. In *Van Drimmelen and Partners v Gowar and others*,[48] the Court held that the employer was not vicariously liable for a delict committed by his employee, which caused personal injuries in a motor vehicle collision, when the employee was going home after work.

In *Daniels v Whitestone Entertainments Ltd*,[49] a steward who was authorized by his employer (the defendant) to evict disorderly persons from a dancehall and to see to it that they did not return had an altercation with the plaintiff. The steward struck the plaintiff in the dancehall, and later assaulted him outside the dancehall. The court held that the employer was liable for the assault that occurred inside the dancehall but not for the assault that occurred outside the dancehall. The decisive factors that were taken into account were the circumstances in which, the time when and the place where the assault was committed. The employee was authorized to evict disorderly persons from the dancehall and to prevent their return. The assault inside the dancehall was done while the employee was carrying out his duties. Having succeeded in evicting the plaintiff, he had no business assaulting the plaintiff outside the dancehall.

The Supreme Court of Appeal reached a similar conclusion in *Costa da Oura Restaurant (Pty) Ltd t/a Umdloti Bush Tavern v Reddy*.[50] The facts in *Daniels v Whitestone* supra bear some similarities to the facts in *Costa da Oura v Reddy*. In *Costa da Oura v Reddy,* the respondent and his girlfriend were patrons in the appellant's restaurant and bar (the Tavern). The respondent was under the impression that one of the appellant's barmen *G* served all the other patrons at the bar, except the respondent and his girlfriend and that *G* had done that intentionally. *G* overheard the respondent telling one of the other barmen that *G* could learn

---

46   *Rossouw v Central News Agency Ltd* 1948 (2) SA 267 (W). See also *SAR &H v Marais* supra.

47   *Carter & Co (Pty) Ltd v McDonald* 1955 (1) SA 202 (A); *H K Manufacturing Co (Pty) Ltd v Sadowitz* 1965 (3) SA 328 (C); *Minister of Law and Order v Ngobo* 1992 (4) SA 922 (A).

48   *Van Drimmelen and Partners v Gowar and others* [2004] 1All SA 175 (SCA).

49   *Daniels v Whitestone Entertainments Ltd* [1942] 2 Lloyd's Rep. 1.

50   *Costa da Oura Restaurant (Pty) Ltd t/a Umdloti Bush Tavern v Reddy* 2003 (4) SA 34 (SCA).

a lesson from the other barmen on how to treat patrons. *G* apparently took offence at the respondent's comments, and got involved in a minor verbal exchange with the respondent. *G* waited outside the Tavern for the respondent and his girlfriend. Without uttering a word to them when they came outside the Tavern, *G* attacked the respondent with his fist and boot. This attack caused physical injuries to the respondent who brought a suit against the appellant on the basis of vicarious liability for *G*'s conduct. It was common cause between the parties that the only issue for determination was whether the appellant was vicariously liable for the conduct of his employee, *G*.

The court below held in favour of the respondent (i.e. plaintiff in the court below). On appeal the Supreme Court of Appeal held unanimously that the assault by *G* outside the appellant's establishment, the Tavern, occurred after *G* had abandoned his duties: it was a personal act of vindictive aggression carried out neither in furtherance of his employer's express or implied authority, nor as incidental to, or in consequence of, anything that *G* was employed to do. In the result, the Court found that *G*'s unprovoked attack on the respondent did not render *G*'s employer (the appellant) vicariously liable.

An employer is equally liable if he ratifies his employee's delict – either by word or conduct – provided that the act was done for the employer and he had knowledge of it.

In indemnity cases, the employee may claim that the employer contributed to the negligence for which he has been held liable and for which he has been called upon to indemnify his employer. On this point, Denning, LJ (as he then was) stated in *Jones v Manchester Corporation*, 'if the servant commits a tort in the course of his employment, then the master is a tortfeasor as well as the servant'.[51] In that case, a patient died in the hospital in circumstances tending to show negligence on the part of the hospital for selecting an inexperienced doctor who also displayed carelessness. It was held that the employer could not claim 100 per cent indemnity from the doctor. The damages were apportioned between the employee and the employer, the former bearing only one-fifth of the total damages.

5.5 Sexual Harassment

Sexual harassment as a wrongful act or conduct in labour law may be described as persistent, troublesome and unsolicited sexual advances or suggestions, by action or conduct, of an individual or individuals against another individual or individuals. Unlike the repealed Labour Act 1992, the Labour Act 2007 expressly prohibits sexual harassment. Section 5(8) provides: 'A person must not, in any employment decision or in the course of an employee's

---

[51] *Jones v Manchester Corporation* [1952] 2 QB 852 at 870. See also *Semtex v Gladstone* [1954] 1 WLR 954.

employment, directly or indirectly sexually harass an employee.' For the purposes of that section, 'employee' includes a prospective employee. The Labour Act defines 'sexual harassment' in s. 5(7)(b) in this way:

> 'sexual harassment' means any unwarranted conduct of a sexual nature towards an employee which violates the dignity of an employee and constitutes a barrier to equality in employment where
>
> (i)   the victim has made it known to the perpetrator that he or she finds the conduct offensive; or
>
> (ii)   the perpetrator should have reasonably realised that the conduct is regarded as unacceptable, taking into account the respective positions of the parties in the place of employment, the nature of their employment relationships and the nature of the place of employment.

Therefore, to constitute a wrongful conduct under the Labour Act 2007, the following crucial elements must exist together. First, the action or conduct must be of a sexual nature and unjustified. Second, the action or conduct must be directed at an employee. Third, the perpetrator must have imposed the action or conduct on the victim. Fourth, the alleged victim must have been an unwilling participant. Finally, the victim himself or herself must have found the action or conduct offensive or unacceptable, and have informed the perpetrator accordingly or the perpetrator ought to have reasonably realized that his or her conduct was unacceptable to the victim, taking into account the relative positions of the perpetrator and the victim in the place of employment, the nature of their employment relationship and the nature of the place of employment.[52] The sex of the perpetrator does not matter.

The South African Industrial Court incisively described sexual harassment in *J v M Ltd* thus:

> If one applies the dictionary meaning of words, sexual harassment would mean to trouble another continually in the sexual sphere. In the employment relationship the word has a slightly different connotation and is very broadly unwanted sexual attention in the employment environment... Conduct which can constitute sexual harassment can range from innuendo, inappropriate gestures, suggestions, or hints or fondling without consent or by force to

---

52   See Bell, *Employment Law in a Nutshell,* p. 34.

its worst form, namely, rape. It is in my opinion also not necessary that the conduct must be repeated. A single act can constitute sexual harassment.[53]

Bracebridge Engineering Ltd v Darby[54] is also authority for the proposition that a single act like those described in *J v M Ltd*, so long as it is sufficiently serious, can constitute sexual harassment.

So great opprobrium is attached to sexual harassment at the workplace in England that persistent and unwanted sexual advances of a male employer towards a female employee was held in *Western Excavating (ECC) Ltd v Sharp*[55] to constitute constructive dismissal. On this aspect, the Labour Act 2007 is identical to English law on the subject, barring the qualification of employer as 'male employer' and 'female employee' in the English case law. According to s. 5(9) of the Labour Act, where sexual harassment is perpetrated by an employer against an employee and that employee resigns as a result of the sexual harassment, the resignation constitutes constructive dismissal; and according to s. 5(1), the mere proof of constructive dismissal, without more, may constitute unfair dismissal within the meaning of s. 33 of the Labour Act.[56]

Sexual harassment must be seen in a serious light because it violates or is capable of violating the dignity and personality of the victim. Besides, it creates a negative atmosphere in the workplace by destroying interpersonal working relations. The Industrial Court put it succinctly in these terms in *J v M Ltd* supra:

> Sexual harassment, depending on the form it takes, will violate the right of body and personality which belongs to every person and which is protected in our legal system both criminally and civilly. An employer undoubtedly has a duty to ensure that its employees are not subjected to this form of violation within the workplace. The victims of harassment find it embarrassing and humiliating. Work performance may suffer and career commitment may be lowered. It is indeed not uncommon for employees to resign rather than subject themselves to further sexual harassment. An employer clearly has an interest in ensuring a happy work environment as that leads to higher productivity.[57]

---

[53] *J v M Ltd* (1989) 10 *ILJ* 755 (IC) at 757D-E.

[54] *Bracebridge Engineering Ltd v Darby* [1990] IRLR 3.

[55] *Western Excavating (ECC) Ltd v Sharp* [1978] 1 All ER 713.

[56] Constructive dismissal is dealt with in chapter 2, para. 2.2.1.5 above, and chapter 6, para. 6.2.1.1 below, and unfair dismissal in chapter 8, para. 8.1 below.

[57] *J v M Ltd* at 758.

Sexual harassment may take the form of the perpetrator following it up with threats of taking specific action detrimental to the victim's career or refraining from taking a specific action that would otherwise promote the victim's career prospects. For instance, a supervisor may follow his or her sexual advances with the threat that if the staff member did not grant him or her sexual favours, he or she would dismiss him or her, transfer him or her to an unfavourable job or duty station, or block the victim's promotion.

As discussed above, sexual harassment has a destructive effect on the dignity and personality of the victim and interpersonal relations at the workplace, and, therefore, tends to poison the working environment. Consequently, the employer bears a duty to ensure that it does not occur in his business, and when it occurs, he must see to it that the wrongdoer is dealt with promptly, decisively and severely.

Thus, in *Grobler v Naspers Bpk and another*,[58] the South African High Court observed that while sexual harassment could probably be regarded as a 'frolic of the employee's own', a number of recent Canadian, United States and English cases had held the employer liable for the sexual harassment of an employee by a co-employee. Accordingly, the Appeal Court came to the conclusion that policy considerations as well as the constitutional imperative to develop the common law justified the extension of vicarious liability circumstances to cover sexual harassment cases. (Vicarious liability of employers for the civil wrongs of their employees is discussed in para. 5.4 above.) In the result, the Court found for the complainant, and decided that an employer can under certain circumstances be held liable for sexual harassment of his employee by a fellow employee.

In *Media 24 Ltd and another v Grobler*,[59] the Court of Appeal confirmed the decision of the High Court in *Grobler v Naspers Bpk and another* supra. The Appeal Court held that the employee had succeeded in establishing a negligent breach by the employer of its legal duty to its employee to ensure a safe working environment in which, among other things, its employees are not sexually harassed by fellow employees. Indeed, according to the Appeal Court, an employer owes a common law duty to its employees to take reasonable care to ensure their safety, which includes protecting them from psychological harm caused, for instance, by sexual harassment by fellow employees.

---

[58] *Grobler v Naspers Bpk and another* [2004] 5 BLLR 455 (C).

[59] *Media 24 Ltd and another v Grobler* [2005] 3 All SA 297 (SCA): this is the citation under which the appeal case is reported.

6 REMEDIES OF EMPLOYEES AND EMPLOYERS

6.1 INTRODUCTION

The focus of this chapter is an examination of remedies that are available to an employer or employee where there has been a breach of the duties that each one owes to the other, i.e. where there has been a breach by either the employer or the employee of the contract of employment. Some of the remedies have either been discussed or mentioned already in chapters 2, 3, 4 and 5. Those that have been discussed in some detail will only be referred to in passing in the present chapter; and those not already discussed will receive in-depth treatment in this and the next chapters. Some remedies will receive in-depth treatment in succeeding chapters.

6.2 REMEDIES OF EMPLOYEES

6.2.1 Termination of Contract by or without Notice

6.2.1.1 Termination without Notice[1]

As a general rule, an employee is entitled to terminate the contract of employment without notice, i.e. summarily, if an employer refuses or fails to discharge his obligations under the contract, e.g. where:

1 the employer fails or refuses to carry out a term which goes to the root of the contract;

2 the employer's conduct evinces an intention that he no longer wishes to be bound by the contract;

3 the employer's conduct towards the employee is such that the employee can no longer reasonably be expected to continue in his employment; or

4 the employer exerts undue influence on the employee to resign.

---

[1] This aspect of the law in terms of the Labour Act 2007 is treated in chapter 7, para. 7.3 below.

If the employee leaves employment because of the existence of any of these situations, the labour law may treat his separation as 'constructive dismissal'. The reason is that although the employee terminates his contract of employment, the termination is in fact caused or prompted by the conduct of the employer.[2] In *Transnamib Limited v Swartz,*[3] Gibson, J accepted counsel's submission on behalf of the respondent that when the employer renders the relationship with the employee so intolerable that the employee has no option but to resign, the termination of the contract is deemed to have been effected by the employer: the termination constitutes constructive dismissal.[4]

As Lord Denning, MR observed in *Woods v W M Car Services (Peterborough) Ltd,* 'The circumstances [of constructive dismissal] are so infinitely various that there can be, and is, no rule of law saying what circumstances justify and what do not. It is a question of fact for the tribunal of fact.'[5] In this connection, the courts have held that an employer's conduct such as that given in the following examples will justify his employee terminating his employment without notice and claiming constructive dismissal:

1   the employer's failure to provide work resulting in ignominy and degradation;[6]

2   variation of the nature of the employee's duties without his consent;[7]

3   unprovoked assault by a representative of the employer on the employee in a depraved and humiliating manner;[8]

4   failure to pay wages that have become due;[9]

5   any other conduct of an employer that drives an employee to resign,[10] e.g. where the employer refuses to listen to the employee and it is shown that the employee has allowed the employer an opportunity to look into (his) complaints but the employer has failed or is unwilling to do so;[11]

6   where an employer creates an unbearable work environment such that an employee is left with no option but to resign;[12] or

---

2   P.A.K. Le Roux and A.van Niekerk, *The South African Law of Unfair Dismissal,* Cape Town, Juta, 1994. p. 84.

3   *Transnamib Limited v Swartz* NLLP 2002 (2) 60 NLC at 61.

4   It is shown in chapter 2, para. 2.2.1.5 above that a unilateral variation of the contract of employment may also have the consequence of constructive dismissal.

5   *Woods v W M Car Services (Peterborough) Ltd* (1982) IRLR (CA) 413 at 415.

6   *In re An Arbitration between Rubel Bronze and Metal Company Ltd and Vos* [1918] 1 KB 315.

7   *Nhlanhla M. K. Vilakati v Attorney-General* Swaziland IC 88/96 (unreported).

8   *Delisile M. Dlamini v Samuel Dlamini t/a Top Hits Record Bar* Swaziland IC 62/97 (unreported).

9   *R v Plank and others* (1900) 17 SC 45 [10 CTR 21].

10   *Amalgamated Beverage Industries (Pty) Ltd v Jonker* 14 *ILJ* 1232 (LAC).

11   *Transnamib v Swartz* supra.

12   *Cymot (Pty) Ltd v McLoud* 2002 NR 391 (LC).

7   where an employer perpetrates sexual harassment against an employee and the employee resigns as a result of the sexual harassment within the meaning of s. 5(7) of the Labour Act 2007.[13]

An employee alleging constructive dismissal bears the onus of proving it; and in order to succeed, he must prove that (i) he terminated the employment contract; (ii) his continued employment became unbearable; (iii) the situation that rendered his employment unbearable was created by the employer; (iv) the termination was the direct result of that situation and the employee had no choice but to terminate the contract of employment. In *Mafomane v Rustenburg Platinum Mines Ltd*,[14] the Labour Court held that the test of whether the employee's continued employment has become intolerable is an objective one. Consequently, the employee must prove that the situation became so intolerable that he could not reasonably be expected to bear it any longer and also that there was no alternative avenue open to him to pursue in the circumstances apart from resigning.

In short, the resignation must be the last resort. The Court held further that whether continued employment has become intolerable or an employee cannot reasonably be expected to bear the intolerable situation is a value judgement, and the appropriate standpoint from which to make such a value judgement is the standpoint of a reasonable person in the place of the employee. It is also important that the situation that makes the continued employment unendurable must be under the control of the employer, not necessarily in the sense that he intentionally caused it. Above all, there must be a causal relationship between the unbearable working environment and the employee's resignation, i.e. his resignation must be the direct result of the unbearable situation. In conclusion, even if the Court or tribunal finds that constructive dismissal took place, such a finding does not necessarily mean that the dismissal is unfair. Constructive dismissal is not inherently unfair. It is up to the employer to prove that the dismissal was valid and fair .[15]

6.2.1.2 Termination by Notice

Under the common law, a contract of employment does not give either the employer or the employee (as parties to the contract) the right to the interminable continuation of their employment relationship: either party can terminate the contract by giving contractual or reasonable notice.[16] Once notice is given – and no reason needs to be given for it – the

---

13   *Ntsabo v Real Security CC* (2003) 24 *ILJ* 234I (LC). Sexual harassment is treated fully in chapter 5, para. 5.5 above.

14   *Mafomane v Rustenburg Platinum Mines Ltd* [2003] 10 BLLR 999 (LC).

15   *Cymot v McLoud*, supra.

16   J. Grogan, *Riekert's Employment Law,* 2nd edn, Cape Town, Juta, 1993, p. 52.

employment relationship comes to an end at the expiration of the notice period. Thus, at common law, every contract of employment is lawfully determinable by contractual or reasonable notice.[17] As we shall see in chapter 7, this position has been modified by statute in respect of contracts of employment subject to the Labour Act 2007.

'Notice' in labour law denotes the formal intimation of the ending of an employment relationship. A notice takes effect when it has been properly served on the intended recipient,[18] i.e. when it comes to the mind of the intended recipient or his authorized representative in terms of the applicable contract of employment or an applicable statute. It is important, therefore, that the employee's notice is given to the employer himself or to an individual having authority to receive it on behalf of the employer. 'Notice period', therefore, means the period between the date on which a notice is duly served (not necessarily the date of the notice) and the date on which it expires.

A fundamental requirement of the giving of notice is that the procedures set out in the applicable contract of employment or an applicable statute should be strictly adhered to. For instance, the contract or statute may provide that notice should be given one month before the employee's date of separation and that the notice should be in writing. The contract or statute may even set out the manner in which notice should be communicated and to whom. Such contractual or statutory provisions are peremptory and any deviation will render the notice invalid. The Labour Act 2007 provides for minimum periods of notice. As indicated above, termination of employment under the Labour Act is given full treatment in the next chapter.

6.2.2 Claim for Wages

An employee may claim wages that are due to him and unpaid. The general rule is that wages do normally become due and payable at the end of the period of hiring. For that reason, it has been held that an employee who unlawfully leaves employment, e.g. where he absconds before the end of the duration of the contract, cannot claim wages.[19] It is different where an employer terminates his employee's service lawfully or unlawfully; in that case, the employee is entitled to claim wages that fell due before his dismissal.[20] Section 11 of the Labour Act 2007 provides for the employee's entitlement to remuneration, and it is discussed in chapter 4, para. 4.3.2 above.

Where an employer prevents the performance of service by his employee by unlawfully dismissing him, the employee can claim wages for the unexpired period. If it is a fixed-term

---

[17] *Joe Gross t/a Joe's Beer House v Meintjies 2005 NR 413 (SC).*

[18] *Clark v African Guarantee and Indemnity Co Ltd 1915 CPD 68.*

[19] *Malan v Van de Merwe 1937 TPD 244; Saunders v Whittle (1976) 33 LT 816.*

[20] *George v Davis [1911] 2 KB 445; and Spenser v Gostelow 1920 AD 617.*

contract, the unexpired period will be the remaining period of the fixed-term, and if it is an indefinite-term contract, then the unexpired period is the period between the date on which the contract was unlawfully terminated and the date on which notice would have expired had it been given lawfully.

6.2.3 Damages

At common law, where an employer is in breach of any of the duties he owes to the employee, or repudiates the contract (see chapter 4 above), the employee may elect to treat the contract as cancelled and sue for damages or ask for specific performance.[21] Damages are not provided for in the Labour Act 2007.

6.2.4 Application for Reinstatement

We saw above that at common law, where an employer breaches any duty he owes to his employee or repudiates the contract, the employee may elect to treat the contract as repudiated and sue for damages or specific performance (para. 6.2.3, above). Indeed, the courts have accepted the proposition that there is nothing in principle to prevent an order of specific performance being granted in respect of a contract of employment.[22]

In *Themba Mdluli and others v Emaswati Coal (Pty) Ltd*,[23] the Swaziland Court of Appeal relied on principles enunciated by *Meyer v Law Society of Transvaal*[24] and *Venter v Abramson*[25] and held that 'once it is accepted that the remedy of specific performance is not excluded as a matter of law in the case of a master and servant contract there should be no objection to apply the rule that, where there has been a fundamental breach by one party, the other party usually has the option to terminate the contract or to keep it alive and demand compliance.'[26]

In the ground-breaking case of *Stewart Wrightson (Pty) Ltd v Thorpe*,[27] the Appellate Division held that where there has been a fundamental breach of the employment contract, the aggrieved party may elect to enforce the contract or terminate it. The position, therefore, is that there is no general principle that precludes specific performance in the enforcement

---

21 Reinstatement as a statutory form of specific performance is discussed in para. 6.2.4 below.

22 *National Union of Textile Workers v Stag Packing (Pty) Ltd & another* 1982 (4) SA 151 (T); Grogan, *Riekert's Employment Law*, p. 60;

23 *Themba Mdluli and others v Emaswati Coal (Pty) Ltd* Swaziland CA 18/96 (unreported).

24 *Meyer v Law Society of Transvaal* 1978 (2) SA 209 (T).

25 *Venter v Abramson* 1952 (3) SA524 (T).

26 *Themba Mdluli v Emaswati Coal* supra at p. 17.

27 *Stewart Wrightson (Pty) Ltd v Thorpe* 1977 (2) SA 943 (A). See also *National Union of Textile Workers v Stag* supra.

of contracts of employment, but the court's power to grant the order is discretionary, and is granted only after all the circumstances of the case have been taken into account.

In England, the common law position that an innocent party to a contract that has been repudiated cannot enforce it because the contract has come to an end was so firm that the furthest the 1971 Industrial Relations Act[28] could go was to permit the labour tribunal to 'recommend', not order, reinstatement where there had been unfair dismissal or victimization of an employee.[29] It was not until the passing of the Employment Rights Act in 1996[30] that the position was changed. In terms of s. 113 of that Act, an employment tribunal may make an order of reinstatement. Similarly, under s. 16 of Swaziland's Industrial Relations Act,[31] the Industrial Court may, in settling any dispute, award an order for reinstatement. Thus, reinstatement as a statutory form of specific performance may be recognized by legislation, for example s. 86(15)(d) of the Labour Act 2007 empowers an arbitrator to make an award of reinstatement (see also chapter 10, para. 10.2.2.1 below).

In order for the courts to exercise their discretion judicially when considering an order of reinstatement, they ought to take into account all the circumstances of the dismissal. For instance, they must determine whether a dismissal is only procedurally unfair, i.e. whether an employer has a 'valid and fair reason' to dismiss but does not follow a fair procedure before dismissing his employee (see chapter 8, paras 8.1 to 8.3 below, where substantive and procedural unfair dismissals are discussed). Moreover, the courts must also determine whether by the nature of the conduct complained of it could be said that mutual trust and confidence between the employer and the employee have clearly disappeared beyond recall.[32] The courts and tribunals will generally find that mutual trust between an employer and his employee has been destroyed beyond repair in cases of fraud, theft and other dishonest acts (chapter 3, para. 3.9.2 above), violent acts and wilful damage to property of the employer (chapter 3, para. 3.9.9 above).

6.2.5 Interdict

An employee may apply for an interdict (equivalent to 'injunction' in English law) to prevent a breach or threatened breach of a contract of employment. An employee who is threatened with any action or conduct in breach of a contract of employment may apply for an interdict *pedente lite* aimed at maintaining the status quo pending proceedings to settle the dispute. Interdict is treated in chapter 10, para. 10.2.2.1 below.

---

[28] Industrial Relations Act 1971 (c. 72).

[29] C.D. Drake, *Labour Law,* 2nd edn, London, Sweet & Maxwell, 1973, paras 272, 296.

[30] Employment Rights Act 1996 (c. 18).

[31] Act No. 1 of 2000.

[32] *Namibia Beverages v Hoaës* NLLP 2002 (2) 380 NLC.

The only point to be made here is that where an employee has already been dismissed, the court dealing with the matter should refuse to grant an interdict because in terms of the Labour Act 2007 there are other remedies whereby the dismissed employee can be adequately protected legally.[33] For instance, an arbitrator can order the reinstatement of the employee, apart from awarding damages or compensation. Besides, it could not have been intended that the unfairness of dismissals should be conclusively determined in interdict applications because in almost all unfair dismissal cases under the Labour Act 2007 there will most invariably be genuine factual disputes.

6.2.6 Strike

It is important to note at the outset three fundamental points with regard to a strike. First, an employee's right to take industrial action in the form of a strike is statutory. Second, the remedy of a strike is not open to a single employee acting alone and on his own behalf to back his demand for improved working conditions for himself. Third, the strike action must be for a specific purpose, namely, as a tool for inducing an employer to accede to proposals of employees where such demands or proposals are the subject of an industrial dispute between the employer and the employees. While the Labour Act 2007 grants employees the right to take industrial action in the form of a strike, it also lays down requirements necessary to make such industrial action lawful. Strikes and other forms of industrial action open to employees are provided for in Chapter 7 of the Labour Act and dealt with here in chapter 13, para. 13.2 below.

6.3 REMEDIES OF THE EMPLOYER

6.3.1 Dismissal

We saw in chapter 3 (where duties of employees are discussed) that at common law an employer may dismiss his employee with or without notice, i.e. summarily, for breaching a fundamental duty he owes to his employer. Therefore, an employer can summarily dismiss an employee who has been guilty of a serious breach of a term of the contract of employment, i.e. a breach that goes to the root of the employment contract. Summary dismissal is, therefore, justified 'where a person has entered into the position of servant, if he does anything incompatible with the due and faithful discharge of his duty to his master'.[34] Thus, at common law, an employer can summarily dismiss his employee if the employee

---

33 See R.H. Christie, *The Law of Contract in South Africa*, 5th edn, Durban, Butterworths, 2006, p. 594.

34 *Pearce v Foster* (1886) 17 QBD 536 at 539, *per* Lord Esher, MR.

has breached an express or an implied fundamental term of their contract of employment, i.e. where he has breached his duty to the employer.[35]

It was also discussed in chapter 3 that the courts have recognized instances or grounds such as the following as entitling an employer to dismiss his employee without notice: e.g. where the employee refuses or fails to render his personal service due to persistent and unexplained absenteeism and lack of punctuality and the employee's wilful and repeated disobedience to lawful and reasonable instructions which can lead to only one inescapable inference, namely, that the employee refuses to be bound by the contract of employment. Besides, certain forms of conduct falling under the rubric of misconduct have been recognized as entitling an employer to dismiss without notice. Notable among them are such dishonest acts as theft, fraud, violent conduct (particularly fighting and assault) and wilful damage to property of the employer, (especially property that is vital to the smooth operation of the employer's business). Yet again, if an employee holds out to his employer that he possesses a particular skill and fails to apply it, this amounts to breach of the contract of employment, justifying summary dismissal.[36]

Apart from the grounds under the common law, which the courts have recognized as justifying summary dismissal, some labour or employment statutes give employers the right to dismiss their employees summarily based on certain specified grounds. For instance, s. 33(8) of Swaziland's Employment Act[37] gives an employer the right to dismiss his employee without notice if the reasons for his dismissal are such as to warrant the immediate cessation of the employer-and-employee relationship and where the employer cannot be expected to take any other course.

The Labour Act 2007 does not expressly spell out the specific causes or grounds that would entitle an employer (or an employee) to cancel the contract of employment summarily. Therefore, the causes or grounds contemplated in s. 30(6)(b) of the Labour Act must be common law grounds and grounds found in different sections of the Labour Act, as well as causes or grounds in any other relevant legislation, e.g. Public Service Act 1995 in respect of public servants. It must be remembered that the Labour Act protects an employee who is subject to this Act from unfair dismissal within the meaning of the Act. (Unfair dismissal is dealt with in chapter 8, para. 8.1 below.)

6.3.2 Non-Payment of Wages

A contract of employment falls within the category of reciprocal contracts. It follows, therefore, that the defence of *exceptio non adimpleti*, i.e. exception on the ground that

---

[35] Grogan, *Riekert's Employment Law,* pp. 30-2, 51.

[36] *Harmer v Cornelius* (1858) 5 CB (NS) 236.

[37] Act No. 5 of 1980.

the claimant, too, is in default and therefore cannot demand performance, is available to an employer sued for wages payable for a period in arrear, if the employee has neither performed nor tendered to perform his obligations under the contract for that period.[38] The claimant employee bears the onus of proving that he has performed his obligation under the contract of employment.[39]

The principle of impossibility of performance in relation to reciprocal contracts, which is that impossibility of performance by one party releases the other party from his reciprocal obligation, also applies to contracts of employment.[40] For instance, as a general rule, if due to illness or injury, an employee is incapable of performing his service under a contract of employment, his employer is not obliged to pay him wages during the period of incapacity. The other side of the coin is that if the employer is incapable of utilizing his employee's services, the employer remains liable to pay wages for the full period of the subsistence of the contract until the employee finds employment elsewhere.[41] However, as was held in *Orman v Saville Sportswear Ltd*,[42] whether an employer remains liable to continue to pay his employee who is absent from work due to sickness will depend upon the express terms of the contract of employment or legislation. For example, as we saw in chapter 4, para. 4.8.2 above, the Labour Act provides for sick leave.

6.3.3 Damages

At common law, where an employee has been guilty of negligence, his employer can bring an action for damages; he may also bring an action for injury or loss caused by the intentional acts of his employee. *Blake v Howkey*[43] is authority for the proposition that the employee's liability arises from the same essentials upon which delictual action is based. By a parity of reasoning, the employer can claim indemnity where he is made liable for his employee's negligence caused to a third party.[44] If an employee is absent from work without lawful excuse, his employer may claim damages calculated upon the cost of providing a relief or substitute employee for the period of his absence.[45] It is important to note once more that the Labour Act 2007 does not provide for the grant of damages.

---

38 *National Union of Textile Workers v Jaguar Shoes (Pty) Ltd* 1987 (1) SA 39 (N).

39 *BK Tooling (Edms) Bpk v Scope Precision Engineering (Edms) Bpk* 1979 (1) SA 391 (A).

40 *Boyd v Stuttaford & Co* 1910 AD 101.

41 Ibid; see also *National Union of Textile Workers v Jaguar Shoes* supra.

42 *Orman v Saville Sportswear Ltd* [1960] 1 WLR 1055. See also chapter 3, para. 3.3 above.

43 *Blake v Howkey* 1912 CPD 817.

44 Vicarious liability of an employer for the delicts of his employee is discussed in chapter 5, para. 5.4 above.

45 *National Coal Board v Galley* [1958] 1 All ER 91.

6.3.4 Specific Performance

We saw previously in this chapter (para. 6.2.4 above) that as a matter of common law, the remedy of specific performance is not excluded in the employer-and-employee relationship. *National Union of Textile Workers v Stag Packings and another*[46] decided that in principle there is nothing that should prevent an employer from seeking an order of specific performance compelling his employee to fulfil his obligation under the contract of employment. But it would seem the courts will be reluctant to order specific performance in the form of reinstatement against an employee in circumstances that tend to show that the employee is being forced to render service, i.e. the employee is being forced into servitude.[47] The courts may also be unwilling to order reinstatement against an employee where in the nature of things, the employer-and-employee relationship has broken down irretrievably as a result of the conduct of either the employee or the employer, making the continuation of the contract of employment not in the best interest of industrial harmony within the employer's business. The Labour Act rather provides for reinstatement, and it is discussed in chapter 10, para. 10.2.2.1 below.

6.3.5 Interdict

As mentioned above, interdict is also treated in chapter 10, para. 10.2.2.1 below. It is enough to mention here that the courts are averse to granting interdict in the employer-and-employee relationship, particularly if it is aimed at restraining the employee from refusing to render personal service to his employer. However, the courts will not be so unwilling to grant the remedy if, for instance, it is aimed at restraining an employee from doing anything that does not further the interests of his employer's business, e.g. where he breaks or is about to break his duty of good faith,[48] or where he breaks or is about to break an agreement in restraint of trade.[49]

6.3.6 Lockout

At common law, an employer is obliged to pay remuneration to his employee so long as he tenders his service.[50] An employer is, therefore, not at liberty to close down his business so as to escape such obligation. Legislation in many countries has changed this; the law grants

---

[46] *National Union Textile Workers v Stag* supra.

[47] Drake, *Labour Law,* para. 271.

[48] *Baker v Gibbons* [1972] 2 All ER 659.

[49] *Roffey v Cateral, Edwards & Goudre (Pty) Ltd* 1977 (4) SA 494 (N). Restraint of trade contracts are dealt with in chapter 3, para. 3.6.2 above.

[50] Grogan, *Riekert's Employment Law,* p. 58.

the employer the right to take industrial action in the form of a lockout where an industrial dispute exists.[51] An employer's right to a lockout is provided in Chapter 7 of the Labour Act 2007. In labour law, a lockout is resorted to with the view to inducing employees to comply with employers' demands, or inducing employees to abandon or modify their demands that are the subject of an industrial dispute. As it is the case with a strike, a lockout qualifies as an industrial action only if it is in furtherance of an industrial dispute (see chapter 13, para. 13.4 below, on lockout).

6.3.7 Secret Profits and Commissions

We saw in chapter, para. 3.6.4 above, that an employee bears a duty to his employer not to use his position in his employer's business to make secret profits and commissions or receive a bribe. If an employee does that, his employer is entitled to the profit, the commission or the bribe, and he can call for an account.[52]

---

[51] For example, under ss 86 and 87 of Swaziland's Industrial Relations Act 2000 (Act 1 of 2000) and Chapter IV of South Africa's Labour Relations Act 1995 (Act No. 66 of 1995).

[52] *Boston Deep Sea Fishing and Ice Co v Ansell* (1889) 39 Ch D 338.

7 TERMINATION OF THE EMPLOYMENT RELATIONSHIP

7.1 INTRODUCTION

Put simply, termination of a contract of employment is the bringing to an end of the contract by, or at the instance of, the employer or the employee or by operation of law.[1] It will be remembered that the duration of a contract of employment depends on the express or implied terms of the contract, and that where there is no express provision, the courts will determine the duration of the contract by ascertaining the intention and conduct of the parties from accepted and known practice in the trade or vocation and surrounding circumstances (see chapter 2, para. 2.2.4 above).

An important point deserves to be made at the outset. In terms of the Labour Act 2007, an employer-and-employee relationship may be deemed to continue beyond the termination of the employment contract, particularly where an employee who has been dismissed challenges the fairness of the dismissal.[2] If that were not the case, it would be illogical or, indeed, untenable for an employee who has been dismissed and, therefore, is no longer an employee, to report a dispute to the Labour Commissioner. In other words, if that person is no longer an 'employee' under the Labour Act, how can he report a dispute under the Act? The Labour Act provides that a conciliator may be appointed to settle such dispute of alleged unfair dismissal, and if the dispute remains unresolved after conciliation, an arbitrator may be appointed to arbitrate the dispute, at the end of which the arbitrator may order reinstatement (see chapter 10, paras 10.1 and 10.2 below).

As Van den Heever AJ stated in *National Automobile & Allied Workers Union (now known as National Union of Metalworkers of SA) v Borg-Warner SA (Pty) Ltd* in relation to the repealed South African Labour Relations Act 1956,[3]

---

1   E. Cameron, H. Cheadle and C. Thompson, *The New Labour Relations Act,* Cape Town, Juta, 1989, p. 143.

2   See *Transport Fleet Management (Pty) Ltd & another v NUMSA and others* [2003] 10 BLLR 975 (LAC). Unfair dismissal is discussed in chapter 8 below.

3   Act No. 28 of 1956.

The relationship envisaged by the Act between 'employer' and 'employee' is therefore clearly not one that terminates as it would at common law. Cases accepting that the provisions of the Act do not relate solely to the enforcement of legal (common-law) rights, are legion. Cf *Marievale Consolidated Mines Ltd v President of the Industrial Court and others* 1986 (2) SA 485 (T) at 498I-499H; *Consolidated Frame Cotton Corporation Ltd v President of the Industrial Court and others* 1986 (3) SA 786 (A); (1986) 7 *ILJ* 489 (A). The fact that the definition is framed in the present tense (by the use of the phrase 'is employed') cannot alter the fact that other sections of the Act already referred to make it clear that ex-employees are also included within its terms. [4]

There is no reason why the principle expressed by Van den Heever, AJ in *National Automobile & Allied Workers Union v Borg-Warner SA (Pty) Ltd*, that an employee who has been dismissed comes within the meaning of 'employee' under the repealed South African Labour Relations Act 1956, must not equally apply to the interpretation and application of 'employee' in the Labour Act 2007, considering the similarity of the key words used in the two statutes. The present chapter discusses the various ways in which a contract of employment may be brought to an end.

7.2 TERMINATION NOT BASED ON NOTICE

7.2.1 Expiration of Contract

As a general rule, where an employee is engaged for a specific period expressed in his contract of employment, the contract comes to an end at the end of that period, i.e. by effluxion of time. The contract comes to an end automatically, and, therefore, there is no need for notice to be given. Thus, 'if the parties agree on a definite time for the expiration of the contract, it follows that no notice of termination is required. The contract expires at the effluxion of time.'[5]

The upshot of the principle is that since such a contract comes to an end by the effluxion of time, an employee cannot be heard to say that he has been dismissed, let alone dismissed unfairly. Thus, an employer's decision not to retain his employee who is on a fixed-term contract of employment for a further term at the expiration of the current term does not

---

[4]   *National Automobile & Allied Workers Union (now known as National Union of Metalworkers of SA) v Borg-Warner SA (Pty) Ltd* (1994) 15 *ILJ* 509 at 518B-D.

[5]   *Tiopaizi v Bulawayo Municipality* (1923) AD 317 at 325.

amount to a dismissal. '[A]n assertion that the decision [not to renew a fixed-term contract of employment] amounted to a dismissal is to do violence to the English language,' stated Silungwe, P in *Hailulu v The Council of the Municipality of Windhoek*.[6]

The likelihood cannot be ruled out that employers may apply this principle unduly and indiscriminately in order to evade a charge of unfair dismissal of their employees. This danger has not escaped the attention of the International Labour Organization (ILO). Little wonder then that Art. 2(3) of the ILO's Termination of Employment Convention 158 of 1982 enjoins State Parties to provide adequate safeguards 'against recourse to contracts of employment for specified periods of time the *aim of which* is to avoid the protection resulting from this Convention'.[7] This provision is reinforced by paragraph 3(1) of the Termination of Employment Recommendation 166 of 1982,[8] which provides guidelines to assist States in developing national policies and practices in conformity with the Convention. Paragraph 3(1) of Recommendation R166 provides: 'Adequate safeguards should be provided against recourse to contracts of employment for a specified period of time *the aim of which* is to avoid the protection resulting from the Termination of Employment Convention, 1982 and this Recommendation.' These ILO instruments are designed against the indiscriminate resort to fixed-term contracts where the object is solely to circumvent the protection provided by the Convention against unfair dismissal. Indeed, in the United Kingdom, s. 95(1)(b) of the Employment Rights Act,[9] treats the expiration of a fixed-term contract without renewal as generally a dismissal. Section 95(1)(b) provides that 'an employee is dismissed by his employer if…he is employed under a contract for a fixed term and that term expires without being renewed under the same contract'.

Judicial thinking these days in South Africa, for instance, appears to take a non-mechanical approach to the expiration of fixed-term contracts to the extent that the courts there are prepared to consider the fairness or otherwise of the conduct of the employer in relation to the ending of the employer-and-employee relationship under a fixed-term contract. In *MAWU v A Mauche (Pty) Ltd t/a Precision Tools*,[10] the Industrial Court found that failure to renew a fixed-term contract *could* amount to an unfair labour practice where the employee had a well-founded expectation that his contract would be renewed. Then, in *Mtshamba & others v Boland Houtnywerhede*,[11] the Industrial Court was also prepared to consider the question of fairness or otherwise of the circumstances in which a fixed-term

---

6   *Hailulu v The Council of the Municipality of Windhoek* 2002 NR 305 (LC) at 310F. The facts of the case are set out below.

7   ILO C158: Termination of Employment Convention, 1982.

8   ILO R166: Termination of Employment Recommendation, 1982.

9   Employment Rights Act 1996 (c.18).

10 *MAWU v A Mauche (Pty) Ltd t/a Precision Tools* (1980) 1 *ILJ* 227 (IC).

11 *Mtshamba & others v Boland Houtnywerhede* (1986) 7 *ILJ* 563 (IC).

contract came to an end. In *Cremark, a Division of Triple P-Chemical Ventures (Pty) Ltd v SACWU and others,*[12] the Labour Appeal Court was prepared to accept the proposal that an employer's discretion to renew or not to renew a fixed-term contract of his employee is not boundless, and that even with fixed-term contracts, termination has to be substantively and procedurally justified.

The Namibian courts have not been prepared to go as far as *Cremark v SACWU* supra. In *Du Toit v The Office of the Prime Minister,*[13] a case determined in terms of the repealed Labour Act 1992, the Labour Court held that *Cremark v SACWU* supra was distinguishable inasmuch as the decision there covers the situation where under the circumstances a '*legitimate expectation*'[14] existed that the fixed-term contract would be renewed upon its expiration and, therefore, a refusal to renew was considered as an unfair labour practice. The Labour Court also observed correctly that there were differences between the South African legislation and Namibia's repealed Labour Act 1992 on the matter of expiration of contract of employment by effluxion of time.

Thus, in *Du Toit v Office of the Prime Minister* supra, the Labour Court observed that s. 45 and s. 46 of the repealed Labour Act 1992 did not generally apply to fixed-term contracts of employment because they came to an end by effluxion of time. Section 45 dealt with an employer's inability in law to dismiss his employee where there is no valid and fair reason and without procedural fairness (see chapter 8, para. 8.1 below, where unfair dismissal is discussed). Section 46 provided for the power of the district labour court and the Labour Court to interfere with termination of a contact, if such termination amounted to a dismissal in terms of s. 45. The reasoning underlying the Labour Court's decision in *Du Toit* can be structured in the following way:

1   *X*'s fixed-term contract of employment came to an end by effluxion of time.

2   The employer did not terminate *X*'s contract.

3   *X* had not been dismissed.

4   The district labour court and the Labour Court could interfere with the termination of *X*'s contact of employment under s. 46 only if the employee was dismissed.

---

12   *Cremark, a Division of Triple P-Chemical Ventures (Pty) Ltd v SACWU and others* (1994) 15 *ILJ* 289 (LAC).

13   *Du Toit v The Office of the Prime Minister* 1996 NR 52 (LC).

14   See the landmark English case of *Schmidt and another v Secretary of State for Home Affairs* [1969] 1 All ER 904, where the term 'legitimate expectation' was first used by Lord Denning, MR. In South Africa the leading case in the development of the term is *Administrator, Transvaal and others v Traub and others* 1989 (4) SA 731 (A). See also *Lisse v Minister of Health and Social Services* 2004 NR 107.

Termination of the Employment Relationship **123**

5   It is only when an employer terminates the contract of employment of his employee that the termination amounts to dismissal for the purposes of s. 45 and s. 46 of the Act.

6   *Ergo, X* has no remedy under s. 45 and s. 46 of the repealed Labour Act 1992.

Silungwe, P came to a similar conclusion in *Hailulu v Municipality of Windhoek* supra. In that case, the learned judge observed that the respondent's non-extension of the statutory fixed term in conformity with s. 27 of the Local Authorities Act,[15] viewed against the backdrop of the undisputed facts, did not amount to a dismissal in terms of s. 45 and s. 46 of the repealed Labour Act 1992 and, therefore, it fell outside the jurisdiction of the District Labour Court. In other words, the respondent's decision not to extend the applicant's term fell outside the ambit of s. 45 and s. 46 of the repealed Labour Act 1992. Consequently, the Labour Court dismissed the applicant's appeal.

The facts of *Hailulu v Municipality of Windhoek* supra are briefly these. The applicant was appointed Chief Executive Officer of the respondent local authority council with effect from 6 June 1994. His employment was governed, among other things, by s. 27 of the Local Authorities Act 1992. Section 27(3)(a) of the Local Authorities Act in material part provides:

s. 27(3)(a)   Subject to the provisions of section 29 –

(i)   (aa) a person who is appointed as chief executive officer or an officer or employee of a local authority council who is promoted to the office of chief executive officer shall occupy that office for a period as from the date of his or her appointment or promotion until two years after the next general election of members of local authority councils, or an election in terms of section 92 (2) (b), as the case may be, has taken place…

(ii)   a period of office referred to in subparagraph (i) may, subject to the provisions of paragraph (b), be extended at the expiry thereof for a further period or successive periods as contemplated in that subparagraph.

s. 27(3)(b)

(b) (i) The local authority council shall in writing inform the chief executive officer concerned at least two calendar months before the expiry of the

---

15   Act No. 23 of 1992.

period contemplated in subparagraph (a) (i) or any previously extended period contemplated in subparagraph (a) (ii) of its intention to retain him or her in service for an extended term, or not.

The general election that followed the applicant's appointment was held on 15 February 1998; therefore, the term contemplated by s. 27 with regard to the applicant was to expire on 15 February 2000. The respondent (the Council) gave the applicant notice in writing at least two months before the expiry of the term set out in s. 27(3) of the Act, inviting the applicant to make representations in writing as to whether he should be retained in service for an extended term. He was requested to address certain matters, which the respondent would take into account when considering the question of whether to renew or extend the applicant's fixed-term contract. The applicant made representations, which the respondent's Council considered. Thereafter the Council unanimously resolved not to extend the term of the applicant upon its expiration.

The respondent gave the applicant notice in writing on 25 November 1999 that his fixed-term contract of employment would expire on 15 February 2000 by effluxion of time. The applicant brought a claim in the district labour court that, among other things, the respondent unlawfully terminated his services and that such termination constituted unfair dismissal. The district labour court dismissed the applicant's complaint of unfair dismissal. He then appealed that decision to the Labour Court. The issue raised on appeal was essentially whether the respondent's decision not to extend the applicant's fixed-term contract upon its expiration on 15 February 2000 constituted a dismissal in terms of the repealed Labour Act 1992. The Labour Court dismissed the appeal.

Significant observations that emerge from these two important Labour Court cases, i.e. *Du Toit v Office of the Prime Minister* supra and *Hailulu v Municipality of Windhoek* supra are these. According to *Du Toit v Office of the Prime Minister*, the only 'possible exception' in which fixed-term contracts expiring by effluxion of time could come under the purview of ss 45 and 46 of the repealed Labour Act 1992 is 'where an expectation of tenure has developed'. According to *Hailulu v Municipality of Windhoek*, under a fixed-term contract of employment the possibility for an extended period was purely at the employer's discretion, but the discretion must be exercised properly, and therefore where there has been no impropriety in the exercise of the discretion, e.g. where there has been no unfair procedure, the employee cannot complain.

It must be noted that 'expectation of tenure' will not in itself lead to an automatic extension or renewal of a fixed-term contract. It is only one of the critical factors, which the employer must take into account when exercising his discretion whether to extend or renew the contract. Thus, the two views turn primarily on whether the employer exercised his discretion properly, i.e. reasonably and fairly. Where a fixed-term contract is governed by statute the discretion is exercised properly where the requirements of the statute have been complied with (as was held to be the case in *Hailulu v Municipality of Windhoek*), and also, where the employer has acted fairly,[16] reasonably, and in good faith, and has taken into account all the relevant factors. It is submitted that where a fixed-term contract of employment is non-statutory, the discretion whether to extend or not to extend the period or to renew or not to renew the contract is exercised properly where the employer has observed the rules of natural justice,[17] and has acted fairly, reasonably, honestly and in good faith, and has taken into account all the relevant factors, e.g. whether legitimate expectation of tenure has developed. Moreover, where the employer is an administrative body, then such a body is expected to comply with the requirements of administrative justice under Art. 18 of the Namibian Constitution.[18]

It is important to stress this crucial point: either of the two views, i.e. concerning 'expectation of tenure' (*Du Toit v Office of the Prime Minister*) and 'the proper exercise of discretion' (*Hailulu v Municipality of Windhoek*), is relevant only in situations where either the non-statutory contract of employment or the statute-governed contract of employment provides for the possibility of an extension or a renewal of a fixed-term contract upon its expiration. Finally, it is submitted that although *Du Toit v Office of the Prime Minister* and *Hailulu v Municipality of Windhoek* were decided in relation to the interpretation and application of ss 45 and 46 of the repealed Labour Act 1992, there is no valid reason why the principles expressed by the Labour Court in those two cases must not apply with equal force to the interpretation and application of s. 33 of the Labour Act 2007, which also deals with unfair dismissal.

Where at the expiration of an employee's fixed-term contract, the employee continues to work with the consent and cooperation of the employer, the employee's contract of employment is deemed to have been tacitly extended for a further term under the same terms and conditions.[19]

It must also be borne in mind that at common law, a party to a fixed term contract has no right to terminate the contract in the absence of a repudiation of the contract by the other party or a breach by the other party that goes to the root of the contract. Furthermore, there

---

16 See *Meyer v Law Society of Transvaal* 1978 (2) SA 209 (T).

17 Rules of natural justice are examined in chapter 8, para. 8.1.3 and chapter 11, para. 11.3.2 below. See also *Meyer v Law Society of Transvaal* supra where the rules of natural justice are explained with great insight.

18 See Collins Parker, 'The "Administrative Justice" provision of the Constitution of the Republic of Namibia: a constitutional protection of judicial review and tribunal adjudication under administrative law', *CILSA* XXIV (1991), p. 88. This is a short monograph on Art. 18 of the Namibian Constitution.

19 *Cronje v Municipality Council of Mariental* NLLP 2004 (4) 129 NSC.

126   Labour Law in Namibia

is no right to terminate a fixed-term contract on notice unless there is an express provision in the contract for such termination.[20]

7.2.2   Performance of Contract

Where a contract of employment has been entered into solely for the carrying out of a specific task, the contract comes to an end upon completion of the task. In such a case, there is clearly no need for notice to be given to end the contract of employment, for indeed, logically there is simply no more service to perform.

7.2.3   As a Result of Supervening Impossibility

The general principle of supervening impossibility in the law of contract applies to contracts of employment, too.[21] Consequently, if performance becomes impossible owing to some supervening event not due to the action or omission of either party, the contract may be discharged. Therefore, if either the employer or the employee is prevented from performing his obligation under the contract due to *vis major* or *causus fortuitis*, a party is entitled to terminate the contract. In such an eventuality, the party is discharged from liability. The supervening impossibility may be due to natural causes or human agency that is unforeseeable, even with reasonable foresight, and unavoidable, even with reasonable care. Acts that constitute supervening impossibility include acts of State in the form of legislative and executive instruments. In *Shlengeman v Meyer, Bridgens & Co,*[22] it was held that the employer of an employee who was given a long custodial sentence is entitled to cancel the contract without notice. In this connection, what is a long prison sentence will depend upon the facts and circumstances of the particular case.

7.2.4   As a Result of Employee's Sickness or Incapacity

As a general rule, the sickness or incapacity of an employee can discharge the contract of employment. The employer's right may be governed by the express term of the contract, under which, for instance, the employer may have the right to cancel the contract, if the employee is absent from work due to sickness or incapacity for a certain period of time. In the absence of express terms, a contract is determined if the sickness would put an end, in a business sense, to their business engagement because it impedes the object of that

---

[20]   *Buthelezi v Municipal Demarcation Board* [2005] 2 BLLR 115 (LAC).

[21]   R.H. Christie, *The Law of Contract in South Africa,* 5th edn, Durban, Butterworths, 2006, pp. 472-5, where the principle is examined.

[22]   *Shlengeman v Meyer, Bridgens & Co* 1920 CPD 494. See also *F C Shepherd & Co Ltd v Jerrom* [1986] IRLR 358.

engagement.[23] Whether the illness or incapacity is capable of discharging the contract depends on a number of factors, notably, the nature of the sickness or incapacity and the duration of absence from work, as well as the nature of service the employee performs in the employer's business.[24]

7.2.5 By Death and Other Causes

The death of either the employee or the employer terminates the contract of employment by operation of law. Section 32(1)(a)(i) of the Labour Act 2007 provides that, subject to a notice given in terms of s. 32(2), the contract of employment terminates automatically (i) one month after the death of the employer, if the employer is an individual, or (ii) one month after the date on which the employer is wound up, if the employer is a juristic person, or (iii) one month after the date on which the partnership is dissolved, if the employer is a partnership, or (iv) a longer period according to the terms of the contract of employment or the applicable collective agreement, as the case may be or during which the employer continues to carry on business. Section 32(2) of the Act provides that at any time during the statutory periods mentioned above, an executor, liquidator or partner may give notice to terminate the employee's contract of employment in accordance with Part F of Chapter 3 of the Act or a collective agreement. Thus, before the termination comes into effect in accordance with the statutory provisions, the law deems it that the contract of employment is still in force. According to s. 32(3) of the Act, and regardless of any provision of any law providing otherwise, an employee whose contract is terminated in circumstances mentioned in s. 32(1), is a preferential creditor in respect of any remuneration due to him or other monies payable to him in terms of the Labour Act.

7.2.6 By Sequestration

The Labour Act 2007 governs termination of a contract of employment, which is subject to the Act, when the employer is sequestrated. In terms of s. 32(1)(a)(i) of the Labour Act, and subject to a notice given in terms of s. 32(2), the contract of employment terminates automatically (i) one month after the sequestration of the employer, if the employer is an individual, or (ii) one month after the date on which the employer is wound up, if the employer is a juristic person, or (iii) one month after the date on which the partnership is dissolved, if the employer is a partnership, or (iv) at the end of a longer period according to the terms of the contract or the applicable collective agreement, as the case may be, or during which the employer continues to carry on business. Section 32(2) of the Act provides that, at any time

---

23   *Jackson v Union Marine Insurance Co* [1874] LR 10 CP.

24   *Marshall v Harland and Wolf* [1972] 1 WLR 899.

during the statutory periods mentioned above, an executor, an administrator, a liquidator or a partner may give notice to terminate the employee's contract of employment in accordance with Part F of Chapter 3 of the Labour Act or a collective agreement. Thus, before the termination takes effect in accordance with the statutory provisions, the law deems that the contract of employment is still in force. According to s. 32(3) of the Act and regardless of any provision of any law providing otherwise, an employee whose contract of employment is terminated in circumstances mentioned in s. 32(1) is a preferential creditor in respect of any remuneration due to him or other monies that are payable to him.

The Insolvency Act 1936[25] governs the effect of insolvency of the employer where the contract of employment is not subject to the Labour Act. In terms of s. 38 of the Insolvency Act, the insolvency of the employer automatically terminates the contract of employment of all his employees, and according to s. 100 of that Act, the remuneration, including bonuses and leave pay, is to some extent, treated as a preferential claim against the employer's insolvent estate.

The insolvency of the employee, on the other hand, will not bring the contract to an end unless an express term of the contract provides otherwise. However, where, due to the nature of the service performed by him, the law precludes the insolvent employee from performing his service to his employer, the employer is entitled to terminate the contract. The employment of a practising legal practitioner who becomes insolvent readily comes to mind.

7.2.7   By Repudiation

An express or implied repudiation of a contract of employment by either party will entitle the other party to terminate the contract. The rights of the employee and those of his employer to terminate the contract of employment where the other party has repudiated the contract are discussed more fully in chapter 6, paras 6.2.1.1 and 6.3.1 above.

7.3   TERMINATION BY NOTICE OR WITHOUT NOTICE

7.3.1   Termination by Notice

Some important introductory remarks were made about notice to terminate a contract of employment in chapter 6, para. 6.2.1.2 above. There is no need to repeat them here. Contrary to popular belief, the mere fact that a post is described as 'pensionable or permanent' does

---

[25]   Act No. 24 of 1936.

not in any way preclude the employer from terminating such contract of employment of the holder of the post by giving him the statutory notice, contractual notice or reasonable notice.[26]

It is important to make the vital point that with regard to the giving of notice, if an employee whose contract of employment is subject to the Labour Act 2007 receives notice to terminate his contract of employment and he does not accept it – which he is entitled to do – the termination constitutes dismissal.[27] In that event, s. 33 of the Labour Act 2007 comes into play;[28] for, according to s. 30(6) of the Labour Act, the fact that an employer has given notice under s. 30(1)–(5) to terminate the contract of employment does not affect the right of the employee to dispute the lawfulness or fairness of the dismissal in terms of the Labour Act or any other law, or the right of an employee or employer to terminate the contract without notice, for any cause recognized by law, to pay money in lieu of notice in accordance with s. 31 of the Act. This provision is supported by s. 33(1) of the Act where it is provided that an employer must not, *whether notice is given or not*, dismiss an employee without a valid and fair reason and without following a fair procedure (see chapter 8, paras 8.1–8.3 below, which deal with unfair dismissal).

In *Meintjies v Joe Gross t/a Joe's Beerhouse* supra, the essence of the dispute between the parties at the Labour Court was whether the termination of the appellant's contract of employment by notice given to him by the respondent in terms of s. 47 of the repealed Labour Act 1992 constituted a 'dismissal' within the meaning of s. 45(1) and s. 46 of that Act. Having undertaken a purposeful and contextual interpretation of the relevant provisions of the repealed Labour Act 1992, Maritz, P (as he then was) observed that 'the Legislature intended the word "dismiss" [in Part VI of the repealed Labour Act 1992] to bear the more general meaning of "dismissal", i.e. an employee's discharge from service by or at the behest of the employer.'[29] He hit the nail on the head, when he observed that it was only when the word 'dismiss' is interpreted to include any termination of a contract of employment by or at the behest of an employer that the notion of 'fairness', which lay at the heart of sound labour relations, was given its rightful place in the structure of the repealed Labour Act 1992. Indeed, if termination of employment by notice was not subject to the test of fairness under ss 45 and 46 of the repealed Labour Act 1992, the President of the Labour

---

26   *McClelland v Northern Ireland General Health Services Board* [1957] 1 WLR 594 (HL).

27   *Meintjies v Joe Gross t/a Joe's Beerhouse* 2003 NR 221 (LC). The principle enunciated by the Labour Court in that case was confirmed by the Supreme Court on appeal in *Joe Gross t/a Joe's Beer House v Meintjies* 2005 NR 413 (SC).

28   Section 33 deals with unfair dismissal and it is discussed in chapter 8, para. 8.1 below.

29   *Meintjies v Joe Gross t/a Joe's Beerhouse* supra at 227I.

Court concluded, 'it would leave it wide open for employers to terminate by notice the employment of unwanted employees for no good reason at all'.[30]

The very words of s. 45, entitled 'Meaning of unfair dismissal and unfair disciplinary actions', puts beyond doubt the correctness of the proposition that termination of employment by notice is subject to the test of fairness under s. 45 and s. 46 of the repealed Act 1992. Section 45(1) provided:

> For purposes of the provisions of section 46, but subject to the provisions of subsection (2) –
>
> (a)   any employee dismissed, *whether or not notice has been given in accordance with any provision of this Act or any term and condition of a contract of employment or of a collective agreement*; [author's italics]
>
> (b)   any disciplinary action taken against any employee, without a valid and fair reason and not in compliance with a fair procedure, shall be regarded to have been dismissed unfairly, as the case may be.

The fact that termination of a contract of employment by an employer complied with the requirements of notice under s. 47(1) of the repealed Labour Act 1992, but had been carried out for an unfair and invalid reason as contemplated in s. 45, did not mean that the termination could not be judicially disapproved by an appropriate order under s. 46 (of the Act), which was designed to deal with unfair dismissals. As Maritz, P rightly pointed out:

> termination by notice provided in s. 47 does not, however, place the employee at the mercy of the employer's will or whims. If the employer acts unfairly in terminating the employee's employment by notice, the employee need not abide by such conduct or accept the notice and is entitled to challenge the fairness of such termination under s. 45 – as he or she may also do when his or her services are terminated at a disciplinary hearing.[31]

In the result, the Labour Court held that the word 'dismiss' in ss 45 and 46 of the repealed Labour Act 1992 meant the termination of a contract of employment by, or at the behest of, an employer. Consequently, the Labour Court set aside the order of the district labour court, dismissing the appellant's (i.e. employee's) claim. The district labour court's decision

---

30   Ibid. at 229C.

31   Ibid. at 233E-F. The Labour Court in *Rabe and another v African Granite (Pty) Ltd* NLLP 2004 (4) NLC 273. found the reasoning in *Meintjies v Joe Gross t/a Joe's Beerhouse* supra, to be correct, and stated that it must be followed.

supported the respondent's (i.e. employer's) position that s. 45 of the repealed Labour Act 1992 did not apply where notice had been given in terms of s. 47 of that Act. The district labour court had wrongly relied on *Du Toit v Office of the Prime Minister*,[32] particularly the statement that the term 'termination' or 'terminate' is used throughout ss 47-52, read with s. 53, and not the words 'dismissal' or 'disciplinary action': in contrast, 'termination' or 'terminate' are not used at all in ss 45 and 46, but only the words 'dismissal' or 'disciplinary action' and, therefore, 'terminate' in s. 48 cannot logically be subject to the 'unfair dismissal' provisions of ss 45 and 46 (of the repealed Labour Act 1992).

The appellant (employer) appealed to the Supreme Court against the judgment of the Labour Court. After reviewing the authorities, the Supreme Court [33] found no ground to fault the conclusions reached by the Labour Court that termination of the respondent's contract of employment by notice given in terms of s. 47 of the repealed Labour Act 1992 constituted a dismissal as contemplated in s. 45(1) of that Act.

The Supreme Court also held that the Labour Court's interpretation of 'termination' and 'dismissal' in the repealed Labour Act was supported by the comment by Cameron, Cheadle and Thompson in a passage from their *The New Labour Relations Act*.[34] 'Dismissal,' the Supreme Court held, 'is the termination of the employment relationship at the behest of the employer. Termination is the wider category encompassing the termination at the instance of the employee, the employer and the operation of law.'[35]

The Labour Court and the Supreme Court were interpreting the relevant provisions of the repealed Labour Act 1992; nevertheless, there is no good reason why the reasoning and conclusions in *Meintjies v Joe Gross* by the Labour Court and the reasoning and conclusions in *Joe Gross v Meintjies* by the Supreme Court must not apply with equal force to the interpretation and application of the word 'dismiss' in s. 33(1) of the Labour Act 2007, seeing that the relevant provisions of s. 45 of the repealed Labour Act 1992 and s. 33 of the Labour Act 2007 are substantially the same.

Section 30(6)(a), read with s. 33(1), of the Labour Act 2007 vindicates this submission. Section 30(6) provides:

> Nothing in this section affects the right –
>
> (a)   of a dismissed employee to dispute the lawfulness or fairness of the dismissal in terms of this Act or any other law; or

---

[32]   *Du Toit v Office of the Prime Minister* supra.

[33]   *Joe Gross t/a Joe's Beer House v Meintjies* supra.

[34]   Cameron, Cheadle and Thompson, *The New Labour Relations Act*, p. 143.

[35]   *Joe Gross v Meintjies* (SC) supra at 428I.

(b)   of an employer or an employee to terminate the contract of employment without notice, for any cause recognised by law…

More significant, the *opening words* of s. 32(1) provides: 'An employer must not, whether notice is given or not, dismiss an employee…' Thus, if an employee does not accept his employee's notice to terminate his contract of employment, then in terms of the Labour Act 2007 the termination constitutes dismissal, and, therefore, is subject to s. 33 of the Act. Accordingly, the giving of notice to the employee by his employer to terminate the contract of employment does not, by that fact alone, take away the employee's right to dispute the lawfulness or fairness of the dismissal in terms of the Labour Act or any other law. Therefore, the mere fact that the employer has given notice to his employee to terminate the contract of employment does not *ipso facto* absolve the employer from his statutory duty to dismiss with a valid and fair reason and according to a fair procedure.[36]

In short, dismissal by notice must be effected for a valid and fair reason. Whether the notice was given in terms of a contract of employment or in terms of the Labour Act or any other written law, there must be a valid and fair reason, bearing in mind that the employer does not have unlimited power to breach a contract of employment with impunity.[37]

Be that as it may, as a general rule, an employer or his employee may terminate the contract of employment by either party giving to the other party notice to terminate the contract. As a general rule, a party is expected to give a reasonable period of notice,[38] and in the absence of an express term in the contract to that effect, what is reasonable is usually determined by frequency of payment of wages. The Labour Act 2007 has modified the general rule concerning the right of parties to a contract of employment that is subject to the Labour Act to agree the length of the period of notice inasmuch as the Labour Act has laid down minimum periods for the giving of notice to terminate contracts of employment that are subject to the Act.

In terms of s. 30(1) of the Labour Act, the length of a period of notice depends upon the length of time an employee has been employed by the employer. The statutory period of notice does not depend on whether an employee is paid on a daily, weekly, fortnightly or monthly basis. The following scheme applies:

1   not less than one day's notice is required, if the employee has been employed for four weeks or less;

---

36   *Joe Gross v Meintjies* supra.

37   *Kiggundu and others v Roads Authority and others* 2007 (1) NR 175 (LC).

38   J. Grogan, *Riekert's Employment Law,* 2nd edn, Cape Town, Juta, 1993, p. 52. See also chapter 6, para. 6.2.1.2 above.

2   not less than one week's notice is required, if the employee has been employed for between four weeks and one year; and

3   one month's notice is required, if the employee has been employed for more than one year.

It must be pointed out that s. 30(1) lays down minimum periods only: according to s. 30(2), agreed periods of notice may be longer than the statutory minima, so long as the contractual periods are of equal duration for both the employer and the employee.

In calculating periods of employment, one has to take the relevant provisions of the Labour Act into account. According to s. 29 of the Act, for the purposes of Part F of Chapter 3 of the Act ('Termination of Employment'), the period of employment includes the following periods:

1   a period during which the employee worked for the employer;

2   a period of leave granted by the employer in terms of the Labour Act;

3   any leave granted in terms of the Labour Act or for any other reason;

4   a period during which an employee is on suspension;

5   in the case of an employee who has been reinstated, the period between the date of his dismissal and the date on which he is reinstated; and

6   a period during which an employee is on a strike, which is in compliance with the Labour Act, or during which his employer takes a lockout action, which is also in compliance with the Act.

Section 30(3) and (4) prescribe the manner in which notice of termination ought to be given and the particulars a notice must contain. The Act provides that a notice of termination must (i) be given in writing, unless the giver of the notice is illiterate, in which case the notice may be given orally; (ii) set out the reasons for the termination, if the giver of the notice is the employer; and (iii) contain the date on which it is given. In the case of a minimum one-day notice, the notice may be given on a working day; in the case of a minimum one-week notice, the notice may be given on or before the last working day; and in the case of a minimum one-month notice, the notice may be given on either the 1st or the 15th of the month.

Section 30(5) of the Act prohibits an employer from giving notice of termination when the employee is on leave to which he is entitled in terms of Part D of Chapter 3 of the Labour

Act or from giving notice in such a way as to make the notice run concurrently with such leave (chapter 4, para. 4.8 above deals with leave to which an employee is entitled in terms of the Labour Act 2007).

As was mentioned above, in terms of s. 30(6) of the Act, there is nothing in s. 30 stopping a dismissed employee from exercising his right under the Labour Act or any law to challenge the lawfulness or fairness of his employer's decision to dismiss him by notice; or preventing an employer or employee from terminating the contract of employment without notice, for any cause recognized by law, or paying money in lieu of notice in terms of s. 31 of the Act (see chapter 6, paras 6.2.1.1 and 6.3.1 above).

Section 31(1) of the Labour Act provides that instead of giving his employee notice to terminate the contract in terms of s. 30 of the Act, an employer may pay his employee the remuneration his employee would have received, if the employee had worked during the period of notice. According to s. 31(2) of the Act, if an employee gives his employer notice to terminate the contract of employment in terms of s. 30 of the Act, the employer may waive the notice; in that case the employer must pay the employee the remuneration to which he would have been entitled had he worked during the period of notice. Lastly, s. 31(3) of the Act provides that instead of giving notice in terms of s. 30, an employee may pay his employer the remuneration that the employer would have paid him had he worked during the period of notice.

A notice terminating a contract of employment must be clear and unambiguous. In *Workers Representative Council v Manzini Town Council* the respondent (employer) sought to terminate the contract of its striking employees in the following terms:

> You are hereby informed that you must return to work by 2.00 p.m. on Monday the 9 October 1989 as the strike in which you are participating is an unlawful strike, failing which you will be deemed to have voluntarily terminated your employment with the Council, the automatic result of which will be your forfeiture of all your internal benefits.[39]

The employees disregarded the notice. The Industrial Court found that the employees had voluntarily terminated their employment. The employees appealed to the Court of Appeal against the Industrial Court's decision. Browde, JA, who delivered the unanimous judgment of the Court of Appeal, observed thus:

---

[39] *Workers Representative Council v Manzini Town Council* Swaziland CA 3/94 (Court of Appeal) at p. 1 (unreported).

The termination of contractual relationships is not a trivial matter and the decision to terminate a contract changes the contractual relationship that the contracting parties have towards each other. This is a step, which might cause serious material prejudice to the party against whom the cancellation is effective. This consideration is, in my view, extremely important and is a valid reason why the act of cancellation of an otherwise valid contract *must be clear and unambiguous*...[40]

Tshabalala v The Minister of Health and others is authority for the proposition that a notice to terminate must be communicated clearly and unambiguously to each and every intended recipient in order for the notice to be valid; for, it is trite law that a decision to terminate a contract must be communicated to the other party.[41] *Rustenburg Town Council v Minister of Labour and others* is also authority for the view that it is only with the consent of the party receiving notice that a notice of termination may be abandoned or withdrawn during its currency.[42]

In terms of the Labour Act 2007, there are two types of notices bearing on termination of contracts of employment. The first is notice given in terms of s. 30 (which has just been discussed); the second is notice given in accordance with s. 34, which concerns collective termination and redundancy and these are dealt with in chapter 8, para. 8.3 below.

7.3.2 Termination without Notice

The rights of an employee and an employer to cancel a contract of employment without notice have already been discussed in chapter 6, paras 6.2.1.1 and 6.3.1 above. There is no need to repeat the discussion here. Suffice it to reiterate that in terms of s. 30(6)(b) of the Labour Act 2007, either the employer or the employee is entitled to terminate a contract of employment without notice 'for any cause recognized by law'. Some of the causes recognized by law are discussed in chapter 6, paras 6.2.1.1 and 6.3.1 above.

7.4 SEVERANCE PAY

Under statute labour or employment law, employers are obliged to pay to their employees certain amounts of money, different from such separation benefits as pension and gratuity,

---

[40] Ibid. at p 12.

[41] *Tshabalala v The Minister of Health and others* 1987 (1) SA 513.

[42] *Rustenburg Town Council v Minister of Labour and others* 1942 TPD 220.

when the contracts of employment come to an end. Such payment is often referred to as severance pay (or allowance). According to s. 34 of Swaziland's Employment Act,[43] for example, if an employer terminates the services of his employee, he must pay to the employee a severance allowance, which is equal to the wages of ten working days for each completed year in excess of one year that the employee has been continuously employed by the employer. Under Swaziland's labour law, severance allowance is payable only where an employer dismisses his employee. It is, therefore, not payable where for instance, an employee resigns. It is also payable only where an employer did not have a fair reason to dismiss an employee within the meaning of s. 36 of the Employment Act, which provides for fair grounds upon which an employer may dismiss his employee.

The grounds for the payment of severance pay in South Africa are extremely restrictive: they are strikingly different from the grounds under Swaziland's Employment Act. According to s. 41 of South Africa's Basic Conditions of Employment Act,[44] an employer is obliged to pay severance pay to an employee whom he dismisses for reasons based on the employer's operational requirements. For the purposes of s. 41, the term 'operational requirements' means requirements based on the economic, technological, structural or similar needs of an employer. Therefore, in South Africa, only a dismissal based on 'operational requirements' attracts the payment of severance pay. However, in terms of s. 41(4), an employee who unreasonably refuses to accept the employer's offer of alternative employment with the employer or any other employer is not entitled to severance pay.

The grounds for the payment of severance pay under the Labour Act 2007, on the other hand, are wider than those under both the Swaziland and South African laws. According to s. 35(1) of the Labour Act, and subject to s. 35(2), an employer is obliged to pay severance pay to an employee who has completed 12 months' continuous service with him, if the employee is dismissed, dies while he is employed, resigns or retires after reaching the age of 65 years. Section 35(2) provides, however, that entitlement to severance pay under s. 35(1) does not apply in the following instances.

1   Where the employee is dismissed fairly on the grounds of misconduct or poor work performance.[45]

2   If the employee refuses to be reinstated after a dismissal.

---

[43]   Act No. 5 of 1980.

[44]   Act No. 75 of 1997.

[45]   See chapter 3, para. 3.9 above, where misconduct is discussed; para. 3.7 above, where competence and efficiency are discussed; and chapter 8, paras 8.1, 8.2 and 8.3 below, where unfair dismissal is discussed.

3   If an employee unreasonably refuses to accept employment, on terms that are not less favourable than those that applied to him immediately before termination of his employment, with a surviving spouse, heir or dependant of a deceased employer within one month of the death of such employer, or with one or more of the former partners within one month of the dissolution of the partnership, if the employer was a partner.

According to s. 35(4) of the Labour Act, when calculating the length of service of an employee for the purpose of payment of severance pay under s. 34(1) and (3), the following rules apply.

1   An employee retains any service acquired before the employer's death, if that employer is an individual and his surviving spouse, heir or dependant subsequently employs the employee.

2   An employee retains any service acquired before the dissolution of a partnership, if the employer is a partnership and it is dissolved, and one or more of the former partners of the partnership subsequently employs the employee.

3   If the business of an employee's employer is transferred to another person and the employee continues in the service of that business after its transfer, the employee retains any service acquired before the transfer of the business.

4   The service of an employee who works for the same employer on a seasonal basis for two or more successive years is regarded as continuous, so long as the period of such service is made up of periods during which the employee actually worked.

'Continuous service' includes any period of employment that an employee works for an employer; any period of leave under the Labour Act; any leave of absence granted in terms of the Labour Act or granted for any other reason; any period of suspension; a period from the date of dismissal to the date of reinstatement, if the employee is reinstated; and the period of a strike or lockout that complies with the Act.

The fact that the contract of employment is terminated by the death of an employee does not absolve the employer from his obligation to pay severance pay under s. 35 of the Labour Act. If the employee dies intestate, the employer must pay the amount to the employee's surviving spouse. If there is no surviving spouse, he must pay the amount to the employee's children, but if there are no surviving children, then he must pay the amount to the employee's estate. According to s. 35(5) of the Act, the payment of severance pay in terms of s. 35 of the Act does not in any way take away the employee's right to any other amount that the employer is obliged to pay to him. Thus the payment of severance pay to an employee does not affect his right to any amounts that he is entitled to receive according to any law.[46]

In terms of s. 35(3) of the Labour Act, the amount of severance pay to which an employee is entitled must be equal to at least one week's remuneration for each year of continuous service with an employer.

---

[46] An identical provision is in s. 41(5) of South Africa's Basic Conditions of Employment Act 1997 (Act No. 75 of 1997).

8 UNFAIR DISMISSAL AND DISCIPLINARY ACTIONS[1]

8.1 UNFAIR DISMISSAL

One outstanding development in statutory labour law has been the introduction of the concept of unfair dismissal and remedies for unfair dismissal. It will be remembered from chapter 6, para. 6.3.1 above, that at common law an employer can dismiss an employee summarily if by his conduct the employee breaches a term of the contract of employment that goes to the root of the contract. We also saw in chapter 7, para. 7.3.1 above, that at common law an employer may decide not to dismiss the employee summarily but rather dismiss by giving due notice. However, under the Labour Act 2007, the question whether a dismissal has been fair or unfair is not anchored in whether due notice has been given: other critical considerations come into play. That is the focus of the present chapter.

In this connection, statute law has modified the common law by introducing the concept of statutory unfair dismissal irrespective of whether a dismissal is, for instance, by notice (see chapter 7, para. 7.3.1 above), is summary or is due to redundancy (see this chapter, para. 8.3 below). Indeed, in some countries, the protection of employees from unfair dismissal is expressed as a statutory right. For instance, s. 94(1) of the United Kingdom's Employment Rights Act[2] provides tersely: 'An employee has the right not to be unfairly dismissed by his employer.' An identical formulation is found in s. 185 of South Africa's Labour Relations Act: 'Every employee has the right not to be unfairly dismissed.[3]

In the interpretation and application of the statutory provision on unfair dismissal, the courts have developed rules and principles of law applicable to the two-fold requirements or tests of substantive fairness and procedural fairness, which an employer who has dismissed his employee must pass in order for the dismissal to be lawful.

The dual requirements of substantive fairness and procedural fairness were provided in s. 45 of the repealed Labour Act 1992. The requirements are repeated in s. 32(1) of the Labour Act 2007 in almost identical terms. It hardly needs saying and it stands to reason,

---

1   For completeness, this chapter should be read with chapters 3, 4 and 6.

2   Employment Rights Act 1996 (c.18).

3   Act No. 66 of 1995.

therefore, that the rules and principles of law developed by the courts in the interpretation and application of s. 45 of the repealed Labour Act 1992 must apply with equal force to the interpretation and application of s. 34 of the Labour Act 2007. By a parity of reasoning, the rules and principles of law developed by the courts with regard to dismissal arising from redundancy under s. 50 of the repealed Labour Act 1992 must also apply with equal force to the interpretation and application of s. 33 of the Labour Act 2007. Consequently, it is those rules and principles of law that will be examined in the present chapter because they offer very useful insights and guides in the interpretation and application of ss 33 and 34 of the Labour Act 2007.

8.1.1   What is Unfair Dismissal?

Section 33 of the Labour Act 2007 provides:

> (1)   An employer must not, whether notice is given or not, dismiss an employee
>
> (a)   without a valid and fair reason; and
>
> (b)   without following –
>
> > (i) the procedure set out in section 34, if the dismissal arises from a reason set out in section 34 (1); or
> >
> > (ii) subject to any code of good practice issued under section 137, a fair procedure, in any other case.[4]

According to s. 33(4) of the Labour Act 2007, just as was the case under s. 46(3) of the repealed Labour Act 1992, an employer bears a different burden of proof from that borne by his employee in any proceedings concerning a dismissal. Section 33(4) provides that in any proceedings concerning dismissal, (i) the employee must establish the existence of the dismissal and (ii) if the existence of the dismissal is established, it is presumed, unless the contrary is proved by the employer, that the dismissal was unfair. Thus, if the employee succeeds in establishing that he was dismissed, there is prima facie proof that the dismissal was unfair; and if the employer fails to prove that the dismissal was for a valid and fair reason and that a fair procedure was followed, the prima facie proof becomes conclusive. The burden that is put on the employer never shifts. In other words, the burden lies on the employer to justify the dismissal in order for the dismissal not to be affected by the prohibition in s. 33(1) of the Act. In sum, 'the burden, whether it be in its strict sense (i.e.

---

4   Similar provisions are found in s. 36, read with s. 42, of Swaziland's Employment Act 1980 (Act No. 5 of 1980).

"burden of proof or true onus")[5] or the lesser form (i.e. "evidential burden")[6], never shifts; the employer must prove that the dismissal was for a valid and fair reason',[7] and that a fair procedure was followed.

Thus, s. 33(1) of the Labour Act 2007, like s. 45(1) of the repealed Labour Act, only approves a dismissal 'that is not only lawful in the technical sense but one which is also fair, meaning one which is not capricious but equitable, conscionable and just.'[8] The first hurdle that an employee who seeks a remedy for unfair dismissal under the Labour Act has to overcome is that he must show that he is an employee within the meaning of s. 1 of the Labour Act. The meaning of employee is discussed fully in chapter 1, para. 1.2 above. Therefore, there is no need to repeat the discussion here. The second hurdle the employee must surmount is that he must show that he was dismissed by the employer within the meaning of s. 33(4)(a) of the Act.[9] Thereafter, it will be the turn of the employer under s. 32(3)(b) to prove that the dismissal is fair; and such proof need not be beyond all reasonable doubt: proof on a balance of probabilities is sufficient.[10] The effect of s. 33(4)(b) is that it firmly places the onus on the employer to rebut the presumption of unfair dismissal.[11]

In *Du Toit v The Office of the Prime Minister*,[12] the Labour Court approved the definition of 'dismissal' by Le Roux and van Niekerk in the following passage: 'A dismissal takes place where the termination of employment is "caused by" the employer or employment is terminated at "the behest of" the employer, irrespective of precisely how this termination takes place in strict contractual terms.'[13]

In *Cross Country Carriers v Farmer*,[14] the respondent (employee) of the appellant (employer) went to South Africa from Namibia on duty. While in South Africa, he had an accident in the employer's truck, driven by a co-employee. Both of them were taken to hospital for treatment and later the police detained them in custody. The respondent's co-employee returned to Namibia, went back to the employers and tendered his service. The employer held a disciplinary hearing, and subsequently dismissed the co-employee. However, the respondent did not return to work to render his service, as he should have

---

5   P.J. Schwikkard, et al., *Principles of Evidence*, 2nd edn, Kenwyn, Juta, 2002, pp. 525-6.

6   Ibid.

7   *Pep Stores (Namibia) (Pty) Ltd v Iyambo and others* 2001 NR 211 at 216H.

8   Ibid at 219C.

9   *Model Pick 'N Pay Family Supermarkets v Mukosho* NLLP 2004 (4) 219 NLC.

10 *Hailemo v Security Force Services* 1996 NR 99.

11 *Swakopmund Hotel & Entertainment Centre v Karibib* NLLP 1998 (1) 213 NLC); *Namibia Beverages v Hoaës* NLLP 2002 (2) 380 NLC; *Pep Stores (Namibia) (Pty) Ltd v Iyambo* 2001 NR 211 (LC).

12 *Du Toit v The Office of the Prime Minister* 1996 NR 52 at 64C-D.

13 P.A.K. Le Roux and A. van Niekerk, *The South African Law of Unfair Dismissa,l* Cape Town, Juta, 1994, p. 83.

14 *Cross Country Carriers v Farmer* NLLP 1998 (1) 226 NLC.

done after being discharged from hospital as his co-employee did: he stayed away from work. The Labour Court found that it could not be said as a matter of law that the respondent was dismissed from his employment; rather he repudiated the contract of employment without any lawful excuse or reason. The Labour Court came to a similar conclusion that the employer had not dismissed the employee in *Johannes Swartbooi v Deon Heunis,*[15] when it confirmed the district labour court's decision that upon the evidence the respondent (employer) had not dismissed the appellant (employee). The Labour Court found that the appellant had reprimanded the employee for idling and loafing. The employee then left his work, and stayed away for two days, but went back to collect his salary. Thereafter, he stayed from work again. When the respondent called the employee, his response was that the employer knew where he lived, and that he could go and fetch him.

Thus, in terms of Labour Act, a dismissal occurs where the employer causes the termination of employment or the contract of employment is terminated at the behest or at the instance of the employer: it does not matter the manner in which the termination takes place.[16] The termination can be carried out summarily (see chapter 7, paras 7.2.9 and 7.3.2 above); it may be due to redundancy (see chapter 7, para. 7.3.1 above, and para. 8.3 below), or it can be brought about by notice. As far as notice is concerned, it will be recalled from chapter 7, para. 7.3.1 above, that according to the Labour Act 2007, if an employee whose contract of employment is subject to that Act does not accept a s. 30 notice terminating his employment, the termination constitutes dismissal.

What then is unfair dismissal, i.e. when is a dismissal an unfair dismissal? The remainder of this paragraph will be devoted to answering this question. Put simply, and in terms of s. 33(1) of the Labour Act 2007, an unfair dismissal occurs where the contract of employment of the employee is terminated without a valid and fair reason and where a fair procedure has not been followed. The test of fair dismissal is, therefore, two-fold, i.e. substantive fairness and procedural fairness, and the two elements are cumulative and not separate.[17] Nevertheless, once it is established that there is no fair and valid reason for dismissing the employee, the enquiry should end there, because considerations of whether the disciplinary proceedings were fairly conducted serve no practical purpose, if, in the first place, there were no fair and valid grounds for dismissal.[18] It is only where the employer has passed the first part of the test, namely, that he has valid and fair reason to dismiss his employee that

---

[15] *Johannes Swartbooi v Deon Heunis* Case No. LCA 6/2001 (unreported).

[16] *Joe Gross t/a Joe's Beer House v Meintjies* 2005 NR 413 (SC).

[17] *SPCA of Namibia v Terblanche* 1996 NR 398. The facts of this case are set out briefly in chapter 10, para. 10.2.2.1 below.

[18] *SPCA of Namibia v Terblanche* supra.

it becomes necessary to consider whether a fair procedure was followed, i.e. whether the disciplinary hearing, for example, was fairly conducted.[19]

In their interpretation and application of the two-fold requirement, the courts have developed various principles. These principles will now be discussed under the headings of 'substantive fairness' and 'procedural fairness'. It cannot be emphasized enough that although the principles have been developed mostly by the courts, they are equally applicable to arbitral tribunals.

8.1.2 Substantive Fairness

In terms of s. 33(1) of the Labour Act 2007, the first part of the two-fold test of fairness, i.e. substantive fairness, has in turn two interrelated components, i.e. the employer's reason for dismissing must not only be valid but it must also be fair. What then is a valid reason? A valid reason is a good and genuine grievance.[20]

The reasons that the employer may have for dismissing his employees are boundless, but they must be good and well grounded; they must not be based on some spurious or indefensible ground. In sum, a dismissal must be based on reasonable grounds: for example, where an employee commits a serious breach of some of his duties that are discussed in chapter 3 above or commits any other serious breach that goes to the root of the contract of employment as mentioned previously (see chapter 6, paras 6.2.1.1 and 6.3.1, above). That is not the end of the matter: the employer may have a 'valid', i.e. a good, reason for dismissing his employee because the employee may have breached his duty as an employee or has breached a fundamental term of the contract, but the reason must also be a 'fair' one. Thus, the Labour Act 2007 only approves of dismissal that is not only lawful in the technical sense, but one that is also fair; meaning one that is not capricious but equitable, conscionable and just.[21]

What then is a 'fair' reason? The fact that the employee has breached any of his duties in terms of the contract of employment or a fundamental term of the contract, which might be a valid reason to dismiss, should not *ipso facto* lead to a dismissal. The employer may only dismiss if, taking into account all the circumstances of the case, it is reasonable, i.e. fair, to dismiss. In *Teixeira v SA Broadcasting Corporation*,[22] the Industrial Court quoted with

---

19 Ibid. at 399.

20 Ibid. at 399I. The courts in South Africa have found the ILO Termination of Employment Recommendation: 119 (1963), to be decisive guidelines when considering what constitutes valid reasons for dismissal: see M.S.M. Brassey, et al., *The New Labour Law*, Cape Town, Juta, 1987, p. 369 and the cases there cited. Section 36 of Swaziland's Employment Act (Act No. 5 of 1980) sets out an exhaustive list of valid reasons or grounds upon which it is fair for an employer to dismiss an employee for the purpose of that Act.

21 *Pep Stores v Iyambo* supra at 219C.

22 *Teixeira v SA Broadcasting Corporation* (1991) 12 *ILJ* 656 (IC) at 657F.

approval this passage from *Govender v SASKO (Pty) Ltd t/a Richards Bay Bakery*: 'The validity of the reason relates to the facts on which the reason is based, whilst the fairness of the reason relates to the gravity of the infraction and whether the sanction imposed was warranted.'[23] Manyarara, AJ observed similarly in *Namibia Breweries v Hoaës* supra thus: 'the concept of substantive fairness involves the issue of validity, i.e. whether there was sufficient evidence placed before the court and the issue of fairness, i.e. whether the sanction was appropriate in the circumstances.'[24] Nevertheless, as Kroon, J stated in *Country Fair Foods (Pty) Ltd v CCMA and others,* 'It remains part of our law that it lies in the first place within the province of the employer to set the standard of conduct by its employees and to determine the sanction with which non-compliance will be visited, interference therewith is only justified in the case of unreasonableness and unfairness.'[25] The Industrial Court has said the same in *Maphetane v Shoprite Checkers (Pty) Ltd*, namely that it is for the employer to determine the standards of conduct required of its employees and the courts should only interfere with any sanction imposed for breach of those standards if it results in any unfairness.[26]

Therefore, a determination of whether there was a fair reason to dismiss turns upon the reasonableness of the decision. However, as was stated in *British Leyland (UK) Ltd v Swift*, it must be remembered in all these cases that there is a band of reasonableness, within which one employer might reasonably take one view and another quite reasonably take a different view.[27] Consequently, what is reasonable will depend largely upon the circumstances of the particular case. In addition, there are different levels of reasonableness; they cannot all be fitted into rigid categories. Therefore, it is important to note that it rests with the court, after weighing all the evidence placed before it, to make its own assessment of what constitutes fair reasons.[28] In any case, a decision to dismiss, which, taking into account all the circumstances of the case, is harsh, arbitrary and unjust is unreasonable.[29] Accordingly, if the employer's decision to dismiss is unreasonable, then he did not have a fair reason to dismiss within the meaning of s. 33(1) of the Labour Act 2007 because 'an unreasonable decision would always be unfair'.[30]

From what has been said, it is clear that the requirement of 'fair reason' involves a consideration of the question whether the ultimate sanction of dismissal, which is the capital

---

23   *Govender v SASKO (Pty) Ltd t/a Richards Bay Bakery* (1990) 11 *ILJ* 1282 (IC) at 1285C-G.

24   *Namibia Breweries v Hoaës* supra at 382.

25   *Country Fair Foods (Pty) Ltd v CCMA and others* [1999] 11 BLLR 1117 (LAC) at 1121E.

26   *Maphetane v Shoprite Checkers (Pty) Ltd* (1996) 17 *ILJ* 964 (IC).

27   *British Leyland (UK) Ltd v Swift* [1981] 1 RLR.

28   *Toyota South Africa (Pty) Ltd v Radebe and others* (2000) 21 *ILJ* 340 (LAC).

29   L. Baxter, *Administrative Law,* Cape Town, Juta, 1984, p. 497.

30   *Frank and another v Chairperson of the Immigration Selection Board* 1999 NR 257 (HC) at 265D.

punishment in labour relations, is suitable, taking into account all the circumstances of the case. The courts must, in that regard, therefore, also decide whether the severity of the penalty was fair.[31] For instance, did the employer consider less harsh sanctions such as a final written warning, a demotion,[32] or a transfer to another job with attendant reduction in rank and remuneration? Did the employer take into account any mitigating factors, e.g. the length of service of the employee, accompanied by a clean record of service? In *Pupkewitz & Sons (Pty) Ltd v Kankara* supra, the Labour Court found that the fact that the employer suffered only potential prejudice ought to have been given some weight as a mitigating factor. A long and unblemished record of good service has also been recognized as a strong mitigating factor.[33] In such a case, a written warning would be just and equitable.[34] However, as the Industrial Court observed in *Lucas Zwane v Tip Top Holdings*, 'one incident of serious and depraved misconduct and misbehaviour, like the one we have found the applicant committed, is capable of cancelling any hitherto unblemished record of good service.'[35]

At times, a consideration of these factors might raise the issue of consistency in the disciplining of employees in the same organization. For instance, an employer may punish an employee who damages his property during a strike – whether or not the strike is in conformity with the Labour Act – more severely than he does the employee's colleague who merely participated peacefully in the strike; for the conduct of the former constitutes misconduct in itself. Moreover, an employee who is also a trade union representative at the workplace may hide from his fellow employees a communication from the Labour Commissioner, warning the employees that the strike they were about to embark upon was illegal and therefore they must desist from engaging in it. Such an employee could be penalized much more severely than the other employees, if the employees did embark upon the strike while under the impression that their strike was in compliance with the Labour Act. In such a situation, if an employer dismisses such an employee (the trade union representative), but does not dismiss the others as well, the employer's action cannot on that count only be said to be unfair or unreasonable.

The view is not inconsistent with the general principle noted by Tip, AJ in *SRV Mill Services (Pty) Ltd v CCMA and others*,[36] that there should be equality of treatment between employees in the application of discipline, but that differing circumstances may justify

---

31 *Pupkewitz & Sons (Pty) Ltd v Kankara* 1997 NR 70.

32 Final written warning is discussed in para. 8.4.2.3 and demotion in para. 8.4.4 below.

33 *Ntshangase v ALUSAF (Pty) Ltd* (1984) 5 *ILJ* 336 (IC); *National Union of Mineworkers and another v East Rand Proprietary Mines Ltd* (1987) 8 *ILJ* 315 (IC).

34 *Mhlume Sugar Company v Jablane James Mbuli* Swaziland CA 1/91 (unreported).

35 *Lucas Zwane v Tip Top Holdings* Swaziland IC 77/95 at p. 7 (unreported). The facts of the case are set out briefly in chapter 3, para. 3.9.6 above.

36 *SRV Mill Services (Pty) Ltd v CCMA and others* [2004] 2 BLLR 184 (LC).

different treatment of different employees. In that case two colleagues, *H* and *A*, failed to report for duty at their shifts, presumably because the vehicle in which they were travelling to work broke down. *H* was brought before a disciplinary hearing for absenting himself from work without permission. He was found guilty and dismissed. *A* was called before a disciplinary hearing some three months later on the same charge but he was not found guilty. *H* contended during arbitration that his dismissal was unfair because the employer had failed to act consistently in the application of discipline. The commissioner found *H*'s contention to be well founded, and ordered his reinstatement with retroactive effect. The employer applied to the Labour Court to review and set aside the commissioner's award. The Labour Court stressed the point that where a challenge on the basis of inconsistency of the application of discipline is raised, the employer bears the onus of showing – as part of proving that the dismissal was fair – that there was no inconsistent disciplining of the employees. On the facts of this case, the Labour Court found that the employer had failed to discharge that onus; consequently, the application for review was dismissed with costs. The principle in *SRV Mill Services v CCMA* was followed by the Labour Appeal Court in *CEPPWAWU and others v Metrofile (Pty) Ltd*,[37] where the Labour Appeal Court held that the respondent's inconsistent application of discipline rendered the dismissal of the employees in question substantively unfair.

The question that a court or a tribunal must decide is this: when should an arbitrator or a court interfere with the employer's decision to impose the ultimate sanction of dismissal? In *Model Pick 'N Pay Family Supermarkets v Mwaala*, Damaseb, AJ (as he then was), approving the standards proposed by Grogan in his work *Dismissal*, set out the following list of useful items – though not an exhaustive list – as guides in determining whether an employer's decision to dismiss was reasonable or unfair; and also observed that the weight to attach to any item would depend largely on the circumstances of the particular case. The items are:

> whether the sanction was in accordance with the employer's disciplinary code; whether a lesser sanction would have served the purpose; whether the employer could reasonably have been expected to continue with the employment relationship; the gravity of the offence; the employee's disciplinary record; the employee's length of service; mitigating factors and the employee's personal circumstances.[38]

---

[37] *CEPPWAWU and others v Metrofile (Pty) Ltd* [2004] 2 BLLR 103 (LAC).

[38] *Model Pick 'N Pay Family Supermarkets v Mwaala* 2003 NR 175 (LC) at 180E-F.

It is important, therefore, to point out that it is not a question of whether a court dealing with the matter would have imposed the sanction of dismissal as the employer did. The question always is rather this: is the dismissal unreasonable, i.e. unfair in the circumstances and, therefore, unjustified? In other words, is the sanction imposed on the employee one which no reasonable employer would have imposed? It must, therefore, be borne in mind that the subjective opinion of the employer regarding the seriousness of the offence with which an employee is charged may not suffice as a yardstick, which should bind the court.[39] As mentioned previously, a court must apply an objective test to determine the seriousness of the offence, to decide whether the sanction of dismissal is an appropriate punishment in the circumstances.

To sum up, not only must the employer have a good and genuine ('valid') reason to dismiss, but also the decision to dismiss must be grounded on reasonableness, i.e. on a just ('fair') reason, taking into account all the circumstances of the particular case. What is a valid and fair reason in relation to dismissal arising from redundancy will be discussed in para. 8.3.2, below.

In terms of s. 33(2) of the Labour Act 2007, if an employee is dismissed on any of the grounds provided in that section, the dismissal is, by that very fact alone, unfair. Such dismissal is discussed in para. 8.2 below. There is a similar provision in s. 187 of South Africa's Labour Relations Act 1995.[40]

8.1.3   Procedural Fairness

An employer cannot lawfully dismiss an employee unless he finds facts upon which the valid and fair reason to dismiss is based and, in pursuit of finding such facts, he must proceed by a fair procedure. Herein lies the inseparability of the dual requirements of substantive fairness and procedural fairness and their cumulative nature.[41] What then is procedural fairness? Procedural fairness is a wide concept. The procedures that different employers will follow in order to determine the facts 'will obviously differ depending on diverse circumstances', but all such enquiries 'will at least have to comply with the *audi alteram partem* rule of natural justice'.[42] Besides, a hearing should be conducted in an impartial manner; otherwise the hearing will be in breach of the other rule of natural justice, i.e. the rule against bias. Brand, AJ explained the rule against bias as follows in *Foster v Chairman, Commission for Administration, and another*:

---

[39]   See *Hendrik Jacobus Van Wyk v Commercial Bank of Namibia Limited* Case No. SA 12/2004 (Supreme Court) (unreported).

[40]   Act No. 66 of 1995.

[41]   *SPCA of Namibia v Terblanche* supra.

[42]   *Kamanya & others v Kuiseb Fish Products Ltd* 1996 NR 123 at 130E.

Regarding the question as to when an administrative decision can be set aside on the ground of bias, a Full Bench of this Division in *Mönnig and Others v Council of Review and Others* 1989 (4) SA 866 (C) decided that the 'reasonable suspicion of bias' test and not the 'likelihood of bias' test is the one to be applied. According to the former, the question is not whether the decision-maker concerned would in fact be partial or impartial. The question is whether an observer in the position of applicant would reasonably suspect that the decision-maker would not be impartial.[43]

Thus, courts will find bias to exist in the following circumstances: if any of the presiding officers of a disciplinary hearing is, for instance, involved in the proceedings as a complainant, a witness or an investigator, or in the preparation or formulation of the charges, or if any one of them has a personal interest in the outcome of the hearing. In addition, bias will be found to exist if any of the presiding officers has had a history of animosity or friction with the employee concerned.[44] In short, the inquirer must act in good faith, and must also respect the rules of natural justice and act fairly. In *Meyer v Law Society, Transvaal*, Nicholas, J explained with great insight that the principles of natural justice

require a domestic tribunal to adopt a procedure which would afford the person a proper hearing by the tribunal, and a proper opportunity of producing his evidence and of stating his contentions, and of correcting or contradicting any prejudicial statements or allegations made against him; to listen fairly to both sides and to observe the principles of fair play; to discharge its duties honestly and impartially; and to act in good faith...[45]

If one extrapolates the natural justice requirements laid down in *Meyer v Law Society* supra and *Foster v Commission for Administration* to the requirements necessary to pass the test of a fair procedure within the meaning of s. 33(1) of the Labour Act 2007, the following principle emerges: a domestic inquiry, which is usually referred to as a disciplinary hearing or inquiry in the employment situation, conducted by an employer so as to find if a valid

---

43 *Foster v Chairman, Commission for Administration, and another* 1991 (4) SA 403 (C) at 411D-E.

44 *Mazian v Transnamib Transport (Pty) Ltd* NLLP 2002 (2) 352 NLC.

45 *Meyer v Law Society, Transvaal* 1978 (2) SA 209 (T) at 212H. See also chapter 11, para. 11.3.2 below, where the rules of natural justice are also discussed.

and fair reason exists for the dismissal of his employee, should respect the rules of natural justice and act fairly. [46]

Besides, where there are express contractual terms governing a disciplinary procedure as, for example, contained in the employer's disciplinary code, it is no defence for an employer to contend that the alternative procedure that he followed was equally fair. An employee is accordingly entitled to insist that the employer abide by his contractual obligation to follow the provisions of the employer's own disciplinary code. The employer's refusal or failure to do so would amount to procedural unfairness.[47] Thus, once an employer has adopted a particular disciplinary code or suchlike rules or regulations – whether unilaterally or after negotiations with a trade union – he is obliged to stick to its provisions meticulously. An employer may, for a good reason, e.g. to attain equitable results, depart from the code and not follow it slavishly but he may not do so to the detriment of an employee.[48]

In England, the doctrine of fairness had made an appearance as far back as 1911 in the important case of *Board of Education v Rice* decided by the House of Lords. In that case, Loreburn, LC said, 'I need not add that in doing either they [decision takers] must act in good faith and fairly listen to both sides, for that is a duty lying upon everyone who decided anything.'[49] Moreover, according to Lord Morris of Borthy-y-Gest, 'Natural justice is but fairness writ large and juridically. It has been described as "fair play in action". Nor is it a leaven to be associated only with judicial or quasi-judicial occasions.'[50]

Although the courts do not expect an employer to handle a disciplinary hearing according to the standards of a court of law, they expect certain minimum requirements to be met if a hearing is to qualify as being procedurally fair. Some of the minimum requirements are as follows.

1 The employer should advise the employee in advance of the precise charge or charges that he or she is to meet at the hearing. This requirement is linked to the need to give to the employee an opportunity to make adequate preparation.

2 The employee should be advised in advance about his right to representation, and the representative must be a representative of his choice, not imposed by the employer or any other person.

---

[46] The courts in South Africa have taken ILO Termination of Employment Recommendation: 119 (1963) on the requirement for a disciplinary hearing to be fair, as decisive guidelines: see Brassey, et al., *The New Labour Law*, p. 369 and the cases there cited.

[47] *Denel (Pty) Ltd v Voster* [2005] 4 BLLR 313 (SCA).

[48] *City of Windhoek v Pieterse* 2002 NR 196 (LC).

[49] *Board of Education v Rice* [1911] AC 179 at 182.

[50] *Furnell v Whangarei High Schools Board* [1973] 660 at 679.

3   The chairperson or presiding official should be impartial; that is to say, he must weigh up the evidence presented before him and make an informed and thought-out decision. There should be no grounds for suspecting that his decision was based on erroneous factors or considerations.

4   The employee must be given ample opportunity to present his case in rebuttal of the charge or charges preferred against him or her and to challenge the assertions of his or her accusers.

5   The employee must be present at the hearing; and it is essential that everything possible be done to enable him to understand the proceedings.

6   There should be a right of appeal, and this should be explained to the employee.[51]

SPCA of Namibia v Terblanche supra also approved the proposition that one of the basic requirements of a fair proceeding is that the employee should be informed of the complaint, and given the chance to answer the charge.[52] In *Kamanya & others v Kuiseb Fish Products Ltd* supra, the Labour Court held that it is a requirement of procedural fairness that the employer who conducts a disciplinary hearing should keep a proper record of the proceedings. This is important because in the absence of a record of the proceedings, or at least notes taken, at the so-called disciplinary hearing or inquiry, the court may be inclined to accept the employee's testimony that he was not given the opportunity to present his case in rebuttal of the charge preferred against him and to challenge the assertions of his accusers by putting questions to them.

In the end, the test is whether the hearings were fair when the proceedings are judged in their broader perspective.[53] In short, there are three requirements of natural justice that have to be complied with during proceedings of a disciplinary hearing: The chargee should know the nature of the accusation against him; he should be given an opportunity to state his case; and the tribunal should act fairly, without bias and in good faith.[54]

It is now time to examine the question whether the *audi alteram partem* rule of natural justice, i.e. the right to be heard, entails the right to an oral hearing in all instances. The landmark English case of *Local Government Board v Arlidge*,[55] the ground-breaking Indian

---

[51] *Food & Allied Workers Union and others v Amalgamated Beverages Industries Ltd* (1994) 15 *ILJ* 630 (IC) at 651A-D.

[52] The facts of *SPCA of Namibia v Terblanche* are set out briefly in para. 10.2.2.1 below.

[53] *Food and Allied Workers Union v Amalgamated Beverages Industries Ltd* supra.

[54] *Anglo American Farms t/a Boschendal Restaurant v Komjwayo* (1992) 13 *ILJ* 573 (LAC). See also chapter 11, para. 11.3.1 below, where the rules are also mentioned.

[55] *Local Government Board v Arlidge* [1915] A C 78 (HL).

case of *A K Gopalan v State*,[56] and the South African case of *Heatherdale Farms (Pty) Ltd v Deputy Minister of Agriculture*,[57] settled the law that the right to be heard does not necessarily entail the right to an oral hearing in all instances. In *Local Government Board v Arlidge*, the respondent contended that since an oral hearing had not been held by the Board to determine his appeal, the principle of natural justice had been breached. The House of Lords rejected this argument and held that the Board was not bound to hear the respondent orally, provided it gave him the opportunity to present his case, which the Board did because the respondent had made a written representation. Baxter explains the principle in this way:

> The vast majority of administrative decisions which comply with natural justice are probably reached after personal, oral representations by the affected party. But the courts incline against requiring oral proceedings and personal presence as a necessary aspect of natural justice, unless the statute provides otherwise. In many cases written submissions would be a perfectly adequate means of conveying one's views, with affidavits and replying affidavits becoming appropriate in cases of greater complexity and formality. It has been pointed out that oral hearings would be quite impractical in some cases. This is especially true with decisions for the whole country.[58]

The High Court has followed the principle expressed by the authorities and Baxter.[59] On this point, Strydom, CJ stated in *Chairperson of the Immigration Selection Board v Frank and another*:

> In the absence of any prescription by the Act, the appellant is at liberty to determine its own procedure, provided of course that it is fair and does not defeat the purpose of the Act (Baxter (*op cit* at 545)). Consequently the Board need not in each instance give an applicant an oral hearing, but may give an applicant an opportunity to deal with the matter in writing.[60]

---

[56] *A K Gopalan v State* AIR 1950 SC 27.

[57] *Heatherdale Farms (Pty) Ltd v Deputy Minister of Agriculture* 1980 (3) SA 476 (T).

[58] Baxter, *Administrative Law*, p. 552.

[59] For example, *Chairperson of Immigration Selection Board v Frank and another* 2001 NR 107 (SC); *Leonard Simasiku v Ministry of Justice* Case No.: LCA 29/2002 (unreported).

[60] *Chairperson of Immigration Selection Board v Frank* (SC) supra at 174H.

152   Labour Law in Namibia

Thus, to insist, for instance, that the *audi alteram partem* rule of natural justice means that in all instances the right to be heard implies the right to an oral hearing, is to allow this efficacious and fundamental principle to 'degenerate into hard and fast rule'.

In *Leonard Simasiku v Ministry of Justice*,[61] one of the grounds of appeal canvassed by the appellant, who was employed as a magistrate, was that he was not given an opportunity to tell his side of the story before the Public Service Commission and the respondent took the decision to discharge him from the Public Service. The Labour Court found that pursuant to s. 26 of the Public Service Act 1995, the Permanent Secretary gave the appellant staff member a copy of the record of proceedings of the disciplinary committee. The record also contained statements and supporting documents relied on by the appellant in mitigation of the punishment recommended by the disciplinary committee. Rejecting the appellant's contention in his ground of appeal, the Labour Court affirmed the principle that written submissions are perfectly adequate where oral hearings would be impracticable, e.g. in this case where the Prime Minister is expected to make decisions for the whole of the Public Service.[62] The Court relied for support on the passage in Baxter, *Administrative Law*,[63] quoted above in the case of *Leonard Simasiku v Ministry of Justice*.[64]

Nevertheless, there is also authority for the proposition that in a disciplinary matter 'physical presence of the affected party *at all stages* is desirable [my italics]'.[65] This is an important qualification to the general principle that the right to be heard does not in all instances imply the right to oral hearing. *Leonard Simasiku v Ministry of Justice* supra is a disciplinary matter, and yet the physical presence of the applicant *at all stages* was denied him. The Court found that since he made written submissions 'in mitigation', the *audi alteram partem* rule of natural justice was satisfied. However, it is submitted that the written submissions by the appellant were not in mitigation of the punishment of dismissal, but the disciplinary committee's recommendation that he 'be removed from the bench and that he be transferred to a different directorate in the Ministry of Justice'.[66] Indeed, the Court found that:

> the Permanent Secretary [Justice] accepted the recommendation [of the disciplinary committee] and also made such a recommendation to the Public Service Commission. However, the Commission decided to dismiss Appellant

---

61   *Leonard Simasiku v Ministry of Justice* supra.

62   Ibid. at p 5.

63   Baxter, *Administrative Law*, p. 552.

64   *Leonard Simasiku v Ministry of Justice* supra, pp. 2-3.

65   Baxter, *Administrative Law*, p. 552 fn. 105, and the case there cited. Indeed, this footnote is actually inserted to the passage relied on by the Court, but the Court's attention was not drawn to it by either counsel.

66   *Leonard Simasiku v Ministry of Justice* supra at p. 1.

and made such recommendation to the Prime Minister who approved the recommendation by the Commission and dismissed the Appellant.[67]

It is clear from the above passage that no opportunity was given to the applicant to make submissions – written or by his physical presence – in respect of the decision to dismiss him from the Public Service. The Public Service Commission denied him his right to natural justice when making its recommendation to the Prime Minister; a recommendation that was totally different from the one made by the disciplinary committee and accepted by the Permanent Secretary: Justice and in respect of which the applicant had made written representations in accordance with s. 26(14) of the Public Service Act 1995. Moreover, the Prime Minister, too, denied the appellant his right to natural justice when he decided to accept the recommendation of the Public Service Commission to dismiss the appellant, a recommendation that, as has been stated above, was totally different from the one made by the disciplinary committee.

Granted, the principle that 'oral proceedings and personal presence' are not always a necessary aspect of natural justice; but it is also correct to state that in disciplinary matters, particularly where dismissal is contemplated, oral proceedings and the personal presence of the affected party is not only desirable but also necessary.[68] In *Leonard Simasiku v Ministry of Justice*, although this crucial qualification to the principle appears in the footnote to the passage relied on by the Labour Court, as has been said above, the Court's attention was not drawn to the qualification by either counsel to the footnote to Baxter's proposition.[69] On the facts of this case and from the analysis made above and relying on the authorities, it is submitted that natural justice was not respected *at all stages* of the disciplinary process. The appellant was not given an oral hearing by the Prime Minister; neither did the Prime Minister give the appellant an opportunity to make a written representation to him when he decided to reject the recommendation of the disciplinary committee and the Permanent Secretary and accept the Public Service Commission's recommendation. The latter recommendation, which, as mentioned above, recommended dismissal, was at variance with the former.

Another equally important question concerning procedural fairness is whether a subsequent internal appeal can remedy a defect in the procedure of an initial disciplinary hearing or inquiry. The Labour Court answered the question in *Kamanya and others v Kuiseb Fish Products Ltd,*[70] in relation to the repealed Labour Act 1992, but there is no good

---

[67] Ibid.

[68] Baxter, *Administrative Law,* p. 552 fn. 105.

[69] *Leonard Simasiku v Ministry of Justice* supra.

[70] *Kamanya and others v Kuiseb Fish Products Ltd* 1996 NR 123 (LC).

reason why those conclusions cannot apply equally to the Labour Act 2007. In that case the Labour Court stated:

> our Labour Act requires a fair hearing and a fair reason for dismissal, whether or not this was done in the course of a single hearing or in the course of more than one hearing and irrespective of whether one of those hearings is labelled an 'appeal' hearing. Surely much depends on the nature of the so-called appeal – e.g. whether it is a full rehearing or whether it is an appeal analogous to the usual appeal on record, which we find in South African criminal and civil procedure.
>
> Furthermore, the appeal in terms of an employer's code, can have in mind the setting aside of the proceedings of the initial disciplinary enquiry, precisely because such initial enquiry was unfair or even a nullity.
>
> Surely in such a case, the appeal itself corrects the procedure and/or result of the initial mutual enquiry, considers the issues *de novo* and comes to its own decision either on the existing evidence, or on new evidence adduced at the rehearing.[71]

Thus, whether a subsequent internal appeal is capable of curing a defect in the procedure of an initial disciplinary hearing depends on the nature of the procedure of the subsequent appeal. In this connection, a court may adjudge the defect to be cured if, for instance, there was a full rehearing, during which the issues were considered anew and the appeal body came to its own decision either on the existing evidence or on additional or new evidence adduced at the appeal hearing.[72]

An equally important question that arises is this: what is the effect of a breach of procedural fairness or natural justice? Both the House of Lords in *Anisminic Ltd v Foreign Compensation Commission,*[73] and *Hoffman-La Roche v Secretary of State for Trade and Industry*[74] and the Privy Council in *Attorney-General v Ryan,*[75] reaffirmed that an order made contrary to natural justice is outside jurisdiction and void. In *Swaziland Federation of Trade Unions v The President of the Industrial Court and the Minister for Enterprise and Employment*, the Court of Appeal of Swaziland was categorical in declaring: 'A clear

---

71 *Kamanya and others v Kuiseb Fish* supra at 125I-6B. The Labour Court also accepted the *Kamanya* approach in *Van Den Heever v Imcor Zinc (Pty) Ltd* NLLP (2004) (4) 257 NLC.

72 *Kamanya and others v Kuiseb Fish* supra.

73 *Anisminic Ltd v Foreign Compensation Commission* [1969] 2 AC 147.

74 *Hoffman-La Roche v Secretary of State for Trade and Industry* [1975] AC 295.

75 *Attorney-General v Ryan* [1980] AC 143.

violation of natural justice will, *in every instance*, violate an order and no room for judicial discretion as to whether to set it aside can, in such instances, exist [my italics].'[76] From the weighty authorities, there is no doubt that a decision taken in breach of natural justice is invalid and of no effect. In this connection, it is worth noting that procedural fairness is 'not a matter of secondary importance'.[77] Consequently, if an employer dismisses his employee without following a fair procedure, the dismissal is unfair and therefore invalid within the meaning of s. 33(1) of the Labour Act 2007.

That the *audi alteram partem* rule is the touchstone of fair hearing and, therefore, cannot be compromised is put beyond doubt. In *Oscar Z. Mamba v Swaziland Development & Savings Bank*,[78] counsel for the respondent (employer) argued that, even if no fair procedure was adopted to determine the guilt of the employee, that should not go against the employer. The reason, counsel contended, was that the applicant had made himself guilty of such gross dereliction of duty that the result in the end would have been the same. Rejecting counsel's argument, Parker, J stated:

> Such an argument begs the question. The hearing was called precisely to determine whether applicant was guilty of the so-called charges. This is not a case where 'for instance the Manager saw one worker stab another in the back on the shop floor'.
>
> In this connection, we have adopted the dictum from *Administrator, Transvaal v Zenzile* 1991 (1) SA 21 (A) at 37C-D, quoted in *Rycroft and Jordaan*, because of its sheer persuasiveness –
>
> 'It is trite…that the fact that an errant employee may have little or nothing to urge in his own defence is a factor alien to the inquiry whether he is entitled to prior hearing. Wade *Administrative Law* 6 ed. puts the matter thus at 533-4: "Procedural objections are often raised by unmeritorious parties. Judges may then be tempted to refuse relief on the ground that a fair hearing could have made no difference to the result. But in principle it is vital that the procedure and the merits should be kept strictly apart, since otherwise the merits may be prejudged unfairly."'[79]

---

[76] *Swaziland Federation of Trade Unions v President of the Industrial Court and Minister of Enterprise and Employment* Swaziland CA 11/91 at p. 17 (unreported).

[77] Collins Parker, 'The "Administrative Justice" provision of the Constitution of the Republic of Namibia: a constitutional protection of judicial review and tribunal adjudication under administrative law', *CILSA* XXIV (1991), p. 96.

[78] *Oscar Z. Mamba v Swaziland Development & Savings Bank* Swaziland IC 81/96 (unreported).

[79] Ibid. at pp. 8-9.

Finally, the following point is worth mentioning: the Labour Act 2007 appears to 'subject' the requirement of 'a fair procedure' under s. 33(1)(b)(ii) to 'any code of good practice' that may be issued by the Minister responsible for Labour in terms of s. 137 of the Act. It is submitted that this stipulation adds little or nothing of significance to the requirement of the age-old and well-tested principle of procedural fairness, whose roots lie deep in the common law principle of natural justice, which is at the core of section 32(1)(b)(ii) of the Act. It is unlikely that the Minister would issue any 'code' that seeks to do away with or whittle down the contents of the common law rules of natural justice that have been the solid and immovable bedrock of due process and fairness for over 500 years in democratic and open societies.[80] Given that the statutory stipulation does not put a different colour on the requirements of natural justice and fairness as the basis of procedural fairness in terms of s. 33 of the Labour Act 2007, it is submitted that any 'code of good practice' issued by the Minister responsible for Labour must aim at fortifying and broadening the procedural requirements of fairness and natural justice (see para. 8.1.3, above, and chapter 11, para. 11.3.2 below, where the principles are also discussed).

8.1.4   Substantive and Procedural Requirements Peremptory

The question arises whether dismissal is unfair where only the requirement for procedural fairness has not been met. It is apparent from the clear and unambiguous words of s. 33(1) and (b) of the Labour Act 2007, that even where an employer succeeds in proving that he had a valid and fair reason for dismissing an employee, the dismissal is unfair if he fails to prove that a fair procedure was followed by him.

As pointed out previously in this chapter, in para. 8.1.3 above, the requirement of procedural fairness cannot be consigned to a secondary position. According to s. 33 of the Labour Act 2007, the dual requirements of substantive fairness and procedural fairness constitute the unbreakable unity of the test for fair dismissal. 'It is trite law', stated Karuaihe, J in *Rossam v Kraatz Welding Engineering (Pty) Ltd*, 'that in order to establish whether the dismissal of the complainant was in accordance with the law this Court has to be satisfied that such dismissal was *both* procedurally and substantively fair [my italics].'[81] The result is that the fulfilment of one requirement does not satisfy the test; it does not matter whether the requirement that was not fulfilled was procedural fairness.

It follows that where the employer has failed to prove on a balance of probabilities that the dismissal of the employee is substantively and procedurally fair, such dismissal is unfair and, therefore, unlawful and invalid within the meaning of s. 33(1) of the Labour Act 2007.

---

80   Collins Parker, *Human Rights Law,* Leicestershire, Upfront Publishing, 2002, pp. 68, 104.

81   *Rossam v Kraatz Welding Engineering (Pty) Ltd* 1998 NR 90 at 92.

The employer must satisfy 'both' requirements: satisfaction of one is not enough. If he fails one limb of the test – no matter which one – he has failed the test of fairness. Whether where the employer satisfies the test of substantive but not procedural fairness, the remedy of reinstatement, for instance, should not be granted has little to do with the fundamental issue of whether the dismissal was unfair in the first place. That consideration only relates to one of the factors that a court may take into account when considering whether reinstatement (see chapter 10, para. 10.2.2.1), for instance, is an appropriate remedy in the circumstances of the case, or when the court or tribunal is considering the quantum of compensation (see chapter 6, para. 6.3.3 above, and chapter 10, para. 10.2.2.1 below).

8.2. Inevitably Unfair Dismissal: Certain Grounds

In terms of s. 33(2) and (3) of the Labour Act 2007, it is inevitably unfair, without proof of unfairness, for an employer to dismiss an employee if the dismissal is based on any of the grounds mentioned in the two subsections. All that the affected employee has to show is that the reason for his dismissal comes under one or more of the grounds set out in s. 33(2) and (3) of the Act.

First, in terms of s. 33(2) of the Labour Act, the law considers a dismissal unfair without proof of the unfairness so long as the employer dismisses the employee because the employee has done one of the following.

1   Disclosed information which he is entitled or required to disclose to another person, e.g. by an order of a court or an arbitrator in any proceedings before the court or the arbitrator.

2   Failed or refused to do anything that his employer has no lawful authority to permit or require him to do, e.g. when the employer requests him to work during any period that he is on his annual leave in terms of the Act.

3   Exercised any right granted by the Act or in terms of a contract of employment or a collective agreement, e.g. for taking leave lawfully due to him under the contract of employment, a collective agreement or the Act.

4   He is or was a member of a trade union.

5   He has taken part in the formation of a trade union.

6   He has participated in the lawful activities of a trade union outside working hours or within working hours with the consent of his employer or in circumstances mentioned in s. 67(4) of the Act, which deals with workplace union representatives.

Second, in terms of s. 33(3) of the Labour Act, the law considers a dismissal unfair, without proof of unfairness, if it can be shown that the employee was dismissed because of the employee's sex, race, colour, ethnic origin, religion, creed or social or economic status, political opinion or marital status. The anti-discrimination grounds are also found in Swaziland's Industrial Relations Act,[82] and in South Africa's Labour Relations Act,[83] and they are some of the grounds that make a dismissal an 'automatically unfair dismissal'. A glaring difference between the Namibian provisions, on the one hand, and the Swaziland and South African provisions, on the other, is this: unlike the Swaziland and South African provisions, the Namibian provisions do not expressly use the term, 'automatically unfair dismissal' anywhere: it is not used in either the text or the title of s. 33 of the Labour Act 2007.

8.3 Redundancy or Collective Termination

'Retrenchment' has usually been used to describe the termination of a contract of employment of employees by their employer because, for instance, the employees have become too many, and so their services are no longer needed, e.g. due to economic downturn of the employer's business.[84] 'Redundancy' has usually been used to describe a termination because of the superfluity of some or all employees due to restructuring of the employer's business or the introduction of new technology, which makes their services no longer suited to the needs of the business.

No purpose will be served by entering into the semantic discussion of the two terms: 'retrenchment' and 'redundancy' may be used complementarily, and not in contradistinction to each other, i.e. 'redundancy' may be used to explain the cause of 'retrenchment'. Consequently, retrenchment or dismissal arising from redundancy, or redundancy for short, should be understood to mean the termination of services of employees by their employer because they have become redundant, that is, superfluous in relation to the needs of the

---

[82]   Act No. 1 of 2000

[83]   Act No. 66 of 1995.

[84]   *Hlongwane and another v Plastix (Pty) Ltd* (1990) 11 *ILJ* 171 (IC).

employer's business.[85] Indeed, s. 34 of Labour Act 2007 provides for dismissal arising from redundancy or collective termination.

Generally, an employer's reasons for terminating the contract of employment of his employees due to redundancy are usually shrouded in secrecy.[86] Nevertheless, even with dismissal due to redundancy or arising from collective termination, a court or tribunal must be satisfied that there are valid and fair reasons for it, not reasons based on extraneous motives, such as the desire to victimize an employee or employees, or irrelevant grounds, such as anti-union reprisal.[87] Thus, as far as redundancy is concerned, what is at issue is not simply whether the employer's decision to dismiss is correct. 'What is at stake here,' the South African Labour Appeal Court stated, 'is not the correctness or otherwise of the decision to retrench, but the fairness thereof.'[88] An employee may become redundant for a number of reasons, notably, because of decline in the economic fortunes of the employer's business, organizational changes in the business, and automation due to technological advancement in the type of business carried on by the employer.

The opening words of s. 50(1) of the repealed Labour Act 1992 recognized a number of ways in which redundancy could arise: (i) re-organization of the employer's business; (ii) transfer of the business to a new owner; (iii) discontinuance of the business; or (iv) contraction of the business. These are all due to economic or technological reasons. Similar words are found in the Labour Act 2007. The opening words of s. 34(1) says it all in this regard; it reads, 'If the reason for an intended dismissal is the reduction of the workforce arising from the reorganization or transfer of the business or the discontinuance or reduction of the business for economic or technological reasons...'

In *Goagoseb v Arechenab Fishing & Development Co (Pty) Ltd*,[89] the Labour Court interpreted and applied s. 50(1) of the repealed Labour Act 1992, which, as we saw above, is almost identical to the words in the *chapeau* of s. 34(3) of the Labour Act 2007. The Labour Court held that for a termination to qualify as a dismissal in terms of s. 50 of the repealed Labour Act 1992, one or more of the grounds mentioned in s. 50(1) must exist. Therefore, where the service of an employee is terminated on the grounds of his advanced age, physical disability or unsatisfactory performance, the dismissal did not amount to a dismissal due to redundancy.[90] There is no valid reason why the principle enunciated in

---

85   *Consolidated Frame Cotton Corp v President, Industrial Court* (1986) 7 *ILJ* 489 (A).

86   *MacLoughlan v Alexander Paterson Ltd* [1968] 1 TR 251; *BCAWU and another v Murray & Roberts Buildings (Tvl) (Pty) Ltd* (1991 12 *ILJ* 112 (LAC).

87   *SA Allied Workers Union and others v Contract Installations (Pty) Ltd & others* (1988) 9 *ILJ* 112 (IC).

88   *NUMSA v Atlantis Diesel Engines (Pty Ltd* (1993) 14 *ILJ* 642 (LAC) at 648D.

89   *Goagoseb v Arechenab Fishing & Development Co (Pty) Ltd* NLLP 2004 (4) 10 NLC.

90   See C. Drake, *Labour Law,* 2nd edn, London, Sweet & Maxwell, 1973, para. 309.

Goagoseb v Arechenab supra should not apply equally to the interpretation and application of the substantially identical provisions of s. 34(1) of the Labour Act 2007.

An important question that arose concerning the interpretation and application of s. 50 of the repealed Labour Act 1992 was whether s. 50 applied where the service of only one employee was terminated. In *Goagoseb v Arechenab* supra, Strydom, JP (as he then was) accepted without deciding that s. 50 applied where the services of only one employee was terminated. The marginal note, i.e. 'Collective termination of contracts of employment', was therefore misleading, according to the Court. In any case, the question is now academic as far as s. 34 of the Labour Act 2007 is concerned. It is clear from the words of the opening lines of s. (34)(1) that a single employee can be dismissed due to redundancy under the Labour Act 2007; *a fortiori*, the very title of s. 34, 'Dismissal arising from collective termination or redundancy', clearly shows the intention of the Parliament that s. 34 applies to the dismissal of a single employee or a group of employees for any of the grounds set out in that section.

Section 34(1) of the Labour Act 2007 sets out procedures that must be followed in the event of dismissal arising from collective termination or redundancy, i.e. where 'the reason for an intended dismissal is the reduction of the workforce arising from the reorganization or transfer of the business or the discontinuance or reduction of the business for economic or technological reasons'.

When in *Vesagie v Namibia Development Corporation*,[91] the High Court was interpreting and applying the word 'intend' in s. 50(1) of the repealed Labour Act 1992, which is used in a similar context as in s. 34(1) of the Labour Act 2007, the High Court held that 'the meaning in the context of s. 50(1) is "[T]o have in mind as a fixed purpose". (See *The Shorter Oxford English Dictionary on Historical Principles* 3rd edn)'[92] It is submitted that the word 'intend' and its derivations in s. 34(1) of the Labour Act 2007 and s. 50(1) of the repealed Labour Act 1992, have the same meaning, if regard is had to the context in which the word is used in the two statutes.

Therefore, according to the scheme of s. 34(1), an employer may make a decision, without the involvement of an exclusive bargaining agent, workplace representatives and the affected employees, to reduce his workforce for any of the reasons set out in the opening words of s. 34(1) of the Labour Act 2007. The employer is then required by s. 34(1)(a) to inform the Labour Commissioner and any trade union that the employer has recognized as the exclusive bargaining agent in respect of the affected employees, at least four weeks before the 'intended dismissals' about: (i) the intended dismissals; (ii) the reasons for the reduction in the workforce; (iii) the number and categories of employees that will be

---

91   *Vesagie v Namibia Development Corporation* 1999 NR 219 (HC).

92   *The Shorter Oxford English Dictionary on Historical Principles* 3rd edn, Oxford, Clarendon Press, 1973, at 225H.

affected; and (iv) the date of the dismissals. If there is no registered trade union recognized as the exclusive bargaining agent in respect of the employees, the employer must give the information to the workplace representative elected in terms of s. 67 of the Act and to the affected employees at least four weeks before the intended dismissals take place. According to s. 34(2), the four-week time limit under s. 34(1)(a) and (b) may be abridged if it is not practicable to give the information within the time limit.

The purpose of informing the Labour Commissioner, the exclusive bargaining agent, workplace representative, and the affected employees, about the intended dismissals is not to require the employer to have prior consultation with them before a decision to terminate owing to redundancy is taken.

Although unlike the opening words of s. 34(1) of the Labour Act 2007, the opening words of s. 50(1) of the repealed Labour Act 1992 state positively that 'Any employer who intends to terminate...' this does not alter the position because in both statutes only an employer can, in the circumstances, intend to dismiss and also advance reasons for the dismissal as required by the Act. Consequently, the interpretation and application of 'intend' in *Vesagie v Namibia Development Corporation* supra should apply equally to the interpretation and application of 'intend' in s. 34(1) of the Labour Act 2007.

In *Vesagie v Namibia Development Corporation* supra, the High Court held that, in terms of s. 50(1)(b) of the repealed Labour Act, it is a foregone conclusion that the terminations due to redundancy would take place but the opportunity was to be given to the exclusive bargaining agent, the workplace representatives or the employees concerned 'to negotiate the conditions on which, and the circumstances under which, the terminations ought to take place with a view to reducing or preventing unfavourable effects'.[93] According to the High Court, this did 'not mean that the terminations themselves must be open to negotiation'.[94] For all intents and purposes, the provisions of s. 50(1)(b) of the repealed Act are not different from s. 34(1)(c) and (d) of the Labour Act 2007 on this issue. That being the case, there is no good reason why the decision in *Vesagie v Namibia Development Corporation* supra on the point should not apply equally to the interpretation and application of s. 34 of the Labour Act 2007.

Section 34(1)(c) provides that the employer must disclose all relevant information necessary to enable the trade union or workplace representatives to negotiate effectively over the intended dismissals. However, in terms of s. 34(3) of the Act, the employer is not required to disclose information that is legally privileged,[95] or information whose

---

93   *Vesagie v Namibia Development Corporation* supra at 226B.

94   Ibid.

95   See M. Milne, 'Discovery and Privilege in Arbitration Proceedings', *JCI Arb,* 60 (1994), pp. 285-8, where the principle of legal privilege is discussed with great insight.

disclosure is prohibited by law or an order of a competent court, or where the information is confidential and its disclosure would cause substantial harm to the employer. Furthermore, according to s. 34(1)(d), the employer must negotiate in good faith with the trade union or workplace representatives on: (i) alternatives to the dismissals; (ii) the criteria for selecting the employees for dismissal; (iii) ways to minimize the dismissals; (iv) the conditions on which the dismissals are to take place; and (v) how to avert the adverse effects of the dismissals. Finally, s. 34(1)(e) provides that the employer must select the employees for dismissal according to selection criteria that are either agreed or fair and objective. The approach of last-in-first-out ('LIFO') has been found to be generally fair and objective.

It is submitted that once the party with whom the employer is obliged to consult in terms of s. 34(1) has been identified, the employer is required by the Act to consult that party to the exclusion of all others. For instance, where an employer informs and consults an exclusive bargaining agent, he is not obliged by law to inform and consult separately with individual employees who are affected by the dismissals and are represented by that exclusive bargaining agent. [96]

As was the case under the repealed Labour Act 1992 (which is discussed above), in terms of the Labour Act 2007, too, an employer is not obliged by law to consult the exclusive bargaining agent, workplace representatives and the affected employees, or, indeed, the Labour Commissioner before a decision to dismiss employees due to redundancy, i.e. for any of the reasons set out in the opening words in s. 34(1), is taken. Nevertheless, the implementation of the decision must take into account the relevant provisions of s. 34 of the Act. Looking at the words in those provisions contextually, it is clear that the primary purpose of the negotiations under s. 34 is for the employer and the trade union or the workplace union representatives to make a genuine and diligent effort to find alternatives to the dismissals, i.e. to prevent the dismissals. This object is in addition to the other aims of the negotiations mentioned in s. 34(d) and (e) of the Act.

As s. 34(4) provides, if after the negotiations the parties fail to agree the matters contemplated in s. 34(1), either party is entitled, within one week after the expiration of the periods referred to in s. 34(1) or (2), to refer the matter to the Labour Commissioner, who must appoint a conciliator to assist the parties to resolve their dispute. Thus, after the employer has unilaterally taken a decision to dismiss employees for any of the reasons in s. 34(1) of the Act, the implementation of the decision is held in abeyance during the periods mentioned in s. 34(1), (4) and (5). More important, during those periods, an employer may

---

[96] See *De Laan v Van Dyck Carpet Company* [2003] 3 BLLR 257 (LC) in which *Sikhosana and others v Sasol Synthetic Fuels* (2000) 21 *ILJ* 649 (LC) was referred to by the South African Labour Court when interpreting similar provisions in South Africa's Labour Relations Act 1995 (Act No. 66 of 1995).

not dismiss employees in terms of s. 34 unless the dispute has been resolved or otherwise disposed of.

It must be borne in mind that the intervention of the Labour Commissioner in terms of s. 34 occurs only after negotiations have failed. Where no negotiations take place at all, the remedy available to an aggrieved employee is to allege an unfair dismissal and take the route provided by s. 33 of the Act. In terms of s. 33(1)(a) and (1) (b) (i), an employer is required to have a 'valid and fair reason' to carry out dismissals based on any of the reasons mentioned in s. 34(1) of the Act, and to follow the procedures set out in the s. 34. If a dismissal arising from collective termination or redundancy is not based on any of those reasons, that dismissal constitutes substantive unfairness, and if the employer fails to follow the procedures, that constitutes procedural unfairness,[97] rendering the dismissal invalid and unlawful.

The Labour Court and arbitrators have the power to enquire into the validity and fairness of any reason for a dismissal due to redundancy under s. 34 of the Labour Act in order to see whether any of the reasons set out in s. 34(1) exists, and if any of them exists, to see whether the decision to dismiss is valid and fair in terms of s. 33(1)(a) of the Act. Moreover, they have the power to determine whether the employer has followed the procedures set out in s. 34 of the Act, so as to pass the test of procedural fairness within the meaning of s. 33(1)(b)(i) of the Labour Act. A dismissal will be procedurally unfair, if for example, an employer failed or refused to disclose all relevant information necessary for a trade union or workplace union representative to engage effectively in negotiations under s. 34(1)(d) of the Act, or failed to negotiate in good faith the matters contained in that subsection. To negotiate in good faith means to negotiate genuinely not perfunctorily, and to negotiate in a spirit of give-and-take.[98]

As in the case of a dismissal due to a cause other than redundancy, in the case of a dismissal due to redundancy, too, if an aggrieved employee alleges that he has been dismissed due to redundancy, he must first show that he is an employee of the employer within the meaning of s. 1 of the Labour Act 2007, and that he has been dismissed. If the employee succeeds in proving these contentions, then it is the turn of the employer to prove two things: he must prove that the dismissal was based on one or more of the grounds mentioned in s. 34(1) of the Labour Act, and also show that he followed the procedure laid down in s. 34 of that Act.

---

[97] *Ntshanga v South African Breweries Ltd* [2003] 8 BLLR 789 (LC); *Mahlinza & others v Zulu Nyala Game Ranch (Pty) Ltd* [2004] 3 BLLR 245 (LC); *Vesagie v Namibia Development Corporation* supra. See also paras 8.1.2 and 8.1.3 above, where substantive unfairness and procedural unfairness, respectively, are discussed.

[98] *African Granite Co (Pty) Ltd v Mineworkers Union of Namibia and others* 1993 NR 9 (LC).

According to s. 189 of South Africa's Labour Relations Act 1995,[99] redundancy occurs when an employer dismisses 'one or more employee for reasons based on operational requirements'. In *General Food Industries Ltd v FAWU*,[100] the South African Labour Appeal Court interpreted s. 189 to mean that in South Africa the provision entitles an employer to dismiss employees for a reason based on its 'operational requirements' without distinguishing between a business striving to survive and a profitable business wishing to increase its profits. It must be borne in mind that the South African requirement is substantially different from the Namibian requirement under s. 34(1) of the Labour Act 2007.

In Namibia, as discussed above, an employer may reduce his workforce through dismissals if the dismissals are due to the reorganization or transfer of the business or the discontinuance or reduction of business that can be justified on economic and technological grounds: these are the valid reasons according to the Act. However, when the issue is whether they are fair, the Labour Court or the arbitrator must determine the question according to general principles of fairness or reasonableness (see para. 8.1.3, above). In this connection, if a business is profitable, in the business sense, then it is not reasonable or fair to reduce the workforce in order to increase profits. In other words, a profitable business has no 'fair' 'economic reason' to reduce its workforce. It would rather be fair for an employer, whose business is striving to survive, in the business sense, i.e. struggling to make and maintain profits, to reduce its workforce in order to turn the business around.[101] It is submitted, the decision in *General Food Industries v FAWU* cannot, therefore, apply to the interpretation and application of s. 34(1) of the Labour Act 2007.

The Labour Act introduces a novel concept that is unknown to the repealed Labour Act 1992: it is 'disguised transfer or continuance of an employer's operation', and it is designed to give added protection to employees against dismissal arising from collective termination or redundancy. According to s. 34(9) of the Labour Act 2007, the concept is defined to include any practice by which or situation in which an employer who runs or operates a business purports to have gone out of business or to have discontinued all or part of its business operation, when in fact those business operations are continued under another name or form or are carried out at another place, and the employer has not disclosed the full facts to the affected employees or their collective bargaining agent. Section 34(7) provides that if there is a disguised transfer or there is continuance of an employer's operation within the meaning of s. 34(9) of a business that employs or employed employees who are to be dismissed or were dismissed in terms of s. 34, the employees or their collective bargaining

---

99   Act No. 66 of 1995.

100   *General Food Industries Ltd v FAWU* [2004] 7 BLLR 667 (LAC).

101   In its ordinary, grammatical sense, 'economic' means, 'maintained for profit': *Concise Oxford University Dictionary* 10th edn.

agent have the right to apply to the Labour Court for appropriate relief, including an order directing the restoration of the operation, directing reinstatement of the employees, or awarding lost and future earnings.

8.4 Unfair Disciplinary Actions other than Dismissal

8.4.1 Introduction

The concept of unfair labour practice, which was unknown to the repealed Labour Act 1992,[102] is now found in Chapter 5 of the Labour Act 2007. According to s. 48 of the Labour Act 2007, a disciplinary action taken by an employer against an employee in violation of s. 33 of the Act constitutes an unfair labour practice, (the other causes of unfair labour practice under ss 49 and 50 are treated in chapter 15 below). Section 33 of the Act, which applies to dismissal of employees (see para 8.1 above), applies with necessary changes by context to disciplinary actions against employees by employers.

At common law, a disciplinary action short of dismissal is not available as a remedy to an employer. This principle is predicated on the notion that an employer is not at liberty to vary the contractual terms – implied or otherwise – without the consent of his employee, particularly if such variation is disadvantageous to the employee (see chapter 2, para. 2.2.1.5, above, where the notion is discussed). Thus a disciplinary action, other than a dismissal, which has the effect of varying a term of the contract of employment without the consent of the employee, runs counter to the well-established common law rule against unilateral variation of contractual terms (see chapter 2, para. 2.2.1.5 above). Statute law has, however, made great inroads into the common law rule inasmuch as disciplinary actions other than dismissal are allowable punitive measures against employees found guilty of offences in the employer-and-employee relationship.[103]

The courts have, indeed, ruled that generally the ultimate sanction of dismissal should be applied only where, taking into account all the circumstances of the situation, it is reasonable to do so. Otherwise, an employer ought to consider less drastic disciplinary actions such as demotion or suspension for a certain period. In *Pupkewitz & Sons (Pty) Ltd v Kankara* supra, the appellant (employer) summarily dismissed the respondent (employee) for gross negligence and prejudicial conduct in that he approved or allowed 100 bags of cement purchased on an obviously falsified invoice to be loaded onto a vehicle. There, Mtambamengwe, J stated that:

---

[102] *Kamanya and others v Kuiseb Fish* supra.

[103] See, for example, s. 26(12)(a)(i)-(iv) of the Public Service Act 1995 (Act No 13 of 1995).

the imposition of a penalty is an exercise of a discretion that should be carried out on a proper weighing of all the factors. The mitigating factors in this case are many and weighty, certainly their cumulative effect *should, if properly considered, have led to the appellant to consider an alternative penalty* [my italics].

The employer is not shown to have considered these factors in this case. It follows that I find nothing to criticise in the conclusion by the magistrate [i.e. district labour court chairperson] that the action taken by the appellant was too harsh in the circumstances of this case.[104]

Labour courts and arbitral tribunals have recognized the following disciplinary actions. The actions are set in the order of least severe to most severe.

8.4.2 Warning

8.4.2.1 Oral Warning

An employer may give an oral warning to an employee for minor offences. An oral warning is informal, and since it is unwritten, there is no formal way in which it may be given. However, it is always advisable that an oral warning is given to an employee in the presence of his immediate supervisor and the representative of the trade union of which the employee is a member, if that is practicable.

8.4.2.2 First Written Warning

The first serious warning is a formal act, i.e. a written warning. A first written warning may be given as a sequel to an oral warning or as the first warning for a serious offence. Unlike an oral warning, a written warning serves as documentary evidence of a warning. It is, therefore, necessary that the employee be made to acknowledge receipt of the written communication. The usual practice is to ask the employee to sign on a copy, which is then kept in his personnel file. In order for the written warning to have probative value, a hearing should be conducted at which the employee is given an opportunity to state his case, including producing witnesses to support his side of the story. However, an oral hearing is not always necessary, particularly if an employee admits his guilt (see para. 8.1.3, above). It is not uncommon for the employer to pile up the employee's record with a series of written warnings before a final one is issued, which is acceptable so long as due process is observed at all times.

---

104 *Pupkewtiz & Sons Ltd v Kankara* supra at 78B-C.

8.4.2.3 Final Written Warning

'Final written warning' is used to describe the last written warning prior to a disciplinary process that might result in dismissal or other severe punitive measure. Consequently, the employer needs to conduct a fair hearing before issuing such a warning. It is the last opportunity offered to a persistently errant employee to mend his ways. Doubtless, a final written warning has serious consequences for the employee. For this reason, courts have recognized the practice whereby the warning is made to last for a fixed period, e.g. six months, so that the offence that gave rise to the warning is not held against the employee indefinitely.[105] Nevertheless, Parker, J observed in *Daniel Matsebula v Swaziland Milling, a Division of Swaki Investment Corporation Limited* thus: 'The purpose of a warning is to warn and encourage an offender to mend his or her ways; it is not to give him or her the licence to continually commit offences as and when the period of a previous warning expires.'[106]

In *Workers Representative Council v Manzini Town Council* (CA) Browde, JA observed that the main purpose of warning is : 'of course, to give the employee the opportunity to mend his ways and in the same way that sufficient time should be given for him to do so. Naturally it would be unfair to dismiss him for wrong-doing or poor performance which has taken place prior to the warning having been given.'[107]

In any case, the fact that an employee has had a series of final written warnings on his record will be an aggravating factor when determining whether there is a fair reason to dismiss when he commits a serious offence that would otherwise have not attracted dismissal. In *Kausiona v Namibian Institute of Mining and Technology*,[108] the Labour Court cautions employees against taking for granted warnings that have expired. The Court noted that whether a warning that had elapsed should be disregarded depended on the circumstances. In that case, the Court observed that the fact that the warning had expired could not be completely ignored when the chairperson (of the district labour court) considered the dismissal of the appellant.

Finally, a final written warning has this effect: an employee who is given a final written warning is put on notice that any further transgression is likely to lead to dismissal.[109] The courts have recognized the principle that for the latest final written warning to count when

---

[105] *National Union of Mineworkers & another v East Rand Proprietary Mines Ltd* (1987) 8 *ILJ* 315 (IC).

[106] *Daniel Matsebula v Swaziland Milling, a Division of Swaki Investment Corporation Limited* Swaziland IC 14/97 at p. 5 (unreported).

[107] *Workers Representative Council v Manzini Town Council* Swaziland CA 3/94 (unreported) at p. 7.

[108] *Kausiona v Namibian Institute of Mining and Technology* NLLP 2004 (4) 43 NLC. The judge referred with approval to B. Perrins, *Harvey on Industrial Relations and Employment Law,* Durban, Lexis Nexis (Issue 156, June 2002), DI 995.

[109] *Model Pick 'N Pay Family Supermarkets* v *Mukosho* supra.

considering a dismissal, the employee should have committed an offence similar to that for which a final written warning was last given,[110] unless otherwise provided in the employer's code of conduct or suchlike instrument.

Such a written warning is distinguishable from a written warning that is given as an alternative to dismissal. This type of final written warning is technically a punishment in itself. Thus, in *Kamanya and others v Kuiseb Fish Products Ltd* supra, the Labour Court stated that while in its opinion the dismissal was an appropriate sanction in terms of the respondent's disciplinary code, a final warning might not have been out of place in view of the provocation.

8.4.3 Suspension

Suspension is used as an appropriate sanction where, although the employee has committed an offence that merits a dismissal, there are mitigating factors in his favour against his dismissal. This type of suspension is a punitive measure: it stands in contradistinction to a suspension that is meted to an employee pending a disciplinary hearing. An employee is entitled to a disciplinary hearing before the first type of suspension ('punitive' suspension') is meted out to him; but he is not so entitled in the case of the second type of suspension ('non-punitive suspension').[111]

8.4.4 Demotion

Demotion has the effect of varying certain provisions of the contract of employment of the employee who is demoted. The courts have accepted demotion as being less severe than dismissal, and so an employer may consider demotion as an alternative to dismissal, particularly in cases where the offence committed by the employee is not as serious as to merit dismissal. An employee who is demoted suffers a reduction in rank with attendant reduction in remuneration and the loss of certain benefits attached to his former rank. Consequently, in addition, he loses seniority in the organization compared to his former peers.[112]

---

[110] J. Grogan, *Riekert's Employment Law,* 2nd edn, Cape Town, Juta, 1993, p. 96 and the cases there cited.

[111] *Raborifi and others v Minister of Justice and Transport* 1991 (4) SA 442 (BG); *Swart and others v Minister of Education and Culture, House of Representatives and another* 1986 (3) SA 331 (C).

[112] See s. 26(12)(a)(iv) of the Public Service Act 1995.

9 INDUSTRIAL DISPUTES

9.1 WHAT IS AN INDUSTRIAL DISPUTE?

Put simply, an 'industrial dispute' is a dispute arising from the employer-and-employee relationship. The term denotes principally a disagreement between an employer (or an organization representing the employer) and an employee (or an organization representing the employee) concerning the employment contract. Doubtless, the search for ways in which industrial disputes can be minimized or solved when such disputes occur, lies at the core of the aims of labour or employment statutes, because the effective resolution or minimizing of industrial disputes is pivotal to sound labour relations and industrial harmony. Consequently, the concept of industrial dispute is at the heart of modern labour or employment law. Labour statutes of many countries provide statutory definitions of what kind of dispute the law recognizes as an industrial dispute.

According to s. 2 of Swaziland's Employment Act,[1] an 'industrial dispute' includes a grievance or a trade dispute, and it means any disagreement over such matters as:

1   the entitlement of any person or group of persons to any benefit under an existing collective agreement;

2   the existence or non-existence of a collective agreement;

3   the dismissal, employment, suspension from employment, re-employment or reinstatement of a person or group of persons;

4   the recognition or non-recognition of an organization, which wants to represent employees in the determination of their terms and conditions of employment;

5   the application or interpretation of any law relating to employment; and

6   the terms and conditions of employment of an employee or the physical conditions under which the employee may be required to work.

---

[1]   Act No. 5 of 1980.

In England, s. 218(1) of the Trade Unions and Labour Relations (Consolidated) Act[2] defines a 'trade dispute' as 'a dispute between workers and their employer which relates wholly or mainly to one or more' matters that are listed in that subsection, e.g. terms and conditions of employment, or the physical conditions in which any workers are required to work; engagement or non-engagement, or termination or suspension of employment or the duties of employment, of one or more workers; allocation of work or the duties of employment between workers or groups of workers; and discipline.

Section 1 of the Labour Act 2007 provides that 'dispute' in labour relations 'means any disagreement between an employer or an employers' organization on the one hand and an employee or a trade union on the other, which disagreement relates to a labour matter'. The definition contains similar words to those found in s. 1 of the repealed Labour Act 1992. However, the Labour Act 2007 does not specifically list the types of disputes that the law recognizes as industrial disputes as Swaziland's Employment Act does.

Apart from the general meaning of 'dispute' in s. 1 of the Labour Act, the Parliament has also set out in different provisions of the Act a restricted meaning of 'dispute' in relation to some specific sections and Parts of the Act. For example, according to s. 80 of the Labour Act, for the purposes of Part B of Chapter 7 of the Act ('Conciliation of Disputes'), 'dispute' means: (i) a dispute of interest (the term is explained in para. 9.2 below); (ii) a dispute relating to affirmative action under the Affirmative Action (Employment) Act[3] that is referred to the Labour Commissioner in terms of s. 45 of that Act; and (iii) a dispute referred for conciliation by either the Minister responsible for Labour under s. 80(1) of the Labour Act relating to disputes affecting the national interest or referred to the Labour Court in terms of s. 117(2)(a) of the Act.

It deserves mentioning that an industrial dispute may exist not only between an employer and his own employees, but it may also exist between that employer and employees who are not employed by him. In *Midland Cold Storage Ltd v Turner,*[4] a group of dockers blocked a cold storage depot outside the dockyard because they believed that the container work that was being carried out there ought to be carried out by them. It was held that an industrial dispute existed between the dockers and the management of the cold storage depot although the dockers were not employees of the cold storage depot. Thus, *Midland Cold Storage Ltd v Turner* supra rejects the idea that for an industrial dispute to exist between an employer and an employee, that employee ought to be his own employee. By the same reasoning, an employer might have a dispute with a union, e.g. over recognition as the exclusive

---

2   Trade Unions and Labour Relations (Consolidated) Act 1992 (c. 52).

3   Act No. 29 of 1998.

4   *Midland Cold Storage Ltd v Turner* [1972] ICR 230.

bargaining agent, even though the employer has no dispute with any of his employees who are members of that union.[5]

At times, the courts have to determine whether what appears to be or is called an industrial dispute is really an industrial dispute in law.[6] For instance, if employees demand that labour legislation be removed or repealed, and the Government refuses to do so; this cannot by any stretch of the imagination constitute an industrial dispute. This must surely be a political demand. It is also not an industrial dispute if the Government refuses to give in to trade union demands for political and constitutional changes in the country.[7]

The facts in *Gouriet v Union of Post Office Workers*[8] also do not reveal an industrial dispute, albeit it involves a labour matter. In *Gouriet v Union of Post Office Workers* the General Secretary of the Union of Post Office Workers of the United Kingdom had threatened that its members were going to stop all transmission of mail from the United Kingdom to apartheid South Africa. An injunction was successfully sued for to restrain the union from going ahead with their action. According to the House of Lords, the intended action was a political action for a political end. Thus, political disputes, even if entered into by employees or their trade unions, are not by that fact alone industrial disputes in law.

From the authorities, it may be stated that for a 'disagreement' that relates to a 'labour matter' to qualify as a dispute within the meaning of s. 1 of the Labour Act 2007, the disagreement must concern the employer-and-employee relationship and any matter reasonably connected with, or incidental to, such relationship. It follows that it must also be the kind of disagreement that is capable of being resolved by an employee, a trade union, an employer or an employers' organization, or that lies within their power to resolve through the application of the Labour Act or any other law on employment or labour relations.

9.2 THE TWO TYPES OF INDUSTRIAL DISPUTE

Industrial disputes fall into two main categories, namely, 'dispute (or conflict) of interest' and 'dispute (or conflict) of right'. Disputes of interest arises where there is disagreement with regard to what ought to be the terms and conditions of employment in a contract of employment or a collective agreement. They are therefore disputes as to new and 'wished-for' terms. Consequently, they are not justiciable: their resolution is left to the

---

5   *Stratford (JT) & Sons v Lindley* [1965] AC 307.

6   See *Conway v Wade* [1909] AC 606; *Handley v Thornton* (1951) 1 WLR 321; *Minister of Enterprise and Employment v Swaziland Federation of Trade Unions* Swaziland IC 163/97 (unreported).

7   See *Minister of Enterprise and Employment v Swaziland Federation of Trade Unions* supra.

8   *Gouriet v Union of Post Office Workers* [1977] 3 All ER 70.

parties to exercise their economic and industrial power. Thus, where employees want new employment rights to be created, they should bargain for them; they cannot refer a dispute in this regard to a court for determination.[9] A dispute of right, on the other hand, concerns the interpretation and application of terms and conditions of employment in a contract of employment, collective agreement or statute: the right relates to benefits or conditions of service to which an employee may be entitled by virtue of legislation or an employment contract or collective agreement.[10] Indeed, by their very nature, it is suitable to have such disputes resolved by the courts.[11]

The Labour Act 2007, indirectly and by implication, recognizes the differentiation between 'dispute of right' and 'dispute of interest', albeit the Act defines only 'dispute of interest' in s 1. According to the Act, a 'dispute of interest'

> means any disagreement between an employer or an employers' organization on the one hand and an employee or a trade union on the other hand, which disagreement relates to a labour matter, but does not include a dispute that this Act or any other Act requires to be resolved by –
>
> (a)   adjudication in the Labour Court or other court of law; or
>
> (b)   arbitration.

In interpreting 'dispute of interest' and 'dispute of right' under the repealed Labour Act 1992, Strydom, JP (as he then was) explained the distinction between disputes of interests and disputes of right in *Smit v Standard Bank Namibia Ltd.*[12] He stated in that case that had the employer changed conditions of employment of the employee

> unilaterally or intimated his intention to do so unilaterally, the dispute between the parties would have fallen fair and square within the definition of 'dispute of right'... But, when employees negotiate for higher wages or better conditions of employment the dispute in such a case is not one relating to rights but is one relating to interests...[13]

---

9   See *Protekon (Pty) Ltd v CCMA and others* [2005] 7 BLLR 703 (LC), which accepted the principle enunciated in *Hospersa and another v Northern Cape Provincial Administration* (2002) 21 *ILJ* 1066 (LAC).

10   *Hospersa and another v Northern Cape Provincial Administration* (2000) 21 *ILJ* 1066 (LAC).

11   C.D. Drake, *Labour Law,* 2nd edn, London, Sweet & Maxwell, 1973, para. 549.

12   *Smit v Standard Bank Namibia Ltd* 1994 NR 366 (LCC).

13   Ibid. at 371E.

The then Judge-President found support for his conclusion in a passage from Wallis's *Labour and Employment Law*.[14]

By implication, upon the authority of *Smit v Standard Bank*, in terms of s. 1 of the Labour Act 2007, a dispute that is excluded from the definition of 'dispute of interest' is an industrial dispute that requires to be resolved by adjudication in a court or by arbitration: such dispute is a dispute of right.

The distinction between dispute of interest and dispute of right is based primarily on the distinction between two processes, namely 'the process of applying and interpreting existing agreements, as against the process of formulating new ones'.[15] The main purpose of the conceptualization of the two types of industrial dispute is to encourage or ensure that employers and employees seek to resolve their disagreement concerning disputes of right peacefully through a tribunal or such adjudicative forum rather than resort to industrial action.[16] The peaceful settlement of industrial disputes is discussed in chapters 10, 11 and 12, below, and the settlement of industrial disputes by industrial action in chapter 13, below.

---

[14] M.J.D. Wallis, *Labour and Employment Law,* Durban, Butterworths, 1992, cited in *Smit v Standard Bank* supra at 372E.

[15] Drake *Labour Law,* para. 549.

[16] Ibid.

10 CONCILIATION, MEDIATION AND ARBITRATION

10.1 CONCILIATION AND MEDIATION

10.1.1 Introduction

Labour statutes in some Commonwealth countries encourage parties to industrial disputes to settle their disputes voluntarily and amicably without the intervention of courts of law.[1] The statutes, therefore, do provide for procedures aimed at the rapid and equitable resolution of disputes outside the courts through alternative dispute resolution mechanisms, i.e. conciliation, mediation and arbitration.

Mediation has been described in broad terms as a procedure whereby a facilitator acceptable to the disputing parties assists the parties to find an agreed solution to their dispute.[2] According to Butler and Finsen,[3] there are two types of mediation procedure, namely, mediation properly so called and conciliation. Some labour experts who are interested in alternative dispute resolution mechanisms are of the view that 'conciliation' involves the intervention of a third party attempting to bring together disputing parties and assisting them to reconcile their differences, but 'mediation' goes further than that. It allows a third party to propose ways in which and terms on which the dispute might be resolved. Others reject the differentiation, arguing that 'conciliation' and 'mediation' are generally interchangeable.

In the face of such lack of consensus, it has been posited that while a distinction appears to be convenient, it is also accurate to argue that usage shows that the two terms are broadly identical.[4] For instance, where the facilitator is not expected to recommend a solution if he fails to assist the parties to agree a solution, he is referred to as a mediator in labour disputes

---

[1] For example, South Africa's Labour Relations Act 1995 (Act No. 66 of 1995); United Kingdom's Employment Rights Act 1996 (c 18) and Employment Rights (Dispute Resolution) Act 1998 (c 8); and Swaziland's Industrial Relations Act 2000 (Act No. 1 of 2000).

[2] See D. Butler & E. Finsen, *Arbitration in South Africa: Law and Practice,* Kenwyn, Juta,1993, p. 10.

[3] Ibid.

[4] B.A. Garner, *A Dictionary of Modern Legal Usage,* 2nd edn, Oxford, Oxford University Press, 1995, p. 554.

176   Labour Law in Namibia

in South Africa. However, if he gives an opinion that does not bind the parties at the end of his facilitation, he is referred to as a conciliator in labour disputes in South Africa.[5]

It serves no practical purpose to enter upon the debate. It has been said that both conciliation and mediation have three common fundamental characteristics: the existence of an agreement under which a facilitator is brought in to assist the parties in reaching an agreement through negotiation; the facilitator is not authorized to impose a solution on the parties; and the process is so flexible that, for instance, the parties can keep it alive until a solution is found or until one of them breaks away from the negotiations.[6] In short, in practice, mediation and conciliation are broadly synonymous: therefore, there is little or no advantage to be gained in pursuing a watertight distinction between the two terms under Namibian labour law. Section 1 of the Labour Act 2007 defines 'conciliation' as including 'mediation' (see para. 10.1.2, below). Consequently, for our purposes, the term 'conciliation' will be used to describe the activities that are common to both conciliation and mediation. Conciliation is therefore used in this book to describe attempts by a third party to facilitate a process whereby two disputing parties are brought together with the aim of assisting them to resolve their differences. The facilitator may or may not put forward proposals by which, and terms on which, in his opinion, the parties may resolve the dispute between them. In any case, the power of a third party, who intervenes between parties to a dispute for the purpose of reconciling them, is determined by agreement between the parties or by statute. Consequently, irrespective of the third party's designation in the agreement, what matters is that both the facilitator and the parties to the dispute must have a clear understanding of the facilitator's functions and powers in terms of their particular agreement.[7]

The Labour Act 2007 introduces a scheme of extensive alternative dispute resolution mechanisms in the form of conciliation, mediation and arbitration. The rest of the present chapter is devoted to a discussion of the mechanisms under the Labour Act.

10.1.2 Statutory Provisions

Section 1 of the Labour Act 2007 defines 'conciliation' to include:

    (a)   mediating the dispute;

    (b)   conducting a fact-finding exercise; and

    (c)   making an advisory award if –

---

[5]   Butler and Finsen, *Arbitration in South Africa,* pp. 10-11.

[6]   L. Street, 'The Language of ADR – its utility in resolving international commercial disputes: the role of the mediator', *Arbitration,* (1992) 58 2(S), p. 18.

[7]   Butler and Finsen, *Arbitration in South Africa,* p. 11.

(i)   it will enhance the prospects of settlement; or

(ii)   the parties to the dispute agree.

Section 82 of the Act provides for the resolution of disputes through conciliation. In terms of s. 82(3) the Labour Commissioner has the discretion to designate a conciliator, from among individuals appointed by the Minister responsible for Labour in terms of s. 82(1) or (2), to attempt to resolve through conciliation a dispute that is referred to him in terms of the Act.

Section 82(1) empowers the Minister, subject to the laws governing the public service, to appoint conciliators to perform the duties and functions under the Act or to exercise the powers vested by the Labour Act on conciliators. Furthermore, in terms of s. 82(2), the Minister may, subject to such terms and conditions as the Minister may determine, also appoint, on a part-time basis, conciliators who may or may not be staff members of the public service in terms of the Public Service Act. A conciliator who is not in full-time employment of the State may be paid fees and allowances at a rate determined by the Minister with the consent of the Minister responsible for Finance. Full-time employees of the State include individuals employed on a full-time basis in the public service, parastatal organizations and local authorities.

According to s. 82(1) a party to a dispute may refer the dispute in the prescribed form to the Labour Commissioner or a labour office. It is a requirement of the Act that a copy of the referral be served on the other parties to the dispute. If he is satisfied that all the parties have received a copy of the referral and, further, that the parties have taken all reasonable steps to resolve or settle their dispute on their own, the Labour Commissioner must (i) refer the dispute to a conciliator to attempt to resolve the dispute through conciliation, (ii) determine the place, date and time of the first conciliation meeting, and (iii) inform the parties accordingly about the appointment of a conciliator and the place, date and time of the first conciliation meeting.

Subject to s. 74(1)(c) and (3) of the Labour Act, s. 82(10) of the Act provides that the conciliator must attempt to resolve the dispute through conciliation within thirty days from the date on which the Labour Commissioner received the referral of the dispute or a longer period agreed in writing by the parties. It is important to point out that the consent of the parties must be in writing: it is not enough that the agreement to extend the thirty-day period is secured orally.

The conciliator must, subject to applicable rules made in terms of the Labour Act, determine the procedures by which conciliation is to be conducted by him. For instance, a conciliator may determine the frequency and number of meetings that may be held within the time limit of thirty days for conciliation to be completed.

Section 82(12) provides that a party to a dispute may either appear in person during conciliation proceedings, or be represented by only (i) a member, an office-bearer or an official of that party's registered trade union or registered employer's organization; (ii) a co-employee, if the party is an employee; (iii) a director, a member or an employee of a juristic person, if the party is a juristic person.

A party is not entitled to be represented by a legal practitioner during conciliation except under the circumstances mentioned in s. 82(13) of the Labour Act. It is submitted that this statutory prohibition is in accord with the common law because at common law a party is not entitled as of right to legal representation before tribunals other than courts of law. [8]

Section 82(13) provides that a conciliator has discretion to permit a legal practitioner to represent a party to a dispute in conciliation proceedings so long as the parties agree or at the request of a party to the dispute, and the conciliator is satisfied that the dispute is so complex that it is appropriate for a party to be represented by a legal practitioner and further that the other party will not be prejudiced.[9] The exclusion of legal practitioners from conciliation is not offensive of one's right to legal representation under the rubric of the right to fair trial under Art. 12(e) of the Namibian Constitution. The reason is that conciliation proceedings do not constitute a trial within the meaning of Art. 12(e): *a fortiori,* the proceedings are not criminal or civil proceedings; neither is conciliation a court or a tribunal.

In addition, a conciliator has the discretion to also permit any individual to represent a party to a dispute during conciliation proceedings if the parties agree or, at the request of a party to the dispute, the conciliator, subject to s. 82(14), is satisfied that that individual will facilitate the effective resolution of the dispute, that he will facilitate the attainment of the objects of the Act, that the individual meets prescribed requirements, and the other party will not be prejudiced. According to s. 82(14) of the Labour Act, in deciding whether to permit an individual to represent a party, a conciliator must take into account applicable guidelines issued by the Minister responsible for Labour in terms of s. 137 of the Act.

A conciliator may, in terms of s. 82(18), subpoena any person to attend a conciliation hearing if in his opinion that person's attendance will assist the resolution of the dispute. A conciliator may also administer an oath or accept an affirmation from any individual called to give evidence, and he may put questions to a witness about any matter relevant to the dispute. Section 82(19) provides that a person who, without lawful excuse, fails

---

[8] *Dabner v South African Railways and Harbours* 1920 AD 583; *Ronald Patrick Kurtz v Nampost Namibia Ltd and another* 2009 (2) NR 696 (LC).

[9] See *Ronald Patrick Kurtz v Nampost* at 702H-706A,where the Labour Court explained the meaning of complex.

to obey a subpoena issued by the conciliator, or refuses to answer a question put to him by the conciliator commits an offence and is liable on conviction to a fine not exceeding N$10,000.00 or to imprisonment for a period not exceeding two years or to both.

According to s. 83 of the Act, certain consequences flow from a party's failure to attend a conciliation meeting. Section 83(1) provides that if a dispute that is referred to conciliation concerns a strike or a lockout in terms of s. 74(1)(a), then s. 74(3) applies to any failure to attend a conciliation meeting. This aspect is discussed under strikes and lockout in chapter 13, paras 13.2 and 13.3, respectively. However, according to s. 83(2), if a dispute concerns any matter other than a strike or a lockout, then the conciliator may dismiss the matter if the party who referred the dispute fails to attend the conciliation meeting. If, on the other hand, it is the other party that fails to attend the conciliation meeting, then the conciliator may determine the dispute in that other party's absence.

Section 83(3) of the Act vests in the Labour Commissioner a discretionary power to reverse a conciliator's decision to dismiss a matter in the absence of a party who referred the dispute to the Labour Commissioner. The Labour Commissioner may exercise his discretion in this regard only if in an application made to him in the prescribed manner, the party who failed to attend the conciliation meeting satisfies him that there are good grounds for his failure to attend the conciliation meeting.

A conciliator should make all efforts to resolve the dispute through any legitimate means, including recourse to any guidelines or code of good practice issued by the Minister responsible for Labour under s. 137 of the Act because the conciliator remains seized with the dispute until it is settled. Nevertheless, according to s. 82(15)(7) of the Act and subject to s. 83 (which deals with consequences of failure to attend conciliation meetings, as we saw above), where, in the opinion of the conciliator, despite his attempts there is no prospect of settlement of the dispute through conciliation at that stage, or where the time limit, including any extension by consent of the parties, in terms of s. 82(10) has expired, the conciliator must issue a certificate indicating that the dispute is unresolved. This is necessary to avoid a situation where conciliation becomes protracted and long drawn out, even though the indications are that there is no prospect of success. When issuing a certificate of unresolved dispute, the conciliator must, if the parties agree, refer the unresolved dispute for arbitration in terms of Part C of Chapter 8 of the Act.

It is important to note that conciliation proceedings before a conciliator under the Labour Act are without prejudice. Consequently, anything that is said or that comes to light during conciliation proceedings, is private and confidential and may, therefore, not be disclosed in subsequent arbitral or judicial proceedings.[10]

---

10   *Hofmeyer v Network Healthcare Holdings (Pty) Limited* [2004] 3 BLLR 232 (LC).

180 Labour Law in Namibia

10.2 ARBITRATION

10.2.1 Introduction

Apart from using conciliation or mediation to resolve a dispute, the parties to the dispute may agree that their dispute be settled by arbitration. Arbitration is a process by which the dispute is determined by a select tribunal instead of a court of law.[11] Arbitration is, therefore, a procedure by which the disputants refer their dispute to a third person, an arbitrator, who as a general rule makes a final decision after he has received and considered evidence and submissions from the disputants.[12] The dispute may be referred to a single arbitrator or to more than one arbitrator sitting together.

While the conciliation process may at its conclusion leave the dispute still unresolved, the aim of an arbitral process is to reach finality, and the award that the arbitrator makes generally binds the parties. An award is the arbitral tribunal's decision on the merits of the dispute, and the meaning of 'finality' is that there is generally no appeal to the courts, even where the award appears to be incorrect.[13] This is the case unless the agreement to refer the dispute to arbitration, or the Act under which the dispute is referred to arbitration, provides otherwise. In other words, the parties do not, barring statutory provisions to the contrary, have a general right to appeal to the court against the arbitrator's award.[14] Indeed, the finality of the arbitrator's award is one of the salient and commendable features of arbitration. Nevertheless, as we shall see in chapter 11 below, in terms of s. 89 of the Labour Act 2007, the Labour Court has the power to determine appeals from an arbitral tribunal award and to review and set aside an arbitral award based on a number of statutory grounds.

The following are, therefore, the main characteristics of arbitration:

1 It is a non-judicial process for solving disputes regarding existing rights of the parties.

2 The parties must, barring a statutory prescription, agree to refer their dispute to arbitration.

3 The parties themselves appoint an arbitrator, or he may be appointed by someone they agree should do the appointment where they have failed to appoint one; or the arbitrator may be appointed in terms of a statute.

---

[11] *Dutch Reform Church v Town Council of Cape Town* (1898) 15 SC 14.

[12] Butler and Finsen, *Arbitration in South Africa*, p. 1.

[13] See D. Butler, 'The need for modern arbitration legislation in Namibia: the available options', Paper presented at the Standard Bank/PAMAN Arbitration Seminar, Windhoek, Namibia (1-2 April 2004), p. 3.

[14] *Clark v African Guarantee and Indemnity Co Ltd* 1915 CPD 68 at 77.

Conciliation, Mediation and Arbitration 181

4   The arbitrator must impartially receive and consider evidence and submissions of the parties and fairly arrive at his decision.

5   The parties agree that the arbitrator's award is final and binding on them and therefore unappealable or such stipulation may be provided by statute.

6   Arbitral proceedings are held in private, and are largely confidential.[15]

These features underscore the difference between arbitration and court proceedings, and the fact that an arbitrator is not a judge or other judicial officer. In addition, compared to judicial proceedings, the main object of arbitral proceedings is the promotion of a cost-effective and a quick way of resolving disputes. For instance, s. 1 of the English Arbitration Act[16] states that arbitration under that Act is founded on the following principles:

1   The object of arbitration is to obtain the fair resolution of disputes by an impartial tribunal without unnecessary delay or expense.

2   The parties should be free to agree how their disputes are resolved, subject only to safeguards as are necessary in the public interest, i.e. the principle of party autonomy.[17]

3   In matters governed by the Act, the court should not intervene except as provided by the Act.

As we saw in the preceding paragraph, a party is not entitled as of right to legal representation during conciliation. However, parties to arbitration are usually legally represented. In conciliation, the conciliator is obliged to attempt to obtain the agreement of the parties to a solution of the dispute that he proposes. However, it is not required of the arbitrator to obtain the agreement of the parties to his stated opinion or award. Seminal to this feature is that while a conciliator proposes a solution, an arbitrator makes an award, or gives an opinion, if the arbitration agreement or statute under which the arbitration takes place provides for the giving of such opinion. Finally, as the term suggests, the burden of a conciliator is generally to enter upon the conciliation with the view to reconciling the parties. But the arbitrator performs a quasi-judicial function, for he is a 'judge' of the evidence presented to him. Although arbitration is generally embarked upon by consent

---

15   Butler and Finsen, *Arbitration in South Africa,* pp. 213-14.

16   Arbitration Act 1996 (c.23).

17   See Butler, 'The need for modern arbitration', p. 2.

of the disputing parties, sometimes a statute compels parties to arbitrate.[18] Compulsory arbitration is also provided for under Part C of Chapter 8 of the Labour Act 2007 and is discussed in para. 10.2.2.1, below.

The following features also distinguish arbitration from conciliation and mediation. An arbitrator is expected to receive evidence and submissions from the parties, which he must consider in order to arrive at a fair decision. An arbitrator, unlike a conciliator or mediator, does not guide the parties to resolve their dispute through negotiation. Unlike a conciliator or mediator, an arbitrator must arrive at a final and binding decision after a judicial evaluation of the evidence and submissions presented to him. Conciliation and mediation are not formal legal proceedings, but arbitral proceedings are legal proceedings governed by the Arbitration Act 1965 or any other statute. Second, the conciliator determines the procedure for conciliation after consultation with the parties. The procedure in arbitral proceedings is in accordance with accepted rules under the Arbitration Act 1965 and supplemented by rules of procedure laid down by some association, and selected by the parties in terms of their arbitration agreement or in accordance with a statute.[19]

10.2.2 Statutory Provisions

The Labour Act 2007 expressly creates two schemes of arbitration: one is provided for under Part C of Chapter 8 of the Act ('Part C arbitration'); the other is private arbitration, which is provided for under Part D of Chapter 8 of the Act ('Part D arbitration'). The basic differences between Part C arbitration and Part D arbitration under the Labour Act are these:

1   a party to a dispute can be dragged to Part C arbitration, while Part D arbitration is resorted to by agreement of the parties to the dispute; and

2   the Labour Act expressly states that Part C arbitrations are tribunals as envisaged in Art. 12(1)(a) of the Namibian Constitution, for the purpose of resolving disputes under the Act.

10.2.2.1 Part C Arbitration

Disputes that are amenable to Part C arbitration are, according to s. 84 of the Labour Act 2007, the following:

---

18   For example, the Expropriation Act 1975 (Act No. 73 of 1975).

19   See, for example, Association of Arbitrators (Southern Africa), *The Rules for the Conduct of Arbitration,* 4th edn, Benmore, Association of Arbitrators (Southern Africa), August 2000.

1 a complaint relating to a breach of a contract of employment or a collective agreement;

2 a dispute referred to the Labour Commissioner in terms of s. 46 of the Affirmative Action (Employment) Act 1998;[20]

3 a dispute referred to arbitration by a conciliator when issuing a certificate of unresolved dispute in terms of s. 82(16) of the Labour Act; and

4 any dispute that is required to be referred to arbitration in terms of the Labour Act.

The fourth category of disputes, i.e. in (4) above, is varied. Some of them are disputes relating to basic conditions of employment that are mentioned in Chapter 3 of the Labour Act, such as remuneration, hours of work, leave, accommodation, and termination of employment. Some of the disputes in the fourth category are also mentioned in Chapter 2 of the Labour Act, concerning prohibition and restriction of child labour, prohibition of forced labour, prohibition of discrimination in employment and freedom of association, and in Chapter 5 of the Act, concerning unfair labour practices (see chapter 8, para. 8.4, above).

As we saw earlier (in para. 10.2.2, above), Part C arbitration is compulsory because any party to a dispute may, unless a relevant collective agreement provides for referral of disputes to a Part D arbitration after certain statutory requirements have been complied with, refer the dispute to arbitration whether or not the other party has agreed that the dispute be resolved by arbitration (see para. 10.2.2.1, above). Part C arbitration tribunals operate under the auspices of the Labour Commissioner, and they have jurisdiction to hear and determine any dispute or any other matter arising from the interpretation and application of the Labour Act. Furthermore, a Part C arbitration tribunal may make any order that is within its power to make in terms of the Act.

The Minister responsible for Labour may, subject to the laws governing the public service, appoint arbitrators to perform the duties and functions of arbitrators under the Act or exercise any powers given to arbitrators by the Act. The Minister has discretion to appoint arbitrators, on such terms and conditions as he may determine, from individuals who may or may not be staff members in the public service under the Public Service Act. He may, on good cause shown, withdraw the appointment of any arbitrator appointed under the Act.

The Labour Commissioner also has discretion to designate from the list of arbitrators appointed by the Minister, one or more arbitrators to constitute an arbitration tribunal to hear and determine disputes. It is worth pointing out that, irrespective of any provision to the contrary in the Public Service Act or any other law, a staff member appointed as arbitrator

---

20 Act No. 29 of 1998. This is how this Act will be referred to in the remainder of this book, without footnoting.

must be independent and impartial in the performance of his duties as arbitrator under the Labour Act.

Arbitral proceedings

Section 86(1) of the Labour Act provides that a party to a dispute that is amenable to Part C arbitration, unless an applicable collective agreement provides for referral of disputes to Part C arbitration, may refer the dispute in writing to the Labour Commissioner or a labour office. If the dispute concerns a dismissal, a party may refer the dispute to the Labour Commissioner or a labour office within six months after the date of the dismissal, or within one year after the dispute arose, if the dispute concerns any matter other than a dismissal. If the Labour Commissioner is satisfied that a copy of the referral has duly been served on every party to the dispute, he must refer the dispute to an arbitrator to attempt to resolve the dispute through arbitration. Thereafter, the Labour Commissioner must determine the place, date and time of the arbitration hearing and, accordingly advise the parties to the dispute about the appointment of the arbitrator and the place, date and time of the arbitral hearing.

Section 86(5) of the Labour Act provides that the arbitrator should not commence arbitration unless the dispute remains unresolved after he has first attempted and failed to resolve the dispute through conciliation or unless conciliation by the conciliator in respect of the same dispute has failed. The arbitrator may, subject to any applicable rules that have been made in terms if the Labour Act, conduct the arbitration in any manner he considers appropriate for the determination of the dispute speedily and fairly. The Labour Act enjoins an arbitrator to consider the merits of a case with few legal formalities. In short, as much as is practicable, the proceedings must be free from formalities known to the courts of law, so long as the arbitrator complies with the rules of natural justice by being fair to both parties.[21]

Like a conciliator, an arbitrator, too, is empowered by s. 86(8) to subpoena any person to attend an arbitral hearing if, in his opinion, that person's attendance will assist in the resolution of the dispute. The arbitrator may also administer an oath to, or accept an affirmation from, any individual called to give evidence, and he may put questions to the witness about any matter relevant to the dispute. Section 86(9) provides that a person who, without lawful excuse, fails to obey a subpoena or who refuses to answer a question put to him by an arbitrator commits an offence and is liable on conviction to a fine not exceeding N$10,000.00 or to imprisonment for a period not exceeding two years or to both.

---

[21] *Bremer Valkan Schiffbau und Maschinenfabrik v South India Shipping Corporation Ltd* [1982] AC 909 ; *Carlisle Place Investments Ltd v Wimpey Construction (UK) Ltd* 15 BLR 109 (QB 1980); *Anshel v Horwitz* 1916 WLD 65; *Meyer v Law Society, Transvaal* 1978 (2) SA 209 (discussed in chapter 8, para. 8.1.3 above). The rules of natural justice are discussed in chapter 8, para. 8.13 above, and chapter 11, para. 11.3.2 below.

Depending on the discretion of an arbitrator or the agreement of the parties as to the way in which a hearing would proceed, a party may give evidence, call witnesses, cross-examine witnesses called by the other party, and make concluding submissions. A remarkable feature of the Labour Act in this regard is that according to s. 86(11), by consent of the parties, the arbitrator may suspend arbitral proceedings and attempt once more to resolve the dispute by conciliation.

Just as is the case in conciliation, in arbitration, too, a party may appear in person, or be represented by only an office-bearer or official of that party's registered trade union or registered employer's organization, or by a co-employee, if the party is an employee, or if the party is a juristic person, an employee of that juristic person. As a general rule, a legal practitioner is not allowed to appear for a party in arbitral proceedings, but may be permitted to do so in circumstances referred to in s. 86(13) of the Act. According to s. 86 (13)(b) of the Act, an arbitrator may permit representation by a legal practitioner, if the parties agree or at the request of a party to the dispute, the arbitrator is satisfied that, due to the complexity of the issues involved, legal representation is appropriate and further that the other party will not be prejudiced.

While arbitration is not a civil (or criminal) trial, at times the issues raised are so complex and difficult that it would assist the arbitrator greatly to come to a fair and reasonable decision if the parties are legally represented. In short, an arbitrator may permit legal representation if it is conducive to the attainment of fairness between the parties, particularly in difficult and complex cases. [22]

Besides, s. 86(13)(b) gives an arbitrator the discretion to permit any individual to represent a party to a dispute during arbitral proceedings if the parties agree or, at the request of a party to the dispute, the arbitrator, subject to s. 86(14), is satisfied that that individual will facilitate the effective resolution of the dispute, that he will facilitate the attainment of the objects of the Act and further that the other party will not be prejudiced. According to s. 86(14) of the Labour Act, in deciding whether to permit an individual to represent a party, an arbitrator must take into account applicable guidelines issued by the Minister responsible for Labour in terms of s. 137 of the Act.

Arbitral awards

In terms of s. 86(15) of the Labour Act 2007, in settling disputes by arbitration, an arbitrator may grant any appropriate award, including the following: (i) an interdict, (ii) a declaratory order, (iii) an order directing the performance of any act that will remedy a wrong, (iv) an

---

22 See *Hamata and another v Chairperson, Peninsular Technikon Internal Disciplinary Committee, and others* 2002 (5) SA 449 (SCA), 2003 24 *ILJ* 1531 (SCA); *Ronald Kurtz v Nampost* supra.

186   Labour Law in Namibia

order of reinstatement of an employee, (v) compensation and (vi) subject to s. 86(16) an order of costs. According to s. 86(18) of the Labour Act, an arbitrator must, within thirty days after the conclusion of an arbitration, grant an award under his signature with concise reasons. Moreover, in making an award, an arbitrator must take into account any code of good practice and guidelines that has been issued in terms of s. 137 of the Labour Act. It remains to deal with awards that an arbitrator is permitted to make under the Labour Act.

Interdict

A full discussion of the law and practice of interdicts is not possible here, and since interdict is not peculiar to labour law, readers are referred to standard works on the subject.[23] Suffice it to mention that an arbitrator has the power to grant an interdict under s. 86(15) (a) of the Labour Act 2007; and by necessary implication, it includes the power to grant interim interdicts and urgent interdicts. An interdict may be interim or final, prohibitory or mandatory, or it may be sought on urgent basis.[24]

In labour matters, a prohibitory interdict may be sought requiring an employee, a trade union, an employer, an employers' organization, or indeed any person exercising power under the Labour Act, e.g. the Labour Commissioner or the Minister responsible for Labour, to abstain from committing a threatened wrong or from continuing to commit an existing wrong under the Labour Act. A mandatory interdict, on the other hand, maybe sought to compel such persons or bodies to perform a duty under the Act or to remedy the effects of an unlawful action already taken purportedly under powers conferred by the Act.[25]

In labour law, it is well settled that the fact that an employee who has been dismissed will suffer financial loss or other hardship if the hearing challenging the dismissal is delayed, is not on that ground alone entitled to have the matter heard as a matter of urgency.[26] In *Nasionale Sorghum Bierbrouery (Edms) Bpk v John NO and others*,[27] the court held that as to the question of whether the requirement of urgency had been fulfilled, the loss of income and medical aid benefits are inherent in any dismissal, whether fair or not, and that there is authority for the view that urgency cannot be founded upon the financial needs of employees. One of the authorities referred to with approval is *Food & Allied Workers*

---

23   An authoritative monograph on the subject is C.B. Prest, *The Law and Practice of Interdicts*, Kenwyn, Juta, 1996. See also H.J. Erasmus, *Superior Court Practice,* Cape Town, Juta, 1994, E8; L de V. van Winsen et al., *Herbstein and van Winsen: The Civil Practice of the Supreme Court of South Africa,* 4th edn, Kenwyn, Juta, 1997.

24   Erasmus *Superior Court Practice* E8-2 and the cases cited. Urgent interdict as a form of urgent relief is mentioned in chapter 11, para. 11.3.4 below.

25   L. Baxter, *Administrative Law,* Cape Town, Juta, 1984, p. 690. Mandatory interdict is known as mandamus where the act to be performed must be carried out not by a private person but by a public body or official.

26   *Aroma Inn (Pty) Ltd v Hypermarket (Pty) Ltd & Another* 1981 (4) SA 108 (C).

27   *Nasionale Sorghum Bierbrouery (Edms) Bpk v John NO and others* (1990) *ILJ* 971 (T).

Union v National Co-operative Dairies Ltd (2),[28] where the applicants (employees) had been dismissed for going on strike. They applied for interim relief, and based the urgency of the application on, among other things, the fact that they would lose income and would have to vacate accommodation supplied by the company. The Industrial Court found that the loss of income is a normal consequence of every dismissal and could therefore not be regarded as an exceptional circumstance to warrant urgent interim relief. The view expressed in *Nasionale Bierbrouery* has been followed by *BHT Water Treatment (Pty) Ltd v Maritz NO & others*.[29]

In *Ludick v Samca Tiles (Pty) Ltd*,[30] the applicant applied on an urgent basis seeking to be reinstated immediately by the respondent on the same conditions he enjoyed before his dismissal. Rejecting the application, Khumalo, J stated: 'Applicant's averment that he was in dire financial circumstances and, if he was not reinstated immediately, an action for his sequestration would follow cannot be a ground for urgency.'[31] The applicant (employee) in *Phineas Vilakati v J D Group (Pty) Ltd*[32] made similar averments. Rejecting the application to treat the matter as one of urgency, Banda, JP had this to say:

> We agree with the Respondent (employer) that the reasons given to justify treating this matter as urgent do not differ from the normal reasons set out by persons who have brought applications of unfair dismissal for determination by the Court. If we were to order that this matter be treated as urgent on the grounds now advanced, then every case now pending before the Court would qualify to be treated as urgent.[33]

The Industrial Court was also prepared to reject a similar application in *Swaziland Agriculture and Plantation Workers Union v United Plantations (Swaziland) Limited*.[34] There, the main argument of counsel for the applicants was that it was not simply a matter of the applicants (employees) coming to the Industrial Court to aver that they had suffered financial loss as a result of their dismissal; it was that their dismissal had been the result of a flagrant breach by the respondent of the Recognition Agreement (between the employees'

---

28 *Food & Allied Workers Union v National Co-operative Dairies Ltd (2)* (1989) 10 *ILJ* 490 (IC).

29 *BHT Water Treatment (Pty) Ltd v Maritz NO & others* (1992) 13 *ILJ* 143 (T).

30 *Ludick v Samca Tiles (Pty) Ltd* 1993 (2) SA 197 (B).

31 Ibid. at 199I.

32 *Phineas Vilakati v J D Group (Pty) Ltd* Swaziland IC 41/97 (unreported).

33 Ibid. at p 2.

34 *Swaziland Agricultural and Plantation Workers Union v United Plantations (Swaziland) Ltd* Swaziland IC 79/98 (unreported).

trade union and the respondent (employer)) and the Disciplinary Code applicable to the employees. Rejecting counsel's argument, Parker, J stated: 'The breach by the respondent of the Recognition Agreement and the Disciplinary Code does not put a different colour on this matter. In the experience of the Court, a good number of disputes for determination arise out of alleged breach by employers of recognition agreements, disciplinary codes or suchlike agreements or arrangements.'[35] A similar observation was made by the Labour Court in *Edwin Beukes and others v National Housing Enterprise*.[36] There, the Labour Court held that the fact that an employee who alleges that he has been retrenched or dismissed unfairly was suffering or would suffer financial, or consequential, hardship because he would be unable to meet his financial obligations if his application were not heard on an urgent basis, does not constitute urgency.

Declaratory order

Section 86 (15)(c) of the Labour Act 2007 empowers an arbitrator to make a declaratory order. It need hardly be said that the requirements for the grant of a declaratory order by an arbitrator and the Labour Court are the same; and they are discussed in chapter 11, para. 11.3.3, below, and so will not be discussed here.

Reinstatement

In terms of s. 86(15)(d) of the Labour Act an arbitrator may order reinstatement (see also chapter 6, para. 6.2.4, above). Arbitral proceedings under the Act are not judicial proceedings, however, like a judge, the arbitrator must exercise his discretion judicially, i.e. fairly and reasonably. After all he would be taking decisions affecting the rights and legally protected interests of individuals. Therefore, when considering an application for reinstatement, the arbitrator must take into account the requirements and considerations that the courts have developed over the years. The Labour Appeal Court observed in *Ubombo Ranches Ltd v President of the Industrial Court and another* that the power to force an employer to reinstate his employee is already a tremendous inroad into the common law principle that employment contracts cannot *normally* be specifically enforced. That being the case, the discretionary power to order reinstatement must be exercised judiciously, even if the exerciser of the discretion is an arbitrator and not a court of law.[37]

---

35 Ibid. at p 3.

36 *Edwin Beukes and others v National Housing Enterprise* Case No.: LC 30/2006 (unreported).

37 *Ubombo Ranches Ltd v President of the Industrial Court and another* 1982-1986 SLR 1 at 9. See also *Pupkewitz Holdings (Pty) Ltd v Petrus Mutanuka and others* LCA/2007 (unreported)

The decision in *SPCA of Namibia v Terblanche*[38] is apposite in this regard. There the appellant (employer), an animal welfare society, which cares for animals (particularly dogs and cats that have no homes), dismissed the respondent (employee) for staying away from work without reason and without a doctor's certificate or other proof. Moreover, when the appellant's veterinarian ordered animals to be put to death by euthanasia, the respondent questioned the decision. At other times, she would obstruct implementation of the decision by removing some of the animals before the arrival of the veterinarian. In addition to such obstructive behaviour, there were complaints that the employee was ill tempered and rude to the public, and she also used obscene language in the presence of clients. As a result, it was contended, some members of the public had kept their distance from the society. The Labour Court accepted the evidence that the employee absented herself from work without permission and for no good reason, and that she interfered with the decisions of the veterinarian. In the result, the Labour Court sitting as an appellate court found that the appellant had a valid and fair reason for dismissing the employee; but since the appellant failed to conduct a fair hearing, the Labour Court found that the process was flawed.

The district labour court (the court of first instance under the repealed Labour Act 1992) had ordered the reinstatement of the dismissed employee after holding that the employee's dismissal was procedurally unfair. At the Labour Court one of the grounds of appeal was that even if the employee was unfairly dismissed, the order that she be reinstated was bad in law because considering the respondent's conduct, it was clear the employer-and-employee relationship had broken down irretrievably.

The Labour Court found that the continued presence of the employee at the employer's premises could result in chaos. It also found that most of the members of the executive committee had been avoiding the appellant's premises because the employee either cold-shouldered them or did not speak to them. That, in the Labour Court's view, showed that it would be difficult for the appellant to resume working with the respondent. From these considerations Gibson, J concluded: 'In my finding this is clearly a most fitting case in which the Court [i.e. the district labour court] could have exercised its discretion to decline to reinstate the respondent in her former position. The working relationships which were shown to have been irretrievably broken down make it essential to terminate the working arrangement with the respondent.'[39]

---

[38]   *SPCA of Namibia v Terblanche* 1996 NR 398.

[39]   Ibid. at 405I-406A.

The Labour Court upheld the decision of the district labour court that the respondent was unfairly dismissed; but in view of the conclusions it had reached, the Court set aside the district labour court's order of reinstatement of the respondent. As the English Court of Appeal in *Chappel & others v The Times Newspaper Ltd & others* stated, 'If one party has no faith in the honesty or integrity or loyalty of the other, to force him to serve or employ that other one is a plain recipe for disaster.'[40]

In the judicial exercise of its or his discretion to reinstate or not to reinstate, a court or an arbitrator must take into account all the relevant circumstances surrounding the case. The following are important factors:

1   the nature of the duty of the employee that was breached;

2   the nature of the misconduct or other offence;

3   how far the breach or misconduct has caused bad blood between the employer and the employee;

4   the likelihood of the employee committing a similar breach or misconduct again, if he was reinstated; or

5   whether because of the length of time that has elapsed between the date of dismissal and judgment of the court or award of the arbitrator, 'it will be unrealistic...to treat the contract [of employment] between the parties as still being in force.'[41]

In *Shiimi v Windhoek Schlachterei (Pty) Ltd,*[42] the Labour Court found that the complainant had been dismissed unfairly. He was dismissed in February 1997 and the Court handed down its decision in February 2000. The Court rejected the complainant's claim for reinstatement. The reasons behind the Court's rejection of the claim are instructive. The evidence was that the appellant drove the vehicle that conveyed carcasses of animals that were part of the respondent's stock in its butchery business. According to the Labour Court, it was unrealistic and completely divorced from the exigencies of commerce to contemplate that someone else had not filled such an important post in the respondent's business. The Court, therefore, held that to dismiss the 'newly' appointed driver (or 'meat-cutter' as the case may be) in order to accommodate the appellant, however worthy the appellant's case might have been, would constitute a grave injustice, and that in any event the evidence

---

40   *Chappel & others v The Times Newspaper Ltd & others* [1995] 2 All ER 233 at 244.

41   *Workers Representative Council v Manzini City Council* Swaziland CA 3/94 at p. 15. (Court of Appeal) (unreported).

42   *Shiimi v Windhoek Schlachterei (Pty) Ltd* NLLP 2002 (2) 244 NLC.

indicated that the relationship between the parties before the appellant's dismissal had seriously deteriorated and therefore re-employment would not have been advisable.

In *Herbert A. Ndlovu v The Chairman, Sigangeni Community Clinic*,[43] the Industrial Court refused to order the reinstatement of the applicant for the following reasons: (i) the applicant employee's advanced age (he was 78 years old); (ii) the long length of time that had elapsed since the employee was dismissed;[44] and more important, (iii) lack of trust between the employer and employee. The Labour Court found that the employer no longer trusted the applicant (who had been employed as a security guard at the respondent's premises (a community health clinic)) because of the applicant's uncooperative attitude and abusive behaviour when the respondent was investigating a burglary that had occurred at the clinic at a time when the applicant was the guard on duty.

The question arises whether an order of reinstatement operates retrospectively, that is to say, does 'reinstatement' have an inherent retrospectivity in its effect? In *Engelbrecht v Transnamib Holdings Ltd*,[45] one of the issues that the Labour Court was called upon to determine was the interpretation of the word 'reinstatement' as used in s. 46(a)(ii) of the repealed Labour Act 1992. The question was whether 'reinstatement' in that section meant reinstatement from the date of dismissal. The Labour Court accepted that from case law of other jurisdictions,[46] the true construction of 'reinstatement' meant putting the employee back in the same position as that in which he had been before he was dismissed, i.e. reinstatement in the employment context in general means no more than putting a person again in his/ her previous job. However, according to the Court, as far as s. 46(1)(a)(ii) of the repealed Labour Act 1992 was concerned, 'reinstatement' 'means reinstatement retrospectively to the date of dismissal or suspension', otherwise, the Labour Court reasoned, the distinction between 're-employment' and 'reinstatement' provided in s. 46 of the repealed Labour Act would have been blurred, something which the Legislature could not have intended. The Supreme Court rejected the Labour Court's interpretation of 'reinstatement' when that case came up on appeal in *Transnamib Holdings Ltd v Engelbrecht*.[47]

The Supreme Court accepted the contention by the appellant's counsel that the word 'reinstatement' refers to putting the dismissed employee back into his or former position at work, and nothing more, and that the Court has the further discretion to award back pay to the reinstated employee to a date as far back as the date of dismissal. The Supreme Court

---

43   *Herbert A. Ndlovu v The Chairman, Sigangeni Community Clinic* Swaziland IC 41/96 (unreported).

44   See also *Shiimi v Windhoek Schlachterei* supra, where the Labour Court observed that reinstatement becomes more and more unreasonable with the lapse of time.

45   *Engelbrecht v Transnamib Holdings Ltd* 2003 NR 40 (LC).

46   The Court cited the Zimbabwean case of *Chegetu Municipality v Manyora* 1997 1 SA 662 (ZSC) and the English case of *Powell Duffryn Ltd v Rhodes* (1946) 1 All ER 666.

47   *Transnamib Holdings Ltd v Engelbrecht* 2005 NR 372 (SC).

observed that 'there is no logical reason why both "reinstatement" and "re-employment" cannot run from the same date'.[48] In order to clarify the point, the Supreme Court explained the essential difference between 'reinstatement' and 're-employment' in this way: 'The essential difference between the two concepts is not the time from which it will run, but that "reinstatement" will relate to the identical job, whereas "re-employment" relates to a similar job, merely comparable to what the employee had prior to the dismissal.'[49] The Supreme Court observed further 'that the mere use of the words "in the position which he or she had or would have been had he or she not been so dismissed" does not necessarily mean that the reinstatement in that "position" runs from the date of dismissal.'[50]

In any case, the Labour Act 2007 does not use the word 're-employment' in any of its provisions. Section 86(15) of the Act provides that an arbitrator may make any appropriate arbitration award '(d) including an order of reinstatement of an employee'. It is submitted that the word 'reinstatement' in s. 86(15)(d) of the Labour Act 2007 ought to bear its ordinary, grammatical meaning in the employment context. McNally, JA expounded the general or ordinary meaning of 'reinstatement' in the employment context with commendable insight thus:

> I conclude therefore that 'reinstatement' in the employment context means no more than putting a person again into his previous job. You cannot put him back into his job yesterday or last year. You can only do it with immediate effect or from some future date. You can, however, remedy the effect of previous injustice by awarding backpay and/or compensation. But mere reinstatement does not necessarily imply that backpay and/or compensation automatically follows.[51]

Doubtless, the Supreme Court's interpretation of 'reinstatement' is materially identical to the Zimbabwean Supreme Court's interpretation. Upon the strength of these high authorities, it is submitted that the term 'reinstatement' in the Labour Act 2007 has no inherent retrospectivity in its application: it means simply putting the employee again into his previous position, i.e. the position he occupied before he was dismissed, with immediate effect or at some future date.

---

[48]   Ibid. at 382C.

[49]   Ibid. at D.

[50]   Ibid. at 381E-G.

[51]   *Chegetu Municipality v Manyora* 1997 (1) SA 662 (ZSC) at 665H.

To sum up, where dismissal has been found to be unfair, and the employee has applied for reinstatement, the arbitrator must refuse to order reinstatement where, taking into account all the circumstances of the case, the employer-and-employee relationship has broken down irretrievably. The arbitrator must also refuse to order reinstatement where another employee, who has been employed in the position that the employee seeking reinstatement had held before his dismissal, will suffer serious injustice or other prejudice. The onus is on the employer to prove on a balance of probabilities that the relationship has broken down irretrievably or that serious injustice or other prejudice would occur if the dismissed employee were reinstated.[52] Finally, where the arbitrator makes an award of reinstatement of an employee, the effect is that the employer must put the employee into his or her previous job with immediate effect or with effect from a future date, as the arbitrator indicates. In other words, the job into which the employer reinstates the employee must have the same job description as the job the employee had occupied previously, with all its financial and other benefits, as at the date of his or her dismissal.[53] This does not necessarily imply that back pay and compensation or compensation follows automatically.[54] The arbitrator's power to award compensation is provided in s. 86(15)(e) of the Labour Act, and is discussed next.

Compensation

An important phenomenon attendant on the statutory creation of labour courts and labour arbitration tribunals is the power of these bodies to grant compensatory remedies in money. Section 86(15)(e) of the Labour Act 2007 empowers an arbitrator to make an award of compensation. Traditionally, compensation in labour law is strictly a remedy for unfair dismissal or other disciplinary measure (e.g. suspension and demotion) arising from the contract of employment, collective agreement or statute.[55]

Compensation consists of:

1   an amount equal to the remuneration that the employer ought to have paid to the employee had he not been dismissed or suffered other unfair disciplinary measure or some other labour injustice; and

2   an amount equal to any losses suffered by the employee because of the dismissal or other disciplinary action or other labour injustice.

---

52   See *Namibia Beverages v Emily* LCA 18/2001 (unreported).

53   See *Transnamib v Engelbrecht* (Supreme Court) supra.

54   Ibid. See also *Chegetu Municipality v Manyora* supra.

55   For example, s. 15 of Swaziland's Industrial Relations Act 2000 (Act No. 1 of 2000) empowers the Industrial Court to award compensation instead of, or in addition to, an order of reinstatement or re-engagement. Similar provisions are in s. 193 of South Africa's Labour Relations Act 1995 (Act No. 66 of 1995).

In *Pep Stores (Namibia) (Pty) Ltd v Iyambo and others*,[56] the Labour Court approved the following passage from *Jacobs v Otis Elevator Co Ltd*[57] on the nature of compensation awarded in the resolution of labour disputes: 'Compensation awarded in labour disputes cannot be equated with civil or delictual damages. The purpose of compensation is not only to provide for the positive or negative interest of the injured party. There is an element of *solatium* present aimed at redressing a labour injustice.'

In terms of s. 46(1)(a)(iii) of the repealed Labour Act 1992, for instance, a district labour court had the power to award compensation to an employee who had been dismissed unfairly. In *Pupkewitz & Sons (Pty) Ltd v Kankara*,[58] the Labour Court interpreted and applied s. 46(1) (a)(iii) of the repealed Labour Act 1992 relating to the power of the district labour court. In that case, Mtambanengwe, J held that in calculating the amount of compensation that was payable to an employee who had been dismissed unfairly, regard should be had to the loss suffered or the amount the dismissed employee would have been paid had he not been dismissed. In terms of s. 46(1)(a)(iii) of the repealed Act 1992, the amount that the court could order fell into two categories. The first was an amount equal to the remuneration that the employee would have been paid had he not been dismissed. The second was an amount equal to any losses suffered by such employee as a consequence of the dismissal. These were two different compensatory awards, and as the Labour Court observed in *Pupkewitz & Sons v Kankara* supra, the two amounts need not be equal.[59] There is no logical reason why this categorization of compensation ought not to apply to compensation that may be awarded under the Labour Act 2007, too: compensation that was awarded under the repealed Labour Act 1992, it is submitted, is equivalent to that provided for in s. 86(15)(e) of the Labour Act 2007, that is, to redress an unfair dismissal or other disciplinary measure or suchlike labour injustice.

Where an arbitrator awards compensation that is equal to the amount of remuneration that would have been paid to the employee had he not been dismissed, it may not be necessary for the employee to lead evidence to establish the amount involved. The amount should be within the employer's domain,[60] but if the amount includes compensation for loss of certain benefits, e.g. medical benefits, then the employee must establish by evidence what the losses entail.[61]

---

[56]   *Pep Stores (Namibia) (Pty) Ltd v Iyambo and others* 2001 NR 211 (LC) at 223F.

[57]   *Jacobs v Otis Elevator Co Ltd* 1997 1 CCMA 7.1.1 08 at 16.

[58]   *Pupkewitz & Sons (Pty) Ltd v Kankara* 1997 NR 70.

[59]   Ibid.

[60]   *Pep Stores v Iyambo and others* supra.

[61]   Ibid.

An arbitrator should award such amount of compensation as he considers reasonable, fair and equitable, regard being had to all the circumstances of the case. Therefore, in determining the amount of compensation, the courts have taken into account the extent to which the claimant's own conduct contributed to the dismissal.[62] The courts have also taken into account the view that compensation must not be calculated in a manner aimed at punishing the employer,[63] or at enriching a claimant because it is awarded based on the principle of *restitutio in integrum*.[64]

The principle applies on the ground that the claimant should not be better off financially as a result of the dismissal than he would have been if there had been no dismissal. In other words, since an award of such compensation is only compensatory, an aggrieved dismissed employee must not be made to profit from it by recovering more than his actual losses. Thus, what the courts should award must be compensation and not gratuity.[65] For these reasons, remuneration from a new job must be brought into account to enable the court to make a proper assessment of compensation. If that was not done it would 'allow the employee to profit unfairly and financially from the "unfair dismissal" by e.g. receiving full pay and benefits from the employer for a period when the employee received an income from other employment engaged in during the same period, made possible by the employee's dismissal'.[66] Thus, the employee is required to prove that he had suffered financial loss as result of the dismissal and that he had taken reasonable steps to mitigate his loss.

Besides, the courts have taken into account any terminal benefits which the claimant may have received from the employer, e.g. leave pay and severance pay.[67] In *Rossam v Kraatz Welding Engineering (Pty)*, [68] Karuaihe, J took into consideration the following factors in deciding what amount was fair under the repealed Labour Act 1992: (i) the fact that the claimant's poor work performance contributed to his dismissal and (ii) the fact that there had not been any serious efforts on the part of the complainant to seek alternative employment. There is no valid reason why these factors should not apply equally to determination of the amount of compensation under the Labour Act 2007. Finally, the courts have also taken into account the fact that such compensation is paid once as a lump sum amount, and, therefore, is bound to impact severely on the employer's financial position.[69]

---

62 *Herbert Ndlovu v Chairman Sigangeni Clinic* supra; *Oscar Z Mamba v Swaziland Development and Savings Bank* Swaziland IC 81/96 (unreported).

63 *Ferodo (Pty) Ltd v de Ruiter* (1993) 14 *ILJ* 974 (LAC).

64 *Addis v Gramophone Co Ltd* [1969] AC 488.

65 *Camdons Realty (Pty) Ltd and Another v Hart* (1993) 14 *ILJ* 1008 (LAC).

66 *Transnamib v Engelbrecht* (SC) supra at 383C.

67 *Ferodo v de Ruiter* supra.

68 *Rossam v Kraatz Welding Engineering (Pty)* 1998 NR 90.

69 *Bold v Brough, Nicholson & Hall Ltd* [1963] 3 All ER 849.

Costs

In terms of the Labour Act 2007 an arbitrator may award costs, but his power to do so is circumscribed by s. 86(16), which provides that an arbitrator may make an order for costs only if a party or his representative at the arbitral proceedings acted frivolously or vexatiously by proceeding with the dispute or defending it, or because of a party's or a party's representative's frivolous or vexatious conduct during the proceedings. Thus, unless in the judgment of an arbitrator a party or his representative acted frivolously or vexatiously in the proceedings, each party to the proceedings is left to bear his own costs. In this way, an arbitrator's discretion to order costs in favour of a successful claimant is circumscribed.

This is a departure from the usual practice in litigation where the general rule is that, in the absence of special circumstances, costs are awarded to the successful party. It has been suggested that the deviation from the general rule is supported by the desire not to frighten away labour disputants who may have genuine and bona fide claims and, therefore, in good faith wish to have their disputes settled by a labour court or an arbitrator. As Basson, A.M. observed in *Chamber of Mines of South Africa v Council of Mining Unions*:

> public policy demands that the industrial court takes into account considerations such as the fact that justice may be denied to parties (especially individual applicant employees) who cannot afford to run the risk of having to pay the other side's costs. The industrial court should be easily accessible to litigants who suffer the effects of unfair labour practices, after all, every man or woman has the right to bring his or her complaints or alleged wrongs before the court and should not be penalized unnecessarily even if the litigant is misguided in bringing his or her application for relief, provided the litigant is bona fide.[70]

The *raison d'être* of the departure from the general rule can also be supported on the basis that an award of costs in labour disputes has the unhealthy tendency to destroy on-going labour relations, which is not conducive to industrial harmony.[71]

A party acts frivolously if he is 'lacking seriousness'[72] in bringing or defending a claim or in referring a dispute to the Labour Commissioner or in defending the reference to an arbitrator. Moreover, a party will be 'lacking seriousness' if, for instance, he delays or is remiss in carrying out any order of the arbitrator during proceedings and the other party

---

[70]   *Chamber of Mines of South Africa v Council of Mining Unions* (1990) 11 *ILJ* 52 (IC) at 77H-I.

[71]   *Ranch Hotel (Pty) Ltd v SACCAWU* (1993) LCD (LAC).

[72]   *The Concise Oxford Dictionary* 10th edn, Oxford, Oxford University Press, 2000.

incurs costs as a result. A party acts vexatiously if he does not have sufficient grounds for his claim or defence and he is motivated by malice and the sheer desire to annoy.[73]

The type of behaviour that qualifies as frivolous or vexatious turns primarily on whether there has been unacceptable conduct on the part of the guilty party entitling the arbitrator to exercise his discretion to award costs against him.[74] In *Seamen and Allied Workers Union v Cadilu Fishing (Pty) Ltd*,[75] the Labour Court granted a costs order against the applicant because the applicant's conduct was found to be vexatious as it sought to make a case based on widespread non-disclosures and, in some instances, on what appeared to be lies. Furthermore, in *Festus Nakanyala v Old Mutual Namibia Ltd*,[76] the Labour Court made a costs order against the applicant, particularly against the deponent of the applicant's founding affidavit, because he approached the Court on behalf of the applicant when he was not authorized to do so and, therefore, by so acting, according to the Court, he had acted vexatiously.

A party will not be found to have acted frivolously or vexatiously just because he is misguided in thinking that he has a good claim, which he pursues vigorously and in good faith.[77]

To sum up, the factors to consider when determining whether a party has acted frivolously or vexatiously are these.

1   Did a party honestly believe that he had a good claim or defence in the dispute?

2   Did a party act in good faith?

3   Was a party driven by some ulterior motive, e.g. the desire to use the proceedings to inflict retaliation for some wrong allegedly done to him by the other party, or did a party have a genuine desire to prosecute a right or to see justice done in the resolution of the dispute?

4   Was the claim or defence in the dispute made with malice or the desire to annoy the other party?

Answers to these questions will greatly assist an arbitrator in exercising his discretion judicially and fairly.

---

[73]   Ibid.

[74]   *Building Construction and Allied Workers Union and others v Group 5/Combrink Construction* (1993) 2 *LCD* 117 (LAC).

[75]   *Seamen and Allied Workers Union v Cadilu Fishing (Pty) Ltd* 2005 NR 257.

[76]   *Festus Nakanyala v Old Mutual Namibia Ltd* Case No.: LC 04/2007 (unreported).

[77]   *Titus Nzima v Swaziland P & T Corp* Swaziland IC 139/95 (unreported).

Order directing the performance of an act

In terms of s. 86(15)(b) of the Labour Act 2007, an arbitrator has the power to make an award directing the performance of any act that will remedy a wrong. While the effect of the statutory remedy under s. 86(15)(b) may be equivalent to the common law order of specific performance, it is not identical to it. An arbitrator's purpose is to remedy any wrong, and an application for such an order can be successful even if technically speaking it does not meet the requirements for the obtaining of the common law order of specific performance (see chapter 6, paras 6.2.4 and 6.3.4, above, where specific performance is briefly discussed).[78] In this regard, it could be said that the provision of a statutory award under s. 86(15)(b) of the Labour Act has the deliberate object of modifying the common law remedy of specific performance for the purposes of the Act.

An award under s. 86(15)(b) of the Act can also be made in the following situation. In terms of s. 50(1)(d), it is an unfair labour practice for an employer or an employer's organization to fail to disclose to a recognized trade union any relevant information that is reasonably required to enable the trade union to consult or bargain collectively effectively in any labour matter (exclusive bargaining agent is treated in chapter 15, para. 15.2, below). If the employer or employer's organization breaks its statutory duty to disclose information that is reasonably required in this regard, an aggrieved trade union may seek relief in arbitration after conciliation to resolve the dispute has been unsuccessful. A trade union may ask an arbitrator to direct an employer or employer's organization to disclose information reasonably required by a trade union, so as to remedy the unfair labour practice of failure to disclose relevant information. The efficacy of an award under this head is this: it can be granted as a remedy to correct a wrong done under this Act, especially where, for instance, an interdict, a declaratory order, an order of reinstatement, or an award of compensation or damages cannot attain the same goal.

Effect of arbitral award

According to s. 87(1) of the Labour Act 2007, an award made in respect of Part C arbitration is binding unless the award is advisory. When a party affected by the award or the Labour Commissioner files it in the Labour Court it becomes an order of the Court. Section 87(2) of the Labour Act provides that if in his award, an arbitrator orders a party to pay a sum of money, the amount attracts interest, and such interest is calculated from the date the award is made and it is calculated at the same rate prescribed from time to time in respect

---

[78] R.H. Christie, *The Law of Contract in South Africa,* 5th edn, Durban, Butterworths, 2006, pp. 530-2.

of judgment debt in terms of the Prescribed Rates of Interest Act 1975,[79] unless the award provides otherwise.

In closing, a party to an arbitral award made under a Part C arbitration may, in terms of s. 90 of the Labour Act, apply to a labour inspector in the prescribed form requesting the inspector to enforce the award by taking any necessary steps in that regard. The steps that the inspector is entitled to take include the institution of execution proceedings on behalf of the applicant.

Variation and rescission

Section 88 of the Labour Act 2007 gives an arbitrator the power in certain circumstances to vary or rescind an award he has made. These provisions are in material respects similar to the provisions in Rule 44 of the High Court Rules.[80] An arbitrator may exercise that power *ex mero motu* within thirty days after service of the award or upon application made by a party within thirty days after service of the award. What this means is that an arbitrator has the discretion whether or not to grant the application for rescission or variation of his award.[81] It goes without saying that an arbitrator ought to exercise his discretion judicially, i.e. he must act fairly and reasonably and in accordance with the ordinary standards of justice and fairness,[82] and in doing so, it will be proper for the arbitrator to take into account all the circumstances of the case.

The first ground upon which the arbitrator may, in terms of s. 88(a) of the Labour Act, vary or rescind an award, is where the award is erroneously sought or made in the absence of a party affected by the award. If the arbitrator is considering making a variation or rescission order *ex mero motu*, he must satisfy himself that the order he wishes to vary or rescind was sought or made erroneously and in the absence of the party disadvantaged by the original order. If he is so satisfied, he must, without carrying on any further enquiry, vary or rescind the award. He need not call upon the party seeking the variation or rescission to show cause why he must vary or rescind the award.[83]

An award is made erroneously if it is not legally competent for the arbitrator to make, e.g. where the arbitrator is under the impression that an unsuccessful conciliation of the dispute has taken place when in truth no conciliation has taken place. As we saw previously, in terms

---

79 Act No. 55 of 1975.

80 Government Notice No. 59 of 1990.

81 *Topol v S Group Management Services (Pty) Ltd* 1988 (1) SA 639 (W); *First National Bank of South Africa Ltd V Van Rensburg* NO 1994 (1) SA 677 (T).

82 *Pretoria North Town Council v A1 Electric Ice-Cream Factory* 1953 (3) SA 1 (T).

83 *Topol* supra. See also *Dawson and Fraser (Pty) Ltd v Havenga Construction (Pty) Ltd* 1993 (3) SA 397 (BGD); *Tshabalala v Peer* 1979 (4) SA 27 (T).

of s. 86(5) of the Labour Act, unless a dispute has already been subjected to conciliation and a certificate of unresolved dispute has been issued in respect of the dispute, and an arbitrator has also attempted unsuccessfully to resolve the dispute through conciliation, an arbitrator is precluded from dealing with the dispute. Yet again, an award is erroneously made where there was an irregularity in the arbitral proceedings. [84]

An award is also sought or made erroneously if at the time the award is made, a fact existed, of which the arbitrator was unaware, and that fact would have influenced the decision, if he had known about it.[85] To illustrate the point: in making an award, the arbitrator is informed by an employee in the absence of his employer, who is the other party, that his contract of employment with the employer ran for twenty years before he was dismissed. It is established later that he was in fact in the employer's employment for ten years. In that case, the arbitrator may vary the award of compensation if the length of service influenced him in determining the amount of compensation.

It is not enough that an award was sought or made erroneously; the award should also have been so sought or made in the absence of the other party in order for an arbitrator to exercise his discretion in this regard either way. Therefore, if an award is sought or made in the presence of all the parties, then the aggrieved party may seek redress on review or appeal before the Labour Court. Appeal and review powers of the Labour Court are discussed in the next chapter.

Section 88(b) of the Labour Act empowers the arbitrator to vary or rescind an award if the terms of the award are ambiguous or the award contains an obvious error or omission. In exercise of his power under s. 88(b), an arbitrator may only vary or rescind the award to the extent that it is necessary to cure an ambiguity, correct an error or fill in an omission, so long as the ambiguity, error or omission is ascribable to him. Besides, the curing of the ambiguity or the correction of the error or the filling in of the omission ought to be necessitated by the fact that the terms of the award do not correctly reflect the true intention of the arbitrator.[86] On that score, the power to vary or rescind an award does not include the power to clarify the award or to correct an error or fill in an omission, which will have the effect of changing the sense and substance of the award.[87]

The circumstances under which the arbitrator may exercise his discretion under this head are many and varied. For example, he may vary or rescind the award where its terms are capable of bearing more than one meaning, or the meaning is obscure or unclear.

---

[84]   *Tshabalala v Peer* supra.

[85]   *Nyingwa v Moolman* NO 1993 (2) SA 508 (TK).

[86]   *First National Bank of South Africa Ltd v Jurgens* 1993 (1) SA 245 (W); *First National Bank of South Africa Ltd v Van Rensburg NO* 1994 (1) SA 677 (T).

[87]   *Marks v Kotze* 1946 AD 29; *S. v Wells* 1990 (1) SA 816 (A).

Circumstances may also occur where there has been a patent error, e.g. a clerical error, an error in an arithmetical calculation, a spelling error and references to the wrong party to the proceedings, e.g. where reference is made to 'employee' instead of 'employer'. Yet, again, the variation or rescission may be necessary because there has been a clear omission in the terms of the award. The critical consideration is that there must clearly be an ambiguity, and the error or omission should be indubitably obvious, patent and plain. 'This exception,' said Trollip, JA in *Firestone South Africa (Pty) Ltd v Genticuro AG,* 'is confined to the mere correction of an error in expressing the judgement or order; it does not extend to altering its intended sense or substance.'[88]

The last ground upon which an arbitrator may vary or rescind an award made by him under s. 88(c) is where the award was made as a result of a mistake common to the parties to the arbitration. Such a situation arises where all the parties have a convergence of minds and share the same mistake,[89] e.g. where the employee and employer, who are parties to the arbitration, jointly make a statement concerning the terms of their contract of employment and the statement is later found to be incorrect. The mistake should be one attributable to the parties collectively. It is not enough that the error is that of one of the parties only or that of an arbitrator, a legal practitioner, a trade union representative or an employee representing one party.[90] Therefore, an award that stands to be rescinded or varied under this head is one which has been ordered based on the common mistake.[91]

An arbitrator's power under this head, it is submitted, includes also the power to vary or rescind consent awards, i.e. where, for example, the arbitral award was made by consent, but the parties consented in *justus error*.[92] However, *'justus error'* that is brought about by innocent misrepresentation is not a sufficient ground for varying or rescinding an order or award.[93]

10.2.2.2 Part D Arbitration

While Part C of Chapter 8 of the Labour Act 2007 is titled in general terms, viz. 'Arbitration of Disputes', the title of s. 91, the only section of Part D, is cast in specific terms, namely, 'Private Arbitration'. Private arbitration (Part D arbitration) comes into play in either of two ways: where the parties agree in writing to submit their dispute in terms of s. 91(2)

---

88   *Firestone South Africa (Pty) Ltd v Genticuro AG* 1977 (4) SA 298 (A) at 307D.

89   *Tshivhase Royal Council v Tshivhase* 1992 (4) SA 852 (A).

90   *De Wet v Western Bank Ltd* 1977 (2) SA 1033 (W); *Childerly Estate Stores v Standard Bank of South Africa* 1924 OPD 163; *Joseph v Joseph* 1951 (3) SA 776 (N).

91   *Tshivhase Royal Council v Tshivhase* supra. See also *Dickenson Motors (Pty) Ltd v Oberholzer* 1952 (1) SA 443 (A).

92   *De Wet v Western Bank Ltd* 1979 (2) SA 1031 (A).

93   I. Isaacs, *Beck's Theory and Principles of Pleadings in Civil Actions,* 5th edn, Durban, Butterworths, 1989, para. 81.

of the Act to arbitration, or where the parties have provided in a collective agreement that any dispute under the Act and arising from the collective agreement must be referred to private arbitration in terms of s. 73 of the Act. In the latter case, the collective agreement becomes the agreement to submit the dispute to arbitration. In this connection, according to s. 91(13) of the Labour Act, if a party to an arbitration agreement refers a dispute to the Labour Commissioner that must be referred to private arbitration, the Labour Commissioner must refer the dispute for arbitration in terms of the arbitration agreement. If a designated arbitrator is not able to act for any reason or his appointment has, on good cause shown, been set aside by the Labour Court under s. 91(6) of the Act, the parties may designate another arbitrator in his place in accordance with the arbitration agreement. However, if the parties are unable to agree to the appointment of a new arbitrator, any party may make an application to the Labour Court in terms of s. 91(4) for a court-appointed arbitrator. The appointment of the arbitrator may be terminated only by consent of the parties to the arbitration agreement, unless the agreement provides otherwise.

Section 91(7) of the Labour Act vests in an arbitrator conducting Part D arbitration the power to subpoena any person to attend the arbitral hearing if, in the arbitrator's opinion, that person's attendance will assist in the resolution of the dispute. Furthermore, an arbitrator has the power to administer an oath to, or accept an affirmation from, any person called to give evidence and the arbitrator may put questions to such witness. Section 86 (9)–(11), which deals with Part C arbitration and discussed in para. 10.2.2.1, above, applies with necessary modifications to Part D arbitration.

An arbitrator who conducts Part D arbitration may make the same awards as those that an arbitrator conducting Part C arbitration may make in terms of s. 86(15)(a)–(e) (which is treated in para 10.2.2.1 above), subject to the arbitration agreement. However, when it comes to the award of costs, the power of an arbitrator conducting Part D arbitration to award costs is different from that of an arbitrator conducting Part C arbitration (see above). The power of the former is subject to the arbitration agreement. If, under the arbitration agreement the arbitrator is empowered to award costs, he must award costs in accordance with the general rule that in the absence of special circumstances costs must be awarded to the successful party.[94] 'Special circumstances', it is submitted, may include whether a party or his representative at the arbitral proceedings acted frivolously or vexatiously within the meaning of s. 86(13) of the Labour Act.

Like an arbitrator conducting Part C arbitration, the arbitrator conducting Part D arbitration must, in terms of s. 91(11) of the Act and unless the arbitration agreement

---

[94] *Fleming v Johnson and Richardson* 1903 TS 318; *Kathrada v Arbitration Tribunal* 1975 (2) SA 673 (A).

provides otherwise, deliver an award with concise reasons under his signature within thirty days after the conclusion of the arbitral proceedings.

Section 91(12) of the Labour Act provides that s. 87(1)(a) and (b)(i), s 88 and s. 89(4)–(9), (10)(b) and (11) (which concern Part C arbitration and are discussed in para. 10.2.2.1, above) apply with necessary modifications to an arbitral award made by a Part D arbitration tribunal.

According to s. 91(14) of the Labour Act, an arbitration agreement in respect of Part D arbitration cannot be terminated except by the consent of the parties or an order of the Labour Court, unless the arbitration agreement provides otherwise. Besides, unless an arbitration agreement provides otherwise, the agreement is not terminated by the death, sequestration or winding up of any party to the agreement. However, in the event of the death, sequestration or winding up of a party, any arbitration that has commenced must be stayed until an executor, administrator, curator, trustee, liquidator or judicial manager has been appointed.

11 INDUSTRIAL DISPUTES AND THE LABOUR COURT

11.1 INTRODUCTION

It will be remembered that in chapter 8, para. 8.2 above, it was stated that disputes of right are better suited to be settled by judicial or quasi-judicial process. One of the policies of the Labour Act 2007 is to encourage the amicable settlement of such disputes by conciliation and arbitration, so as to attain harmonious labour relations. The Labour Court is meant to complement conciliation and arbitration in the implementation of the Labour Act.

Some Commonwealth African countries like Kenya, Botswana, South Africa, Swaziland and Zambia, have established labour or industrial courts for the purpose of settling industrial disputes. Kenya was one of the first of the former British colonies in eastern and southern Africa to pass comprehensive industrial relations legislation in 1965. Under the Kenyan Act, the Industrial Court was established as 'the pivot of the new' dispensation.[1] In Namibia, the Labour Court is established by the Labour Act 2007, and it is discussed in this chapter.

11.2 ESTABLISHMENT AND COMPOSITION OF THE LABOUR COURT

Section 115 of the Labour Act 2007 provides that the Labour Court which was established by s. 15 of the repealed Labour Act 1992 will continue to exist and operate, subject to Part D of Chapter 9 of the Act, which provides for the establishment, composition, jurisdiction and rules of court of the Labour Court under the Labour Act 2007. The Labour Court under the repealed 1992 Act was presided over by judges of the High Court who were styled 'Presidents', and was primarily a labour appeal court, and, therefore, heard appeals from district labour courts that were presided over by magistrates.

Section s. 116 of the Labour Act provides that the Judge-President must assign judges or acting judges of the High Court to the Labour Court. What the Labour Act 2007 has done

---

[1] C. Okpaluba, 'Collective Labour Rights and Industrial Relations Legislation of Swaziland', in C. Okpaluba et al. (eds), *Human Rights in Swaziland: A Legal Response,* Mbabane, University of Swaziland, 1997, fn. 98.

206   Labour Law in Namibia

is to constitute a court, presided over by judges or acting judges of the High Court, within the meaning of Art. 78, read with Arts. 80 and 82, of the Namibian Constitution, and vests it with exclusive review and appellate jurisdiction in terms of ss 117 and 118 of the Labour Act. The jurisdiction of the Labour Court is discussed next.

11.3   EXCLUSIVE JURISDICTION OF THE LABOUR COURT

11.3.1 Appeal and Review Powers of the Labour Court

From the outset, it is important to emphasize the point that there is a clear distinction between 'review' and 'appeal'.[2] In *Attorney-General for NSW, ex el. Chopin v North Sydney Municipal Council*, Street, CJ declared: 'This court is not hearing an appeal against the desirability or wisdom of the council's decision. The sole matter falling for decision is whether the council has the power permanently to prevent through traffic passing along a residential road.'[3]

In reviewing the decisions of persons or bodies or inferior tribunals, the courts are only concerned with the lawfulness of the decision complained of; but, when determining an appeal, the courts are entitled to go into the merits of the decision or action. Accordingly, as a general rule, appeal deals with merits rather than legality and fairness.[4] In other words, 'review relates to the conduct of the proceedings and not the result of it'. [5]

The reason is simply that if the court went into the merits of the decision, it would be substituting itself for the person or body to whom or to which the Legislature in its wisdom has given the power to make the decision in question, unless the statute granting the power provides otherwise. 'It is well settled,' wrote Professor Willis, 'that where an administrative body is vested by statute with powers of decision the courts cannot, *in the absence of express statutory authority*, interfere with their exercise; they can only see to it that the body does not exceed its jurisdiction [my italics].'[6] Thus, review of the exercise of a statutory power is undertaken mainly on the basis of the principles of *ultra vires* or legality, fairness and natural justice.[7] The proposition is well put by Lord Hailsham LC in the following passage

---

2   See L.de V. Van Winsen, et al., *Herbstein and Van Winsen: The Civil Practice of the Supreme Court of South Africa,* 4th edn, Kenwyn, Juta, 1997, pp. 932-7, where the main distinguishing features are discussed.

3   *Attorney-General for NSW, ex el. Chopin v North Sydney Municipal Council* [1973] 1 NSW LR 186 at 194.

4   R.J.F. Gordon, *Judicial Review: Law and Procedure,* London, Sweet & Maxwell, 1985, para. 2-19; L. Baxter, *Administrative Law,* Cape Town, Juta, 1984, p. 305.

5   *S v Bushebi* 1998 239 NR (SC) at 241F, *per* Leon, AJA. See also *Ellis v Morgan, Ellis v Dessai* 1909 TS 576 at 581, where the distinction is also explained.

6   J. Willis, AdministrativeLaw and the British American Act', *Harvard Law Review,* 1939, 53, 274.

7   Gordon, *Judicial Review,* para. 1-01. Rules of natural justice are explained in chapter 10, para. 10.3.2 above.

from *Chief Constable of North Wales Police v Evans*: 'It is important to remember in every case that the purpose [of review]…is to ensure that the individual is given fair treatment by the authority to which he has been subjected and it is no part of that purpose to substitute the opinion of the judiciary or of individual judges for that of the authority constituted by law to decide the matters in question.'[8] However, as Professor Willis reminds us,[9] in review proceedings, the Court may, if permitted to do so by 'express statutory authority', substitute its decision for that of the body or tribunal.

Therefore, in any proceedings under s. 117 of the Labour Act, it must be clear to the Labour Court whether it is determining an appeal or undertaking a review. This is crucial because appeal proceedings are different from review proceedings. In explaining the distinction between the two proceedings, Hoff, AJ (as he then was), in *Ellen Louw v The Chairperson, District Labour Court and JP Snyman & Partners (Namibia) (Pty) Ltd* observed:

> Where the reason [i.e. to have the judgment set aside] is that the court came to a wrong conclusion on the facts or the law, the appropriate procedure is by way of appeal. Where however the real grievance is against the method of the trial, it is proper to bring the case on review. The … distinction depends, therefore, on whether it is the result only or rather the method of the trial which is to be attacked. The giving of a judgment not justified by the evidence would be a matter of appeal and not review upon this test.
>
> The second main distinction between procedure on appeal and procedure on review is that in the case of the former, the matter is usually a question of argument on the record alone, whereas in a review the irregularity generally does not appear from the record. In an appeal the parties are absolutely bound by the four corners of the record, whereas in a review it is competent for the parties to travel outside the record to bring extrinsic evidence to prove the irregularity or illegality.[10]

In terms of s. 117(1)(b) of the Act, the Labour Court has exclusive jurisdiction to review arbitral awards made in terms of the Act, decisions of the Minister responsible for Labour, the Permanent Secretary responsible for Labour, the Labour Commissioner or any other body or official in the exercise of powers conferred by the Labour Act or any other Act relating to

---

8   *Chief Constable of North Wales Police v Evans* [1982] 1 WLR 1155 at 1160

9   Willis, 'Administrative Law', p. 274.

10   *Ellen Louw v The Chairperson, District Labour Court and JP Snyman & Partners (Namibia) (Pty) Ltd* Case No.: LCA 27/1998 at p. 11 (unreported).

labour or employment which the Minister administers, e.g. the Workmen's Compensation Act 1941,[11] as amended by the Employees Compensation Act 1995.[12]

Besides, according to s. 117(1)(c), irrespective of a provision in any Act, the Labour Court has power to review any decision of any body or official provided for in terms of any other Act, if the decision concerns a matter within the scope of the Labour Act 2007. For instance, in this regard, the Court has power to review the decision of a disciplinary committee or inquiry set up by a private employer or a public service institution to enquire into an alleged misconduct of an employee of the private employer or the public service institution, so as to determine whether the dismissal is unfair in terms of the Labour Act (unfair dismissal is discussed in chapter 8).

In *Feinberg v African Bank Ltd & another*,[13] an application was made to the High Court to review the findings of the chairperson of the disciplinary enquiry, which enquired into the applicant's alleged misconduct, namely, failure to carry out a reasonable and lawful instruction. The applicant was dismissed following the disciplinary inquiry. Rejecting the respondent's submission that it is the Labour Court, not the High Court, which has jurisdiction to hear such application, the South African High Court held that the Labour Court has exclusive review jurisdiction only over the performance or purported performance of any function provided for in the Labour Relations Act.[14] Since the findings of the disciplinary inquiry were not referred to in the Labour Relations Act at all, the High Court reasoned that the Labour Court did not have jurisdiction to review decisions of such bodies: it was the High Court that had jurisdiction. It is submitted that in terms of s. 117(1)(c) of the Labour Act 2007, the decision in *Feinberg v African Bank* supra cannot apply in Namibia, because the Labour Court, which is a division of the High Court, has exclusive jurisdiction to review the decisions of disciplinary bodies or officials, so long as the decision concerns a matter within the purview of the Labour Act.

The principles, which ought to guide the Labour Court in exercising its power of review under the common law, are set out concisely by the High Court in *Federal Convention of Namibia v Speaker, National Assembly of Namibia and others*:

> Where there is a statutory duty on a public officer and, in giving his decision or ruling in pursuance thereof, he acts *mala fide* or fails to apply his mind or takes into account irrelevant or extraneous facts or is prompted or influenced by

---

11   Act No. 30 of 1941.

12   Act No. 5 of 1995.

13   *Feinberg v African Bank Ltd & another* [2004] 10 BLLR 1039 (T).

14   Act No. 66 of 1995.

improper or incorrect information or motives, the High Court of Namibia has inherent jurisdiction (see Art 78(4) of the Constitution of Namibia) to review the decision or ruling, to set it aside and to return the matter to the public officer or simply to correct it. [15]

Moreover, where the decisions were taken by administrative bodies and administrative officials, the Labour Court should take into account the 'administrative justice' requirements in Art. 18 of the Namibian Constitution, which reinforce the common law principles.[16] As Levy, J correctly pointed out in *Frank and another v Chairperson of the Immigration Selection Board*, Art. 18 'does not repeal the common law. In fact it embraces it.'[17]

Equally important in this regard is that s. 117(1)(c) of the Labour Act reinforces the Labour Court's common law power of review and buttresses the common law principles of review like those discussed. The section also extends the subjects amenable to review by the Labour Court to include any other person or body, apart from administrative bodies and officials, e.g. private bodies such as trade unions and private employers, as well as officials of trade unions and private bodies.

It remains to deal with the Labour Court's appellate power. According to s. 117(1)(a) of the Labour Act 2007, the Labour Court has exclusive jurisdiction to hear and determine appeals against decisions made by the Labour Commissioner in terms of the Labour Act, appeals arising from arbitral awards in terms of s. 89 of the Act and arising from compliance orders in terms of s. 126 of the Act.

According to s. 89(1)(a) of the Act, a party aggrieved by an arbitral award made in terms of s. 86 of the Act, may appeal to the Labour Court against the award on a question of law only;[18] or in terms of s. 89(1)(b), on a question of fact, law or mixed fact and law, in the case of an award made in a dispute, which was initially referred to the Labour Commissioner in terms of s. 7(1)(a) of the Act. Section 7 of the Act concerns the protection of the fundamental rights referred to in that section. In addition, s. 89(2) of the Act provides that a party who wishes to appeal against an arbitral award must note an appeal within thirty days after the award is served on him. Nevertheless, in terms of s. 89(3), the Labour Court may, on good cause shown, condone an appeal noted out of time.

---

15 *Federal Convention of Namibia v Speaker, National Assembly of Namibia and others* 1994 (1) SA 177 (NmH) at 197G. The same principles are set out in the landmark case of *African Realty Trust v Johannesburg Municipality* 1906 TH 179 at 182.

16 See Collins Parker, 'The "Administrative Justice" provision of the Constitution of the Republic of Namibia: a constitutional protection of judicial review and tribunal adjudication, under administrative law', *CILSA, XXIV* (1991), a monograph on Art. 18 of the Namibian Constitution.

17 *Frank and another v Chairperson of the Immigration Selection Board* 1999 NR 257 (HC) at 265E.

18 *Faustino Moises Paulo v Shoprite Namibia (Pty) Ltd* Case No. LCA 02/2010 (unreported)

Furthermore, s. 89(6) of the Act provides that the noting of an appeal or the making of an application for review does operate to suspend any part of an award that is adverse to the interests of an employee, but it does not operate to suspend any part of an award that is adverse to the interests of the employer. Nevertheless, an employer against whom an adverse award has been made may apply to the Labour Court for an order varying the effect of s. 89(6), and the Court may make any appropriate order. According to s. 89(8), in considering the employer's application, the Court must take into account any irreparable harm that would affect the employee and employer, respectively, if the award or any part of it were to be suspended or not suspended. Additionally, if the balance of irreparable harm favours neither the employer nor the employee, the Court must determine the matter in favour of the employee. In this connection, s. 89(9) of the Act provides that the Court may order that all or a part of the award be suspended. In making such an order the Court may attach conditions to the order, including, but not limited to, conditions requiring the payment of a monetary award into Court or requiring the continuation of the employer's obligation to pay remuneration to the employee pending the determination of the appeal or review, even if the employee is not working during that time.

Finally, s. 89(4) of the Labour Act provides that a party aggrieved by an arbitral award and who alleges a defect in the arbitral proceedings may apply to the Labour Court for an order reviewing and setting aside the award. The setting aside of arbitral awards is discussed next.

11.3.2 Setting Aside of Arbitral Awards

In terms of s. 89(4) of the Labour Act 2007, a party to a dispute who alleges a defect in arbitral proceedings may apply to the Labour Court for an order reviewing and setting aside the award within thirty days after the award is served on him, unless the alleged defect involves corruption. If the aggrieved party alleges that the defect involves corruption, then he must make the application within six weeks after he becomes aware of the corruption.

According to s. 89(5) of the Labour Act 2007, a 'defect' referred to in s. 89(4) means that:

1   the arbitrator has committed misconduct in relation to the duties of an arbitrator;

2   the arbitrator has committed a gross irregularity in the conduct of the arbitration;

3   the arbitrator has exceeded his power;

4   the award has been obtained improperly.

Without forcing meaning, it is submitted that the term 'defect' under the Labour Act connotes grounds for determining whether the arbitral proceedings are defective. For this reason, those grounds are substantially the same as the grounds provided in s. 33(1) of the Arbitration Act 1965,[19] upon which the High Court may review and set aside an arbitrator's award.

It is now proposed to examine the four grounds on which an allegation of a defect in arbitral proceedings can be maintained or proved in support of an application to review and set aside an award in terms of the Labour Act 2007. It is further proposed to use the provisions in the Arbitration Act as points of reference because it is convenient and neat to do so. However, *a fortiori*, it is appropriate to take that approach because, as mentioned previously, the four grounds in the Labour Act are substantially the same as the four grounds for reviewing and setting aside an arbitral award under the Arbitration Act 1965. It must be kept in mind that the party who alleges that there has been a defect in the proceedings bears the onus of proving the claim.[20]

Misconduct

In terms of s. 89(5)(a)(i) of the Labour Act (and similarly s. 33(1)(a) of the Arbitration Act), the award of an arbitrator may be set aside where the defect in the proceedings is as a result of misconduct on the part of an arbitrator in relation to his duties as arbitrator, i.e. the 'wrongful or improper misconduct'[21] of the arbitrator. According to Butler and Finsen,[22] misconduct in this sense means a dishonest act or any act or omission involving moral improbity on the part of the arbitrator. Indeed, the courts have consistently taken the line that a mistake of fact or law in the award is not misconduct within the meaning of s. 33(1)(a) of the Arbitration Act and therefore does not warrant the setting aside of the award.[23] It is submitted that the same conclusion must apply to the interpretation and application of s. 89(5)(a)(i) of the Labour Act.

As far back as 1915, in the case of *Dickenson & Brown v Fisher's Executors* supra, the Appellate Division held that a bona fide mistake of law or fact made by an arbitrator could not be characterized as misconduct.[24] In *Clark v African Guarantee and Indemnity Co Ltd,*

---

19   Act 42 of 1965. This is how this Act will be referred to in the rest of the book without footnoting.

20   *Total Support Management (Pty) Ltd and another v Diversified Health Systems (SA) (Pty) Ltd and another* 2002 (4) SA 661 (SCA).

21   *Dickenson & Brown v Fisher's Executors* 1915 AD 166 at 176.

22   D. Butler and E. Finsen, *Arbitration in South Africa: Law and Practice,* Kenwyn, Juta, 1993, pp. 292-3.

23   See, for example, *Dickenson & Brown v Fisher's Executors* supra; *Bester v Easigas (Pty) Ltd* 1993 (1) SA 30 (C); *Hyperchemicals International (Pty) Ltd and another v Maybaker Agrichem (Pty) Ltd and another* 1992 (1) SA 89 (W).

24   *Dickenson & Brown v Fisher's Executors* supra.

Gardiner, J stated that so long as the arbitrator has taken evidence and has fairly considered it, the Court will not set aside the conclusions made by him on the evidence before him, merely because in the court's view he has drawn inferences which are possible but are not acceptable to the Court.[25] Then, in *Total Support Management (Pty) and another v Diversified Health Systems (SA) (Pty) Ltd and another*,[26] the Supreme Court of Appeal confirmed earlier authorities that the basis on which an award may be set aside due to misconduct on the part of the arbitrator is a very narrow one. A gross or manifest mistake is not sufficient; at best it provides evidence of misconduct. Moreover, the party alleging misconduct on the part of the arbitrator has to prove wrongful and improper conduct, dishonesty, *mala fides*, partiality or moral turpitude. In that case, Smalberger, ADP stated concisely:

> Proof that the second respondent [the arbitrator] misconducted himself in relation to his duties or committed gross irregularity in the conduct of the arbitration is a prerequisite for setting aside the award. The onus rests upon the appellants in this regard. As appears from the authorities to which I have referred, the basis on which an award will be set aside on the grounds of misconduct is a very narrow one. A gross or manifest mistake is not *per se* misconduct. At best it provides evidence of misconduct (*Dickenson & Brown v Fisher's Executors (supra* at 176)) which, taken alone or in conjunction with other considerations, will ultimately have to be sufficiently compelling to justify an inference (as the most likely inference) of what has variously been described as 'wrongful and improper conduct' (*Dickenson & Brown v Fisher's Executors (supra* at 176)), 'dishonesty' and '*mala fides* or partiality' (*Donner v Ehrlich (supra* at 10–1) and 'moral turpitude' (*Kolber and another v Sourcecom Solutions (Pty) and others (supra* at 1108A)).[27]

Gross irregularity

According to s. 89(5)(a)(ii) of the Labour Act (and similarly s. 33(1)(b) of the Arbitration Act), an arbitrator's award may also be set aside where there has been a defect in the proceedings because the arbitrator has committed a gross irregularity, i.e. irregularity of a serious nature, in the conduct of the arbitration. Gross irregularity will be found to exist where there has been a breach of a rule of natural justice resulting in the aggrieved party not

---

25 *Clark v African Guarantee and Indemnity Co Ltd* 1915 CPD 68 at 77-8.

26 *Total Support Management v Diversified Health Systems* supra.

27 Ibid. at 672 F-H.

having had his case heard and fairly determined.[28] There are three rules of natural justice. First, the *audi alteram partem* rule, which states that the other party must also be heard. Second, the rule that the one who decides must not be biased, i.e. he must not decide in his own case. To these two rules of natural justice must be added a third that has been developed over the years, namely, that 'justice should not only be done, but should also manifestly and undoubtedly be seen to be done.'[29]

We are, however, reminded that 'natural justice is a somewhat elastic concept,' and, therefore, while natural justice requires that the procedure before a tribunal which is acting judicially must be fair in all circumstances, this fundamental principle must not be allowed to degenerate into hard and fast rules.[30] Under this head, it is important to note that the admission of inadmissible evidence does not in itself amount to gross irregularity. It has been said that unless it can be shown that inadmissible evidence allowed by the arbitrator has had a significant effect on the result of the arbitration, the Court will be reluctant to set aside the award solely on that ground.[31]

It is worth noting that under this head, as the Labour Act provides, the irregularity committed by the arbitrator must be 'gross'. Accordingly, it is submitted, an irregularity that is calculated to prejudice a party is 'gross irregularity' within the meaning of s. 89(5)(a)(ii) of the Act. Therefore, the Labour Court will not interfere with the decision of an arbitrator unless satisfied that the complaining party has suffered some prejudice as a result. The test of prejudice in this regard was laid down by *Jockey Club of South Africa and others v Feldman.*[32] In the words of Tindall, JA:

> In respect of civil cases a test has been formulated by various decisions in provincial courts, for instance, *Stemmer v Sabina* 1910 TS 479, and *Ablansky v Bulman* 1915 TPD 71, where it was held that if the irregularity complained of is calculated to prejudice a party he is entitled to have the proceedings set aside unless the court is satisfied that the irregularity did not prejudice him. This, in my judgment, is the correct test and we adopt it. I may mention that the concluding remarks of Solomon JA in his judgment in *Meyers v South African Railways* 1924 AD 85, lend support to the view that this is also the

---

28   *Bester v Easigas (Pty) Ltd* 1993 (1) SA 30 (C), at 43.

29   *R v Sussex Justices, ex parte McCarthy* [1924] 1 KB 256 at 259. See also *Meyer v Law Society, Transvaal* 1978 (2) SA 209 (T) at 212H.

30   C.D. Binnington, 'Dispute Resolution in the Construction Industry', Paper presented at the Standard Bank/PAMAN Arbitration Seminar, Windhoek, Namibia (1-2 April 2004), p.9.

31   M. Milne, 'Discovery and Privilege in Arbitration Proceedings', *JCI Arb* 60 (1994), p. 285.

32   *Jockey Club of South Africa and others v Feldman* 1942 AD 340.

test to be applied in the case of proceedings before statutory tribunals. In my judgment the same test is applicable to proceedings before a private tribunal.[33]

Exceeding power

An award may also be set aside under s. 89(5)(a)(iii) of the Labour Act (and similarly s. 33(1)(b) of the Arbitration Act), where the basis of the defect complained of is the arbitrator exceeding his powers under the arbitration agreement,[34] or in terms of the Labour Act pursuant to which the arbitration is conducted.[35] The arbitrator must restrict himself to the dispute that is brought before him: he cannot decide issues or matters that are not raised in the referral. For instance, it will be *ultra vires* the powers of the arbitrator if he considers a counter-claim where the defendant has not advanced any counter-claim, or where the arbitrator awards costs where the arbitration agreement excludes an award of costs to any party to the arbitration.

Defective proceedings

In terms of s. 89(5)(b) of the Labour Act (and similarly s. 33(1)(b) of the Arbitration Act), an award may be set aside because of defective proceedings based on the award having been obtained improperly, e.g. through corruption, fraud or bribery.[36]

The courts have held that the grounds for reviewing and setting aside the award of an arbitrator in an arbitration governed by the Arbitration Act are limited to the grounds set out in s. 33 of that Act. By similar reasoning, the grounds on which the Labour Court may set aside an arbitrator's award under the Labour Act are those set out in s. 89(4) of the Act. The list of grounds is also exhaustive. This view is supported by the fact that s. 89(5) of the Act defines the word 'defect' by using the verb 'means'. When 'means' is used to define a word or a term, then the Legislature intended that the meaning given is expressed in a complete form, and, therefore, no part of the intended meaning is left out.[37] Consequently, there is no room for additional grounds on which an alleged 'defect' in arbitration proceedings can be based as far as the Labour Act 2007 is concerned.

It is important to note that, for the Labour Court to exercise its power to review an arbitral award, there must be in existence a proper record of the arbitral proceedings. In *Coates*

---

33   Ibid. at 359.

34   *Allied Mineral Development Corporation (Pty) Ltd v Gemsbok Vlei Kwartsiet (Edms) Bpk* 1968 (1) SA 7 (C).

35   *Cape Town Municipality v Yeld* 1978 (4) SA 802 (C).

36   *Graaf-Reinet Municipality v Jansen* 1917 CPD 604.

37   G.C. Thornton, *Legislative Drafting,* 3rd edn, London, Butterworths, 1987, p. 175. The principle is also mentioned in chapter 13, para. 13.2.1 below.

SA (Pty) Ltd v CCMA and others,[38] the third respondent (employee) was dismissed for insubordination. He referred the dispute to the South African Commission for Conciliation, Mediation and Arbitration (CCMA). At the arbitration, his dismissal was held to be unfair. The applicant (employer) applied for the review of the arbitral award, even though the record of the arbitral proceedings was not available. The Labour Court held that the matter could not be determined by it without a record.

According to s. 89(10) of the Labour Act, if the Labour Court sets aside an arbitral award, it may (i) in the case of an appeal, determine the dispute in any manner it considers appropriate; (ii) refer the dispute back to the arbitrator or direct that a new arbitrator be designated; or (iii) make any order it considers appropriate concerning procedures to be followed for determining the dispute.

11.3.3 Declaratory Orders

The Labour Court has exclusive jurisdiction under s. 117(1)(d) of the Labour Act 2007 to make a declaratory order in respect of a matter under the Labour Act, collective agreement, contract of employment or wage order, so long as the declaratory order is the only relief sought. It follows that a declaration order must relate to a right under the Act, a collective agreement, a contract of employment or wage order. Additionally, the interest of the applicant or claimant must be real not abstract or speculative.[39] The Labour Court may therefore decline to issue a declaratory order if in its opinion the interests in issue are hypothetical, abstract or speculative,[40] or if the result of a declaration would in effect be a decision on a matter that is only of academic interest to the claimant.[41] Generally, a declaratory order is of particular importance where other remedies cannot be obtained.

11.3.4 Urgent Relief

According to s. 117(1)(e) of the Labour Act, the Labour Court may grant urgent relief in respect of a dispute, including urgent interdict pending resolution of the dispute in terms of Chapter 8 of the Act, which deals with prevention and resolution of disputes under the Act (see chapter 10, para. 10.2.2.1 above, where interdict is briefly discussed). Section 79 of the Act provides that the Labour Court must not grant an urgent interdict, interdicting a strike,

---

38 *Coates SA (Pty) Ltd v CCMA and others* [2004] 4 BLLR 252 (LC). The award was nevertheless set aside and the matter remitted to the CCMA for a rehearing because the Labour Court found that there was a prima facie case against the employee.

39 *Durban City Council v Association of Building Societies* 1942 AD 27.

40 *Shaba v Officer Commanding, Temporary Police Camp, Wagendrift Dam* 1995 (4) SA 1 (A); *Rowe v Assistant Magistrate, Pretoria and another* 1925 TPD 36.

41 *Adbro Investments Co Ltd v Minister of Interior and others* 1959 (3) SA 292 (T).

picket or lockout that is not in compliance with Chapter 7 of the Labour Act (which deals with strikes, picket and lockouts) unless all these conditions have been met, that is to say:

1   the applicant has given to the respondent a written notice of his intention to apply for an interdict, together with copies of all relevant documents;

2   the applicant has served a copy of the notice and of the application on the Labour Commissioner; and

3   the respondent has been given a reasonable opportunity to be heard before the Court makes its decision.

Moreover, the Labour Court may request a police report referred to in s. 117(2)(b) of the Act before making an order.

11.3.5   Exclusive Jurisdiction in Respect of Other Matters

In terms of s. 117(1)(f) of the Labour Act, the Labour Court also has exclusive jurisdiction to grant an order to enforce an arbitration agreement. Additionally, under s. 117(1)(g), the Labour Court has exclusive jurisdiction to hear and determine any other matter in respect of which it is given the power to do so under the Labour Act. Furthermore, the Labour Court has exclusive jurisdiction to make an order, which the circumstances may require in order to give effect to the objects of the Act, which are found in both the long title and the preamble of the Act. Finally, the Labour Court also has exclusive jurisdiction to generally deal with all matters necessary or incidental to the Court's functions under the Act concerning any labour matter – whether the matter is governed by the Labour Act, any other law or the common law.

11.4. The Labour Court's Power to Order Costs

According to s. 118 of the Labour Act 2007 and despite any other law, in proceedings before it, the Labour Court must not make an order as to costs against any party unless that party has acted in a frivolous or vexatious manner by instituting, carrying on with, or defending, those proceedings. The limitation placed by the Act on the Labour Court's power to make orders as to costs is materially identical to the limitation that the Act places on an arbitrator's power to order costs; and it is discussed in chapter 10 (see para. 10.2.2.1 above) where what essentially constitutes frivolous or vexatious manner in instituting, carrying on or defending arbitration proceedings is explained. It is submitted that the same explanation and considerations apply equally to what constitutes frivolous and vexatious manner in instituting, going on with or defending proceedings in the Labour Court.

11.5 The Labour Court's Power of Referral

Apart from its exclusive power, the Labour Court has power of referral. In this regard, in terms of s. 117(2) of the Act, the Labour Court may refer to the Labour Commissioner, for conciliation in terms of Part C of Chapter 8 of the Act, a dispute referred to in s. 117(1) (c) and (d) of the Act. The Labour Court may also request the Inspector General of the Namibian Police to give a situation report on any damage to life, health or safety of persons arising from a strike or lockout (strike and lockout are discussed in chapter 13, paras 13.2.1 and 13.4 respectively).

11.6 Rules Board

Section 119(1) of the Labour Act 2007 provides that the Labour Court's Rules Board established by s. 22 of the repealed Act 1992 will continue to operate under the name 'Labour Court Rules Board'. The Labour Court Rules Board, under the Labour Act, consists of a High Court judge, designated by the Judge-President, as the chairperson; two legal practitioners with expertise and experience in labour law, appointed by the Judge-President; an individual appointed by the Minister responsible for Justice to represent the Ministry responsible for Justice; an individual appointed by the Minister responsible for Labour to represent the Ministry responsible for Labour; and two individuals nominated by the Labour Advisory Council.

The Labour Court Rules Board is responsible for advising the Judge-President on Rules of the High Court to regulate the conduct of proceedings in the Labour Court, with the view to effecting speedy and fair disposal of matters before the Labour Court. According to s. 119(4) where those rules do not make provision for the procedure to be followed in any matter before the Labour Court, the High Court Rules apply.[42]

---

42 High Court Rules 1990 (Government Notice No. 59 of 1990).

11.7 General Powers of the Labour Court

As was mentioned above (see para. 11.2), the Labour Act 2007 provides that in the exercise of its powers, the Labour Court possesses all the powers of the High Court.

12 AGREEMENT TO SETTLE INDUSTRIAL DISPUTES

An employer who faces a claim for unfair dismissal may oppose the claim by arguing that there is no dispute remaining between him and the employee requiring determination by the court, or arbitration or conciliation, because the dispute has already been settled. The usual argument is that the employee has accepted a monetary payment 'in full and final settlement' of his claim. But such contention cannot oust the power of an arbitrator or the Labour Court to consider the matter to see, if indeed, there has been a settlement and, therefore, no dispute to determine. The reason is obvious. With the enormous economic power that an employer wields over his employee, a passive acceptance of such assertions will work real injustice and unfairness against employees who by any consideration are the weaker parties in labour or employment relationships. An arbitrator or the Labour Court must, therefore, consider the merits of an employer's claim in order to determine whether there has indeed been a full and final settlement of the dispute by the parties themselves. For, on the other hand, not to do so but to disregard the employer's statement out of hand, will also not be conducive to the spirit and objects of the Labour Act 2007, viz. the need for employees and employers to attempt to settle their differences amicably outside the courts for the sake of sound labour relations and fair employment practices, as well as industrial peace and harmony.

The usual question that has come up for determination is whether a document purporting to be documentary proof of the full and final settlement of a dispute between an employer and an employee, constitutes a mere acknowledgement of receipt of an amount of money or a binding contract of waiver or *acceptilatio*. In *Eric Mthandazo Mahlalela v Ubombo Ranches Ltd*,[1] the Court of Appeal was called upon to determine such issue. In that case, the appellant (employee) sued the respondent (employer) in the High Court claiming Emalangeni 406,406.00 by way of damages for repudiation or breach of a contract of employment. The respondent raised by way of special plea an allegation that, on 3 May 1991, the appellant had entered into an agreement with the respondent wherein it was agreed that having received an amount of Emalangeni 2,869.08, the appellant would have no further claims arising from his employment or the termination of the contract of employment.

---

1   *Eric Mthandazo Mahlalela v Ubombo Ranches Ltd* Swaziland CA 32 /1995 (unreported).

The document, which the employer contended barred the appellant from pursuing his claim for damages, was phrased as follows:

UBOMBO RANCHES LIMITED
SHORT RECEIPT

I, E. Mahlalela do hereby certify that I have this 3rd day of May 1991 received the sum of E2, 869.08 (two thousand eight hundred and sixty nine Emalangeni and eight cents) from Ubombo Ranches Limited which is in full and final settlement of all that was due to me up to and including the 25th day of March 1991.

I also certify that having received the above stated amount, I shall have no further claims against the above named Company arising from my employment or the termination of my employment.

Signature of Recipient: E. Mahlalela

Date: 3.5.1992

Signature of Witness: Illegible

Occupation: Salaries Accountant

Schreiner, JA, who delivered the unanimous judgment of the Court of Appeal, observed:

If the document is a receipt and nothing more it would not constitute a final bar to further proceedings: it would have evidentiary value only. However, if notwithstanding the designation by the Respondent as a receipt, it constitutes by its terms a binding contract of waiver or *acceptilatio* the special plea must be upheld and the appeal dismissed.[2]

Having found that 'as a matter of principle there should be no objection to a document constituting a simple receipt and, additionally, a contract of abandonment, acquiescence, release, renunciation, surrender or waiver', the learned Judge of Appeal concluded that waiver 'can only occur when the person foregoing a right contractually agrees to do so'.[3] After considering the evidence that was led at the High Court and the terms of the document set out above, Schreiner, JA found that there was no doubt that a contract was concluded.

---

2   Ibid, at p 2.
3   Ibid.

He went on to state, 'In these circumstances a contract was concluded in the terms of the document and it is not open to the Appellant to set up a private (mental) reservation as to the effect of his signature. I do not think that any issue of unilateral mistake can arise on the above evidence.[4] In the result, the Court of Appeal upheld the plea and dismissed the appeal with costs.

The decision in *Eric Mahlalela v Ubombo* was followed by the Industrial Court in *Job Matsebula & others v Intercon Construction (Pty) Limited.*[5] In *Job Matsebula v Intercon,* the Industrial Court refused to accept the view expressed by the Industrial Court in *PPWAWU & others v Delma (Pty) Ltd,*[6] that the common law principle relating to the termination of obligations through compromise did not apply to a statutory claim such as compensation for unfair dismissal. The Industrial Court found support for its rejection of the *PPWAWU v Delma* view from *Ubombo Ranches Ltd v President of the Industrial Court and another,*[7] where Will, CJ, had stated that 'the common law can only be regarded as having been amended or repealed by the legislature by very clear language.' In *Mbombe & another v Foodcon Fishing Product,*[8] the Labour Court, under the repealed Labour Act 1992, was tasked with determining the validity or otherwise of a similar 'settlement note' in an appeal from the district labour court. The provisions of the note were similar in many material respects to the provisions of the note in *Eric Mahlalela v Ubombo* supra. In *Mbome v Foodcon,* after a complaint had been served on the respondent, a 'written agreement' was purportedly entered into between the complainants (appellants) and the respondent. The appellants' representative and the respondent's representative signed the agreement, which was worded in the following terms:

STATEMENT

The undersigned hereby declares that an amount of N$700.00 (Seven Hundred Namibian Dollars) is payable to the following persons:

1. Shihepo Ndshitiwa

2. Mbome Amon

This amount is in lieu and in full and final settlement of any possible claims emanating from the dismissal from the Maris Stella and the Company's employ on the grounds of assault and damage to Company property.

---

4   Ibid. at p 5.

5   *Job Matsebula & others v Intercon Construction (Pty) Limited* Swaziland IC 16/94 (unreported).

6   *PPWAWU & others v Delma (Pty) Ltd* (1980) 10 *ILJ* 420 (IC).

7   *Ubombo Ranches Ltd v President of the Industrial Court and another* 1982-1986 SLR 1 at 26.

8   *Mbome & another v Foodcon Fishing Product* NLLP 2002 (2) 202 NLC.

The representative of the respondent sent a facsimile message to the appellants' representative. The message read: 'In the light of the second appended statement which we signed, please notify me whether Form 2 is still valid. Should this not be valid, as we have agreed, I would appreciate if you could assist in withdrawing the case on the prescribed form at Mr. Seibeb's office.' The appellants' representative did not reply to the message.

Meanwhile, the appellants had received and paid into their bank account cheques in the amount of N\$725.77, but the complaint was not withdrawn: it came before the district labour court for trial. The respondent's counsel handed in the 'settlement note' and raised a point *in limine* that the complaint should be dismissed because the settlement agreement represented a full and final settlement of the dispute between the parties. The appellants' representative argued contrariwise: he contended that the N\$725.77 was paid to the appellants because they had waited for too long for the appellants to make a decision on their complaint. He added that the complainants' representative who was illiterate had signed the agreement thinking that it was a receipt in respect of the cheques they received. The district labour court ruled that the settlement note was an agreement showing that a full and final settlement of the dispute between the parties had been reached. Mainga, J accepted the decision of the district labour court that the dispute between the parties had been settled finally by the parties in terms of the settlement note. The learned judge ruled that since it had not been shown that it was induced by fraud, duress or misrepresentation, the agreement was valid and its terms were conclusive. According to him, to reject each and every such agreement 'would mean that no dismissal disputes could be settled prior to a court action and that would be contrary to the purpose of the Labour (Relations) Act which encourages the settlement of disputes through negotiation and agreement'.[9]

It is submitted that the principles enunciated in *Mbome v Foodcon, Eric Mahlalela v Ubombo, Job Matsebula v Intercon* and *Ubombo Ranches v President of the Industrial Court* supra, should apply with equal force to the interpretation and application of suchlike settlement agreements made under the Labour Act 2007. It hardly needs saying that the consideration of full-and-final-settlement agreements turns largely upon the facts of the particular case. What is important, therefore, is that where the full-and-final-settlement argument is set up, the Court must ascertain whether the agreement which led to the settlement can stand up in law.[10] For instance, considering the incidence of illiteracy among some employees, the arbitrator and the Labour Court must take into account whether the agreement was entered into voluntarily and whether the employee had a reasonably informed mind when he entered into the agreement.[11]

---

9   *Mbombe v Foodcon* supra at 206-207.

10   *Job Matsebula v Intercon* supra at p. 11.

11   P.A.K. Le Roux and A.Van Niekerk, *The South African Law of Unfair Dismissal,* Cape Town, Juta, 1994, p. 93 and the cases there cited.

13 DISPUTES OF INTEREST AND INDUSTRIAL ACTION

13.1 INTRODUCTION

We saw in chapters 9, 10 and 11 that in the face of an industrial dispute of rights, the parties to the dispute may resort to an amicable way of resolving or settling the dispute. In terms of the Labour Act 2007, the dispute may be referred to conciliation; if the dispute remains unresolved after conciliation, the dispute may be referred to arbitration, and an arbitrator's decision in the matter is subject to the Labour Court's appellate or review powers. These are amicable ways of resolving industrial disputes of rights without resorting to industrial 'hostilities', so to speak. In labour relations today, there are three widely acceptable acts of 'hostilities' that parties to industrial disputes of interest may resort to: employees may strike or picket, and employers may resort to lockout. These industrial actions are discussed now.

13.2 STRIKE

13.2.1 What is a Strike?

Put simply, a strike in labour or employment relations is a joint action of a group of employees, whereby they withdraw their labour totally or partially, with the aim of inducing an employer to accept their joint demands. According to s. 1 of the Labour Act 2007:

> 'strike' means a total or partial stoppage, disruption or retardation of work by employees if the stoppage, disruption or retardation is to compel their employer, any other employer or an employers' organization to which the employer belongs, to accept, modify or abandon any demand that may form the subject matter of a dispute.

224   Labour Law in Namibia

Similar provisions are found in s. 213 of South Africa's Labour Relations Act[1] and s. 2 of Swaziland's Industrial Relations Act.[2] According to the Swaziland Act, 'strike' is defined as:

> a complete or partial stoppage of work or slow down of work carried out in concert by two or more employees or any other concerted act on their part designed to restrict their output of work against their employer, if such action is done with a view to inducing compliance with any demand or with a view to inducing the abandonment or modification of any demand concerned with the employer-employee relationship.

The following key elements are discernible in the definition of 'strike' in the Labour Act 2007, and all those elements ought to be present together in order for an industrial action to qualify as a strike for the purposes of the Labour Act: First, there must be a collective withdrawal of labour, disruption of work or retardation of work (usually referred to as 'go slow') – partial or total – by employees acting in concert. Consequently, the withdrawal of labour, disruption of work or retardation of work, by one employee acting alone or by a number of employees acting not in concert and with a common purpose but separately, falls outside the definition. Such action is, therefore, not a strike within the meaning of the Labour Act. Second, the aim of the collective act or omission by the employees must be to achieve a stated objective, namely, to induce their employer, or any other employer, or employers' organization to which that employer belongs, to accept certain demands. Finally, it is necessary that the demand should be the subject matter of an industrial dispute, i.e. employees or their trade union must declare a dispute.

The narrowness of the definition is borne out by the fact that a concerted and collective stoppage, disruption or retardation of work resorted to when there is in law no declared industrial dispute, is not a strike within the meaning of the Labour Act 2007. For example, employees of an employer cannot just wake up one morning and unexpectedly go on a strike. Therefore, for there to be a strike for the purposes of the Labour Act, the employees must declare a dispute, and such dispute must be a dispute of interest, which is discussed in chapter 9 (see para. 9.2 above). An identical condition was provided in s. 79(2)(a)(ii)(aa) of the repealed Labour Act 1992, which laid down that parties should not resort to a strike or lockout if the dispute between them related to a dispute of right. This was the case, albeit in the definition of 'strike' under s. 1 of the repealed Labour Act, reference was made in wide terms to 'any dispute'. It is only if the dispute between the parties relates to an interest

---

[1]   Act No. 66 of 1995.

[2]   Act No. 1 of 2000.

that a lockout and a strike as part of the negotiating process would be permissible.[3] The formulation in the Labour Act 2007 is excessively cautious.

A very significant word in the formulation of the definition of 'strike' in the Labour Act 2007 is 'means'. As was explained in chapter 10 (see para. 10.3.2 above), when 'means' is used to define a word or a term, then the Legislature intended that the meaning given is expressed in a complete form, and, therefore, no part of the intended meaning is left out.[4] Consequently, the word 'strike' in the Labour Act ought to be given a restrictive meaning because, as a general rule, where it is the intention of the Legislature that the definition it has formulated is not exhaustive of the items listed in the formulation, it has made its intention known by the use of the word 'includes' instead of 'means'.[5] The meaning of 'strike' in the Labour Act 2007 has been expressed in a complete form: no part of the intended meaning has been omitted. Therefore, the statutory definition prevails: Parliament could not have intended otherwise.[6]

A strike that is for a political end, for instance, is, therefore, not a 'strike' under the Labour Act. In this connection, a strike or 'rolling mass action' by employees – the Swaziland equivalent of the South African 'mass stay-away' – to press for political or constitutional reforms is not a strike, as was held in *Minister of Enterprise and Employment v Swaziland Federation of Trade Unions*.[7]

In South Africa, 'stay-away' is a term used to describe a collective action taken by employees, whereby they absent themselves from work, not with the aim of compelling an employer to comply with an industrial demand, but to pursue a political agenda.[8] In *Monareng v Midrand Motolek CC*,[9] Kachelhoffer, AM approved what Balbulia, M had stated about 'stay-aways' in *National Union of Mineworkers v Amcoal Collieries & Industrial Operations Ltd*: '''[s]tay-aways'' has been coined by trade unionists in South Africa to denote a specie of industrial action which elsewhere in the world is simply known as political strike: "Stay-aways" are akin to general strikes which, too, have strong political overtones.'[10] It was said of the South African law that a stay-away is not a strike for the

---

3   *Smit v Standard Bank Namibia Limited* 1994 NR 366 (LC).

4   G.C. Thornton, *Legislative Drafting,* 3rd edn, London, Butterworths, 1987, p. 175.

5   This is usually the case but, if the well-known primary meaning of the term covers all the items in the list, then the purpose of the list is rather to make the definition of the term more precise by the use of the word 'includes'. In that case 'includes' may also signify an exhaustive list. (See *De Reuck v Director of Public Prosecutions, Witwatersrand Local Division, and others* 2004 (1) SA 403 (CC)).

6   *Canca v Mount Frere Municipality* 1984 (2) SA 830 (Tk).

7   *Minister of Enterprise and Employment v Swaziland Federation of Trade Unions* Swaziland IC 163/97 (unreported). See chapter 9, para. 9.1 above, where the case is discussed in connection with disputes that are not industrial disputes in labour law.

8   P.A.K. Le Roux and A. Van Niekerk, *The South African Law of Unfair Dismissal,* Cape Town, Juta, 1994, p. 311.

9   *Monareng v Midrand Motolek CC* (1991) 12 *ILJ* 1348 (IC).

10   *National Union of Mineworkers v Amcoal Collieries & Industrial Operations Ltd* (1990) 11 *ILJ* 1295 (IC) at 1305C.

purposes of s. 1 of South Africa's repealed Labour Relations Act.[11] In *R v Tshongongo and others*,[12] Van Winsen, J interpreted similar provisions under s. 18(5) of the Black Labour Relations Regulations Act[13] (as substituted by s. 1 of Black Labour (Settlement of Disputes) Amendment Act).[14] In that case, he enunciated the principle that the words of the statute 'clearly refer to matters in connection with which the employers can be compelled or indeed agree to or comply with demands made by the employees, in other words, matters which it lies with the employers to remedy'.[15] Indeed, only those having political power 'can be compelled or indeed agree to or comply with' political demands.

To sum up, for the purposes of the Labour Act 2007, a strike is an industrial action taken by employees as parties to an industrial dispute of interest.

The statutory definition is at the same time wide. It covers a withdrawal of labour, disruption of work and retardation of work by employees who are parties to a dispute with their own employer and wish to compel him or an employers' organization to which he belongs to accede to their industrial demand. However, it also covers a withdrawal of labour, disruption of work and retardation of work by employees aimed at compelling, through their employer or directly, another employer or an employers' organization to which that employer belongs, to accede to their demands. The first instance is referred to as a 'primary boycott' and the second as a 'secondary boycott'[16] or 'secondary strike'[17]. The decision in *Midland Cold Storage Ltd v Turner,*[18] discussed in chapter 9 (see para. 9.1 above), explains this point.

13.2.2 The Right to Strike

The courts have recognized striking as an essential ingredient of the negotiating process.[19] In *National Union of Mineworkers v East Rand Gold & Uranium Co Ltd* supra, the Appellate Division of the Supreme Court held that collective bargaining is the preferred means of promoting good labour relations and resolving disputes, and that the strike weapon is an essential and integral part of collective bargaining. Lord Wright put it clearly and concisely in this way in *Crofter Harris Tweed Co v Veitch*: 'Where the rights of labour are concerned, the rights of the employer are conditioned by the rights of the men to give or withhold their

---

11   J. Grogan, *Riekert's Employment Law,* 2nd edn, Cape Town, Juta, 1993, p. 35.

12   *R v Tshongongo and others* 1957 (2) SA 486 (C).

13   Act No, 48 of 1953.

14   Act No. 59 of 1955.

15   *R v Tshongongo* supra at 490A.

16   C.D. Drake, *Labour Law,* 2nd edn, London, Sweet & Maxwell, 1973, para. 561.

17   See s. 66 of South Africa's Labour Relations Act 1995 (Act No. 66 of 1995).

18   *Midland Cold Storage Ltd v Turner* [1972] ICR 230.

19   *Smi v Standard Bankt* supra; *Barlows Manufacturing Co Ltd v Metals & Allied Workers Union & others* (1990) 11 *ILJ* 35 (T); *National Union of Mineworkers v East Rand Gold and Uranium Co Ltd* (1991) 12 *ILJ* 1221 (A).

services. The right of workmen to strike is an essential element in the principle of collective bargaining.'[20]

A strike is, therefore, a sharp economic instrument used as the last resort to propel parties to an industrial dispute to come to some agreement at the negotiating table. It has, therefore, become an indispensable tool in labour relations. Considering the huge economic power employers wield over employees, there must be a corresponding leverage at the disposal of employees, to enable them to take on the massive power of employers in negotiations, so as to bring about some equilibrium in the employer-and-employee relationship. However, there cannot be such balance in labour or employment relations, in general, and collective bargaining, in particular, unless employees acting collectively and in concert have the right to strike. Herein, it is submitted, lies the *raison d'être* of the right of employees to strike.

It must, nevertheless, be borne in mind that the right to strike is a statutory innovation in employer-employee relationship. At common law, the withdrawal of services by employees for any reason amounts to a fundamental breach or repudiation of the contract of employment, entitling the employer to summarily dismiss the employees,[21] apart from any remedies the employer may have in delict, contract and criminal law.

There is no International Labour Organization (ILO) Convention, including those dealing with freedom of association, that specifically and clearly provides for the right of employees to strike. It is only by recourse to some ingenious application of the purposive approach to interpretation,[22] that the Committee on Freedom of Association of the Governing Body of the ILO came up with the view that certain ILO Conventions guarantee employees the right to strike. The Committee has interpreted a provision in Art. 3 of the Freedom of Association and the Protection of the Rights to Organize Convention,[23] which calls on public authorities to refrain from any interference which would restrict the right of workers 'to organize their...activities' as giving employees the right to strike. The basis of the argument is that 'activities' of employees include industrial action.[24]

The Namibian Constitution, in a way, guarantees the right to strike.[25] Article 21(1)(f) of the Constitution protects employees from being visited with penal sanctions solely for going on strike. It is rather s. 74(1)(a) of the Labour Act 2007 that expressly gives employees the right to strike. Section 74(1)(a) provides: 'every party to a dispute of interest has the right

---

20   *Crofter Harris Tweed Co v Veitch* [1942] AC 435 at 463.

21   *R. v Smit* 1955 (1) SA 239 (C); *Tshabalala v the Minister of Health and others* 1987 (1) SA 513 (W).

22   See G.E. Devenish, *Interpretation of Statutes,* Cape Town, Juta, 1992, pp. 35-9.

23   ILO C87. Freedom of Association and Protection of the Right to Organize Convention, 1948.

24   International Labour Organization, *Digest of Decisions and Principles of the Freedom of Association Committee of the Governing Body of the ILO,* 3rd edn, Geneva, ILO, 1985, paras 262-4.

25   Compare with the right to strike in South Africa, which is expressly guaranteed by s. 23(2) of that country's Constitution (Act 108 of 1996).

to strike.' However, the exercise of the right is circumscribed, as it is conditional upon the fulfilment of clearly laid down conditions under the Act.

In interpreting and applying the relevant provisions of Swaziland's repealed Industrial Relations Act,[26] on the right to strike in *Nantex Textile Swaziland (Pty) Ltd v Swaziland Manufacturers and Allied Workers Union and others*, Parker, J stated: 'The right to strike as guaranteed by the 1996 Act cannot be an absolute and unfettered right. It has never been so in any jurisdiction that we know of.'[27] Relying on Art. 8(1)(d) of the United Nations International Covenant on Economic, Social and Cultural Rights,[28] he went on to observe, 'Under international human rights law, the right to strike can lawfully be circumscribed.'[29]

The restrictions to the right to strike are in the form of substantive and procedural conditions that must be fulfilled in order for a strike to be lawful for the purposes of the Labour Act 2007, and in order for employees to bring themselves under the protection that the Act provides for striking employees. Indeed, it is important to note that the right being discussed is only the right to strike without being dismissed by the employer solely for participating in a strike, and without incurring penal sanctions solely for going on strike.[30] The main conditions under s. 74 of the Labour Act are as follows.

1   There must be an industrial dispute of interest to which the party desirous of going on strike is a party (dispute of interest is discussed in chapter 9, para. 9.2 above).

2   The dispute ought to have been referred to the Labour Commissioner for conciliation in accordance with s. 82 of the Act.

3   A party may strike only if the party attended a conciliation meeting conveyed by a conciliator appointed by the Labour Commissioner.

4   The dispute has remained unresolved despite efforts of a conciliator, at the end of (i) a period of thirty days from the date of the referral; or (ii) if it is applicable, a longer period determined in terms of s. 74(3)(a); or (iii) if it is applicable, a shorter period determined in terms of s. 74(3)(b).

5   After the end of the applicable period referred to in s. 74(1)(c) of the Act, a party has given a 48-hour notice in the prescribed form to the Labour Commissioner and to the parties to the dispute.

---

26   Act No. 1 of 1996.

27   *Nantex Textile Swaziland (Pty) Ltd v Swaziland Manufacturers and Allied Workers Union and others* Swaziland IC 140/97 at p. 14 (unreported).

28   Namibia became a State Party to this Covenant in 1994.

29   *Nantex Textile Swaziland v Swaziland Manufacturers & Allied Workers Union* supra at p. 14.

30   M.S.M. Brassey, et al., *The New Labour Law,* Cape Town, Juta, 1987, p. 124.

6 A strike must comply with rules governing the conduct of that strike or any rules determined by a conciliator in terms of s. 74(2) of the Act. According to this subsection if a dispute referred to in terms of s. 74(1) cannot be resolved, a conciliator referred to in s. 82(9)(a) must endeavour to make the parties reach an agreement on rules to govern the conduct of the strike; and if the parties are unable to agree the rules, the conciliator must make the rules in accordance with any guidelines or code of good practice published by the Minister responsible for Labour in terms of s. 137 of the Labour Act.[31]

The provisions on referral of disputes, unresolved disputes, notices of commencement of strikes and rules made to regulate the strikes are peremptory for the purposes of s. 74 of the Labour Act. Consequently, if a party breaches any of the conditions or procedures, the ensuing strike will not be in compliance with the Labour Act. For instance, employees intending to strike cannot be seen to short-circuit, as it were, the dispute-reporting and strike-notice procedures. Any short cut is a breach of the clear provisions of s. 74 of the Labour Act, rendering the strike not being in conformity with the Labour Act.

In *Nantex Textile Swaziland v Swaziland Manufacturers and Allied Workers Union* supra, the effect of non-compliance with the dispute-reporting and strike-notice provisions of Swaziland's repealed Industrial Relations Act,[32] which are similar to those in s. 74(1) of the Labour Act 2007, came up for consideration. In that case, counsel for the respondents argued that the fact that there had not been a strict adherence to the provisions of the Act – even if they were peremptory – should not render the strike unlawful. The Industrial Court rejected the argument as ill founded, and in the result declared the strike by the respondents unlawful.

It is, thus, not permissible for employees intending to strike to do anything that is in contravention of the laid-down statutory procedures because this would detract from what the Act clearly requires.[33] Innes, CJ stated the applicable law succinctly in *Schierhout v Minister of Justice* in this way: 'It is a fundamental principle of our law that a thing done contrary to the direct provisions of the law is void and of no effect.'[34]

---

[31] See ' Codes of Good Practice on Industrial Actions and Picketing', GN 208 in GG4J61 of 19 October 2009.

[32] Act No. 1 of 1996.

[33] See *Republican Party of Namibia and Congress of Democrats v Electoral Commission of Namibia and others* Case No. SA 387/2005 (Supreme Court) at p. 92 (unreported).

[34] *Schierhout v Minister of Justice* 1926 AD 99 at 109-110.

13.2.3 Protection of Strikers

We saw earlier in para. 13.2.2 above that Art. 21(1)(f) of the Namibian Constitution protects strikers from being subjected to penal sanctions solely for participating in a strike. The constitutional protection is available both to strikers who participate in a strike that is in compliance with the Labour Act, i.e. lawful strike action, and those who participate in a strike that is not, i.e. unlawful strike action. However, the Constitution does not protect strikers from dismissal or action in delict or contract. Section 33(2)(c)(i) of the Labour Act 2007, on the other hand, protects employees who participate in lawful strike action from dismissal, and s. 76(1), read with s. 76(5), of the Labour Act makes them immune from proceedings in action in delict or contract or from any other civil proceedings *solely* for engaging in a strike that complies with the requirements of the Labour Act. However an employer is not obliged by the Act to remunerate an employee for services that the employee does not render during such a strike.

The immunity also does not cover acts that constitute defamation or a criminal offence during a strike; it matters not if the strike complies with the Act. Thus, an employee who makes or publishes a statement defamatory of, for example, the employer or his representative, cannot escape liability even if he makes or publishes the statement to advance the course of the strike. Similarly, an employee who, for instance, assaults the human resources manager of his employer, even if he thought he did so in furtherance of a strike – whether or not it is a lawful strike action in terms of the Labour Act – will not escape criminal liability. In *CEPPWAWU and others v Metrofile (Pty) Ltd,*[35] the Labour Appeal Court confirmed the principle that the right to engage in a strike that was protected by statute did not permit employees to take part in wrongful conduct. If they did, the employer was entitled to take disciplinary action against those who committed the acts of misconduct. In addition, as far as the Labour Appeal Court was concerned, it was fair for an employer not to wait for the strike to end before instituting disciplinary proceedings. The reason was that unlawful conduct carried out during a strike gave the striking employees an unjustified advantage, and an employer was not expected to put up with such misconduct indefinitely.

The protection offered by the Labour Act aims at encouraging the observance of the Act and at discouraging employees from bringing about industrial disharmony through strikes that are not in conformity with the Labour Act. Of course, it does not mean that an employer is entitled to dismiss employees merely for taking part in an unlawful strike action, i.e. a strike that is not in conformity with the Labour Act, without any questions asked. In *SACWU & others v Pharma Natura (Pty) Ltd,*[36] the Industrial Court stated that it was prepared to

---

35 *CEPPWAWU and others v Metrofile (Pty) Ltd* [2004] 2 BLLR 103 (LAC).

36 *SACWU & others v Pharma Natura (Pty) Ltd* (1986) 7 *ILJ* 696 (IC).

protect employees who had engaged in an illegal strike where exceptional factors existed. According to the Industrial Court, the following factors merit consideration in this regard. The courts must look at the circumstances that gave rise to the strike to see if the employees did not create them. The courts must also consider the conditions under which the employees performed their services to see whether the strike was the only reasonable option open to them, that is, whether no alternative reasonable avenues were open to them. In *National Union of Mineworkers v Amcoal Collieries* supra where the applicants had engaged in an unlawful strike, Jacob, AM stated:

> I should add that there is ample authority for the view that this court can in suitable circumstances come to the assistance of illegal strikers, but there must be special circumstances to excuse their behaviour. They must show some justification 'which will purge their action and give them "clean hands"'. Nothing in this case leads me to the conclusion that the applicants had no option other than to participate in the strike. They are therefore not entitled to relief on the basis of equity.[37]

It is necessary for an arbitrator or the Labour Court to determine whether the employer's decision to dismiss was fair, considering all the circumstances of the case, despite the fact that the employees took unlawful strike action. An enquiry into such issues as those underlying the consideration in *SAWCU v Pharma Natura* and *National Union of Mineworkers v Amcoal Collieries* will be of assistance. Indeed, in *National Union of Mineworkers v Amcoal Collieries*, those strikers who were not on final warning for previous disciplinary breaches received either warnings as first offenders, or severe warnings as second offenders, in terms of the employer's disciplinary code. However, those who were likely to receive a final warning or those who were likely to be dismissed, were invited to a disciplinary hearing before the employer took the decision to dismiss some of them.

Thus, it is fair and reasonable for an employer to hear the side of the story of those who participated in an unlawful strike action before taking disciplinary action against them. This goes to support the view that there is nothing unfair in dealing with such employees on an individual basis as was held in *National Union of Mineworkers v Amcoal Collieries* supra and *Reckitt & Colman (SA) (Pty) Ltd v Chemical Workers Industrial Union and others*.[38] In *Reckitt & Colman v Chemical Workers Union,* Harms, J stated categorically: 'There is

---

37   *National Union of Mineworkers v Amcoal Collieries* (1991) 12 *ILJ* (IC) 1340 at 1347A-B.

38   *Reckitt & Colman (SA) (Pty) Ltd v Chemical Workers Industrial Union and others* (1991) 12 *ILJ* 806 (LAC).

obviously no general rule to the effect that selective disciplinary action is per se unfair.'[39] It depends on the circumstances. An employer's selective disciplinary action can be justified on the ground that it is fair and reasonable for him to take into account relevant factors concerning individual employees that may become known during disciplinary enquiries. An employer can take into account the employee's service record, including his disciplinary record, in order to see whether the employee has an unblemished service record, his length of service and his conduct during the illegal strike.

There is authority for the proposition that labour or employment legislation like the Labour Act 2007 does not contemplate the wholesale dismissal of all employees who participate in an unlawful strike action or who commit any other wrong.[40] In *Pep Stores (Namibia) (Pty) Ltd v Iyambo and others*,[41] the appellant (employer) dismissed its employees for poor performance. The reason for their dismissal was collective guilt for stock losses in his business which the employer attributed to the employees. The district labour court under the repealed Labour Act 1992 set aside the employer's decision to dismiss the employees. The employer appealed to the Labour Court against the decision of the labour court based on substantive unfairness on the part of the employer. The Labour Court found that, in dismissing the employees based on suspected collective act of misconduct, the appellant breached the provisions of collective responsibility in the collective agreement because it failed to prove the individual guilt of every employee in question. As the Labour Court observed, in Namibia such conduct of the employer is viewed with disapproval because it violates the right to be presumed innocent until proven guilty, guaranteed by the Namibian Constitution. Moreover, it goes against the common law.[42]

There is also authority for the proposition that the issuance of general information not communicated to anyone in particular which indiscriminately terminates the employment of striking employees is invalid and unfair.[43] In *Tshabalala v Minister of Health* supra, two student nurses and a pupil nurse applied for a temporary order declaring that the chief superintendent of the hospital where they were employees had unlawfully dismissed them. In addition, they sought an interdict to prevent their eviction from the hostels in which they lived.

---

[39] Ibid. at 813G.

[40] *Workers Representative Council v Manzini Town Council* Swaziland CA 3/94 (Court of Appeal) (unreported) at p.14 where Browde, JA endorsed the decision by Amissah, JP in *National Amalgamated Local & Central Government & Parastatal Manual Workers Union v Attorney-General* Botswana CA 26/93 (unreported).

[41] *Pep Stores (Namibia) (Pty) Ltd v Iyambo and others* 2001 NR 211 (LC).

[42] Ibid.

[43] *Workers Representative Council v Manzini Town Council* (Court of Appeal) supra; and *Tshabalala v Minister of Health* supra.

The nurses had engaged in a strike after the chief matron had declined to consider their grievances. The chief superintendent later informed the 900 or so nurses that they had been dismissed summarily with effect from the day before the strike. The first applicant had been on leave; the second denied participating in the strike, while the third admitted he had taken part in the strike. The case fell under South Africa's Nursing Act,[44] which declared strikes by nurses to be unlawful and criminal, and under the Hospital Ordinance,[45] in terms of which an employee whose employment was subject to the Nursing Act, and was on probation and went on strike, was guilty of misconduct rendering him subject to summary dismissal. Goldstone, J (as he then was) stated:

> In my judgment, the notice to terminate was not given by the chief superintendent clearly or unambiguously to any of the students. The chief superintendent was not entitled to issue a general order terminating the employment of all the students and leave it to those who participated in the strike action to determine for themselves whether the termination applied to them or not.[46]

In the result, the learned judge held that the notice of termination was invalid and ineffective in respect of all the students. On the question of exercise of discretion by the chief superintendent under the Ordinance to dismiss, the court held that the chief superintendent was obliged to give careful and *bona fide* consideration to the case of each individual in respect of whom he was considering dismissal. According to the Court, the chief superintendent ought to have given each such person the right to be heard, and should certainly have had regard to whether the facts established that the individual participated in the unlawful strike action.

In terms of s. 76(4) of the Labour Act 2007, an employee is entitled to resume employment within three days after a strike has ended or after he became aware, or could reasonably have become aware, that the strike had ended. This right does not apply where the employer dismisses the employee for a valid and fair reason. (Unfair dismissal has been dealt with already in chapter 8.)

Finally, there is another important protection offered by the Labour Act 2007 (under s. 76(3) of the Act) to an employee who participates in a lawful strike action in terms of the Act. Irrespective of any provision in a contract of employment or collective agreement, an employer must not require an employee who is not participating in a strike that complies

---

44   Act No. 50 of 1978.

45   No. 14 of 1958.

46   *Tshabalala v Minister of Health* supra at 521B.

with Chapter 7 of the Labour Act or whom the employer has not locked out, to do the work of a striking employee or one who has been locked out, unless the work is necessary to prevent a danger to the life, personal safety or health of any individual. Furthermore, an employer must not hire any individual, for the purpose in whole or in part, of performing the work of a striking employee or one who has been locked out.

13.2.4 Circumstances under which Strikes are Prohibited

Section 75 of the Labour Act 2007 lists the circumstances in which strikes are prohibited. The effect of the provision is that a strike that takes place under any of those circumstances is unlawful as far as the Labour Act is concerned. The circumstances are where:

1. the provisions of s. 74 of the Act have not been complied with;
2. the dispute in question is one that a party has the right under the Labour Act to refer to arbitration or other adjudication for determination;
3. the parties to the dispute have agreed to refer it to arbitration;
4. the issue in the dispute is governed by an arbitral award or an order of a competent court of law; or
5. the dispute is between parties engaged in a service designated as an essential service in terms of s. 77 of the Act.

Item (1) is discussed above in para. 13.2.2. Items (2), (3) and (4) are dealt with in chapter 10 above. It now remains to deal with item (5).

13.2.5 Designation of Essential Services

According to the International Labour Organization (ILO), essential services are those services whose interruption endangers the life, personal safety or health of the whole or part of the population.[47] Such services include the rendering of health services; the provision of water, electricity and telephone facilities; and services rendered by air traffic controllers.[48]

In terms of s. 1 of the Labour Act 2007, '"essential service" means a service the interruption of which would endanger the life, personal safety or health of the whole or any part of the population of Namibia and which has been designated as such in terms of section 77'. The Act borrows the definition of essential service from the ILO formulation.

---

[47] ILO, *Digest of Decisions and Principles of the Freedom of Association Committee,* para. 393.

[48] C. Cooper, 'Strikes in Essential Services', *ILJ* 903 (1994), p. 905.

Section 77(1) of the Act provides that the Essential Services Committee must recommend to the Labour Advisory Council all or a part of a service to be an essential service if, in the opinion of the Committee, the interruption of that service would endanger the life, personal safety or health of the whole or any part of the population of Namibia.

Section 77(2) sets out requirements, which the Essential Services Committee must take into account when considering whether to designate a service as an essential service. First, except in the case of an urgent application made in terms of s. 77(12) of the Act, the Committee must give notice in the *Gazette* of any investigation it intends to carry out in order to determine whether an entire service or a part of it should be designated as an essential service. The Committee must indicate in the notice the service, or part of it, that is the subject of its investigation. The notice should also invite interested parties to make written submissions to the Committee within a period specified in the notice. In addition, the notice should indicate the date on which, the time at which, and the venue where the Committee will receive oral representations at a public hearing from those who have made written submissions.

After it has considered written submissions and oral representations, the Committee may decide whether to recommend the designation of the whole, or part, of a service that is the subject of the investigation as an essential service, and must forward its report to and recommendations to the Labour Advisory Council. According to s. 77(6), in addition to publishing the notices in the *Gazette*, the Committee or the Minister responsible for Labour must, through any other means available, publish the information contained in the *Gazette* notice so as to ensure that individuals whose interests are affected by the notice receive the information. It is submitted that the Minister may publish the notice in the local dailies, the *Namibia Review* or the Ministry of Labour's *Newsletter*.

After considering a report of the Essential Services Committee, the Labour Advisory Council must forward its recommendations to the Minister responsible for Labour. When the Minister receives the recommendations, he must consider them. If the Minister decides to designate any part of a service as an essential service, he must publish a notice to that effect in the *Gazette*. It goes without saying that in taking any decision, the Minister is not bound by the recommendations of the Labour Advisory Council.

A person may refer to the Essential Services Committee, in writing, a dispute concerning whether an employee or an employer is engaged in an essential service, except a dispute referred under s. 77(12) of the Act.

The Essential Services Committee has discretion under s. 77(7) of the Act to recommend to the Labour Advisory Council to vary or cancel any designation made, as long as the procedures for consultation and the publication of notices under s. 77 are followed with necessary modifications.

After the Committee or the Minister, as the case may be, has published the notices mentioned previously in terms of s. 77(2)(a) or 77(6), every interested person is entitled to inspect any written representations made in pursuance of the notices. A party that refers a dispute to the Committee must satisfy the Committee that he has served a copy of the referral on all parties to the dispute. Section 77(1)–(5) applies with necessary modifications to disputes referred to the Essential Services Committee.

If a party to a dispute of interest asserts that the dispute relates to a service that should be designated as an essential service, that party must in terms of s. 77(12) refer the matter to the Committee for urgent consideration no later than the date on which the dispute is referred to the Labour Commissioner in accordance with s. 82 of the Act. Section 82 deals with resolution of disputes through conciliation (this is treated in chapter 10, para. 10.1 above).

The Committee must consider the matter in accordance with s. 77(2) and (3) of the Act, and make its recommendation to the Labour Advisory Council within fourteen days of the referral of the dispute. After considering the report of the Essential Services Committee, the Labour Advisory Council must in turn forward its recommendations to the Minister responsible for Labour within fourteen days after receiving the Committee's report. Thereafter, the Minister must decide whether to designate the whole or a part of the service as an essential service and must, within fourteen days from the date of receipt of the Labour Advisory Council's recommendation, inform the parties concerned of his decision. In making his decision the Minister must take into account the requirements set out in s. 77(4) and (6) of the Act.

The Act provides that an employer who is a party to a dispute referred to the Essential Services Committee in terms of s. 77(12) may not take lockout action until the Minister has made his decision. By the same token, a trade union that is a party to the dispute, may also not take strike action until the Minister has made his decision.

It will be remembered from para. 13.2.4 above, that an employee must not participate in a strike action and an employer in a lockout action if the employee or the employer is engaged in an essential service. Such an employee may, in terms of s. 75(e) of the Labour Act, refer the dispute to the Labour Commissioner who, in turn, may refer the dispute for determination by an arbitrator under a Part C arbitration or Part D arbitration in terms of Chapter 8 of the Act (these are dealt with in chapter 10 above). However, the Labour Commissioner may refer the dispute to arbitration only if the person who referred the dispute to him satisfies him that he has served a copy of the referral on every party to the dispute.

13.3 Picket

Industrial strike and picket are two connected actions in the armoury of employees who engage in industrial action. In *Navachab Joint Venture t/a Navachab Gold Mine v Mineworkers Union of Namibia & others*, Strydom, JP (as he then was) observed (with reference to picketing under the repealed Labour Act 1992) that:

> those who picket must be able and must be in a position to give effect to stated objects. As it was put by Benjamin, Jacobs and Abertyn *Strikes, Lockouts and Arbitration in South African Labour Law*, p. 55: 'The major justification picketing has is in the right to freedom of speech and peaceful protest.' [49]

The right to picket was recognized in England as far back as 1906 by s. 2 of the Trade Disputes Act:[50] the right is now recognized by the Trade Unions and Labour Relations (Consolidation) Act.[51] Section 220(1) of the latter Act states:

> It is lawful for a person in contemplation or furtherance of a trade dispute to attend – (a) at or near his own place of work, or (b) if he is an official of a trade union, at or near the place of work of a member of the union whom he is accompanying and whom he represents, for the purpose only of peacefully persuading any person to work or abstain from working.

'Picket' is not expressly defined in the Labour Act 2007; nevertheless, like the English statute, the Labour Act provides for the right to picket. Section 76(2) of the Labour Act provides that any law notwithstanding, an employee or a member or an official of a registered trade union may, in furtherance of a strike that is in compliance with Chapter 7 of the Act, hold a picket at or near the place of employment so as to peacefully communicate information and persuade any individual not to work.

Thus in terms of the Labour Act, a picket must meet certain minimum requirements.

1   A picket must be conducted in a peaceful manner: a violent or intimidating picket is not in compliance with the Labour Act.

---

[49]   *Navachab Joint Venture t/a Navachab Gold Mine v Mineworkers Union of Namibia & others* 1995 NR 225 (LC) at 229G-H.

[50]   1906 (6 Edw. 7, c. 47). Similar provisions are found in s. 107 of Swaziland's Industrial Relations Act 2000 (Act No. 1 of 2000).

[51]   Trade Unions and Labour Relations (Consolidation) Act 1992 (c. 52.)

2   A picket must have the aim of advancing the course of a strike that is in conformity with the Labour Act.

3   A picket must be for the purpose of communicating information and persuading an individual not to work. The most popular form of picket is the carrying of placards by striking employees and other authorized persons at the place of employment. The placards usually bear inscriptions highlighting the dispute and the employees' demands.

4   A picket must be for persuading individuals not to work.[52] Such persons may be fellow employees, or scab employees or any other person. A picket is, therefore, a tool for employees to use for peaceful communication and persuasion during a strike.

5   The attendance of picketers must be 'at or near the place of employment', i.e. outside the premises: it cannot be carried out at or near a person's residence, unless it is also the place of employment. The term 'place of employment' is wide enough to cover a picket at or near the premises of an employer by picketers who may not be his employees, as where the dockers in *Midland Cold Storage Ltd v Turner* were found to have a dispute with the owners of the container depot who were not the dockers' employers.[53]

A picket on a highway, railway, runway and such public transport facilities constitutes a trespass, because it is likely to interfere with the safe flow of transport on the facilities. A sedentary or ambulatory picket has to be conducted in such a manner so as not to obstruct persons going about their lawful errands or exercising their right to freedom of movement guaranteed to them by the Namibian Constitution. Picketing on a runway, for instance, will endanger the life and safety of air travellers and, therefore, the Legislature could not have intended that such conduct is a lawful form of picketing.

In *Navachab v Mineworkers Union of Namibia* supra, the Labour Court referred with approval to the interpretation of the phrase 'at or near' in three English cases.[54] In one of them, *British Airports Authority v Ashton and others*, the Labour Court considered the words 'at or near an employer's premises' and stated that that 'does not in terms confer a right to attend on land against the will of the owner of the land. It would be astonishing if Parliament intended that such right should be implied.'[55] Relying on the three English cases, Strydom, JP (as he then was) came to the following conclusion:

---

52   See *Navachab v Mineworkers Union of Namibia* supra.

53   *Midland Cold Storage Ltd v Turner* [1972] ICR 230, which is discussed in chapter 9, para. 9.1 above.

54   *Broome v DPP* (1974) 1 All ER 314 (CA); *LARKIN v Belfast Harbour Commissioners* (1908) IR 214; *British Airports Authority v Ashton and others* [1983] 3 All ER 6 (QB).

55   *British Airports Authority v Ashton* supra at 13-14.

A review of the decided cases and comments thereon by writers on the subject show that the act of picketing took place, and was understood to take place, outside the premises or property of the employer. This was not changed by introduction into statutes of the words 'at or near'. In fact the use of these words further, in my opinion, strengthened the meaning given to the term picketing because the general grammatical meaning of those words does not mean 'on the premises' or 'within' such geographical area.[56]

13.4 LOCKOUT

In labour or employment relations, a lockout action is in contrast to a strike action, as a form of industrial action. A lockout is the exclusion of employees from their workplace or the suspension of work by one or more employers, in contemplation or furtherance of an industrial dispute. Section 2 of Swaziland's Industrial Relations Act 2000 defines 'lockout' as 'a total or partial refusal by an employer or group of employers to allow his or their employees to work, if such refusal is done with a view to inducing compliance with any demand or with a view to inducing the abandonment or modification of any demand'. The Swaziland formulation is substantially the same as the Namibian formulation. According to s. 1 of the Labour Act 2007, '"lockout" means a total or partial refusal by one or more employers to allow their employees to work, if the refusal is to compel those employees or employees of any other employer to accept, modify or abandon any demand that may form the subject matter of a dispute.'

Like a strike, a lockout is in compliance with the Labour Act if the lockout has one of the foregoing statutorily stipulated purposes in view. Again, just as employees have the right to strike, employers, too, have the right to take lockout action in terms of s. 76 of the Labour Act. The considerations relating to the right to strike discussed previously (see para. 13.2.2 above) apply with necessary modifications to the right to lockout. Similarly, the aspects of statutory protection offered to strikers (see para. 13.2.3 above) apply with necessary modifications to employers engaged in a lockout. Finally, circumstances under which some strikes are prohibited (see para. 13.2.4, above) also apply with necessary modifications to lockouts. For instance, like a strike, an employer must not take a lockout action if the dispute he and employees have relates to a dispute of right. Thus, it is only when a dispute relates to a dispute of interest that a lockout as a part of the negotiating process would be permissible.[57]

---

56   *Navachab v Mineworkers Union of Namibia* supra at 231B-C.

57   *Smit v Standard Bank Namibia* supra.

It is not intended to discuss lockout any further. Lockouts are less frequent than strikes. Indeed, out of twenty-seven reported labour law cases brought before the Labour Court under the repealed Labour Act 1992 over a period of about two years, only one concerned a lockout.[58]

---

[58] For instance, the author, sitting as a Judge of the Industrial Court of Swaziland, handled about 160 matters in a period of about two years: not even one of them involved a lockout.

14 TRADE UNIONS AND EMPLOYERS' ORGANIZATIONS

14.1 INTRODUCTION

Present-day economies do have certain characteristics that impact significantly on employer-and-employee relationships. Businesses are carried out in the form of huge local and international corporations – either as small separate entities or conglomerates. A corporation today is not managed directly by its owners but by a host of professional business managers, employing many other professionals. Corporations have, therefore, replaced many of the one-individual or the small-scale businesses of two or three centuries ago that were managed by their proprietors. Besides, modern governments have also become employers on a large scale. Indeed, in most developing countries, governments are the largest employers, employing a multitude of individuals in the civil service, local government authorities, parastatals and other State institutions.

Despite the stiff competition among employers in the business world, most employers have seen fit to form or join employers' associations with the aim of promoting and defending their common interests vis-à-vis employees. Their common interests at times involve ways and means of countering all manner of demands by employees. It was mentioned in chapter 13 (see para. 13.2.2 above) that employers have always wielded enormous economic power over their employees, not to mention the tremendous economic and political power of modern governments over their employees. Employees have, therefore, also found it necessary, if not imperative, to bind together into employees' organizations aimed at safeguarding and promoting their interests in the face of the vast economic power that private employers and their associations exercise over employees, coupled with the overwhelming economic and political power that governments bring to bear upon their own employees. However, it has not been all plain sailing for employees. The common law notion of the master-and-servant relationship does not take kindly to employees' organizations: it considers such organizations at the workplace as unlawful and irritating combinations.

The provenance of free and lawful organization of employees into trade unions, therefore, lies in statute law, e.g. Trade Unions Act (Malawi),[1] Trade Unions Ordinance (Tanzania),[2] Trade Unions Act (United Kingdom),[3] and in Namibia, the Wage and Industrial Conciliation Ordinance.[4] In some countries, the statutory right to form or join trade unions is buttressed by constitutional provisions, e.g. s. 23(2)(a) of the Constitution of South Africa,[5] Art. 21(1) of the Constitution of Zambia[6] and s. 21(1) of the Constitution of Zimbabwe.[7] In Namibia, the human right to form or join trade unions is guaranteed by Art. 21(e) of the Namibian Constitution.

The rest of the present chapter is devoted to a discussion of trade unions, particularly as provided for under Chapter 6 of the Labour Act 2007. It is not intended to discuss employers' organizations. Suffice it to mention that the topics that are discussed in relation to trade unions under the Labour Act apply with necessary modifications to employers' organizations: indeed, Chapter 6 of the Act is entitled 'Trade Unions and Employers' Organizations'.

14.2 What is a Trade Union?

A trade union may be described as an organization of employees whose principal object is the regulation of relations between its members, on the one hand, and their employers or employers' associations of which the employers are members, on the other hand. According to s. 1 of the Labour Act 2007 a '"trade union" means an association of employees whose principal purpose is to regulate relations between employees and their employers.'[8] Chapter 6 of the Labour Act has established the legal framework for the formation and registration of trade unions and other matters connected with, or incidental to, trade union rights and activities.

---

[1]   Cap. 54.01 of the Laws of Malawi.

[2]   Trade Unions Ordinance 1932.

[3]   Trade Unions Act 1871 (c. 31).

[4]   Act No. 35 of 1952.

[5]   Act No. 108 of 1996.

[6]   1996.

[7]   As amended, 1 August 1985.

[8]   See s. 2 of Swaziland's Industrial Relations Act (No. 1 of 2000), which defines a 'trade union' as 'a combination of employees, the principal purpose of which is the regulation of relations between employees and employers'.

14.3 THE RIGHT TO FORM OR JOIN A TRADE UNION

The right to join or form a trade union is a genus of the wider human right to freedom of association, which is recognized in international human rights law. Article 22(1) of the United Nations International Covenant on Civil and Political Rights (ICCPR) provides: 'Everyone shall have the right to freedom of association with others, including the right to form and join trade unions for the protection of his interests.'[9] The International Labour Organization (ILO) Freedom of Association and Protection of the Right to Organize Convention consolidates the enjoyment of the right.[10] Article 2 of the Convention provides: 'Workers and employers, without distinction, whatsoever, shall have the right to establish and, subject to the rules of the organization concerned, to join organizations of their own choosing without previous authorization.' Since the Convention is a treaty, it is binding on States that are parties to it. Therefore, State Parties to the Convention are obliged to bring their domestic laws and practices into conformity with it. Such a process ensures that the international labour standards established in the Convention are implemented through national laws and practices. Being a party to ILO Convention 87, Namibia has taken the legislative measures under the Labour Act necessary to implement certain key aspects of the Convention.

Article 21(1)(e) of the Namibian Constitution, which is in accord with Namibia's international obligations under the ILO Convention 87 and the ICCPR, guarantees an employee's right to form or join a trade union of his choice. The relevant part of Art. 21(1) (e) of the Constitution provides: 'All persons shall have the right to freedom of association, which shall include freedom to form and join...unions, including trade unions.' Doubtless, the right to freedom of association includes the right to freedom of non-association, and, *a priori*, the right to terminate membership of any association. An employer will therefore be violating an individual's constitutional right guaranteed under Art. 21(1)(e), if he attaches non-membership of a trade union as a precondition of employment or continued employment. Therefore, an employer's insistence that an employee can only keep his employment if he is not, or has not been, a member of a trade union, is tainted by illegality according to Art. 21(1) of the Constitution and s. 32(2) of the Labour Act 2007. As we saw in chapter 8, para. 8.2 above, it is automatically unfair under s. 33(2)(d), (e) and (f) of the Labour Act for an employer to dismiss an employee because that employee belongs, or has belonged, to a trade union, or has taken part in the formation of a trade union, or has participated in the lawful

---

9   Namibia became a State Party to the Covenant in 1994.

10   ILO C87 Freedom of Association and Protection of the Right to Organize Convention, 1948.

activities of a trade union outside working hours or during working hours, with the consent of the employer.

The result of this is that the concept of the 'closed shop' is alien to Namibian labour law. According to the principle of 'closed shop', an individual is required to be a member of a particular union before obtaining employment or after obtaining employment in a particular industry. The former is referred to as pre-entry closed shop and the later post-entry closed shop.[11] In terms of s. 26 of South Africa's Labour Relations Act 1995,[12] a representative trade union and an employer or employer's organization could conclude a collective agreement, to be known as a closed-shop agreement, which required all employees covered by the agreement to be members of that trade union. Similarly, what is referred to in the United States as the 'yellow-dog contract',[13] will also be unconstitutional and unlawful in Namibia. Under such contract of employment, the employer requires his employees to renounce their right to form or join a trade union.[14]

14.4 Unionizable Employees

The Labour Act 2007 does not prescribe the minimum number of employees required to form a trade union.[15] Nevertheless, it cannot be doubted that for any trade union to be viable, financially strong and effective, it has to be able to attract a large number of paying members: a trade union with only a handful of members is doomed to fail.

Another important issue that has bedevilled the formation of trade unions is the question as to which employees qualify to be members of trade unions. In other words, which categories of employees are 'unionizable'? The answer to this question has real practical relevance during collective bargaining, which is discussed in the next chapter. The question that often crops up, particularly during collective bargaining, is whether it is practicable or, indeed, fair to an employer that some of his own employees (who, by virtue of their managerial position in his enterprise, do represent the employer during collective bargaining with a trade union) should be members of that trade union? Such managers, as well as their personal assistants, in most cases belong to the management component of the enterprise.[16]

---

[11] C.D. Drake *Labour Law* 2nd edn, London, Sweet & Maxwell, 1973, para. 143.

[12] Act No. 66 of 1995.

[13] Today such contracts are generally illegal, having been outlawed by the Wagner Act of 1935 (see B.A. Garner *A Dictionary of Modern Legal Usage,* 2nd edn, Oxford, Oxford University Press, 1995, p. 947).

[14] Drake *Labour Law,* para. 509.

[15] Cf. s.26(2) of Swaziland's Industrial Relations Act 2000 (Act No. 1 of 2000), which prescribes the minimum number of employees required to form an industry (or trade) union.

[16] See P. Blunt *Organizational Theory and Behaviour: An African Perspective,* London, Longman, 1983, pp. 121-2.

As far as the right to join or form trade unions under the Labour Act 2007 is concerned, there is nothing preventing an employee who is a manager of an organization from forming or joining a trade union of his choice or, indeed, becoming an office-bearer of such a trade union. What may be unconscionable is such an employee being placed under undue pressure to disclose his employer's confidential information or being made a member of the negotiating team representing his trade union in negotiations with his own employer where it is part of his duties as an employee to negotiate on behalf of his employer or assist his employer in negotiations with the same trade union.[17]

In *Keshwar v SANCA* supra, the South African Industrial Court declared unfair the dismissal of an employee who was a manager and who was dismissed after she had refused to resign as the elected chairperson of the association of her fellow employees. The gravamen of the employer's contention was that the position of the employee in the union was incompatible with her managerial responsibilities. The Industrial Court rejected the argument that an employee who is in the management cadre ought, as a general rule, to be prevented from becoming an office-bearer of a trade union, which is active in the undertaking of his employer.

Be that as it may, the employee's right to join or form a trade union of his choice, and to be elected to office, may be limited by certain aspects of the employee's duty to his employer, which are discussed in chapter 3 above. The right may be limited by the employee's duty at common law to render the service for which he was employed and not to divulge to unauthorized persons confidential information gained in the course of employment. As the Industrial Court observed in *Keshwar v SANCA* supra, an employee may not participate in those union activities which would make it impossible or extremely difficult to perform the tasks entrusted to him by his master.

It is not merely the title that one carries in an enterprise that qualifies one as an employee in a management position. The title may be a useful indicator, but it is by no means the decisive consideration. The duties performed by an employee in a particular post are a determining factor. For instance, an employee is considered as having managerial responsibilities if he:

1   has power to define policy and make rules and enforce such policy and rules through commands to subordinates;[18]

2   exercises sufficient discretion in carrying out his functions;

3   exercises authority over subordinates;

---

17   *Keshwar v SANCA* 1991 12 *ILJ* 816 (IC).

18   Ibid.

4   participates in the formulation of enterprise policies and strategies for the implementation of those policies;[19]

5   is involved in the supervision of work either directly or indirectly through subordinates;

6   is responsible for governing the relationship between the enterprise and organizations external to it;

7   is charged with the responsibility of determining direction, amount, and pace of change in enterprise activities.[20]

However it may be, as we have seen, in terms of the Namibian Constitution and the Labour Act 2007, all employees have the right to join or form trade unions. Nevertheless, it would be proper that an employee who holds a managerial position ought to be excluded from collective bargaining by both sides in the interest of industrial harmony and fair play, if his union and his employer are engaged in collective bargaining. This should be the case where, for instance, his inclusion in a bargaining unit would lead to a conflict of interest and thereby make the rendering of his service to his employer in terms of his contract of employment difficult or impossible.[21]

14.5 REGISTRATION

In terms of s. 57(1) of the Labour Act 2007, any trade union may apply to the Labour Commissioner for registration. It is worth pointing out that as a matter of law, it is not mandatory to register a trade union with the Labour Commissioner in order for it to be a lawful employee organization. The provisions governing registration for the purposes of the Labour Act are rather permissive and empowering: they grant to registered trade unions certain status and rights, which unregistered trade unions do not enjoy. (Consequences of registration and rights of registered trade unions are discussed in para. 14.7 below.)

The foremost requirement for registration is that the trade union must adopt a constitution that complies with the requirements set out in s. 53 of the Act. The provisions of the constitution of a trade union must not, as provided in s. 53(3), be inconsistent with the human rights provisions in Chapter 3 of the Namibian Constitution or any other law. Neither should the constitution of a trade union impede the attainment of the objects of any law, or be an instrument for avoiding an obligation imposed by any law.

---

19   *SA Society of Bank Officials v Standard Bank South Africa Ltd* (1994) 15 *ILJ* 332 (IC).

20   Blunt *Organizational Theory and Behaviou,r* pp. 165-6.

21   *SA Society of Bank Officials v Standard Bank* supra.

According to s. 57(1) of the Labour Act, a trade union that has adopted a constitution that complies with s 53 of the Labour Act and that wishes to apply for registration, may submit an application to the Labour Commissioner in a prescribed form. The application must be accompanied by three copies of its constitution, each duly certified as true and correct copies of the constitution by both the chairperson and secretary of the trade union. The Labour Commissioner may ask for further information if, in his opinion, such further information is required to enable him to make a decision. In terms of s. 57(5) of the Act, the Minister responsible for Labour may make regulations prescribing further requirements or conditions to be satisfied by a trade union applying for registration under Chapter 6 of the Act. Section 57 (3) provides that the Labour Commissioner has a statutory duty to consider every application and any further information given by the applicant; and if the application meets the requirements for registration set out in s. 53(2) and (3) of the Act, he must register the trade union, and issue the union with a prescribed certificate of registration.

If the Labour Commissioner refuses to register a trade union, he must give notice of his decision and the reasons for it. It is submitted that even without the specific statutory requirement that the Labour Commissioner must give reasons for his decision, upon the authority of *Frank and another v Chairperson of the Immigration Selection Board*[22] and *Katofa v Administrator-General for South West Africa and another*,[23] the Labour Commissioner is obliged by common law and Art. 18 of the Namibian Constitution to give reasons for his refusal to register a trade union. The reason why the Labour Commissioner must give reasons for his refusal to register a trade union is not far to seek. As Levy, J stated in *Frank and another* supra, 'an unfair or unreasonable decision entitles an aggrieved person to redress by the court but the court cannot judge what is reasonable or unreasonable unless the administrative body gives its reasons for arriving at its decision.'[24] In *Katofa v Administrator-General for SWA*, the High Court considered whether the Administrator-General (for South West Africa – now Namibia) could be compelled to give reasons for the arrest and detention of *K*. The statutory provision required the Administrator-General to be 'satisfied' that *K* had 'committed or attempted to commit or in any manner promoted the commission of the violence or intimidation referred to in s. 2(1)(a) and (c) of the relevant statute'. The Administrator-General refused to give reasons. The Court held that to be 'satisfied', the Administrator-General must have reason to be satisfied. In other words, objective reasonable grounds must exist to make him satisfied.

Section 63 of the Labour Act provides that a person aggrieved by a decision of the Labour Commissioner under Part B of Chapter 6 of the Act may appeal to the Labour Court against the decision.

---

22   *Frank and another v Chairperson of the Immigration Selection Board* 1999 NR 257 (H C).

23   *Katofa v Administrator-General for South West Africa & another* 1985 (4) SA 211 (SWA).

24   *Frank v Immigration Selection Board s*upra at 265E.

14.6 Elements of the Constitution of a Trade Union

Section 53(2) of the Labour Act 2007 sets out an obligatory list of items that a union must provide in its constitution before its application for registration can be considered. These items are discussed next.

14.6.1 Name of the Trade Union

The constitution of a trade union must state the name of the union. The name chosen must not be identical with the name of a trade union that has already been registered; neither should the name be insulting, profane or odious.

14.6.2 Objects of the Trade Union

The constitution of a trade union must declare the objects of the union. A trade union must not be for a criminal or other unlawful purpose; neither should a trade union be formed with the aim of obstructing the implementation of, for instance, the Labour Act or any other law. A trade union whose sole object is to gain and maintain political power is not a trade union for the purpose of the Act, and cannot therefore be registered. It does not mean that a trade union is barred from expressing itself vigorously and openly in support of one political party or another; neither is it wrong nor improper for a trade union to openly support a particular political view or aim. There is ample evidence of the invaluable role played by trade unions in the nationalist struggle for freedom and independence in Africa.[25] Indeed, trade unions continue to play an important role in post-colonial politics in Africa and elsewhere.[26]

14.6.3 Industry or Industries in its Scope

The constitution must prescribe the industry or industries in the trade union's scope, i.e. in which the trade union will be active. Unlike, for instance, the situation in Swaziland where s. 29 of the Industrial Relations Act[27] confines a trade union to only one particular undertaking, industry or trade in which that union can represent employees, in Namibia the Labour Act does not restrict a trade union to only one industry.

---

[25] See W. Tordoff, *Government and Politics in Africa,* London, Macmillan, 1984, p. 58.

[26] In Swaziland, the Swaziland Federation of Trade Unions spearheads the movement for multi-party democracy. In South Africa, the triadic relationship between the ruling party (the African National Congress (ANC)), the South African Communist Party (SACP) and the Congress of South African Trade Unions (COSATU) is well known. In Namibia, the National Union of Namibian Workers (NUNW), a federation of a number of trade unions, is affiliated to the ruling party, the SWAPO Party. This arrangement gives the NUNW a noticeable and invaluable voice in government and politics in Namibia in the interests of its members.

[27] Act No. 1 of 2000.

14.6.4 Qualification for Admission to Membership

The constitution of a trade union must prescribe the qualifications for membership. The question that arises is whether a trade union can reject the application of an employee for membership. The general rule is that an applicant who is an employee in the industry or undertaking that is within the scope of the union, and who meets the qualifications requisite for membership according to that trade union's constitution, should not be excluded from membership arbitrarily or upon discriminatory grounds.[28] In *NAGLE v Fielden*,[29] where a female jockey trainer was excluded from the Jockey Club (an association of jockeys), Lord Denning, MR observed that a person should not be shut out of such organization 'at the whim of those having the governance of' the organization.[30] The Court found that the exclusion would be unlawful because it was arbitrary and unreasonable.

The decision of a trade union like that of any other private or contractual body is subject to those principles of administrative law that are designed to protect individuals from abuse of power. As a general rule, private or contractual bodies like trade unions, which exercise power over their members, must observe the common law requirements of natural justice and fairness just as public bodies are expected to do.[31] The courts will, however, uphold the rules governing admission of members so long as the rules are not discriminatory or do not violate any provision of the Namibian Constitution or any other law. In *Faramus v Film Artistes Association*,[32] the House of Lords did not find fault with a rule of an association which rendered anyone unfit for admission, if such an individual had been convicted of a criminal offence, other than a traffic offence not punishable by imprisonment.

14.6.5 Membership Fees

The constitution of a trade union must provide for the payment of union membership fees (i.e. dues and the method of determining those fees and fees and other payments by members). Fees and other payments exacted from members must be for the legitimate objects of the trade union. It will be ultra vires for a trade union to ask its members to pay, for instance, a political levy, i.e. a levy meant as a contribution to the funds of a political party. In *Amalgamated Society of Railway Servants v Osborne*,[33] the House of Lords applied the doctrine of ultra vires to unions and held that a rule providing for a political levy was null and void.

---

28   Drake *Labour Law,* para. 252.

29   *NAGLE v Fielden* [1966] 2 QB 633.

30   Ibid. at 644.

31   L. Baxter *Administrative Law,* Cape Town, Juta, 1984, p. 101.

32   *Faramus v Film Artistes Association* [1964] 2 AC 925.

33   *Amalgamated Society of Railway Servants v Osborne* [1910] AC 87 (HL).

The constitution must also make provision that prescribes that a member of good standing is one who is not more than three months in arrears with the payment of fees due in terms of the union's constitution. Thus the maximum period of arrears permissible under the Labour Act is three months. The constitution must also prescribe that only a member of good standing is entitled to nominate candidates for any office or vote, or be voted for, in the election of an office-bearer or official of the union. The upshot of these stipulations is that one must be a member of good standing for one to participate in the election of office-bearers or officials, either as a candidate or a voter.

14.6.6 Termination of Membership

The constitution must specify the circumstances under which membership may terminate and also prescribe the procedure governing termination of membership. The constitution must essentially provide for voluntary and involuntary termination. With regard to voluntary termination, the constitution must provide for circumstances under which, and procedures by which, a member may terminate his membership voluntarily. For instance, it may provide that a member must give reasonable notice in writing to terminate membership, indicate the person authorized to receive the notice on behalf of the trade union, and the mode of transmission of the notice.

As regards involuntary termination, the circumstances under which, and the procedures by which, termination may take place must include the provision that a member has the right to be heard before a decision to terminate his membership is taken, as well as the right of, and procedures for, appeal. The right to be heard, it is submitted, entails the member being informed in writing of the allegations made against him, being given the opportunity to respond in writing to the allegations, being given the opportunity to cross-examine witnesses so as to controvert adverse evidence, where necessary or expedient, and being afforded the opportunity to bring witnesses to testify on his behalf (see chapter 8, para. 8.1.3 and chapter 11, para. 11.3.2 above, where the rules of natural justice are discussed). In short, the termination of one's membership of a trade union must be substantively and procedurally fair, i.e. the decision to terminate must be based on valid, reasonable, and fair grounds, and the procedure leading up to the termination must be fair. In *Bonsor v Musicians' Union*,[34] the House of Lords held that a member of a registered trade union whose membership has wrongfully been terminated is entitled to any appropriate relief.

---

34   *Bonsor v Musicians' Union* [1956] AC 104 (HL).

14.6.7 Office-Bearers and Officials

The constitution must prescribe the functions of its office-bearers and officials. It must also prescribe the procedures to be followed in the election and appointment of officials and office-bearers, as the case may be, the terms of their appointment and the circumstances and manner in which they may be removed from office. It must also provide for the appointment of officials and the circumstances and manner in which they may be appointed.

Doubtless, there is a distinction between office-bearers and officials of a trade union. Office-bearers are the elected officers of the trade union; their primary functions are to make policies and direct and supervise the implementation of the policies. Office-bearers, therefore, include such elective officers as the president, chairperson, secretary-general, treasurer and the national and sub-national organizers. Officials, on the other hand, are those appointed to advise the office-bearers in making policies and to implement those policies. They are primarily employees of the trade union and are responsible for the day-to-day administration and management of a trade union. In other words, officials are the staff of the trade union: they include technical and administrative support staff, such as legal advisors, economists and clerical and secretariat staff. The requirements of observance of natural justice and fairness must also apply to a decision to remove an office-bearer from office or dismiss officials (see chapter 8, para. 8.1.3 and chapter 11, para. 11.3.2 above, where the rules of natural justice are also discussed).

The constitution must also contain a provision that prescribes that no person who has been convicted by a competent court of an offence of which dishonesty is an element, and for which that person has been sentenced to a term of imprisonment without the option of a fine should stand for election to the position of office-bearer.

14.6.8 Workplace Representatives

The constitution must make provision prescribing the procedure for nomination and election of health and safety representatives. Section 43 of the Labour Act provides that where there are more than 10 but fewer than 101 employees at a workplace, the employees are entitled to elect from among their number at least one health and safety representative. Where there are 101 or more employees, they are entitled to elect from among their number at least one health and safety representative for the first 100 employees in the workplace and at least one additional representative for each additional 100 employees, or a part of that number. Nevertheless, an employer and employees, or a trade union representing the employees, may agree to elect a greater number of health and safety representatives. Section 43(2), (3) and (4) provide for the conduct of election of health and safety representatives, their tenure of office and provision of facilities necessary to enable them to carry out their functions.

Furthermore, s. 44 provides for their rights and powers. The constitution must also prescribe the procedure for the nomination and election of workplace representatives. Section 67 of the Act provides for, among other things, the conduct of election of workplace representatives, their functions, powers and activities.

14.6.9 Meetings

The constitution must prescribe that there must be at least one general meeting of members every three years, and that such meetings are open to all members. These are ordinary meetings. Therefore, nothing prevents a trade union from convening as many extra-ordinary meetings as necessary and practicable. The constitution must also prescribe the procedure for convening and conducting meetings of members and of office-bearers, as well as the manner in which ballots are to be conducted. These provisions should deal, for instance, with such procedural matters as the giving of notice, which must indicate the agenda, the time and venue of the meeting, the manner of voting at meetings and the kind of majorities required to carry decisions,[35] and the power of the chairperson of a meeting to cast a casting vote in addition to his deliberate vote, where there is equality of votes.[36] This is necessary because at common law the chairperson of a meeting has no casting vote: the power to cast a casting vote must be expressly conferred on him. The constitution must also prescribe the quorum of meetings and the manner in which minutes of meetings are to be kept.

14.6.10   Financial Provisions and Acquisition and Control of Property

The constitution must provide for the banking and investing of union funds, and stipulate the purposes for which the funds may be used. It must also provide that no payment may be made to an official or employee without the prior approval of its governing body granted under the hand of the chairperson, except payment of salaries and expenses incurred by them in the course of their duties. The constitution must also indicate the end of the trade union's financial year. The constitution must also make provision for the acquisition and control of property.

---

[35] Sir S. Shaw and Judge D. Smith *The Law of Meetings,* 5th edn, Estover, MacDonald and Evans, 1979, p. 98; M.M. Ncube and C. Parker *Comparative Electoral Systems and Political Consequences for Independent Namibia,* Lusaka, UN Institute for Namibia, 1989, pp. 28-31, where the different kinds of majorities are discussed. For a brief discussion of the nature and essentials of meetings, voting and sense of meetings, and decisions and resolutions that may not be binding, see Collins Parker *A Manual of Public Management,* Windhoek, Aim Publications, 2003, Chapter 10.

[36] *Bishop of Chichester v Horward* (1787) 1 T Rep 650; *Noel v Longbottom* 1894 1 QB 771; A. Lewin *The Law, Procedure and Conduct of Meetings in South Africa,* Cape Town, Juta, 1975, p. 61.

14.6.11   Affiliation and Amalgamation

The constitution must prescribe procedures whereby the trade union may affiliate or amalgamate with another trade union. Affiliation denotes connection with one or more trade unions, while amalgamation denotes combining or uniting with one or more trade unions to form one single organization.

Thus, where affiliation is achieved, the trade union retains its independent existence, structure and organization. If, on the other hand, amalgamation is created, then that trade union loses its independent identity: its structure and organization are merged with those of the other trade union or trade unions with which it amalgamates to form one organization; thereby creating a single organizational structure. It is therefore feasible for X union to be affiliated with other trade unions so as to form a federation, comprising two or more trade unions, even though those trade unions are active in industries and undertakings outside X union's scope of activity. However, where X union amalgamates with one or more trade unions active in industries and undertakings that are totally outside X union's scope of activity, in practice, X union is made to sacrifice its interests for the interests of the whole, which may not necessarily be identical to its own. Trade unions will, therefore, do well to bear these observations in mind when taking a decision on affiliation or amalgamation.

14.6.12   Amendment of Constitution

The constitution must make provision that prescribes a procedure for amending the constitution. An amendment of a constitution must comply with statutory procedures under s. 54 of the Labour Act. According to s. 54(1) of the Act, any change to the constitution of a trade union takes effect only when the Labour Commissioner approves the change.

In terms of s. 54(2), a trade union desirous of amending any provision of its constitution may apply to the Labour Commissioner for approval of the amendment, by submitting to him a duly completed prescribed form, the prescribed number of copies of the resolution containing the wording of the amendment, and a certificate signed by the chairperson of the trade union, stating that the resolution was passed in accordance with the union's constitution.

The Labour Commissioner may, in terms of s. 54(3), ask for further information that supports the application. It is peremptory for the Labour Commissioner to consider an application, together with any further information supplied to him by the trade union. If the Labour Commissioner is satisfied that a proposed amendment meets the requirements under s. 53, he must approve the amendment by issuing the prescribed certificate, approving the change. If an amendment concerns a change of name of the union, the Labour Commissioner must issue a new certificate of registration, reflecting the new name. As provided in s. 54(5), if the Labour Commissioner refuses to approve an amendment, he must give a written notice of his decision and reasons for it. Section 53(2)–(5) applies with necessary modifications to an application to amend a constitution of a registered trade union under s. 54.

14.6.13 Winding up of a Trade Union

Finally, the constitution of a trade union must prescribe the procedure for the winding up of the trade union. Section 55 of the Labour Act governs the winding up of a trade union. The Labour Court may order a trade union to be wound up if any of the following circumstances exist.

1   If the union has resolved to wind up its affairs and has applied to the Court to make an order giving effect to the resolution (i.e. voluntary winding-up).

2   If the Labour Commissioner or any member of the trade union has applied to the Court for an order to wind up the union, and the Court is satisfied that due to some problem that cannot be remedied, the trade union is no longer able to function as a trade union (i.e. involuntary winding-up).

3   If a person has applied to the Labour Court for an order to wind up the trade union because the trade union is insolvent (i.e. winding-up due to insolvency); in which case the Insolvency Act 1936[37] applies, but any reference in that Act to the court must be interpreted as a reference to the Labour Court.

14.7 Consequences of Registration and Rights of Registered Trade Unions

According to s. 59(1) of the Labour Act 2007, upon receiving its certificate of registration, a trade union becomes a juristic person. It becomes a new species of body corporate having separate legal personality and the power to hold and dispose of property, to sue and be sued and to enter into contracts in its own name. Consequently, a member, an office-bearer or an official of a registered union is not personally liable for any liability or obligation incurred in good faith by the union solely because of being a member, an office-bearer or official of the trade union.

---

[37]   Act No 24 of 1936.

According to s. 59 of the Labour Act, certain notable rights accrue to a trade union upon registration.

1　　A trade union is entitled to institute proceedings or 'bring a case' on behalf of its members and to represent its members in any proceedings brought under the Act.

2　　A trade union has the right of access to an employer's premises in terms of s. 65 of the Labour Act.

3　　A registered trade union is entitled to have union fees deducted on its behalf in terms of s. 66 of the Labour Act.

4　　A registered trade union is entitled to form federations with other registered trade unions.

5　　A trade union has the right to affiliate with, and participate in the activities of, federations formed with other trade unions.

6　　A trade union has the right to affiliate with, and participate in the activities of, any international workers' organization and, subject to any applicable law governing exchange control, to make contributions to such an organization and to receive financial assistance from such organization.

7　　A registered trade union recognized as an exclusive bargaining agent in terms of s. 64 of the Labour Act is entitled to negotiate terms of, and enter into, a collective agreement with an employer or a registered employers' organization. (Exclusive bargaining agent is dealt with in chapter 15, para. 15.2 below, and collective agreement in para. 15.5.)

8　　A registered trade union is entitled to report to the Labour Commissioner any dispute, which has arisen between an employer and that employer's employees who are members of the trade union.

The other set of consequences of registration is in the form of obligations. According to s. 60 of the Labour Act, every registered trade union must do the following things.

1　　It must maintain a register of its members in the prescribed form.

2　　It must keep proper books of accounts.

3　　It must prepare at the end of each of its financial year a statement of income and expenditure for that year and a balance sheet showing its financial position at the end of the year.

4   It must within six months after the end of its financial year make the statement of income and expenditure, and the balance sheet and the audit report referred to above available to members of the trade union and also submit an annual return in the prescribed form to the Labour Commissioner.

5   It must submit the statement of income and expenditure and the balance sheet to a meeting of its members or their representatives in terms of its constitution.

14.8 Consequences of Registration and Individual Membership Rights

The basic provisions, which every constitution of a trade union wishing to be registered must contain (see para. 14.6, above), and some of the consequences of registration and trade union rights (see para. 14.7) in terms of the Labour Act, help to protect the rights of individual members of registered trade unions. Without a doubt, many of those statutory stipulations constitute a deliberate attempt by the Labour Act 2007 to safeguard the rights of individual members of registered trade unions, too. One basic and supremely important right inferred from those provisions is this: a member of good standing of a registered trade union should not be subjected to arbitrary or unlawful interference with his right to participate directly or indirectly in the governance of the trade union. In this regard, such a member has the right to do the following.

1   He may put forward his candidature for any office in the organization – at the national and sub-national levels, and to hold office when successful in elections. For instance, it will be an arbitrary or unlawful decision if the member is excluded from standing as a candidate in a union election to elect an officer-bearer solely because of, e.g. his sex, race, colour, ethnic origin, religion, creed, or social or economic status or political belief and affiliation.

2   He is entitled to nominate candidates who wish to be elected as office-bearers.

3   He is entitled to vote in any election of office-bearers and participate in any ballot to determine decisions affecting the union.

4   He has the right to attend and participate in meetings of the union at the national level and meetings of a section or branch so long as he belongs to that section or branch.

However, as discussed previously (para. 14.6.5 above), according to s. 53(2)(g)(ii) of the Labour Act, only a member of good standing is entitled to nominate candidates, or put up himself as a candidate, for any office or vote in an election of an office-bearer or official. In addition, according to s. 53(2)(g)(iii), a member who has been convicted of an offence of which dishonesty is an element and sentenced to imprisonment without the option of a fine is ineligible to seek election to the position of office-bearer.

14.9 Cancellation of Registration of Trade Union

14.9.1 Cancellation in Terms of Section 61 of the Labour Act

The status of a trade union as a registered union does not endure indefinitely. First, according to s. 61 of the Labour Act 2007, the Labour Commissioner must give notice in writing to a registered trade union that he has reason to believe that that trade union is no longer complying with its obligations under Part B of Chapter 6 of the Act. In the notice, the Labour Commissioner must invite the trade union to make representations to him. Section 61(3) provides that after considering the representations made to him by the trade union, the Labour Commissioner may issue a compliance order, which may include steps required to rectify the union's non-compliance. If a trade union fails to comply with a compliance order, the Labour Commissioner may do one of two things: he may cancel its registration or apply to the Labour Court for an order to compel the trade union to comply with the compliance order, which may include an order suspending the trade union's registration pending its compliance.

14.9.2 Cancellation in Terms of Section 62 of the Labour Act

Section 62(1) of the Labour Act provides that if a registered trade union fails to comply a provision of its constitution, the Labour Commissioner or a member of the trade union may apply to the Labour Court for relief. In this regard, the Labour Court may grant an order directing the trade union and its officials and office-bearers to comply with the provision in its constitution to the extent indicated in the order, or cancelling the trade union's registration, or the Court may grant such further relief as it may deem necessary.

Furthermore, according to s. 62(2) of the Labour Act, if a violation or material irregularity occurs concerning an election held in terms of the constitution, rules or by-laws of the registered trade union, or if any person influences the outcome of an election by unlawful means, the Labour Commissioner or a member of the trade union may apply to the Labour Court for relief. The Labour Court may make an order declaring such election to be null and void, directing the holding of a further election as specified, providing for interim arrangements in relation to the affairs of the trade union pending the outcome of any further election, or the Court may grant such further relief at it may deem necessary.

15 COLLECTIVE BARGAINING AND AGREEMENTS

15.1 INTRODUCTION

The Labour Act 2007 now provides for the concept of unfair labour practice, which as we saw in chapter 8 above, was unknown to the repealed Labour Act 1992.[1] Chapter 5 of that Act is entitled 'Unfair Labour Practices'. Section 49 lists practices of an employee or a trade union, and s. 50 practices of an employer or employers' organization that are unfair labour practices for the purposes of the Act. Some of the practices concern collective bargaining, which is one of the topics discussed in the present chapter.

We saw in chapter 14 (para. 14.7 above), that upon registration, a trade union acquires certain statutory rights. In addition to acquiring those rights, which are immediate, a registered trade union may seek recognition as the exclusive bargaining agent in the industry or industries within its scope. Those rights and the rights attaching to a trade union as the exclusive bargaining agent inure as collective rights: they do not attach to individual members of the trade union.[2]

The basis of collective bargaining is the desire of employers and employees to bargain freely with minimum State interference; nevertheless, State intervention in the form of legislation is considered to be conducive to sound labour or employment relations. The *raison d'être* of trade unions is the need for employees to present a united and collective front in their dealings with employers who, on any scale, have overwhelming economic power. Doubtless, the main purpose of a trade union is to secure suitable conditions for its individual members.[3] It, therefore, makes great sense for the State to intervene and facilitate the process of collective bargaining by means of legislation so as to promote the attainment of industrial peace and harmony.

The machinery of collective bargaining has the effect of replacing the arrangement whereby remuneration and other terms and conditions of service of employees are negotiated between the employer and his employees individually. Since the 1970s, there has been a

---

[1]   *Kamanya and others v Kuiseb Fish Products Ltd* 1996 NR 123 (LC) at 125E.

[2]   *Mutual & Federal Insurance Co v Bank, Insurance, Finance & Assurance Workers Union* (1996) 17 *ILJ* 241 (A).

[3]   *SA Association of Municipal Employees v Minister of Labour* 1948 (1) SA 528 (T) at 537-8.

great increase in the practice of collective bargaining over the negotiation of individual contracts of employment.[4] The desired result of collective bargaining is the making of collective agreements, which is discussed in para. 15.5 below. In *National Union of Mineworkers v East Rand Gold & Uranium Co Ltd*, Goldstone, J (as he then was) observed about collective bargaining under South Africa's repealed Labour Relations Act[5] that the 'fundamental philosophy of the Act is that collective bargaining is the means preferred by the legislature for the maintenance of good labour relations and for the resolution of labour disputes.[6] This 'fundamental philosophy', it is submitted, is one of the foundational features and one of the objects of the Labour Act 2007; since one of the objects of the Act is spelt out in the Preamble as 'promoting an orderly system of free collective bargaining'.

In *National Union of Mineworkers v East Rand Gold & Uranium* supra, Goldstone, J (as he then was) stated:

> In Davie & Freedland *Labour Law: Text and Materials* one reads at 112-3:
>
> 'By collective bargaining we mean those social structures whereby employers (either alone or in coalition with other employers) bargain with the representatives of their employees about terms and conditions of employment, about rules governing the working environment (e.g. the ratio of apprentices to skilled men) and about the procedures that should govern the relations between union and employer. Such bargaining is called "collective" bargaining because on the workers' side the representative acts on behalf of a group of workers.'[7]

During collective bargaining, the representatives of employees and the representatives of the employer bargain about such substantive matters as terms and conditions of employment and such procedural matters as the procedures that should govern the relations between the employer and the trade union and disciplinary inquiries. The word 'collective' is, therefore, used to denote the representativeness of the bargaining teams.

15.2 Exclusive Bargaining Agents

In terms of the Labour Act 2007, only a registered trade union can aspire to become the sole bargaining agent of employees in any industry or undertaking. It is when a trade union has

---

4   C. Drake, *Labour Law,* 2nd edn, London, Sweet & Maxwell, 1973, para. 499.

5   Act No. 28 of 1956.

6   *National Union of Mineworkers v East Rand Gold & Uranium Co Ltd* (1991) 12 *ILJ* 1221 (A) at 1236J-1237A.

7   Ibid. at 1237A-B.

been recognized as the sole bargaining agent that it can undertake 'collective bargaining' with the employer who has recognized the trade union as such. It is, therefore, necessary for a trade union to attract large numbers of employees into its membership so that it can claim exclusive recognition by the employer of the right to engage in bargaining on behalf of his employees. Recognition of trade unions for the purpose of collective bargaining is a statutory innovation.[8]

As s. 64 of the Labour Act 2007 provides, a registered trade union that represents the majority of employees in an appropriate bargaining unit is entitled to recognition as the exclusive bargaining agent of the employees in that bargaining unit for the purpose of negotiating a collective agreement on any matter of mutual interest. 'Bargaining unit' is not defined by the Act: the term denotes an ascertainable category of employees in an industry or industries having the same employer or the same group of employers. To illustrate the point, both the Public Service Union of Namibia (PSUN) and the Namibian Public Workers Union (NAPWU) are, for example, active in the civil service. Each union has a substantial number of civil servants as its members; the employer of the civil service is the Government; and the civil service is an undertaking. Consequently, the civil service is a bargaining unit.

In terms of s. 64(2) of the Labour Act, a trade union which claims such recognition must be a registered trade union, which represents the majority of employees in the bargaining unit, or where an arbitrator has, in terms of s. 64(9) of the Act, declared that such trade union represents the majority of employees in the bargaining unit. In this regard, 'majority' means a simple majority. If two or more trade unions claim recognition, then there is a recognition dispute. Such dispute can be resolved by the employer holding a ballot under the supervision of the Labour Commissioner to determine which union has the best claim. This is what the Government did in July 1997 in terms of the repealed Labour Act 1992, in order to decide whether to recognize the Namibia Public Workers Union (NAPWU) or the Public Service Union of Namibia (PSUN) as the exclusive bargaining agent of civil servants. The result of the ballot favoured NAPWU.

A registered trade union, wishing to be recognized as the exclusive bargaining agent in an appropriate bargaining unit, may deliver a request on a prescribed form in terms of s. 64(3) of the Labour Act to an employer, for recognition as the exclusive bargaining agent of all or a part of the employees of the employer. Or it may deliver a request to an employer's organization for such recognition in respect of the employees of the members of that employers' organization. The trade union in question is obliged by s. 64(4) of the Labour Act to submit to the Labour Commissioner a copy of the request, proof that the request has

---

8   For example, in Swaziland, collective bargaining is provided under s. 42 of Swaziland's Industrial Relations Act 2000 (Act No. 1 of 2002).

been submitted to the employer and, if requested by the Labour Commissioner, proof that in truth the trade union represents the majority of the employees within the bargaining unit. Such proof may be obtained in one of two ways: (i) through either the taking of a ballot of the employees under the supervision of the Labour Commissioner; or (ii) through any other manner agreed between the trade union and the employer or employers' organization.

According to s. 64(5) of the Act, upon receipt of the request, the employer or the employers' organization is obliged to respond to the trade union in a prescribed form within thirty days of receipt of the request. The response must take the form of a notification stating either:

1   that the employer or the employers' organization recognizes the trade union as the exclusive bargaining agent of the employees in the bargaining unit, as proposed by the trade union, or as agreed by the union and the employer; or

2   that it refuses to recognize the union as the exclusive bargaining agent on the basis that it disputes the appropriateness of the proposed bargaining unit, or it disputes whether that union represents the majority of employees in the proposed bargaining unit.

Where the employer or the employers' organization fails to respond to the union's request within thirty days as required by s. 64(5) of the Act or refuses to recognize the union in terms of s. 64,(5), the union may take it that a dispute exists. In that event the union may refer its request in the prescribed form to the Labour Commissioner as a dispute.

When referring the dispute to the Labour Commissioner, the trade union must satisfy the Labour Commissioner that a copy of the notice of the dispute has been served on all the parties to the dispute. If the Labour Commissioner is so satisfied, he must refer the dispute to an arbitrator to attempt to resolve the dispute through arbitration. At the conclusion of the arbitration, the arbitrator may make an order declaring the trade union to be recognized as the exclusive bargaining agent of the employees in the agreed bargaining unit or in an appropriate bargaining unit. However, the arbitrator may make such order only if he is satisfied that the trade union represents the majority of employees in the agreed bargaining unit or in a bargaining unit that the arbitrator considers to be appropriate. In determining the appropriateness of a bargaining unit, an arbitrator must take into account the employer's organizational structure and the need to have a bargaining unit that contributes to orderly and effective collective bargaining, and one that would create minimum fragmentation of the employer's organizational structure.

The status 'exclusive bargaining agent' does not attach to a trade union for an indefinite period because, according to s. 64(11) of the Labour Act, if by the estimation of the employer or the employers' organization concerned the trade union no longer represents the majority of the employees in the bargaining unit, the employer or employers' organization must do the following: the employer or the employer's organization must give to the trade union notice in the prescribed form, urging the union to obtain the support of the majority of employees within three months of receipt of the notice. If at the expiration of three months the union has failed to obtain that majority, then the employer or the employers' organization must withdraw the recognition of the trade union as the exclusive bargaining agent.

As s. 64(12) provides, if there is a dispute concerning the withdrawal of recognition under s. 64(11), any party to the dispute may refer the dispute in writing to the Labour Commissioner. In that event, s. 62(7)–(10), which are discussed above, apply with necessary modifications, and the arbitrator has the power to make any appropriate order, including declaring that the trade union represents a majority of the employees in the bargaining unit, giving the trade union a further opportunity to obtain the necessary majority, altering the bargaining unit, or withdrawing recognition of the trade union as the exclusive bargaining agent of the employees in the bargaining unit. The Act does not state the amount of time the arbitrator may give to a trade union for the purpose of obtaining the required majority. Nonetheless, a trade union's effort in this regard cannot go on indefinitely: it must obtain the required majority within a reasonable time. What is a reasonable time will depend largely upon the circumstances of the particular case: for instance, the need to prevent disruption of operations at the employer's business and the need to promote orderly and effective collective bargaining are critical considerations.

One important point needs to be stressed. According to s. 64(14), a trade union, which has been recognized as an exclusive bargaining agent in respect of the bargaining unit concerned, has a duty to represent, for the purposes set out in s. 64(1) of the Act, the interests of every employee falling within the bargaining unit, irrespective of whether they are members of that trade union. The Labour Court held that the identical provisions in s. 58(1) of the repealed Labour Act 1992 were constitutional, and not offensive of the rules of natural justice.[9] It is submitted that there is no valid reason why that decision should not apply with equal force to the interpretation and application of the identical provisions in s. 64(14) of the Labour Act 2007.

One final point: as far as a particular bargaining unit is concerned, a registered trade union can be recognized as the union holding the right to bargain on behalf of all employees of the particular bargaining unit to the exclusion of all else, i.e. to the exclusion of other

---

9   *Pep Stores (Namibia) (Pty) Ltd v Iyambo and others* 2001 NR 211 (LC).

trade unions or individual employees. However, the conferment of the status of 'exclusive bargaining agent' on, for example, trade union X, does not preclude the employer from consulting with trade union Y and trade union Z, which are also registered trade unions active in the bargaining unit, on matters of mutual interest, because 'consulting' is not 'bargaining'. Suppose, for instance, the Government is considering amending a statute, e.g. the Affirmative Action (Employment) Act 1998,[10] or passing a statute, e.g. the Sexual Harassment in the Public Service Bill, and the Government wishes to consult as many interested parties as possible. The Labour Act does not prohibit the Government from consulting other registered trade unions representing public servants, apart from NAPWU. What the Government qua employer is precluded from doing in terms of the Labour Act is to attempt to bargain with such trade unions, together with NAPWU, for the purpose of negotiating a collective agreement or negotiating remuneration and other terms and conditions of public servants.

15.3 DISCLOSURE OF INFORMATION

Collective bargaining is a serious matter in labour or employment relations; it is based on the voluntary will of the representatives of employees, on the one hand, and the representatives of employers or employers' organizations, on the other, to settle amicably any matter of mutual interest. Therefore, having access to adequate, correct and all relevant information is one of the hallmarks of genuine collective bargaining. It leads to both the employer and the trade union in question understanding each other's position and circumstances, and it enables the union to appreciate the true financial constraints the employer is facing in order for it to make practical and reasonable demands.

Some countries, e.g. Swaziland, South Africa and United Kingdom, have found it necessary to oblige employers by statutory provisions to disclose all relevant information to trade union representatives during collective bargaining. Like the United Kingdom, Swaziland has provided for the disclosure of information in a non-enforceable Code of Practice annexed to its Industrial Relations Act 2000.[11] The importance of full disclosure for the purpose of collective bargaining is recognized by the Code of Practice. In terms of s. 109 of that Act, the Code is not legally binding but the Industrial Court, the Conciliation, Mediation and Arbitration Commission, or any other person, may take the Code into account in arriving at a decision under that Act.

---

10 Act No. 29 of 1998.

11 Act No. 1 of 2000.

In the United Kingdom, s. 181 of the Trade Unions and Labour Relations (Consolidation) Act[12] places certain obligations on the employer engaged in collective bargaining. The employer is obliged by that Act to disclose to the representatives of the relevant trade union all information relating to the employer's undertaking, which is in his possession, without which the trade union's bargaining team would be gravely handicapped and hindered during the bargaining process. The employer is also obliged to disclose such information as is conducive to the practice of sound industrial relations for the purpose of collective bargaining. In determining what constitutes good industrial relations with regard to full disclosures, one is referred to a Code of Practice issued by the Advisory, Conciliation and Arbitration Service (ACAS). The Code contains such matters as the importance of union representatives getting adequate information, and management acceding to reasonable union requests for information. According to the Code of Practice, information relating to the employer's undertaking, which are relevant in collective bargaining are: (i) principles and structure of pay and benefit systems; (ii) policies on recruitment, training and promotion; number of employees analysed according to grade, department, location, age, sex, etc.; (iii) productivity and efficiency data; (iv) cost structure; and (v) gross and net profits. Failure to observe the Code does not by itself render anyone liable to face judicial or quasi-judicial proceedings. Nevertheless, the Act requires any relevant provisions of the Code to be taken into account in proceedings before the Central Arbitration Committee.

South Africa's Labour Relations Act 1995,[13] on the other hand, provides for the disclosure of information for the purposes of collective bargaining in the following terms under s. 16(3): 'whenever an employer is consulting or bargaining with a representative trade union, the employer must disclose to the representative trade union all relevant information that will allow the representative trade union to engage effectively in consultation or collective bargaining.'

The Labour Act 2007 does not provide for specific items comparable to those contained in the United Kingdom's Code of Practice. The requirements under the Labour Act concerning disclosure of information for the purpose of collective bargaining are, rather, comparable to those contained in the South African statute. As provided in s. 50(1)(d) of the Labour Act 2007, it is an unfair labour practice for an employer or an employers' organization, subject to s. 50(2)–(7), to fail to disclose to a recognized trade union any relevant information that is reasonably required to enable the trade union to consult or bargain collectively in respect of any labour matter.

---

12   Trade Unions and Labour Relations (Consolidation) Act 1992 (c.52).

13   Act No. 66 of 1995.

266 Labour Law in Namibia

When disclosing information, the employer must bring to the attention of the recognized trade union representative or workplace union representative, in writing, whether any of the disclosed information is confidential. According to s. 50(2)(b) of the Labour Act, an employer is not required to disclose every piece of information; he is not so required if:

1   the information is legally privileged;[14]

2   the employer is prohibited by any law or an order of a competent court from disclosing the information;

3   the information is confidential and its disclosure might cause substantial harm to an employee or the employer; or

4   the information is private and personal to an employee and the employee has not consented to its disclosure.

Section 50(3) of the Act provides that, in any dispute about disclosure of information, the first thing an arbitrator must decide is whether the information in question is relevant, i.e. relevant to the process of bargaining. If an arbitrator decides that the information requested is relevant but confidential according to s. 50(2)(b)(iii) of the Act, or it is private and personal information relating to an employee in terms of s. 50(2)(b)(iv), then the arbitrator must balance the harm the disclosure is likely to cause against the harm that failure to disclose is likely to cause to the ability of the workplace union representative to perform his functions, or the ability of the trade union to engage effectively in consultations or collective bargaining. If the arbitrator decides that the harm favours disclosure, the arbitrator may order disclosure on terms aimed at limiting the harm likely to be caused to the employer or employee.

One important point deserves to be made in connection with reasonable requests for adequate, correct and all relevant information. It is submitted that it is a reasonable request for a trade union to ask for information on the financial plans and general financial position of an employer.[15] However, it is an unreasonable request for trade union representatives to ask for detailed information on the remuneration of each employee at management level. Such information is not relevant because it will not assist the union representatives in negotiating for higher remuneration and better conditions and terms for employees who do not occupy managerial positions in the bargaining unit.

---

14   See M. Milne, 'Discovery and Privilege in Arbitration Proceedings', *JCI Arb* 60 (1994), pp. 285-8, where legal privilege is discussed with insight and clarity.

15   For example, the Swaziland's Code of Practice provides that it would be a reasonable request if the trade union asks for information supplied to shareholders or published in annual reports.

It must be borne in mind that wage differentiation in relation to categories of employees in any organization depends upon a myriad of factors, for example:

1.   minimum education and specialist training or experience required for a particular job;

2.   requisite knowledge of a branch of science and technology at university or other tertiary level;

3.   ability to carry out or direct research into new products;

4.   whether an employee directs the work of a major functional department of the employer's enterprise;

5.   whether an employee takes decisions leading to important changes in the enterprise; and

6.   whether an employee plays any policy-making role.[16]

In addition, the payment of high remuneration to certain categories of employees depends upon factors, most of which, notably market forces, are outside the control of any employer.

For instance, in a country where there is a shortage of skilled and experienced specialist individuals like scientists, technologists, business administration experts, corporate lawyers and chartered accountants, there is great competition for such experts. Therefore, an employer who wishes to do well in his business by competing well with similar businesses will have to offer competitive remuneration to such experts so as to be able to attract and retain them. Consequently, the fact that a factory manager, a chartered accountant, a corporate lawyer, a research scientist or a technologist receives high remuneration does not simply mean that the employer is extravagant, or is capable of paying high remuneration to other employees, too.

Section 50(6) of the Labour Act provides a precaution against breach of confidentiality in respect of information disclosed to a recognized trade union or workplace union representatives in terms of s. 50 of the Act. When making an order, an arbitrator must take into account any breach of confidentiality in respect of information disclosed to the workplace union representative or the recognized trade union in terms of s. 50 and may refuse to order the disclosure of the information for a period specified in the award. In a dispute about alleged breach of confidentiality, an arbitrator may order that the right to disclosure of information in that workplace be withdrawn for a period specified in the award.

---

16 See P. Blunt, *Organizational Theory and Behaviour: An African Perspective,* London, Longman, 1983, pp. 126-32.

268 Labour Law in Namibia

It will be a breach of confidentiality if, for instance, the workplace union representative or the recognized trade union disclosed any confidential information to an unauthorized person, or if the information was used for a purpose other than enabling the trade union or workplace union representative of the recognized trade union to consult or bargain collectively.

15.4 Duty to Bargain in Good Faith

According to s. 49(1)(b) of the Labour Act 2007, it is an unfair labour practice for a registered trade union to refuse to bargain collectively when a provision of the Labour Act or a collective agreement requires the union to bargain collectively. It is equally an unfair labour practice according to s. 50(1) of the Act for an employer or an employer's organization to refuse to bargain collectively when a provision of the Labour Act or a collective agreement requires the employer or the organization to bargain collectively. It is also an unfair labour practice for the parties to bargain in bad faith.

The duty of employees and employers engaged in collective bargaining to bargain in good faith is a crucial feature in labour or employment legislation of many countries because it promotes industrial harmony.[17] For, what is the purpose of such statutes, including Namibia's Labour Act, to provide elaborately for collective bargaining if it is not expected of the parties to engage in genuine and serious bargaining? Goldstone, JA (as he then was) observed tersely in *National Union of Mineworkers v East Rand Gold & Uranium* supra: 'the very stuff of collective bargaining is the duty to bargain in good faith.'[18]

To bargain half-heartedly or bargain perfunctorily with no intention of reaching an agreement, or to refuse to accede to a reasonable request for relevant information required in the interest of effective bargaining, is to bargain in bad faith. Relying on textual authorities, Gibson, J noted in *Namdeb Diamond Corporation (Pty) Ltd v Mineworkers Union of Namibia* that 'good faith' in collective bargaining is inconsistent with stubbornness and unwillingness to yield a position that cannot be supported on economic or other relevant considerations.[19] But 'good faith', the learned judge observed further, 'does not compel a party to agree each and every proposal; neither does it require a party to make a concession anyhow'.[20]

---

17 C. Okpaluba, 'Labour Adjudication in Swaziland: The Exclusive Jurisdiction of the Industrial Court', *JAL* 43 (1999), 184-200.

18 *National Union of Mineworkers v East Rand Gold & Uranium* supra at 1237E.

19 *Namdeb Diamond Corporation (Pty) Ltd v Mineworkers Union of Namibia* NLLP 2002 (2) 188 NLC.

20 Ibid. at 198.

An employer bargains in bad faith if, for instance, in the middle of bargaining on remuneration or other terms and conditions of employment, the employer unilaterally changes rates of remuneration or other terms, because by doing so he gives the impression that he has all along had no intention of reaching an agreement with the trade union representatives. It matters not if the new rates and terms are better than pre-bargaining ones.[21] Thus, where an impasse is reached in good faith, the employer may not put a better offer to the employees than he put to their union. However, where the impasse is reached because of bad faith on the part of the trade union representatives, the position may be different: in that case, direct negotiation with individual employees would not be unfair, unjust or inequitable.[22]

15.5 COLLECTIVE AGREEMENT

The true aim of parties to a collective bargaining is generally to reach agreement in the form of a collective agreement. As provided in s. 1 of the Labour Act 2007,

> 'collective agreement' means a written agreement concerning the terms and conditions of employment or any other matter of mutual interest, concluded by –
>
> (a)   one or more registered trade unions, on the one hand, and
>
> (b)   on the other hand –
>
>   (i)   one or more employers;
>
>   (ii)   one or more registered employees' organizations; or
>
>   (iii)   one or more employers and one or more registered employers' organization;

The 'terms and conditions' in the definition refer to terms and conditions under which an employee is required by his contract of employment or a collective agreement to render his service to his employer. The Labour Act does not spell out what 'any matter' is. It is submitted that 'any matter' must be understood to connote administrative or procedural matters under the Labour Act or agreed under a collective agreement, e.g. (i) machinery for consultation regarding future terms and conditions of employment; (ii) procedures for the

---

21   *National Union of Mineworkers v East Rand Gold & Uranium* supra.

22   Ibid.

prevention of disputes; (iii) methods of settling or resolving disputes between the employer and his employees; (iv) procedures for the airing of grievances by individual employees or by the trade union recognized as the exclusive bargaining agent; and (v) procedures relating to dismissal or any other disciplinary action. Indeed, s. 73(1) of the Labour Act provides that every collective agreement must provide for a dispute-resolution mechanism, including arbitration, for the resolution of any dispute arising from the interpretation, application or enforcement of the collective agreement in accordance with Part C or Part D of Chapter 8 of the Act, unless provision is made in another collective agreement for the resolution of such disputes. (Part C arbitration and Part D arbitration are treated in chapter 10, para 10.2.2.)

According to s. 70(1) of the Labour Act 2007, a collective agreement binds the following: parties to the agreement, members of any registered trade union that is a party to the agreement, members of any registered employers' organization that is a party to the agreement, employees in a recognized bargaining unit, if a trade union that is a party to the agreement has been recognized as an exclusive bargaining agent in terms of s. 64 of the Act, and any other employees, employers, registered trade unions or employers' organizations to whom the agreement has been extended in terms of s. 71 of the Act.

Furthermore, according to s. 70(2), a collective agreement binds every member of a registered trade union and every member of a registered employer's organization that are parties to the agreement during the subsistence of the agreement. That is the case so long as such a member was a member at the time the agreement came into force, or he becomes a member after the agreement comes into force. It matters not whether such a person continues to be a member of the registered trade union or registered employer's organization while the agreement is in force.

In this way, an employee of the bargaining unit in which a registered trade union has been recognized as the exclusive bargaining unit in terms of s. 64(1) is 'subjugated by legislation into the straight jacket of majoritarianism or an enforced collective representation'.[23] Indeed, s. 70(1), read with s. 64(1), of the Labour Act effectively amends the common law tenet that a person may not contract for another unless that other person has authorized him to do so.[24] Thus, under the Labour Act, a registered trade union recognized as the exclusive bargaining agent in respect of a recognized bargaining unit, is empowered by legislation to contract on behalf of all employees in that bargaining unit – whether or not they are members of that trade union or irrespective of whether the non-members of the trade union have agreed that the exclusive bargaining agent should represent them. (See para. 15.2 above, where it

---

[23] *Radio Television Electronic & Allied Workers Union v Tedelex (Pty) Ltd and another* (1990) 11*ILJ* 1272 (IC) at 1282B.

[24] Ibid. at 1276A.

is shown that these provisions are not unconstitutional or offensive of the rules of natural justice.)

Section 70(3) of the Labour Act provides that the provisions of a collective agreement relating to terms and conditions of employment, subject to s. 70(4), vary every contract of employment between an employee and an employer who are bound by the collective agreement. In that case, those terms and conditions are deemed to have been incorporated into the contract of employment. Moreover, according to s. 70(4) of the Act, unless it expressly states otherwise, a collective agreement does not preclude the conclusion of a contract of employment that contains terms and conditions that are more favourable than those contained in the collective agreement, so long as an employer who enters into the contract of employment does so in good faith and also without weakening or undermining collective bargaining or the status of the registered trade union concerned.

Despite the general definition of 'collective agreement' in s. 1 of the Labour Act, s. 71(1) provides for a definition that is specific and exclusive to s. 71, which deals with extension of collective agreements to persons who otherwise are not parties to the agreements. Thus, according to s. 71(1) of the Act, for the purposes of s. 71, a 'collective agreement' means an agreement between an employer or a registered employers' organization, and a registered trade union that is recognized by that employer or employers' organization, as the exclusive bargaining agent in a bargaining unit in terms of s. 64 of the Act. Section 71 provides for a procedure by which a collective agreement may be extended to cover some other employers and employees who are not members of the parties to agreement.

Section 71(2) provides that parties to a collective agreement may, in the prescribed form, request the Minister responsible for Labour to extend that collective agreement to cover employers and employees who are not members of the parties to the agreement, so long as such employers and employees fall within the industry to which the agreement relates. After he has received a request, the Minister must publish the request in the *Gazette*. The *Gazette* publication must invite objections to the request from those who are minded to object within a period specified in the *Gazette* notice; the period must not exceed thirty days from the date of publication of the request in the *Gazette*. The Minister is also obliged to serve on the parties to the collective agreement any objections received by him, and invite responses to any objections within a maximum period of fourteen days from the date of the invitation.

Section 71(4)(a) of the Act provides that the Minister must not extend a collective agreement unless he has considered both the objections and the responses that he has received and unless he is satisfied that:

1   the agreement is not in conflict with the Namibian Constitution or any other law;

2   the agreement is not, on the whole, less favourable than the terms and conditions of employment enjoyed by the employees immediately before the conclusion of the agreement;

3   the agreement provides arbitration to resolve disputes about the interpretation, application and enforcement of the agreement; and

4   the request to extend the agreement complies with the relevant provisions of s. 71.

Section 71(5) provides that if the agreement meets all the foregoing requirements, the Minister must extend that collective agreement for a fixed period by notice in the *Gazette*, directed to the parties mentioned in s. 71(2).

Thereafter, as provided in s. 71(6), after a notice referred to in s. 71(5) has been published, the Minister may, at the request of the parties to the collective agreement, publish a further notice in the *Gazette*, extending the period specified in the earlier notice for a further period determined by him. However, if the period specified in the earlier notice extending the collective agreement has already expired, the Minister may declare a new date. The Minister may publish a further notice cancelling all or part of the first notice published in terms of s. 71(5). It must be borne in mind s. 71(2)–(5) of the Act apply with necessary modifications to the publication of any notice published in terms of s. 71(6)(a) or (b) of the Act.

There is a further requirement concerning publication of information under s. 71. Section 71(8) provides that, in addition to publishing the information in the *Gazette*, the Minister must, where appropriate, publish the same information through other available means with the view to ensuring that the intended recipients of the information receive it. In this connection, the Minister can, it is submitted, publish the information in the local dailies, the *Namibia Review* and the Ministry responsible for Labour's *Newsletter* or suchlike news bulletin.

In terms of s. 72(2) of the Labour Act, a person bound by an extension of a collective agreement in virtue of s. 71 may apply in the prescribed form to the Minister to be exempted from the extension of that collective agreement. If he is satisfied that special circumstances exist justifying an exemption, the Minister may in writing grant the applicant's request with or without conditions. Section 72(3) obliges the Minister to serve a copy of any exemption granted on the parties to the collective agreement.

15.6 Disputes Regarding Collective Agreement

It was mentioned in para. 15.5 above, that an important administrative or procedural item that s. 73(1) of the Labour Act 2007 requires to be provided for in a collective agreement, is a dispute resolution mechanism, including arbitration, whereby a dispute about the interpretation, application or enforcement of a collective agreement may be resolved in accordance with Part C or Part D of the Chapter 8 of the Act. As we saw previously, this deals with arbitration, unless another collective agreement provides for the resolution of that dispute. According to s. 73(2) of the Act, if such dispute arises and the collective agreement does not provide for a dispute resolution mechanism for the resolution of the dispute, or the mechanism provided is not operative, any party to the dispute may refer the dispute to the Labour Commissioner. The Labour Commissioner must not entertain the referral unless he is satisfied that the applicant has served a copy of the referral on every other party to the dispute. Finally, according to s. 73(4), the Labour Commissioner may refer the dispute to an arbitrator to arbitrate the dispute in accordance with Part C of Chapter 8 of the Labour Act, or refer the matter for arbitration in accordance with Part D of Chapter 8 of the Act. (Part C arbitration and Part D arbitration are treated in chapter 10 above.)

16 TRANSITIONAL PROVISIONS OF THE LABOUR ACT 2007

The Labour Act 2007 provides transitional provisions in Schedule 1. The function of the transitional provisions is to preserve for specified periods some of the provisions of the repealed Labour Act 1992 (previous Act) and the 2004 Act,[1] including provisions relating to certain rights, obligations or interests under the previous Act that are subsisting and which would otherwise cease to have effect as a result of the coming into force of the Labour Act or a relevant provision of it. Thus, Schedule 1 makes special provisions, in the form of deeming clauses, for the application of the Labour Act to certain circumstances and situations that existed prior to that Act or a relevant provision of it coming into operation.[2] It is not proposed to deal with the transitional provisions in any detail, except to note that Schedule 1 deals with the following matters:

1   definitions for the purposes of the schedule;

2   general preservation of rights, duties, regulations, notices and other instruments;

3   continuation of time;

4   application and notices concerning continuous work and overtime;

5   applications and notices concerning Sunday or public holiday work;

6   remuneration deposited with the Permanent Secretary responsible for Labour;

7   health and safety representatives;

8   registration of trade unions and employers' organizations;

9   collective bargaining;

10   strikes, lockouts and essential services;

11   wages commission, wage orders and exemptions;

12   Labour Commissioner and Labour Inspectors;

13   references in other laws; and

14   resolution of other transitional matters.

---

[1]   The Labour Act 2004 (Act No. 15 of 2004). This Act was passed but was not brought into operation.

[2]   See G.C Thornton, *Legislative Drafting,* 3rd edn, London, Butterworths, 1987, p. 319.

APPENDIX I
TABLE OF STATUTES

NAMIBIA

Affirmative Action (Employment) Act 1998 (Act No. 29 of 1998)

Age of Majority Act 1972 (Act No. 57 of 1972)

Anti-Corruption Act 2003 (Act No. 8 of 2003)

Apprenticeship Ordinance 1938 (Ordinance No. 12 of 1938)

Arbitration Act 1965 (Act No. 42 of 1965)

Companies Act 1973 (Act No. 61 of 1973)

Defence Act 2002 (Act No. 1 of 2002)

Development Corporation Act 1993 (Act No. 18 of 1993)

Employees Compensation Act, 1995 (Act No. 5 of 1995)

High Court Act 1990 (Act No. 16 of 1990)

High Court Rules 1990 (Government Notice No. 59 of 1990)

Income Tax Act 1981 (Act No. 24 of 1981)

Income Tax Amendment Act 1996 (Act No. 12 of 1996)

Insolvency Act 1936 (Act No. 24 of 1936)

Labour Act 1992 (Act No. 6 of 1992)

Labour Act 2004 (Act No. 15 of 2004)

Labour Act 2007 (Act No. 11 of 2007)

Local Authorities Act 1992 (Act No. 23 of 1992)

Medical and Dental Act 2004 (Act No. 10 of 2004)

Merchant Shipping Act 1951 (Act No. 57 of 1951)

Namibia Central Intelligence Service Act 1997 (Act No. 10 of 1997)

Namibia Development Corporation Act 1993 (Act No. 18 of 1993)

Namibian Constitution 1990

National Pensions Act 1992 (Act No. 10 of 1992)

Police Act 1990 (Act No. 19 0f 1990)

Prescribed Rates of Interest Act 1975 (Act No. 55 of 1975)

Prisons Service Act 1998 (Act No. 17 of 1998)

Public Service Act 1995 (Act No. 13 of 1995)

Regional Councils Act 1992 (Act No. 22 of 1992)

Social Security Act, 1994 (Act No. 34 of 1994)

Wage and Industrial Conciliation Ordinance 1952 (Ordinance No. 35 of 1952)

Water Act 1956 (Act No. 54 of 1956)

Workmen's Compensation Act 1941 (Act No. 30 of 1941)

SOUTH AFRICA

Basic Conditions of Employment Act 1983 (Act No. 3 of 1983)

Basic Conditions of Employment Act 1997 (Act No. 75 of 1997)

Black Labour Relations Regulations Act 1953 (Act No. 48 of 1953)

Black Labour (Settlement of Disputes) Amendment Act 1955 (Act No. 59 of 1955)

Constitution of South Africa 1996 (Act No. 108 of 1996)

Expropriation Act 1975 (Act No. 63 of 1975)

Hospital Ordinance 1958 (Ordinance No. 14 of 1958)

Labour Relations Act 1956 (Act No. 28 of 1956)

Labour Relations Act 1995 (Act No. 66 of 1995)

Nursing Act 1978 (Act No. 50 of 1978)

OTHER COMMONWEALTH COUNTRIES

Botswana

Trade Unions and Employers Organizations Act, 1972 (Botswana)

Malawi

Trade Unions Act; Cap 54:01 (Malawi)

Swaziland

Employment Act 1980 (Act No. 5 of 1980) (Swaziland)

Industrial Relations Act 1996 (Act No. 1 of 1996) (Swaziland)

Industrial Relations Act 2000 (Act No. 1 of 2000) (Swaziland)

Workmen's Compensation Act 1983 (Act No. 7 of 1983) (Swaziland)

Tanzania

Trade Unions Ordinance, 1932 (Tanzania)

United Kingdom

Arbitration Act 1996 (c. 23) (UK)

Employment Relations Act 1999 (c. 26) (UK)

Employment Rights Act 1996 (c. 18) (UK)

Employment Rights (Dispute Resolution) Act 1998 (c. 8) (UK)

Employment Tribunals Act 1996 (c. 17) (UK)

Payment Wages Act 1960 (8 & 9 Eliz. 2, c. 37) (UK)

Health and Safety at Work, etc. Act 1974 (c. 37) (UK)

Industrial Relations Act 1971 (c.72) (UK)

Trade Disputes Act, 1906 (6 Edw. 7, c.47) (UK)

Trade Unions Act, 1871 (24 & 35 Vict. c. 31) (UK)

Trade Unions and Labour Relations (Consolidated) (Act) 1992 (c. 52) (UK)

Truck Act 1831 (1 & 2 Will. 4, c.37) (UK)

Truck Act 1887 (50 & 51 Vict. c. 46) (UK)

Truck Act 1896 (59 & 60 Vict. c. 48) (UK)

Truck Act, 1940 (3 & 4 Geo. 6, c. 38) (UK)

Zambia

Employment Act Cap 512 (Laws of Zambia)

Constitution of Zambia 1996

Zimbabwe

Constitution of Zimbabwe 1980

APPENDIX II
TABLE OF CASES

ACTWUSA & others v J M Jacobsohn (Pty) Ltd (1970) 11 *ILJ* 107 (IC)

Adampol (Pty) Ltd v Administrator, Transvaal 1989 (3) SA 733 (A)

Adbro Investment Co Ltd v Minister of Interior and others 1959 (3) SA 292(T)

Addis v Gramophone Co Ltd [1969] AC 488

Administrator, Transvaal and others v Traub and others 1989 (4) SA 731 (A)

African Granite Co (Pty) Ltd v Mineworkers Union of Namibia & others 1993 NR 91 (LC)

African Realty Trust v Johannesburg Municipality 1906 TH 179

A K Gopalan v State AIR 1950 SC 27

Alfred MacAlpine & Sons (Pty) Ltd v Transvaal Provincial Administration 1974 (3) SA 506 (A)

Allied Mineral Development Corporation (Pty) Ltd v Gemsbok Vlei Kwartsiet (Edm) 1968 (1) SA 7 (C)

Ally v Dinath 1984 (2) SA 451 (TPD)

Alpine Caterers Namibia (Pty) Ltd v Owen and others 1991 NR 310

Amalgamated Beverage Industries (Pty) Ltd v Jonker 14 *ILJ* 1232 (LAC)

Amalgamated Society of Railway Servants v Osborne [1910] AC 87 (HL)

Anbeenco (Pty) Ltd and SACCAWU (1991) ARB 8.14.10

Anglo American Farms t/a Boschendal Restaurant v Komjwayo (1992) 13 *ILJ* 573 (LAC)

Anisminic Ltd v Foreign Compensation Commission [1969] 2 AC 147

Anshel v Horwitz 1916 WLD 65

Aroma Inn (Pty) Ltd v Hypermarket (Pty) Ltd & Another 1981 (4) SA 108 (C)

Attorney-General v H R H Prince Augustus of Hannover [1957] 2 All ER 45 (HL)

Attorney-General v Ryan [1980] AC 143

Attorney-General for NSW ex rel. Chopin v North Sydney Municipal Council [1973] 1 NSW LR 186

Baker v Gibbons [1972] 2 All ER 659

282   Labour Law in Namibia

Bank voor Handel en Scheepvaart NV v Slatford and Another [1953] 1 QB 497

Barkhuizen v Napier 2007 (5) SA 323 (CC)

*Barlows Manufacturing Co Ltd v Metals & Allied Workers Union & others (*1990) 11 *ILJ* 35 (T)

Basson v Chilwan and others 1993 (3) SA 742 (A)

Basson and others v The Ministry of Fisheries and Marine Resources NLLP 2004 (4) 58 NLC

Bauer t/a Hrabovsky Bottlestore v Piebrock t/a L'Dorado Clothing Shop 1999 NR 157

Bauman v Hulton Press Ltd [1952] 2 All ER 1121

BCAWU and another v Murray & Roberts Buildings (Tvl) (Pty) Ltd (1991) 12 *ILJ* 112 (LAC)

Beach v Read Corrugated Cases Ltd [1956] All ER 652

Beier Ltd v SACTWU (1991) ARB 8.9.8

Beral Swaziland (Pty) Ltd v Swaziland Manufacturing & Allied Workers Union Swaziland IC Case No. 108/87 (unreported)

Bester v Easigas (Pty) Ltd 1993 (1) SA 30 (C)

BHT Water Treatment (Pty) Ltd v Maritz NO & others (1992) 13 *ILJ* 143 (T)

Billingham v Huges [1949]1 All ER 684

Bishop of Chichester v Horward (1787) 1 T Rep 65

BK Tooling (Edms) Bpk v Scope Precision Engineering (Edms) Bpk 1979 (1) SA 391 (A)

Blackburn v Krohn (1885) 2 Searle 209

Blake v Howkey 1912 CPD 817

Board of Education v Rice [1911] AC 179

Bok v The Transvaal Gold Exploration and Land Co (1883) 1 SAR 75

Bold v Brough, Nicholson & Hall Ltd [1963] 3 All ER 849

Bonsor v Musicians' Union [1956] AC 104 (HL)

Borcherds v C W Pearce & F Sheward t/a Lubrite Distributors (1991) 12 ILJ 383 (IC)

Borcherds v C W Pearce & J Sheward t/a Lubrite Distributors (1993) 14 *ILJ* 1262 (LAC)

Boston Deep Sea Fishing and Ice Co v Ansell (1889) 39 Ch D 338

Botha v Maree 1964 (I) SA 168 (O)

Boulting v Association of Cinematograph, Television and Allied Technicians [1963] 2 QB 606 (CA)

Appendix II Table of Cases **283**

Boyd v Stuttaford & Co 1910 AD 101

Brace v Calder [1895] 2 QB 253

Bracebridge Engineering Ltd v Darby [1990] IRLR 3

Braude v Pretoria City Council 1981 (1) SA 680 (T)

Breen v Amalgamated Engineering Union [1971] 1 All ER 1148

Bremer Valkan Schiffbau und Maschinenfabrik v South India Shipping Corporation Ltd [1982] AC 909

British Airports Authority v Ashton and others [1983] 3 All ER 6 (QB)

British Leyland (UK) Ltd v Swift [1981] 1 RLR 91

British Transport Commission v Gourley [1955] 2 All ER 652

Broome v DPP (1974) 1 All ER 314 (CA)

Brown v Hicks (1902) 19 SC 314

Brown v Sessell 1908 TS 1137

Bucher v Kalahari Express Airlines NLLP (2002) (2) 104 NLC

Building Construction and Allied Workers Union and others v Group5/Combrink Construction (1993) 2 *LCD* 117 (LAC)

Buthelezi v Municipal Demarcation Board [2005] 2 BLLR 115 (LAC)

Buthelezi & others v Labour for Africa (Pty) Ltd 1991 12 *ILJ* 587

Cabinet for the Interim Government of South West Africa v Bessinger and others 1989 (1) SA 618 (SWA)

Camdons Realty (Pty) Ltd and another v Hart (1993) 14 *ILJ* 1008 (LAC)

Canadian Pacific Railway v Loskhart [1942] AC 591

Canca v Mount Frere Municipality 1984 (2) SA 830 (Tk)

Cape Town Municipality v Yeld 1978 (4) SA 802 (C)

Capital Estate and General Agencies (Pty) Ltd v Holiday Inns Inc 1977 (2) SA 677 (A)

Carlisle Place Investment Ltd v Wimpey Construction (UK) Ltd 15 BLR 109 (QB 1980)

Carol v Bird (1800) 3 Esp 201

Carter & Co (Pty) Ltd v McDonald 1955 (1) SA 202 (A)

Cassidy v Ministry of Health [1951] 2 KB 353

Catholic Commission for Justice and Peace v Attorney-General Zimbabwe 1993 (2) SACR 432 (ZS)

CCAWUSA v Metro Cash & Carry Ltd (1992) 1 LCD 28 (IC)

CCAWUSA v Wooltru Ltd t/a Woolworths (Randburg) (1989) 10 *ILJ* 311 (IC)

CDM (Pty) Ltd v Mineworkers Union of Namibia and others 1994 NR 180 (LC)

Central News Agency (Pty) Ltd v Commercial Catering & Allied Workers Union & another (1991) 12 *ILJ* 340 (LAC)

Century Insurance Co Ltd v Northern Island Road Transport Board [1942] AC 509

CEPPWAWU and others v Metrofile (Pty) Ltd [2004] 2 BLLR 103 (LAC)

Chairperson of the Immigration Selection Board v Frank and another 2001 NR 107 (SC)

Chamber of Mines of South Africa v Council of Mining Unions (1990) 11 *ILJ* 52 (IC)

Chappel & others v Times Newspaper Ltd & others [1995] 2 All ER 233

Chegetu Municipality v Manyora 1997 (1) SA 662 (ZSC)

Chemical Workers Industrial Union & another v AECI Paints (Pty) Ltd (1988) 9 *ILJ* 1046 (IC)

Chief Constable of North Wales Police v Evans [1982] 1 WLR 1155

Childerly Estate Stores v Standard Bank of South Africa 1924 OPD 163

Christopher H. Dlamini v Inter Africa Supplies (SWD) Limited Swaziland IC 81/96 (unreported)

City of Windhoek v Pieterse 2000 NR 196 (LC)

Clark v African Guarantee and Indemnity Co Ltd 1915 CPD 68

Clark v Coronel Ltd [1972] IRR 208

Cloete v Smith 1971 (1) SA 453

Coates SA (Pty) Ltd v CCMA and others [2004] 4 BLLR 252 (LC)

Coin Security (Cape) v Vukani Guards & Allied Workers Union 1989 (4) SA 234 (C)

Collier v Sunday Referee Publishing Co Ltd [1940] 4 All ER 234

Colonial Mutual Life Assurance Society Ltd v MacDonald 1931 AD 412

Commercial Bank of Namibia v Van Wyk NLLP 2004 (4) 250 NLC

Commercial Plastics Ltd v Vincent [1965] 1 QB 623

Conradie v Rossouw 1919 AD 279

Consolidated Frame Cotton Corp v President, Industrial Court (1986) 7 *ILJ* 489 (A)

Conway v Wade [1909] AC 606

Costa da Oura Restaurant (Pty) Ltd t/a Umdloti Bush Tavern v Reddy [2003] (4) SA 34 (SCA)

Country Fair Foods (Pty) Ltd v CCMA and others [1999] 11 BLLR 1117

Appendix II   Table of Cases   **285**

Cowey v Liberian Operations Ltd [1966] 2 Lloyd Reports 45

Cremark, a Division of Tripple P-Chemical Ventures (Pty) Ltd v SACWU & Others (1994) 15 *ILJ* 289 (LAC)

Creswell and others v Board of Inland Revenue [1984] 2 All ER 713

Crofter Harris Tweed Co v Veitch [1942] AC 435

Cronje v Municipality Council of Mariental NLLP 2004 (4) 129 NSC

Crook v Pedersen Ltd 1927 WLD 62

Cross Country Carriers v Farmer NLLP 1998 (1) 226 NLC

Crown Chickens (Pty) Ltd t/a Rocklands Poultry v Kapp [2002] 6 BLLR 493 (LC)

Cymot (Pty) Ltd v McLoud 2002 NR 391 (LC)

Dabner v South Africa Railways and Harbours 1920 AD 583

Daewoo Heavy Industries (SA) (Pty) Ltd v Banks and others 2004 (4) SA 458 (C)

Daniel Matsebula v Swaziland Milling, a Division of Swaki Investment Corporation Ltd Swaziland IC 14/97 (unreported)

Daniels v Whitestone Entertainment Ltd [1942] 2 Lloyd's Rep 1

Dawson and Fraser (Pty) Ltd v Havenga Construction (Pty) Ltd 1993 (3) SA 397 (BGD)

De Beer v Thomson and Son 1918 TPD 70

De Laan v Van Dyck Carpet Company [2003] 3 BLLR 257 (LC)

De Reuck v Director of Public Prosecutions, Witwatersrand Local Division, and others 2004 (1) SA 403 (CC)

De Wet v Western Bank Ltd 1977 (2) SA 1033 (W)

De Wet v Western Bank Ltd 1979 (2) SA 1031 (A)

Delisile M. Dlamini v Samuel Dlamini t/a Top Hits Record Bar Swaziland IC 62/97 (unreported)

Dempsey v Home & Property (1995) 16 *ILJ* 378 (LAC)

Denel (Pty) Ltd v Gerber [2005] 9 BLLR 849 (LAC)

Denel (Pty) v Voster [2005] 4 BLLR 313 (SCA)

Denham v Midland Employers Mutual Assurance Ltd [1955] 2 QB 437; [1955] 2 All ER 561

Denny v SA Loan, Mortgage and Mercantile Agency Co Ltd 3 EDC 47

Dickenson & Brown v Fisher's Executors 1915 AD 166

Dickenson Motors (Pty) Ltd v Oberholzer 1952 (1) SA 443 (A)

Donaldson v Webber 4 HCG 403

Dowden and Pook Ltd v Pook [1904] 1 KB 45

Du Toit v The Office of the Prime Minister 1996 NR 52 (LC)

Durban City Council v Association of Building Societies 1942 AD 27

Dutch Reform Church v Town Council of Cape Town (1898) 15 SC 14

East London Municipal Council v Thompson 1944 AD 61

Edwards v Bairstow [1956] AC 14

Edwin Beukes and others v National Housing Enterprise Case No.: LC 30/2006

Ellen Louw v The Chairperson, District Labour Court and JP Snyman & Partners (Namibia) (Pty) Ltd Case No. LCA 27/98 (unreported)

Ellerines Furniture Namibia (Pty) Ltd t/a Furncity Furniture v De Vos NLLP 2004 (4) 35 NLC

Ellis v Morgan, Ellis v Dessai 1909 TS 576

Ellis Park Stadium Ltd v Minister of Justice and another 1989 (3) SA 898 (T)

Enderby v Frenchay (1994) 69 CMLR 8

Engelbrecht and others v Hennes 2007 (1) NR 236 (LC)

Engelbrecht v Transnamib Holdings Ltd 2003 NR 40 (LC)

Empangeni Transport (Pty) Ltd v Zulu (1992) 13 *ILJ* 352 (IC)

Erasmus v Afrikander Proprietary Mines Ltd 1976 (1) SA 950 (W)

Eric Mthandazo Mahlalela v Ubombo Ranches Ltd Swaziland CA 32/1995 (unreported)

Erongo Mining & Exploration Company Limited t/a Navachab Gold Mine v Mineworkers Union of Namibia (NUM) and another 2000 NR 70 (LC)

Esso Petroleum Co. v Harper's Garage (Sturport) Ltd [1968] AC 269

Estate Duminy v Hofmeyr & Sons Ltd 1925 CPD 115

Estate van der Byl v Swanepoel 1927 AD 141

Faberlan v McKay & Fraser 1920 WLD 24

Fana Ndaba v Thekwini Wholesalers Swaziland IC 7/97 (unreported)

Faramus v Film Artistes Association [1964] 2 AC 925

Faustino Moises Paulo v Shoprite Namibia (Pty) Ltd Case No. LCA 02/2010 (unreported)

Fawcett Security Operations v Omar Enterprises (Pvt) Ltd 1992 (4) SA 425 (ZSC)

F C Shepherd & Co Ltd Jerrom [1986] IRLR 358

Federal Convention of Namibia v Speaker, National Assembly of Namibia and others 1994 (1) SA 177

Feinberg v African Bank Ltd & another [2004] 10 BLLR 1039 (T)

Ferodo (Pty) Ltd v de Ruiter (1993) 14 *ILJ* 974 (LAC)

Festus Nakanyala v Old Mutual Namibia Ltd Case No.: LC 04/2007 (unreported)

Firestone South Africa (Pty) Ltd v Genticuro AG 1977 SA (4) 298 (A)

First National Bank of South Africa Ltd v Jurgens 1993 (I) SA 245 (W)

First National Bank of South Africa Ltd v Van Rensburg NO 1994 (1) SA 677(T)

Fleming v Johnson and Richardson 1903 TS 318

Food & Allied Workers Union v National Co-operative Dairies Ltd (2) (1989) 10 *ILJ* 490 (IC)

*Food & Allied Workers Union and others v Amalgamated Beverages Industries Ltd (*1994) 15 *ILJ* 630 (IC)

Foodcon (Pty) Ltd v Schwartz NLLP 2002 (2) 181 NLC

Forwarding African Transport Services CC t/a F.A.T.S. v Manica Africa (Pty) Ltd and others [2004] 4 All SA 527 (D)

Foster v Chairman, Commission for Administration, and another 1991 (4) SA 403 (C)

Francis v Robert 1973 (1) SA 507 (RA)

Frank and another v Chairperson of the Immigration Selection Board 1999 NR 257 (HC)

Freeman v Standard Bank of South Africa Ltd 1905 TH 26

Friedlander v Hodes 1944 CPD 169

Furnell v Whangarei High Schools Board [1973] AC 660

Ganes and another v Telecom Namibia Ltd 2004 (3) SA 615 (SCA)

Gascol Conversions Ltd v Mercer [1974] ICR 420

General Food Industries Ltd v FAWU [2004] 7 BLLR 667 (LAC)

George v Davies [1911] 2 KB 445

Gerry Bouwer Motors (Pty) v Preller 1940 TPD 130

Gibbins v Williams, Muller Wright & Mostert Ingelyf 1987 (2) SA 82 (T)

Gliksman v Transvaal Provincial Institute of the Institute of South African Architects and another 1951 (4) SA 56 (W)

Goagoseb v Arechenab Fishing & Development Co (Pty) Ltd NLLP 2004 (4) 10 NLC

Goldberg v Durban City Council 1970 (3) SA 325 (W)

Golden Grapefruits (Pty) Ltd v Fotoplate (Pty) Ltd 1973 (2) SA 642 (C)

Gouriet v Union of Post Office Workers [1977] 3 All ER 70

Govender v SASKO (Pty) Ltd t/a Richards Bay Bakery (1990) 11 *ILJ* 1282 (IC)

Graaf-Reinet Municipality v Jansen 1917 CPD 604

Grobler v Naspers Bpk and another [2004] 5 BLLR 455 (C)

Habenicht v Chairman of the Board of Namwater Ltd and others NLLP 2004 (4) 18 NHC

Hailemo v Security Force Services 1996 NR 99 (LC)

Hailulu v The Council of the Municipality of Windhoek 2002 NR 305 (LC)

Halgreen v Natal Building Society (1986) 7 *ILJ* 769 (IC)

Hall (HM Inspector of Taxes) v Lorimer [1994] IRLR 171

Hamata and another v Chairperson, Peninsula Technikon Internal Disciplinary Committee, and others 2002 (5) SA 449 (SCA), 2003 24 *ILJ* 1531 (SCA)

Handley v Thornton 1951 1 WLR 321

Hannah v Government of the Republic of Namibia 2000 NR 46 (LC), 2000 (4) SA 940 (NmH)

Harmer v Cornelius (1858) 5 CB (NS) 236

Harnischfeger Corporation v Appleton 1993 (4) SA 479 (A)

Harrismith Building Society v Taylor 1938 OPD 36

Harvey v O'Dell [1958] 1 All ER 657

Haynes v Doman [1899] 2 ch.13

Heatherdale Farms (Pty) Ltd v Deputy Minister of Agriculture 1980 (3) SA 476 (T)

Hedley Byrne & Co Ltd v Heller & Partner Ltd [1963] 2 All ER 575

Hendrik Jacobus Van Wyk v Commercial Bank of Namibia Limited Case No. SA12/2004 (unreported)

Herbert A. Ndlovu v The Chairman, Sigangeni Community Clinic Swaziland IC 41/96 (unreported)

Hill v C. A. Parson & Co Ltd [1972] 1 Ch 305

Hilton v Thomas Burton (Rhodes) Ltd [1961] WLR 70

Hivac Ltd v Park Royal Scientific Instruments Ltd [1946] Ch 169

HK Manufacturing Co (Pty) Ltd v Sadowitz 1965 (3) SA 328 (C)

Hlongwane and another v Plastix (Pty) Ltd (1990) 11 *ILJ* 171 (IC)

Hoffman-La Roche v Secretary of State for Trade and Industry [1975] AC 295

Hofmeyer v Network Healthcare Holdings (Pty) Limited [2004] 3 BLLR 232 (LC)

Hollington v F H Hewthorn & Co Ltd [1942] 3 All ER 35

Appendix II   Table of Cases

Hospersa and another v Northern Cape Provincial Administration (2000) 21 *ILJ* 1066 (LAC)

Huntley v Thorton [1951] 1 WLR 321

Hurt v Sheffield Corporation (1916) 85 LJKB 1684

Hyperchemicals International (Pty) Ltd and another v Maybaker Agrichem (Pty) Ltd and another 1992 (1) SA 89 (W)

Ibhayi City Council v Yantolo (1991) 12 *ILJ* 1005 (E)

In re An Arbitration between Rubel Bronze and Metal Company Ltd and Vos [1918] 1 KB 315

Interstate Matsebulas Bus Service and TGWU (1991) ARB 10.4.6

Isaacs v Centre Guards CC t/a Town Centre Security [2004] 3 BLLR 288 (C)

Isaacs v Isaacs 1949 (1) SA 952 (C)

Isaacson v Walsh & Walsh (1903) 20 SC 56

J v M Ltd (1989) 10 *IJL* 755 (IC)

Jackson v Union Marine Insurance Co [1874] LR 10 CP

Jacobs v Otis Elevator Co Ltd 1997 1 CCMA 7.1.1 08

J Louw and Co (Pty) Ltd v Richter and others 1987 (2) SA 237 (N)

Job Matsebula and others v Intercon Construction Limited Swaziland IC 16/94 (unreported)

Jockey Club of South Africa and others v Feldman 1942 AD 340

Joe Gross t/a Joe's Beer House v Meintjies 2005 NR 413 (SC)

Joel Melamed and Hurwitz v Cleveland Estates Ltd; Joel Melamed and Hurwitz v Vorner Investments (Pty) Ltd 1984 (3) SA 155 (A)

Johannes Swartbooi v Deon Heunis Case No.: LCA 6/2001 (unreported)

Johannesburg Consolidated Investment Company Ltd v Johannesburg Town Council 1903 TS 111

Johannesburg Municipality v O'Sullivan 1923 AD 201

Jones v Manchester Corporation [1952] 2 QB 852

Jonker v Amalgamated Beverage Industries (1993) 14 *ILJ* 199 (IC)

Joseph Matse v Swaziland Breweries Ltd Swaziland IC 102/96

Joseph v Joseph 1951 (3) SA 776 (N)

Kamanya & others v Kuiseb Fish Products Ltd 1996 NR 123 (LC)

Kaplin v Penkin 1933 CPD 233

Kathrada v Arbitration Tribunal 1975 (2) SA 673 (A)

Katofa v Administrator-General for South West Africa & another 1985 (4) SA 211(SWA)

Kauesa v Minister of Home Affairs 1985 (2) SA 51 (NmH)

Kausiona v Namibia Institute of Mining and Technology NLLP 2004 (4) 43 NLC

Kearney v Whitehaven Colliery Co [1893] 1 QB 700

Kenyon v Darwen Cotton Manufacturing Co [1936] 1 All ER 310

Keshwar v SANCA (1991) 12 *ILJ* 816 (IC)

Khan v Rainbow Chicken Farms (1985) 6 *ILJ* 60 (IC)

Khoza v Minister of Justice 1964 (3) SA 78 (W)

Kiggundu and others v Roads Authority and others 2007 (1) NR 175 (LC)

Kinemas Ltd v Berman 1932 AD 246

Knox D'Arcy Limited and another v Shaw and another 1996 (2) SA 651 (W)

Kruger v Office of the Prime Minister & another 1996 NR 321 (LC)

Kurtz v Nampost Namibia Ltd and another 2009 (2) 696 (LC)

Land Securities plc v Westminster City Council [1993] 4 ALL ER 124

Lane v Shire Roofing Co (Oxford) Ltd [1995] IRLR 493

LARKIN v Belfast Harbour Commissioners (1908) IR 214

Laws v London Chronicle (1959) 1 WLR 698

Lee v Chung and Shun Shing Construction & Engineering Co Ltd [1990] IRLR 236

Lee v Lee's Air Farming Ltd (1961) AC 12

Leonard Simasiku v Ministry of Justice Case No.: LCA 29/2002 (unreported)

Lisse v The Minister of Health and Social Services 2004 NR 107

Lister v Ramford Ice and Cold Storage Co Ltd [1957] AC 55

Lloyd v Grace, Smith & Co [1912] AC 716

Local Governments Board v Arlidge (1915) AC 78

Louw v University of Cape Town 1945 CPD 373

Lucas Zwane v Tip Top Holdings Swaziland IC 77/95 (unreported)

Ludick v Samca Tiles (Pty) Ltd 1993 (2) SA 197 (B)

Luna Meubel Vervaardigers v Makin t/a Makin's Furniture Manufacturers 1977 (4) SA 135 (W)

Lunt v University of Cape Town and another 1989 (2) SA 438 C

Appendix II   Table of Cases   **291**

Machine Moving International (Pty) Ltd and TGWU (1990) *ARB* 1.4.2

MacLoughlan v Alexander Paterson Ltd [1968] 1 TR 251

Madayi v Timpson Bata (Pty) Ltd (1987) 8 *ILJ* 494 (IC)

Madlala v Vynne & Tedder t/a Thorville Engineering (1990) 11 *ILJ* 394 (IC)

Mafomane v Rustenburg Platinum Mines Ltd [2003] 10 BLLR 999 (LC)

Magawo v Caledon Divisional Council 1972 (3) SA 365 (C)

Magna Alloys and Research (SA) (Pty) Ltd v Ellis 1984 (4) SA 874 (A)

Mqhayi v Van Leer SA (Pty) Ltd (1984) 5 *ILJ* 179 (IC)

Mahlangu v CIM Detlak, Gallant v CIM Detlak (1986) 7 *ILJ* 346 (IC)

Mahlinza & others v Zulu Nyala Game Ranch (Pty) Ltd [2004] BLLR 245 (LC)

Malan v Van der Merwe 1937 TPD 244

Manzini City Council v Workers Representative Council Swaziland IC 92/89 (unreported)

Maphetane v Shoprite Checkers (Pty) Ltd (1996) 17 *ILJ* 964 (1C).

Marks v Kotze 1946 AD 29

Marriot v Oxford & District Cooperative Society (No.2) [1970] 1 QB 187

Marshall v Harland and Wolf [1972] 1 WLR 899

Mason v Provident Clothing Supply Ltd [1913] AC 724

Masondo & others v Bestform (SA) (Pty) Ltd (1986) 7 *ILJ* 448 (IC)

Mawu v A Mauche (Pty) Ltd t/a Precision Tools (1980) 1 *ILJ* 227 (IC)

Mazian v Transnamib transport (Pty) Ltd NLLP 2002 (2) 352 NLC

Mbome and others v Foodcon Fishing Product NLLP 2002 (2) 202 NLC

McClelland v Northern Ireland General Health Services Board [1957] 1 WLR 594 (HL)

McLeod & Co v Dunnell, Ebden & Co (1868) 1 Buch 182

MEC: Department of Finance, Economic Affairs & Tourism, Northern Province v Mahumani (2004) 25 *ILJ* 2311 (SCA)

Media 24 Ltd and another v Grobler [2005] 3 All SA 297 (SCA)

Meintjies v Joe Gross t/a Joe's Beerhouse 2003 NR 221 (LC)

Metcash Trading Ltd t/a Metro Cash and Carry v Fobb and another (1998) *ILJ* 1516 (LC)

Metropolitan Namibia Ltd v Haimbili NLLP 2004 (4) 110 NLC

Meyer v Law Society, Transvaal 1978 (2) SA 209 (T)

Meythal v Baxter 1916 OPD 122

Mhlume Sugar Company v Jablane James Mbuli Swaziland CA 1/91 (unreported)

Midland Cold Storage Ltd v Turner [1972] ICR 230

Minister of Enterprise and Employment v Swaziland Federation of Trade Unions Swaziland IC 163/97 (unreported)

Minister of Justice v Khoza 1966 (1) SA 410

Minister of Law and Order v Committee of the Church of Summit 1994 (3) SA 89 (B)

Minister of Law and Order and Others v Ngobo 1992 (4) SA 822 (A)

Minister of Police v Mbilini 1983 (3) SA 705 (A)

Mkize v Maartens 1914 AD 382

Mkhosi Madolo and Babazile Dlamini v Write Solutions Consortium Swaziland IC 72/96 (unreported)

Model Pick 'N Pay Family Supermarkets v Mukosho NLLP 2004 (4) 219 NLC

Model Pick 'N Pay Family Supermarkets v Mwaala 2003 NR 175 (LC)

Moghamat v Central Guards [2004] 1 All SA 221 (C)

Mokoena and Others v Administrator, Transvaal 1988 (4) SA 912 (W)

Monareng v Midrand Motolek CC (1991) 12 *ILJ* 1348 (IC)

Montreal Locomotive Works Ltd v Montreal and Attorney-General for Canada [1947] 1 DLR 161

Morren v Swinton & Pendlebury Borough Council [1965] 1 WLR 576

Morrish v Henlys (Folkestone) Ltd [1973] ICR 482

Mthembu and others v Claude Neon Lights (1992) 13 *ILJ* 422 (IC)

Mtshamba & others v Boland Houtnywerhede (1986) 7 *ILJ* 563 (IC)

Müller v President of the Republic of Namibia and another 1999 NR 190 (SC)

Municipality of Windhoek v Van Wyk and others 1999 NR 315 (LC)

Mutual & Federal Insurance Co v Bank, Insurance, Finance & Assurance Workers Union (1996) 17 *ILJ* 241 (A)

Mwellie v Minister of Works, Transport and Communication and another 1995 (9) BCLR 1118 (NmH)

Mweuhange v Cabinet of the Interim Government of South West Africa 1989 (1) SA 976 (SWA)

Nadasen v CG Smith Sugar Ltd (1992) 13 IJL 1571 (IC)

NAGLE v Fielden [1966] 2 QB 633

Namdeb Diamond Corporation (Pty) Ltd v Mineworkers Union of Namibia NLLP 2002 (2) 188 NLC

Namibia Beverages v Emily LCA 18/2001 (unreported)

Namibia Beverages v Hoaës NLLP 2002 (2) 380 NLC

Namibia Development Corporation v Vesagie NLLP 1998 (1) 166 NLC

Namibia Post Limited v Hans Eiman Case No.: LCA 13/2005 (unreported)

Namibia Seamen and Allied Workers Union v Cadilu Fishing (Pty) 2005 NR 257 (LC)

Namibia Seamen and Allied Workers Union v Lalandi Fishing (Pty) Ltd and others 2003 NR 71 (LC)

Nanditume v Minister of Defence 2000 NR 103 (LC)

Nantex Textile Swaziland (Pty) Ltd v Swaziland Manufacturers and Allied Workers Union and others Swaziland IC 140/97 (unreported)

Napier v National Business Agency [1951] 2 All ER 204

Nasionale Sorghum Bierbrouery (Edms) Bpk v John NO & others (1990) 11 *ILJ* 971 (IC)

National Amalgamated Local & Central Government & Parastatal Manual Workers Union v Attorney-General Botswana CA 26/93 (unreported)

National Automobile & Allied Workers Union (now known as National Union of Metalworkers of SA) v Borg-Warner SA (Pty) Ltd (1994) 15 *ILJ* 509 (A)

National Coal Board v Galley [1958] 1 All ER 91

National Union Metal Workers of SA and another v Bonar Long NTC (SA) (Pty) Ltd 1990 11 *ILJ* 1447 (IC)

National Union of Mineworkers v Amcoal Collieries & Industrial Operations (1990) 11 *ILJ* 1295 (IC)

National Union of Mineworkers & others v Amcoal Collieries & Industrial Operations Ltd (1991) 12 *ILJ* 1340 (IC)

National Union of Mineworkers & another v East Rand Proprietary Mines Ltd (1987) 8 *ILJ* 315 (IC)

National Union of Mineworkers v East Rand Gold & Uranium Co Ltd (1991) 12 *ILJ* 1221 (A)

National Union of Textile Workers v Jaguar Shoes (Pty) Ltd 1987 (1) SA 39 (N)

National Union of Textile Workers v Stag Packing (Pty) Ltd & another 1982 (4) SA151 (T)

Navachab Joint Venture t/a Navachab Gold Mine v Mineworkers Union of Namibia & others 1995 NR 225 (LC)

Navarro v Moregrand Ltd [1951] 2 TLR 674

Ndamase v Fyfe-King NO 1939 EDL 259

Negro v Continental Spinning & Knitting Mills 1954 (2) SA 203 (W)

Nel v Minister of Defence 1979 (2) SA 246 (R)

Nhlanhla M K Vilakati v Attorney-General Swaziland IC 88/96 (unreported)

Nkumbula v Attorney-General of Zambia (1972) ZR 204

Noel v Longbottom 1894 1 QB 771

Nokes v Doncaster Amalgamated Collieries Ltd [1940] AC 1014

North Riding Garages Ltd v Butterwick [1967] 2 QB 56

Ntsabo v Real Security CC (2003) 24 *ILJ* 2341 (LC)

Ntshanga v South African Breweries Ltd [2003] 8 BLLR 789 (LC)

Ntshangase v ALUSAF (Pty) Ltd (1984) 5 *ILJ* 336

NUMSA v Atlantis Diesel Engines (Pty) Ltd (1993) 14 *ILJ* 642 (LAC)

Nyingwa v Moolman NO 1993 (2) SA 508 (TK)

OA-Eib v Swakopmund Hotel and Entertainment Centre 1999 NR 137 (LC)

Oak Industries S.A. (Pty) Ltd v John NO & another 1987 (3) SA 702 (N)

Ocean Diamond Mining SA v Louw NLLP 2002 (2) 276 RSA HC (C)

O'Kelly v Trusthouse Forte plc [1983] 2 All ER 456

Ongevallekommissaris v Onderlinge Versekeringsgenootskap AVBOB 1996 (4) SA 446 (A)

O'Reilly v Graff-Reinetse Kooperatiewe Winkels Bpk (1991) 12 *ILJ* 1360 (IC)

O'Reilly v Mackman [1982] 3 All ER 1124 (HL)

Orman v Saville Sportswear Ltd [1960] 1 WLR 1055

Oscar Z Mamba v Swaziland Development and Savings Bank Swaziland IC 81/96 (unreported)

Ottoman Bank v Chakarian [1930] AC 277

Park v Wilson & Clyde Co Ltd 1928 SC 121

Patz v Greene & Co 1907 TS 427

Paxton v Namib Rand Desert Trails (Pty) Ltd 1996 NR 109 (LC)

Pearce v Brooks (1866) 1 Ex 213

Pearce v Foster (1886) 17 QBD 536

Pelunsky v Teron 1913 WLD 34

Penman v Fife Coal Co [1936] AC 45

Pep Stores (Namibia) (Pty) Ltd v Iyambo and others 2001 NR 211 (LC)

Pepper v Webb [1969] 1WLR 514

Performing Rights Society Ltd v Mitchell and Booker (Palais de Danse) Ltd [1924] 1 KB 762

Phillips v Fieldstone Africa (Pty) Ltd and another [2004] 1 All SA 150 (SCA)

Phineas Vilakati v J D Group (Pty) Ltd Swaziland IC 41/97 (unreported)

Plascon-Evans Paints Ltd v Van Riebeeck Paints (Pty) Ltd 1984 (3) SA 623 (A)

Potchefstroom Municipal Council v Bouwer NO 1958 (4) SA 382 (T)

Powell Duffryn Ltd v Rhodes (1946) 1 All ER 666

PPWAWU & others v Delma (Pty) Ltd (1980) 10 *ILJ* 420 (IC)

Pratt v Cook, Son & Cook (St. Paul's) Ltd [1940] AC 437

Pretoria North Town Council v A1 Electric Ice-Cream Factory 1953 (3) SA 1 (T)

Prinsloo v Van der Linde and another 1997 (3) SA 1012 (CC)

Prism Holdings Ltd and another v Liversage and others 2004 (2) SA 478 (W)

Protekon (Pty) Ltd v CCMA and others [2005] 7 BLLR 703 (LC)

Pupkewitz & Sons (Pty) Ltd v Kankara 1997 NR 70

Pupkewitz Holdings (Pty) Ltd v Petrus Mutanuka and others LCA 47/2007 (unreported)

Queensland Stations (Pty) Ltd v Federal Commissioner of Taxation (1945) 70 CLR 539

R. v Feun 1954 (I) SA 58 (T)

R v Plank and others (1900) 17 SC 45 [10 CTR 21]

R v Smit 1955 (1) SA 239 (C)

R v Sussex Justices, ex parte McCarthy [1924] 1 KB 256

R. v Tshongongo and others 1957 (2) SA 486 (C)

Rabe and another v African Granite (Pty) Ltd NLLP 2004 (4) 273 NLC

Raborifi and others v Minister of Justice and Transport 1991 (4) SA 442 (B)

Radio Television Electronic & Allied Workers Union v Tedelex (Pty) Ltd & another (1990) 11 *ILJ* 1272 (IC)

Ranch Hotel (Pty) Ltd v SACCAWU (1993) *LCD* (LAC)

Raymore Limited v TGWU [1989] 3 All ER 583 (CA)

Ready Mixed Concrete (South East) v Minister of Pensions [1968] 2 QB 497

Reckitt & Colman (SA) (Pty) Ltd v Chemical Workers Industrial Union & others (1991) 12 *ILJ* 806 (LAC)

Redman v Colbeck 1917 EDL 35

Reed v Richmond Local Board 1923 AD 50

Reigate v Union Manufacturing Co (Ramsbottom) [1918] 1 KB 592

Republican Party of Namibia and Congress of Democrats v Electoral Commission of Namibia and others Case No. SA: 387/2005 (Supreme Court) (unreported)

Rex v Nay 1934 TPD 52

Robinson v George Sorby Ltd (1960) 2 ITR 148

Roe v Ministry of Health [1954] 2 WLR 915

Roffey v Cateral, Edwards & Goudre (Pty) Ltd 1977 (4) SA 494 (N)

Rossam v Kraatz Welding Engineering (Pty) Ltd 1998 NR 90 (LC)

Rossouw v Central New Agency Ltd 1948 (2) SA 267 (W)

Rossouw v Minister of Mines and Minister of Justice 1928 TPD 741

Rowe v Assistant Magistrate, Pretoria and another 1925 TPD 36

Rumingo and others v Van Wyk 1997 NR 102 (HC)

Rustenburg Town Council v Minister of Labour and others 1942 TPD 220

S v Bushebi 198 NR 239 (SC)

S. v Wells 1990 (1) SA 816 (A)

SA Allied Workers Union and others v Contract Installations (Pty) Ltd & others (1988) 9 *ILJ* 112 (IC)

SA Allied Workers Union & others v Dorbyl Automotive Products (Pty) Ltd (1988) 9 *ILJ* 680 (IC)

SA Association of Municipal Employees v Minister of Labour 1948 (1) SA 528 (T)

SA Breweries Ltd v FAWU and others (1992) 1 *LCD* 16 (LAC)

SA Chemical Workers Union and others v Sentrachem (1988) 9 *ILJ* 410 (IC)

SA Master Dental Technicians Association v Dental Association of SA & others 1970 (3) SA 733 (A)

SA Society of Bank Officials v Standard Bank South African Ltd (1994) 15 *ILJ* 332 (IC)

SACWU & others v Noristan Holdings Ltd and others (1987) 8 *ILJ* 682 (IC)

SACWU & others v Pharma Natura (Pty) Ltd (1986) 7 *ILJ* 696 (IC)

Sagar v Ridehalgh [1931] 1 Ch 310

SALDCDAWU v Advance Laundries t/a Stork Napkins (1985) 6 *ILJ* 544 (IC)

Salt and another v Smith 1990 NR 87

Sanders v Parry [1967] 2 All ER 145

SAR & H v Marais 1950 (4) SA 610 (A)

Sasfin (Pty) Ltd v Beukes 1987 (1) SA1 (A)

Saunders v Whittle (1876) 33 LT 816

SCAW Metals Ltd v Vermuelen (1993) 14 *ILJ* 672 (LAC)

Schierhout v Minister of Justice 1926 AD 99

Schmidt and another v Secretary of State for Home Affairs [1969] 1 All ER 904

Schneir & London Ltd v Bennet 1927 TPD 346

Seamen and Allied Workers Union v Cadilu Fishing (Pty) Ltd 2005 NR 257

Secretary of State for India v Bank of India [1938] LR 65 IA

Semtex v Gladstone [1954] 1 WLR 945

Setlogelo v Setlogelo 1914 AD 221

Shaba v Officer Commanding, Temporary Police Camp, Wagendrift Dam 1995 (4) SA 1 (A)

Shifidi v Administrator-General for South West Africa 1989 (4) 631 (SWA)

Shiimi v Windhoek Schlachterei (Pty) Ltd NLLP 2002 (2) 224 NLC

Shlengeman v Meyer, Bridgens & Co 1920 CPD 494

Short v Henderson Ltd [1946] 174 LT 417

Sibongile Nxumalo and others v Attorney-General and others Swaziland CA 25/96, 28/96, 29/96, 30/96 (consolidated) (unreported)

Sikhosana and others v Sasol Synthetic Fuels (2000) 21 *ILJ* 649 (LC)

Smit v Standard Bank Namibia Ltd 1994 NR 366 (LC)

Smit v Workmen's Compensation Commissioner 1979 (1) SA 51 (A)

SPCA of Namibia v Terblanche 1996 NR 398 (LC)

Spencer v Gostelow 1920 AD 617

Springs Town Council v MacDonald 1967 (3) SA 229 (W)

SRV Mill Services (Pty) Ltd v CCMA & others [2004] 2 BLLR 103 184 (LC)

Standard Bank of SA Ltd v Commission for Conciliation, Mediation and Arbitration and others (1998) 19 *ILJ* 903 (LC)

Standard Bank of South Africa and others v Ocean Commodities Inc and others 1983 (1) SA 276 (A)

Stein v Rising Tide Productions CC 2002 (5) SA 199 (C)

Stellenbosch Farmers Winery Ltd v Stellenvale Winery (Pty) Ltd 1957 (4) SA 234 (C)

Sterling Engineering Co v Patchett [1955] AC 534

Stevenson, Jordan and Harrison Ltd v MacDonald and Evans [1952] 1 TLR 100

Stewart Wrightson (Pty) v Thorpe 1974 (4) SA 67 (D)

Stewart Wrightson (Pty) Ltd v Thorpe 1977 (2) SA 943 (A)

Strachan v Prinsloo 1925 TDP 709

Stratford (JT) & Sons v Lindley [1965] AC 307

Street v Dublin 1961 (2) SA 4 (W)

Susan Dlamini v President of the Industrial Court and Melmans Pharmacy (Pty) Ltd Swaziland ICA Case No. 13/88 (unreported)

Swakopmund Hotel and Entertainment Centre v Karibib NLLP 1998 (1) 213 NLC

Swart and others v Minister of Education and Culture, House of Representatives, and another 1986 (3) SA 331 (C)

Swaziland Agricultural and Plantation Workers Union v United Plantations (Swaziland) Ltd Swaziland IC 79 /98 (unreported)

Swaziland Dairies (Pty) Ltd v Meyer 1970-1976 SLR 91

Swaziland Federation of Trade Unions v President of the Industrial Court and Minister of Enterprise and Employment Swaziland CA 11/91 (unreported)

Swaziland Transport & Allied Workers Union v Tracar Swaziland IC 16/94 (unreported)

System Floors (UK) Ltd v Daniel [1982] ICR 54

Teixeira v SA Broadcasting Corporation (1991) 12 *ILJ* 656 (IC)

The Free Press of Namibia (Pty) Ltd v Cabinet of the Interim Government of South West Africa 1987 (1) SA 614 (SWA)

The President of the Methodist Conference v Parfitt [1984] IRLR 141

The Queen v Walker 72 LT MC 207

The State v A.M.C.A. Services (Pty) Ltd 1962 (4) SA 537 (A)

Themba Mdluli and Others v Emaswati Coal (Pty) Ltd Swaziland CA 18/96 (unreported)

Tiger Bakeries Ltd v Food & Allied Workers Union & others (1988) 9 *ILJ* 82 (W)

Tiopaizi v Bulawayo Municipality 1923 AD 317

Titus Nzima v Swaziland P &T Corp Swaziland IC 139/95 (unreported)

Topol v S Group Management Services (Pty) Ltd 1988 (1) SA 639 (W)

Appendix II Table of Cases **299**

Total Support Management (Pty) and another v Diversified Health Systems (SA) (Pty) Ltd and another 2002 (4) SA 661 (SCA)

Toyota South Africa (Pty) Ltd v Radebe and others 2000 21 *ILJ* 340 (LAC)

Transnamib Holdings Ltd v Engelbrecht 2005 NR 372 (SC)

Transnamib Ltd v Imcor Zinc (Pty) Ltd (Moly-Copper Mining and Exploration (SWA) Ltd and another Intervening) 1994 NR 11

Transnamib Ltd v Swartz NLLP 2002 (2) 60 NLC

Transnet Bpk v Voorsitter Nasionale Vervoerkommissie 1995 (3) SA 844 (T)

Transport Fleet Management (Pty) Ltd & another v NUMSA and others [2003] 10 BLLR 975 (LAC)

Tshabalala v the Minister of Health and others 1987 (1) SA 513 (W)

Tshabalala v Moroka Swallows Football Club Ltd (1991) 12 *ILJ* 389 (IC)

Tshabalala v Peer 1979 (4) SA 27 (T)

Tshivhase Royal Council v Tshivhase 1992 (4) SA 852 (A)

Turiff Construction Ltd v Bryant (1967) KIR 659

Turner v Sawdon & Co [1901] 2 KB 653

Ubombo Ranches v Pan Attendants Swaziland CA 6/90 (unreported)

Ubombo Ranches Ltd v President of the Industrial Court and another 1982-1986 SLR 1

Union of India v Prathiba Bonnerjea (1976) AIR SC 690

V & A Waterfront Properties and another v Helicopter and Marine Service (Pty) Ltd and others [2004] 2 All SA 664 (C)

Van Den Heever v Imcor Zinc (Pty) Ltd NLLP 2004 (4) 257 NLC

Van der Merwe v Colonial Government (1904) 21 SC 520

Van Drimmelen and Partners v Gowar and others [2004] 1 All SA 175 (SCA)

Van Wyk and another v Rumingo and others NLLP 2004 (4) 1 NLC

Venter v Abramson 1952 (3) SA 524 (T)

Vesagie v Namibia Development Corporation 1999 NR 219 (HC)

Von Molkte v Costa Areosa (Pty) Ltd 1975 (1) SA 255 (C)

Walter McNaughton (Pty) Ltd v Schwartz and others [2003] 1 All SA 770 (C)

Webb v East (1880) LR 5 Ex 108

Western Excavating (ECC) Ltd v Sharp [1978] 1 All ER 713

Whitehead v Woolworths (Pty) Ltd (1999) 20 *ILJ* 2133 (LC)

Wilson & Clyde Coal Co v English [1938] AC 57

Wlotzkasbaken Home Owners' Association and another v Erongo Regional Council and others 2007 (2) NR 799

Woods v W M Car Services (Peterborough) Ltd (1982) 1 RLR 413

Workers Representative Council v Manzini City Council Swaziland IC 92/89 (unreported)

Workers Representative Council v Manzini Town Council Swaziland CA 3/94 (unreported)

Wyeth SA (Pty) Ltd v Manqele and others [2005] 6 BLLR 523 (LAC)

Yetton v Eastwood Froy Ltd [1966] 3 All ER 353

Yewens v Noakes (1880) 6 QBD 530

Yoffe v Koppies District Licensing Board 1948 (3) SA 743 (O)

Zimbabwe Township Developers (Pvt) Ltd v Lou's Show (Pvt) Ltd 1984 (2) SA 778 (ZS)

BIBLIOGRAPHY

Anderman, S. D. *Law of Unfair Dismissal,* 2nd edn, Durban, Butterworths, 1985.

Association of Arbitrators (Southern Africa). *The Rules for the Conduct of Arbitration,* 4th edn, Benmore, Association of Arbitrators, August 2000.

Baxter, Lawrence. *Administrative Law,* Cape Town, Juta & Co, 1984.

Beech, Warren and Peart, Susan. 'Case Note' *De Rebus* 405 (October 2001), 54-55.

Bell, Andrew C. *Employment Law in a Nutshell,* London, Sweet & Maxwell, 2000.

Binnington, Chris D. 'Dispute Resolution in the Construction Industry', Paper presented at the Standard Bank/PAMAN Arbitration Seminar, Windhoek, Namibia, 1-2 April 2004.

Blunt, Peter. *Organizational Theory and Behaviour : An African Perspective*, London & New York, Longman, 1983.

Boberg, P.Q.R. *The Law of Delict*, vol I, Cape Town, Juta & Co, 1984.

Brassey, M.S.M. et al. *The New Labour Law*, Cape Town, Juta & Co, 1987.

Butler, David. 'The need for modern arbitration legislation in Namibia: the available options', Paper presented at the Standard Bank/PAMAN Arbitration Seminar, Windhoek, Namibia, 1-2 April 2004.

Butler, David and Eyvind Finsen. *Arbitration in South Africa: Law and Practice*, Kenwyn, Juta & Co, 1993.

Cameron, E., Cheadle, H. and Thompson, C. *The New Labour Relations Act*, Cape Town, Juta & Co, 1989.

Cheadle, H. et al. *Current Labour Law*, Cape Town, Juta & Co, 1991.

Christie, R.H. *The Law of Contract in South Africa*, 5th edn, Durban, Butterworths, 2006.

Cooper, Carol. 'Strikes in Essential Services', *ILJ* 903 (1994).

Cox, Archibald. 'The Duty to Bargain in Good Faith', *Harvard Law Review* 71 (1958), 1401.

Davies, P. and Freedland. M. *Labour Legislation and Public Policy*, Oxford, Clarendon Press, 1993.

Devenish, G E. *Interpretation of Statutes*, Cape Town, Juta & Co, 1992.

Drake, Charles D. *Labour Law,* 2nd edn, London, Sweet & Maxwell, 1973.

Edgar, S.G.G. *Craies on Statute Law*, 7th edn, London, Sweet & Maxwell, 1971.

Else-Mitchell, Justice R. 'Administrative Law', in R.N. Spann et al. (eds) *Public Administration in Australia*, Government Printer, New South Wales, 1975.

Employment Equity Commission of Namibia. *The Employers' Guidelines to the Affirmative Action (Employment) Act 1998 (Act No. 29 of 1998)*, revised edn, Windhoek, 2002.

Erasmus, H.J. *Superior Court Practice*, Cape Town, Juta & Co, 1994.

Finkin, M.W. et al. *Legal Protection for the Individual Employee*, St. Paul Minne, West Publishing, 1989.

Garner, Bryan A. *A Dictionary of Modern Legal Usage*, 2nd edn, New York & Oxford, Oxford University Press, 1995.

Gibons, J.T.R. *South African Mercantile and Company Law*, 5th edn, Cape Town, Juta & Co, 1983.

Gordon, R.J.F. *Judicial Review: Law and Procedure*, London, Sweet & Maxwell, 1985.

Grogan, John. *Riekert's Employment Law*, 2nd edn, Cape Town, Juta & Co, 1993.

Grogan, John. *Dismissal*, Cape Town, Juta & Co, 2002.

International Labour Organization (ILO). *Digest of Decisions and Principles of the Freedom of Association Committee of the Governing Body of the ILO*, 3rd edn, Geneva, ILO, 1985.

ILO. C29 Forced Labour Convention, 1930.

ILO. C87 Freedom of Association and Protection of the Right to Organize Convention, 1948.

ILO. C111 Employment and Occupation Convention, 1958

ILO. R119 Termination of Employment Recommendation, 1963.

ILO. C158 Termination of Employment Convention, 1982.

ILO. R166 Termination of Employment Recommendation, 1982.

Issacks, I. *Beck's Theory and Principles of Pleadings in Civil Actions,* 5th edn, Durban, Butterworths, 1989.

Jackson, Helen. *Aids in Africa: Continent in Crisis*, Harare, SAFAIDS, 2002.

Joubert, W.A. *The Law of South Africa (LAWSA)*, vol.3, Durban, Butterworths, 1985.

Landman, A. et al. *Labour Law,* (Study Guide) LWB 403-4/LBL 200-J, Pretoria, UNISA.

Le Roux, P.A.K. and Van Niekerk, André. *The South African Law of Unfair Dismissal*, Cape Town, Juta & Co, 1994.

Letsika, Qhalehang. 'Restraint of trade clauses', *De Rebus* 425 (August 2003), 26-31.

Lewin, Arthur. *The Law, Procedure and Conduct of Meetings in South Africa*, Cape Town, Juta & Co, 1975.

Lewis, T. Ellis. *Winfield on Tort,* 6th edn, London, Sweet & Maxwell, 1954.

Lockton, Deborah. *Employment Law*, 3rd edn, London, Butterworths, 2000.

Lowe, Robert. *Commercial Law*, 4th edn, London, Sweet & Maxwell, 1973.

McKerron, R.G. *The Law of Delict*, Cape Town, Juta & Co, 1971.

Millin, Philip and George Wille. *Wille and Millin's Mercantile Law of South Africa*, 7th edn, Johannesburg, Hortas Ltd, 1967.

Milne, Michael. 'Discovery and Privilege in Arbitration Proceedings', *JCI Arb* 60, 1994, 285-8.

Mureinik, Etienne. 'The Contract of Service: An Easy Test for Hard Cases', *SALJ* 97, 246.

Ncube, Mtshana M. and Parker, Collins. *Comparative Electoral Systems and Political Consequences for Independent Namibia*, Lusaka, UN Institute for Namibia, 1989.

Neethling, J. et al. *Law of Delict*, 2nd edn, Durban, Butterworths, 1990.

Okpaluba, Chuks. 'Collective Labour Rights and Industrial Relations Legislation of Swaziland', in Chuks Okpaluba, et al. (eds), *Human Rights in Swaziland: A Legal Response*, Mbabane, University of Swaziland, 1997.

Okpaluba, Chuks. 'Labour Adjudication in Swaziland: The Exclusive Jurisdiction of the Industrial Court', *JAL* 43 (1999), 184-200.

Oosthuizen, Martin. 'Racist language in the workplace', *De Rebus* 431 (March 2004), 45-6.

Parker, Collins. 'Executive Discretion and Personal Freedom', LL.M. Thesis, Dalhousie University, 1979.

Parker, Collins. 'The "Administrative Justice" provision of the Constitution of the Republic of Namibia: a constitutional protection of judicial review and tribunal adjudication under administrative law', *CILSA* XXIV (1991), 88.

Parker, Collins. *Human Rights Law,* Leicestershire, Upfront Publishing, 2002.

Parker, Collins. *A Manual of Public Management*, Windhoek, Aim Publications, 2003.

Perrins, B. *Harvey on Industrial Relations and Employment Law,* Durban, Lexis Nexis (Issue 156, June 2002), DI 995.

Perrit, H.H. *Employee Dismissal, Law and Practice*, 3rd edn, Chichester, John Wiley and Sons, 1992.

Prest, C. B. *The Law and Practice of Interdicts*, Kenwyn, Juta & Co, 1996.

Rycroft, A. and Jordaan, B. *A Guide to South African Labour Law*, 2nd edn, Cape Town: Juta & Co, 1992.

Schwikkard, P.J. et al. *Principles of Evidence*, 2nd edn, Kenwyn, Juta & Co, 2002.

Shaw, Sir Sebag and Smith, Judge Dennis. *The Law of Meetings*, 5th edn, Estover, MacDonald and Evans, 1979.

Snyman, A.R. *Criminal Law*, 3rd edn, Durban, Butterworths, 1995.

Street, L. 'The Language of ADR – its utility in resolving international commercial disputes: the role of the mediator', *Arbitration* (1992) 58 2 (S), 17-22.

Tajgman, David. *International Labour Standards in Southern Africa*, Southern Africa Monographs 49/4, Institute of Development and Labour Law, University of Cape Town.

The Namibian, Windhoek.

The Concise Oxford Dictionary, 10th edn, Oxford, Clarendon Press, 2000.

The Shorter Oxford English Dictionary on Historical Principles, 3rd edn, Oxford, Clarendon Press, 1973.

Thornton, G.C. *Legislative Drafting*, 3rd edn, London, Butterworths, 1987.

Tordoff, William. *Government and Politics in Africa,* London, Macmillan, 1984.

Van Winsen, L. de V. et al. *Herbstein and Van Winsen: The Civil Practice of the Supreme Court of South Africa*, 4th edn, Kenwyn, Juta & Co, 1997.

Visser, P.J and Potgeiter, J.M. *Law of Damages*, Cape Town, Juta Law, 2003.

Wade, H.W.R. and Forsyth, C.F. *Administrative Law,* Oxford, Oxford University Press, 2000.

Wallis, M.J.D. *Labour and Employment Law,* Durban, Butterworths, 1992.

Willis, John. 'Administrative Law and the British American Act', *Harvard Law Review* 53 (1939), 251.

INDEX

absconding by employee   44

absenteeism   42, 44

accident   96-7, 102

     arising from and in the course of employment   97

accommodation   75, 90

administrative bodies   209

affirmative action   94-5, 170, 183

agreements   64, 173, 260, 271

     closed-shop   244

     recognition   169, 259-63

     'yellow-dog'   244

     see also collective agreements

appeal   129, 150, 152-4, 180, 205-7, 209-10, 215, 221

arbitration   175, 180-2, 201-2, 211, 214, 237, 262, 264-6

     Arbitration Act 1965   182, 211-13, 214

     contrast with conciliation   119, 170, 175-85, 198-200, 205, 223, 236

     contrast with mediation   175, 215

     Part C arbitration under Labour Act 2004   182-4, 198-9, 202-3, 236, 270, 273

     private arbitration under Labour Act 2004   182, 202

     see also Labour Court

arbitrator   21, 62, 112-13, 119, 146, 157, 164, 180-6, 210-16, 219, 222-3, 231, 236, 261-7, 273

arbitrator's power to award   193

audi alteram partem   147, 150-5, 213

ballot   256, 261-2

     exclusive bargaining agents   95, 160-2, 170, 259, 261-4, 270, 271

     trade union   75, 95, 145, 149, 157-8, 160-3, 166, 170-2, 178, 198, 201, 237, 242-70 bargaining   95, 160-2, 164, 226-7, 244, 246, 259-66, 268-1

basic wages   72, 80-4, 89

    see also remuneration

bias   147-8, 150

breach of trust by employee   27, 42-3, 48, 50, 54-6, 64, 98, 106-7, 112-14, 143-4, 147, 190

Certificate of Employment or Service   76

child labour   30, 183

    prohibition of in terms of Labour Act 2004   9, 24, 27, 30, 74, 79, 82-3, 183

closed shop, *see* agreement, closed-shop

code of good practice under Labour Act 2004   140, 156, 179, 186, 229

    arbitrator's award   180-1, 211-12, 214

    conciliation   119, 170, 175-82, 184, 199-200, 205, 217, 219, 223, 228

    picketing   237-9

    see also fairness, procedural

Code of Practice (UK)   264-5

collective agreements   29, 75, 127-8, 130, 157, 169, 171-2, 183-4, 202, 215, 232-3, 244, 255, 261, 264, 268-73

collective bargaining   95, 164, 226-7, 244, 246, 259-66, 268-71, 275

    disclosure of information   60, 162, 264-8

    duty to bargain in good faith   268

    exclusive bargaining agent   95, 160-2, 170, 255, 259-64, 270-1

    unfair labour practice   32, 121-2, 165, 198, 259, 265, 268

common law   1, 2, 4, 10-12, 14, 16, 18, 21-2, 26, 28, 30, 36, 38-42, 52, 57, 63-5, 69, 70, 72, 75-6, 79, 84, 90, 96, 106, 109-16, 120, 125, 139, 156, 165-6, 178, 188, 198, 208-9, 221, 227, 232, 241, 245, 247, 249, 252, 270

compensation   87, 97, 113, 157, 186, 192-5, 198, 200, 221

    arbitrator's power to award   193

conciliation   119, 170, 175-85, 198-200, 205, 219, 223, 228, 236

    contrast with arbitration   175-6, 179-86, 198-203, 210, 212-15, 219, 223

    contrast with mediation   175-6, 180, 182

    Labour Act 2004   275, 277

representation of parties during conciliation   178, 181, 185

consideration   3, 13, 14, 36

constructive dismissal   32-4, 105, 108-9

continuity of employment

    death   4, 87-8, 127, 137-8, 203

    dissolution   137

    transfer   92, 106, 137, 145, 159-60, 164

    winding-up   254

contract of employment   2, 4, 9, 13-17, 20, 22, 25-39, 42, 44-50, 55-6, 63-72, 78-9, 84, 86, 88-90, 96-8, 107-16, 119-39, 142-3, 157-9, 165, 168-72, 183, 193, 200-1, 215, 219, 227, 233, 244, 246, 206, 269-72

    definition   5, 15, 20-1, 25-6

    duration   26, 28-9, 38, 80-1, 110, 119, 127, 133

    freedom of association   38, 77, 110-11, 120-22, 124-6

    Freedom of Contract   26-7

    illegal contracts   27, 31, 74, 232, 244

    personal nature   3, 4, 18, 22, 25-7, 30, 37, 39, 41-5, 48, 69, 102, 114, 116

    repudiation   32, 34, 46-7, 70-1, 125, 128, 219, 227

    restraint of trade clauses   63-6, 116

    statutory intervention   15-16, 19, 22-3, 25, 27, 39, 45, 72, 74-6, 84, 110-13, 123, 125, 127-9, 132-3, 139, 156, 178, 180, 183, 193, 198, 206-7, 247, 259, 261, 264

    suspensive conditions   20

    terms of   20-1, 25-8, 30-2, 34-38, 41-2, 44-6, 50, 56, 69, 70-1, 88, 92, 96, 107, 113-15, 119, 126-8, 131-2, 149, 164-5, 201, 269

        express   13, 15, 20, 25, 28, 37, 41, 46, 48, 50, 72, 114-15, 119, 126-8, 132, 149

        implied   13, 15, 19-20, 25, 28, 30-1, 38, 41, 46, 50, 69, 71-2, 97-8, 114, 119, 165

    variation   31, 34, 199

    written statement of particulars   29, 73

    see also collective agreements; common law; redundancy; termination of employment contract criminal sanctions   1, 19, 55, 60, 62, 227, 230, 233

damages   12, 71, 97-8, 103, 111, 113, 115-16, 145, 194, 198, 219-20

    compensation   3, 7, 10, 41, 87, 97, 193-4, 208

    employer's liability   97, 99

    power   6, 11, 13, 33, 39-40, 132

death   87-8, 127, 137, 203

declaratory order   185, 188, 198, 215

delict   1, 96-7, 99-100, 102-3, 227, 230

    immunity   230

    liability   1, 77, 97-101, 103, 106, 115, 126, 230

demotion   34, 92, 145, 165, 168, 193

disciplinary hearing   141, 143, 146, 148-9, 150, 154, 168

    Public Service Act 1995   44, 47, 62, 75, 114, 152-3, 177, 183-4, 261, 264

disciplinary measures   193-4

discrimination, prohibited grounds of dismissal   24, 91-5, 158, 183

    see also fairness, substantive; International Labour Organization; notice; redundancy; reinstatement; unfair dismissal

dismissal   13, 32-4, 39, 42-62, 77, 92, 105, 108-14, 119-25, 129-33, 136, 139-49, 152-69, 184, 186-95, 208, 215, 219, 221, 230, 232-3, 270

    see also constructive dismissal

duty of care   77

    see also negligence

employee   1-150, 155-60, 163-72, 178, 185-95, 200-1, 208, 210, 219, 222, 224, 227, 230-7, 241, 243, 245-6, 248-9, 252, 259, 263, 266-71

    approaches and tests for identifying   5, 10, 14, 16

    as director   11, 49, 178

    association of employees *see* trade unions

    duties

        duty to exercise   56

        fiduciary   49

indemnity 97-8, 115

inventions 48

not to make secret profit and commissions 49

obedience 35, 45

to adopt to new methods 52

ejection from accommodation provided by employer 90, 183, 187

guaranteee of skill and knowledge 4, 13, 36-7, 48, 50, 98, 114

independent contractor, contrasted with 2, 3, 5, 9, 10, 15-16, 18-19, 21

remedies against employer 37, 107, 113, 139, 193, 215, 227

right to be given work by employer 22, 26, 32-3, 70, 108

who is an employee 2, 22

see also dismissal; contract of employment; redundancy; unfair dismissal

Employees Compensation Act 1995 201

employer 1-9, 12, 14, 16-20, 22, 25-90, 93-150, 154-72, 178, 185-195, 198, 200-1, 208, 210, 215, 219-20, 223-46, 251, 255, 259-71

association 242

dismissal, *see* dismissal

duties

board and lodging of employee 90

disclosure of information, *see* collective bargaining

indemnity 97-8, 103, 115

see also health and safety; severence pay; testimonial

remedies against employer 37, 107, 113, 139, 193, 215, 227

vicarious 97, 99, 103, 106

who is an employer 22

in terms of common law, *see* common law

employment contract, *see* contract of employment

employment law 1, 135, 169

see also labour law

equity, *see* Labour Court

essential services committee 234-6, 275

European Court of Justice   93

exclusive bargaining agents   95

fairness   2, 119, 121-2, 129-32, 134, 139-44, 147, 149-50, 153-9, 163-4, 185, 199, 206, 249

     natural justice, relationship with, *see* natural justice

     procedural fairness   112, 122, 139-43, 147, 149-50, 153-7, 163-4, 228

     substantive fairness   139-44, 147, 156-7, 163, 228, 232

fixed-term contract, *see* contract of employment, freedom of association

full and final settlement   219-22

garnishee order   75

health and safety   96-7, 251, 275

     employee's duty   97

     employer's duty   96

     legislation   86-7, 96

HIV and AIDS   91

     discrimination   91-3

hours of work   29, 42, 73, 79, 183

illness   42, 44-5, 72, 76, 86-8, 115, 127

income tax   9, 75

independent contractor   2, 3, 5, 9-10, 15-16, 18-19, 21

industrial action   113, 117, 173, 224, 225-7, 237, 239

     ballot   252, 256, 261-2

industrial disputes   169-73, 175, 205, 219, 223, 225

     disputes of interest   171-2

     disputes of right   172-3, 205

     resolution by industrial action   169, 171, 175-8, 181, 184-5, 202, 215, 273

Industrial Revolution   7

injury   29, 42, 44-5, 76, 86-7, 96-7, 100, 115

insolvency   128, 254

   see also employee; employer

insulting language   57

interdict   112-13, 116, 185-6, 198, 215-16, 232

   final   186

   interim   186

   prohibitory   186

   to restrain lockouts   216

   to restrain strikes   216

   urgent   186-8, 215-7

International Labour Organization (ILO)   26-7, 91, 94, 121, 227, 234, 243

   conventions   227

      essential services (1985)   234-7, 275

      forced labour (1930)   26-7, 183

      freedom of association and protection of the right to organize (1948)   2, 183, 227, 243

      right to strike, no convention specifically on   113, 145, 223-37

   Namibia as a State Party of   243

intimidation by employee   59, 247

Labour Commissioner   119, 145, 160-3, 170, 177, 179, 183-4, 186, 196, 198, 202, 207-9, 216-17, 228-9, 236-7, 246-7, 253-7, 261-3, 273, 275

   exclusive bargaining agents   95, 160-2, 198, 255, 259

   registration of trade unions   242, 246-7, 248, 253-7, 259, 275

Labour Court   9, 18, 32, 47, 50-1, 53-54, 59, 93, 109, 122-5, 129-31, 141-42, 145-6, 150, 152-4, 159, 162-5, 167-8, 170, 172, 180, 188-91, 194, 197-8, 200, 202-3, 205-10, 213-23, 231-2, 238, 240, 247, 254, 257, 263

   judges presiding over   205-7

   Rules Board   217

labour law   1-2, 4-5, 29-30, 36, 41, 75, 99, 103, 108, 110, 117, 139, 176, 186, 193, 244

leave

   annual   30, 78, 84-8, 157

312   Labour Law in Namibia

compassionate   78, 87-8

maternity   30, 78, 85, 87-9

public holiday   80-5, 275

sick   29-30, 44, 78, 85-9, 115

letter of reference, *see* testimonial

letting and hiring   2, 3, 4, 36, 110

    see also contract of employment

LIFO (last in first out)   162

local authorities   123, 177

locatio conductio of Roman law   2-4, 14, 16, 36

lockout   1, 117, 133, 137, 179, 216-17, 223-25, 236, 239, 240

maintenance order   75

majoritarianism   270

    see also collective agreements

managerial prerogative   34-5

master and servant relationship   1, 4, 6, 8, 13, 69, 111

mediation   175-6, 180, 182, 264

    constrasted with conciliation   119, 170, 175-85, 198-200, 205, 219, 223, 228

    contrasted with arbitration   172-6, 179-86, 192-3, 198-203, 210, 212-15, 223, 236, 262, 272

misconduct   33, 42, 47, 52, 56-62, 75, 114, 136, 145, 190, 208-12, 230-3

Namibian Public Workers Union (NAPWU)   261, 264

natural justice   125, 147-56, 184, 212-13, 249-50, 263, 271

    see also fairness

negligence   56

    damages, as remedy of, *see* damages

    employee's liability   99, 115

    employer's liability   97, 99

      see also vicarious liability

standard of care 56

notice 27, 29, 32, 38, 45, 90, 107, 109, 110-14, 120, 126-35, 139, 140, 142, 167, 216

fair notice

payment in lieu 84

reasonable notice 109-10, 129, 250

statutory notice 129

termination by notice 130

termination without notice 107, 135

see also dismissal; unfair dismissal

overtime 30, 37, 80-2, 275

pacta sunt servanda 65

picketing 237-9

promotion 59, 92, 106, 123, 265

public servants 114, 264

as administrative officials *see* administrative officials

misconduct of, under Public Service Act 1995, *see* misconduct

Public Service Union of Namibia (PSUN) 261

racist remarks 59-60

redundancy 52, 89, 92, 135, 139-40, 142, 147, 158-64

ILO 27, 91, 94, 121, 227, 234, 243

maternity leave 30, 78, 85, 87-9

offer of suitable alternative employment 145

onus of proof 20, 51, 56, 64, 66-7, 88, 109, 115, 141, 146, 193, 211-12

selection criteria, *see* LIFO

substantive fairness, with regard to 139, 142-4, 147, 156

see also dismissal; unfair dismissal

re-employment 169, 190-2

reinstatement 112-13, 116, 119, 137, 146, 157, 165, 169, 186, 188-93, 198

314   Labour Law in Namibia

     in relation to specific performance   71, 111-12, 116, 198

remuneration   13-14, 16, 21, 24-30, 35-41, 71-8, 82-9, 92, 94, 110, 116, 127-8, 134, 138, 145, 168, 183, 193-4, 210, 266-7, 269, 275

     essential element in employment contracts in English common law   14, 38

     essential element in employment contracts under Labour Act 2004   14, 38

     mode of payment   13-14, 28, 38, 71-5, 81, 84, 87, 136-8, 210

     permitted deductions from   75

     prohibited deductions from   74-5

retrenchment, *see* redundancy

rolling mass action   225

separation   63, 67, 86, 108, 110

severance pay   135-8, 195

sexual harassment   21, 24, 52, 103-6, 109

     improper behaviour   52

sickness   29, 44-5, 87, 115, 126-7

social security   75

specific performance, *see* reinstatement

stay-aways   225

strike   1, 61, 113, 117, 133, 137, 145, 179, 223-39

     criminal liability, arising from   230

     illegal strike   231-2

     immunity   230

     interdict to restrain   112, 116, 185-6, 232

     International Covenant on Civil and Political Rights   243

     violence   58-9, 247

     see also common law; conciliation

summary dismissal, *see* dismissal

Sunday work   80, 82-3, 275

suspension of employee   59, 92, 133, 137, 165, 168-70, 191, 193, 239

     disciplinary measure   193-4

termination of employment contract   4, 32, 38, 65, 76-8, 86-8, 92, 110, 129-37, 141-2, 158-60, 163-4, 170, 183, 219-221, 233

    by notice   129-34, 139, 142

    by repudiation   128

    disciplinary measure   193-4

    due to effluxion of time   120, 122, 124

    due to insolvency of employee   128

    illness   42, 44-5, 72, 76, 86-8, 115, 127

    notice period   109

    on completion of task   126

    permanent or indefinite period contracts   25-6, 37-8, 111

    see also dismissal; unfair dismissal; redundancy

terms and conditions of employment, *see* contract of employment

testimonial   63, 76-8

    consequences of false or incorrect statements in   77-8

theft   55, 60, 112, 114

trade unions   30, 75, 95, 145, 149, 157-8, 160-3, 166, 170-2, 178, 185-6, 188, 198, 201, 224, 236-7, 242-71

    admission to membership   249-50, 256

    bypassing by employers during collective bargaining   95, 226-7, 244, 246, 259-66, 268-9, 271

    consequences of registration   254, 256

    constitutional right to organize   30

    exclusive bargaining agents   95, 260

    individual membership rights   256

    joining   2, 30, 39, 53, 63, 241-6

    membership, exclusion where employee eligible   243, 249-50, 261

    office-bearers   250-2, 256-7

    officials   250-1, 257

    political   91, 92, 171, 225-6, 241, 248-9, 256

    political parties   248-9

    termination of membership   250

ultra vires, principle of   206, 214, 249

unfair dismissal   51, 105, 112-14, 119, 121-2, 124-5, 130-1, 136, 139, 141-2, 158, 163, 187, 193-5, 208, 219, 221

administrative law principles, relevance of   125, 155, 209, 249

arbitration, and   172-3, 175-6, 179-86, 192-3, 198-205, 210, 212-17, 219, 223, 234, 236, 262, 272-3

as a result of absence of valid and fair reasons for dismissal, *see* fairness, substantive

as a result of unfair procedure, *see* fairness, procedural

automatically unfair dismissal   120, 158

code of good practice   140, 156, 179, 186, 229

conciliation   119, 170, 175-85, 198-200, 205, 217, 219, 223, 228

onus   20, 109, 115, 141, 146

participation in strike   61, 113, 133, 145, 224, 228, 230-1, 233-4, 236-7

pregnancy   89, 91

redundancy   52, 89, 92, 135, 139, 142, 158-64

remedies

compensation   87, 97, 113, 157, 186, 193-5, 198, 200, 221

damages   71, 97-8, 103, 111, 113, 115, 194, 198, 219, 220

declaratory order   185, 188, 198, 215

reinstatement   112-13, 116, 119, 137, 146, 157, 165, 169, 186, 188-93, 198

right not to be dismissed unfairly   43, 109, 114, 125, 132

strike   61, 113, 117, 133, 145, 187, 223-39

see also constructive dismissal; contract of employment, freedom of association; natural justice; notice

unfair labour practice   32, 121-2, 165, 198, 259, 265, 268

collective bargaining   95, 226-7, 244, 246, 259-66, 268-9, 271, 275

remedies   37, 107, 113, 139, 193, 215, 227

what constitutes   143-4, 265

unfairness, *see* fairness

United States of America   106, 244

variation of employment contract   31-5, 70, 108, 165

consequence of unilateral variation   32, 44, 165

vicarious liability   97, 99, 103, 106

    in relation to employee   115

    'scope and course of employment'   35, 38, 41, 46, 48-50, 68, 97-103

warning   145, 166-8, 231

    as punitive measure   167-8

    final written warning   145, 167-8

    oral   166

    purpose of   143, 167

    written   132, 145, 166-8

    Workmen's Compensation Act 1941   97, 208

work   16-17, 21-2, 26, 29, 43-5, 69-71, 79-87

    employee's duty to perform   37, 42, 47-9, 52, 97, 245

    employer's duty to provide   70-1, 96

workplace representatives   160-2, 252

    collective bargaining   95, 164, 244, 246, 259-66, 268-9, 271, 275

    role in promoting health and safety at workplace   96, 251, 275

    role in redundancy procedures   158-64

ABOUT THE AUTHOR

Collins Parker BA (Hons) LLB (Hons) LLM PhD MBIM FArb practised law as an advocate in Zambia. He is an admitted legal practitioner of the High Court of Namibia. He was Chief: Legal Services and International Cooperation and Coordinator of the SADC Legal Sector. He was one of the counsel for Namibia in the *Case concerning Kasikili/Sedudu Island* at the International Court of Justice. Before that he was a Judge of the Industrial Court of the Kingdom of Swaziland. He has been a Judge of the High Court of Namibia since November 2006.

His other publications are *Comparative Electoral Systems and Political Consequences: Options for an Independent Namibia* (Lusaka: UN Institute for Namibia, 1989, (Co-author)); *Human Rights Law* (Leicestershire, UK, Upfront Publishing, 2002); *A Manual of Public Management* (Windhoek, Aim Publications, 2003). He has also written various learned articles on law, including 'Legal Control of Executive Decisions through the Natural Justice Rule of Fair Hearing: the Practical Approach' ((1984) 10 *Journal of Zambia Law Association* 35); 'The "Administrative Justice" Provision of the Constitution of the Republic of Namibia: A Constitutional Protection of Judicial Review and Tribunal Adjudication under Administrative Law' ((1991) 24 *Comparative and International Law Journal of SA* 88); 'Legal Aspects of Access to Land and Land Tenure in Namibia' (*Lesotho Law Journal* (1991) Vol. 7 No. 1); 'Administrative law in Namibia, its current state, challenges, and proposals for law reform' ((2009) 42 *Comparative and International Law Journal of SA* 115).